Tatsuki Fujimoto

I love *Hereditary*!

Tatsuki Fujimoto won Honorable Mention in the
November 2013 Shueisha Crown Newcomers' Awards for
his debut one-shot story *Love Is Blind*. His first series,
Fire Punch, ran for eight volumes. *Chainsaw Man* began
serialization in 2019 in *Weekly Shonen Jump*.

3

SHONEN JUMP Manga Edition

Story & Art TATSUKI FUJIMOTO

Translation/AMANDA HALEY
Touch-Up Art & Lettering/SABRINA HEEP
Design/JULIAN [JR] ROBINSON
Editor/ALEXIS KIRSCH

CHAINSAW MAN © 2019 by Tatsuki Fujimoto
All rights reserved.
First published in Japan in 2019 by SHUEISHA Inc., Tokyo.
English translation rights arranged by SHUEISHA Inc.

The stories, characters and incidents mentioned in this publication are
entirely fictional.

Printed in the U.S.A.

Published by VIZ Media, LLC
P.O. Box 77010
San Francisco, CA 94107

10 9 8 7 6 5 4 3 2 1
First printing, February 2021

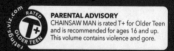

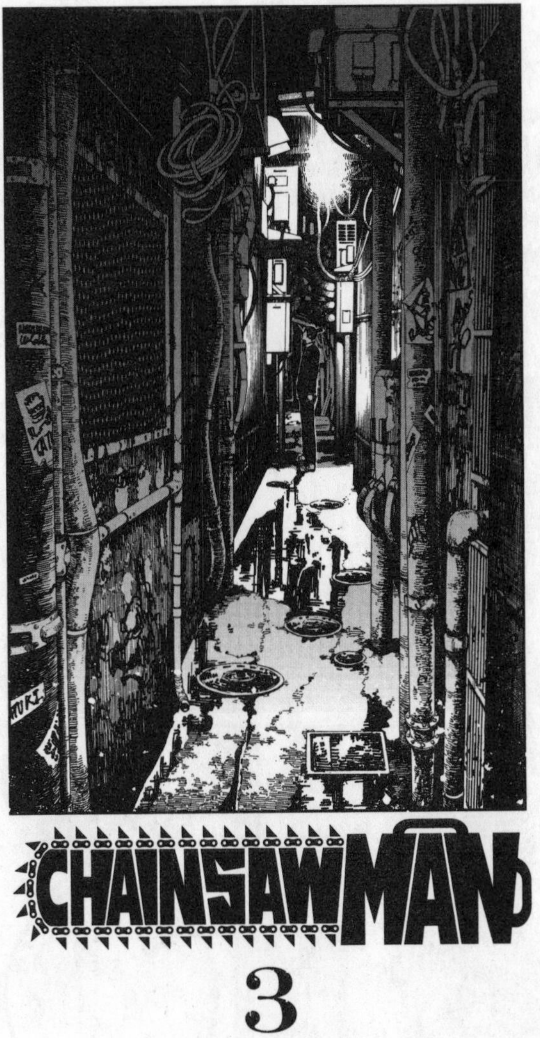

CHAINSAW MAN

3

KILL DENJI

Tatsuki Fujimoto

CHARACTERS

Denji

A young man-slash-Chainsaw Devil who carries his partner Pochita inside him. He's always true to his desires. Likes Makima, the first person to ever treat him like a human being.

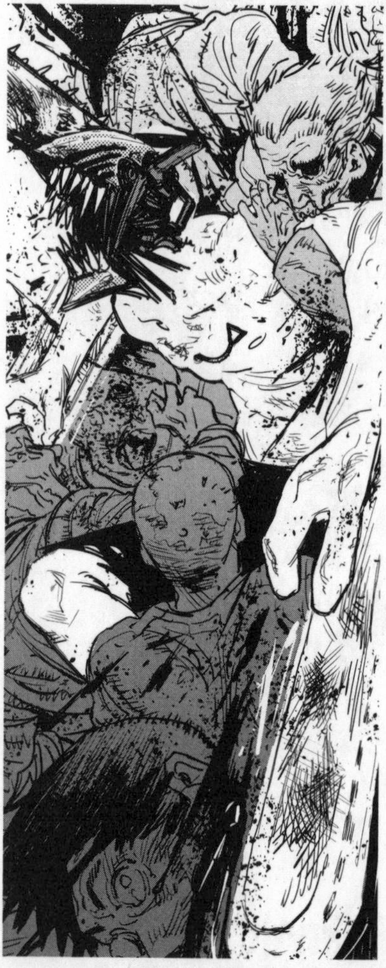

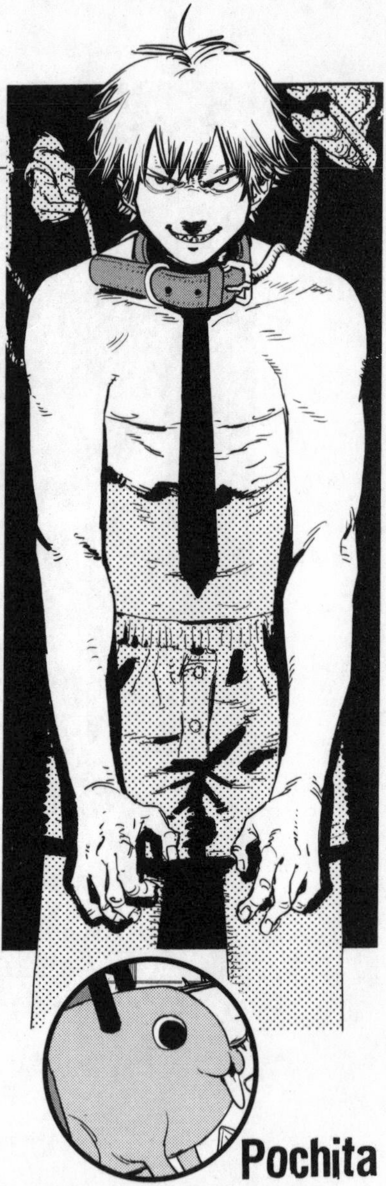

Pochita

Chainsaw Devil. Gave up his heart to Denji, becoming part of his body.

Makima

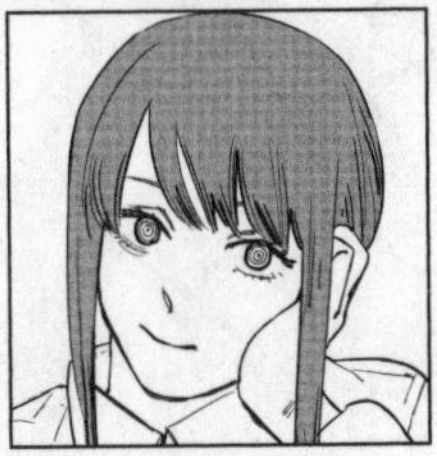

The mysterious woman in charge of Public Safety Devil Extermination Special Division 4. Can smell devil scents.

Aki Hayakawa

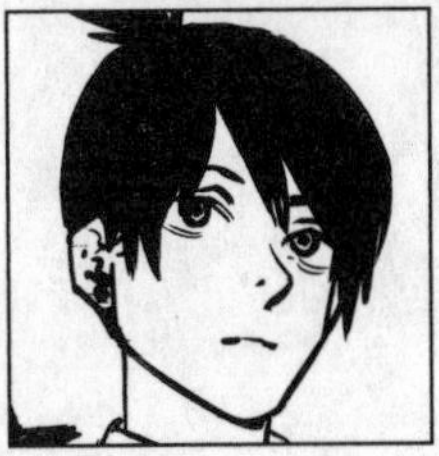

Makima's loyal subordinate. Denji's senior at Public Safety by three years, he's assigned to keep an eye on him.

Himeno

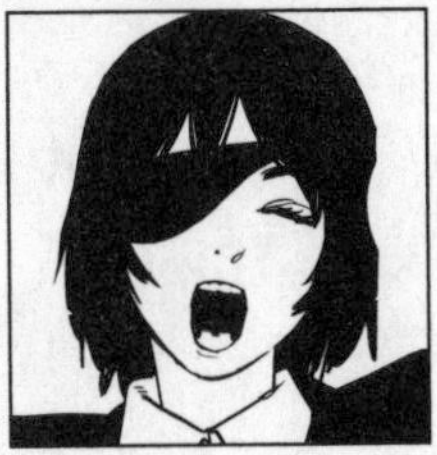

Hayakawa's work senior and paired with him as his buddy. Contracted with the Ghost Devil.

Power

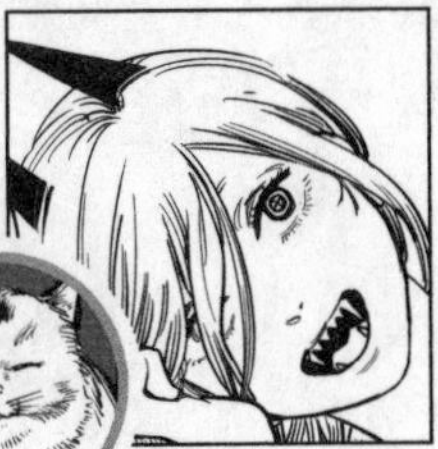

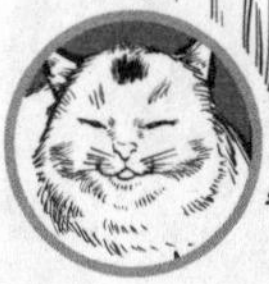

Blood Devil Fiend. Egotistical and prone to going out of control. Her cat Meowy is her only friend.

Arai

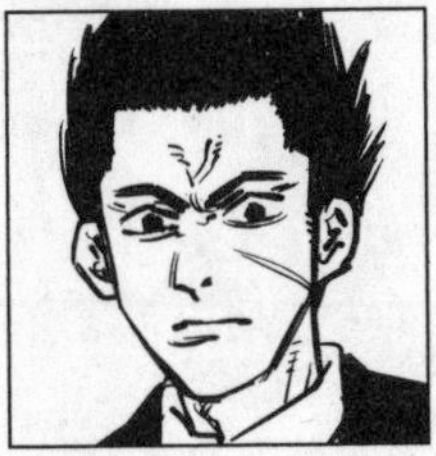

Himeno's uptight, hot-blooded subordinate. Doesn't trust Denji and Power.

Kobeni

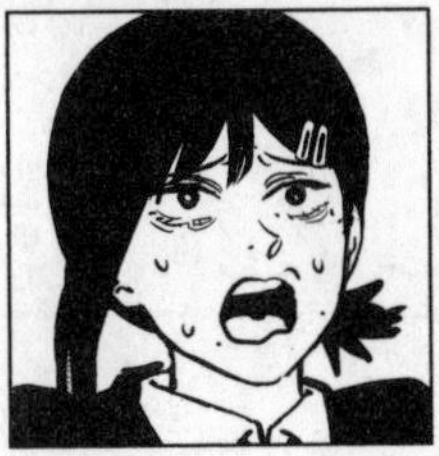

A timid new recruit. Though mentally frail, her boss Himeno thinks she has talent.

STORY

Denji is a young man who hunts devils with his pet devil-dog Pochita. To pay off his debts, Denji is forced to live in extreme poverty and worked like a dog, only to be betrayed and killed on the job without ever getting to live a decent life. But Pochita, at the cost of the pooch's own life, brings Denji back—as Chainsaw Man! After Denji buzzes through all their attackers, he's taken in by the mysterious Makima, and begins a new life as a Public Safety Devil Hunter.

Denji defeats the Bat Devil and rescues Power, so as promised, she lets him squeeze her breasts! His first handful of boob turns out to be a big letdown. But when Makima tells a disillusioned Denji about the strongest devil, the Gun Devil, her offer to grant Denji any one wish if he can kill the Gun Devil brings his motivation back big-time! Denji and the members of Special Division 4 are soon dispatched to a hotel where a devil that's ingested a piece of the Gun Devil has been sighted. Himeno gives Denji some extra motivation with a promise of her own: If he's the one to defeat this devil, she'll kiss him with tongue! However, the mission goes awry when a devil traps the group on the hotel's eighth floor with a mysterious power. As the extreme situation wears everyone down, the devil offers them a deal: let it eat Denji and it will let them go...

CONTENTS

[17] Kill Denji — 007

[18] Chainsaw vs. Eternity — 027

[19] Nobel Prize — 047

[20] Drinking — 067

[21] Taste of a Kiss — 087

[22] Cola-Flavored Chupa Chups — 107

[23] Gunfire — 127

[24] Curse — 147

[25] Ghost, Snake, Chainsaw — 167

Chapter 17: Kill Denji

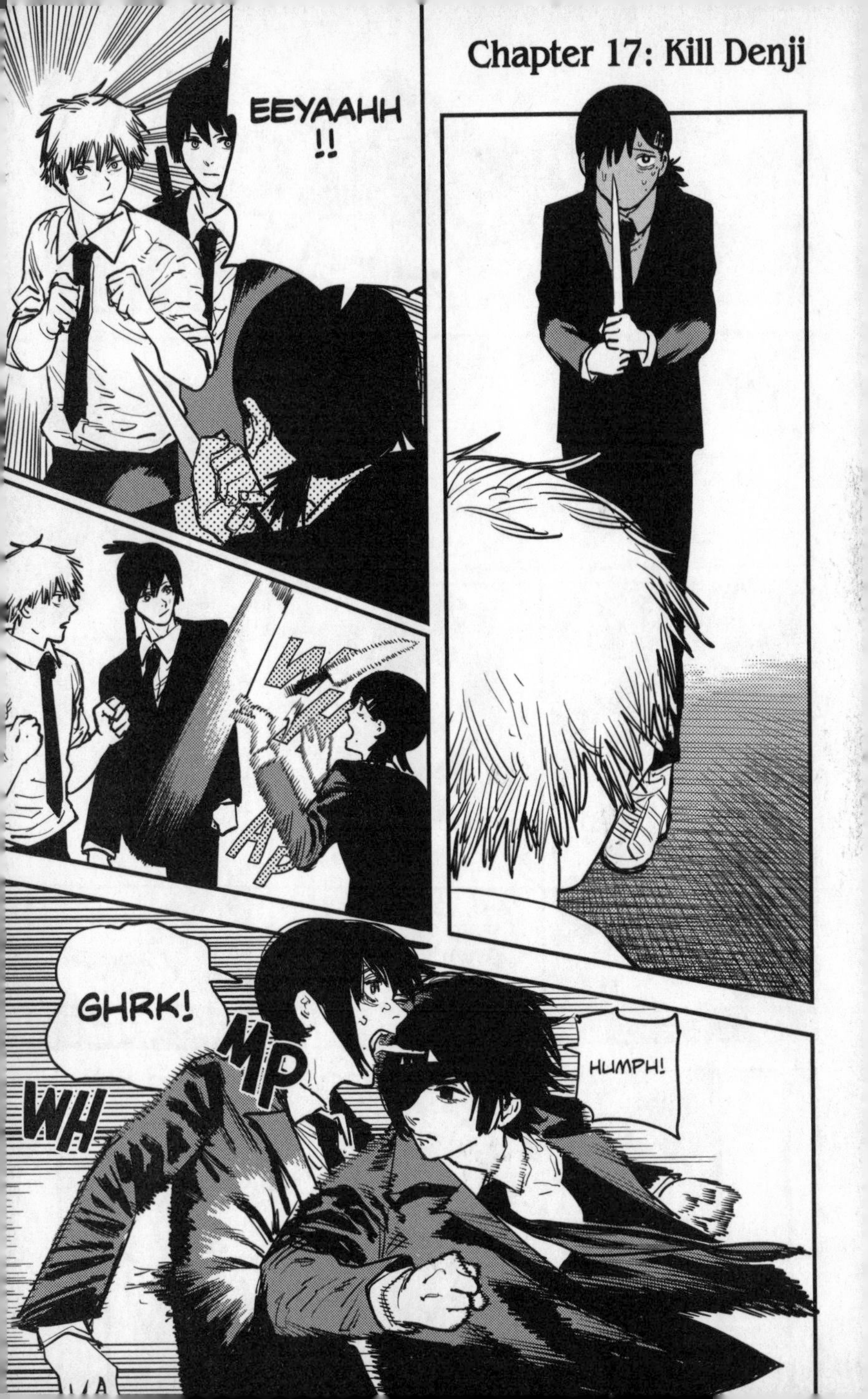
EEYAAHH!!
WHAP
HUMPH!
GHRK!
WH
MP

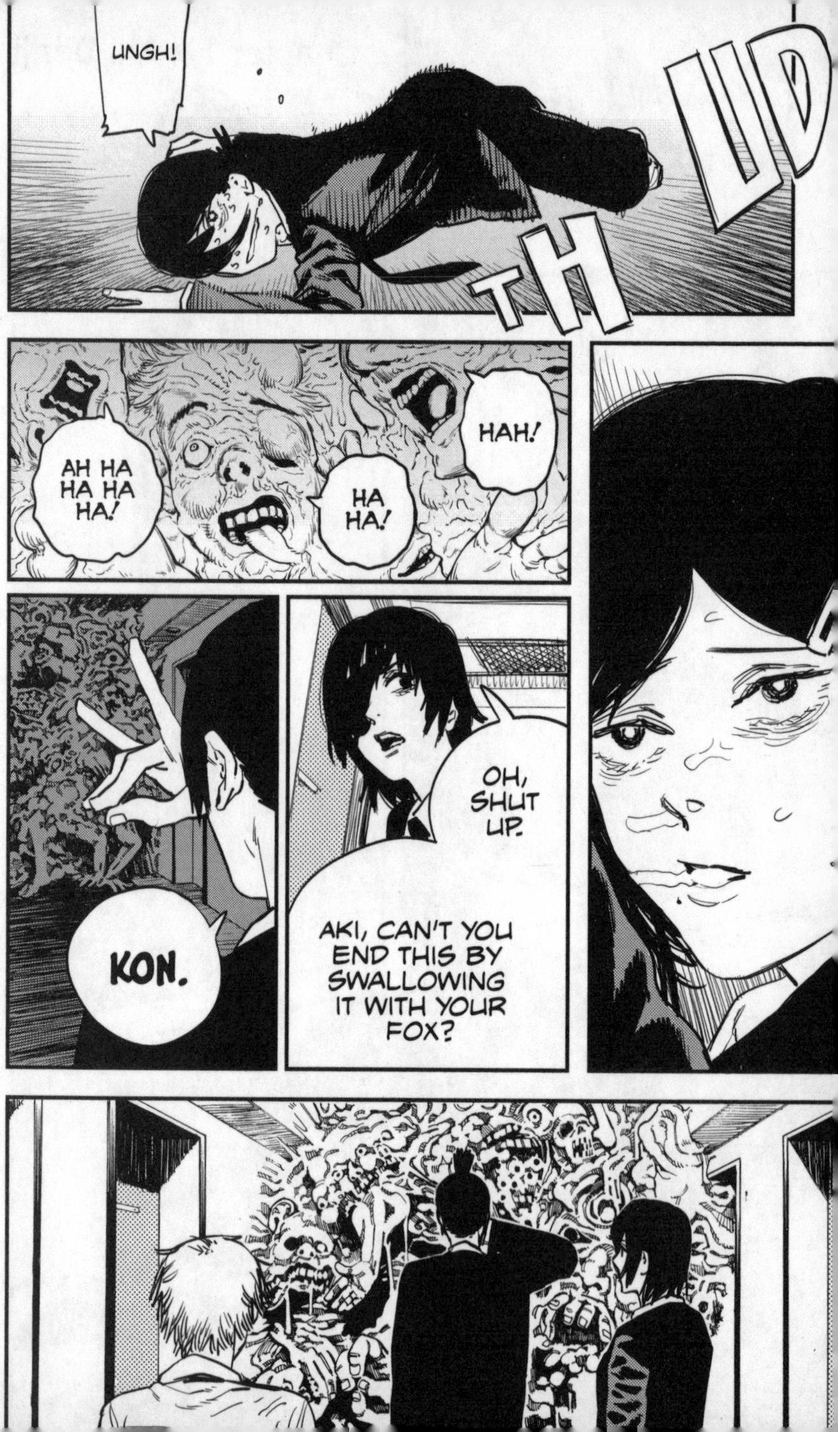
UNGH!
THUD
HAH!
HA HA!
AH HA HA HA HA!
OH, SHUT UP.
AKI, CAN'T YOU END THIS BY SWALLOWING IT WITH YOUR FOX?
KON.

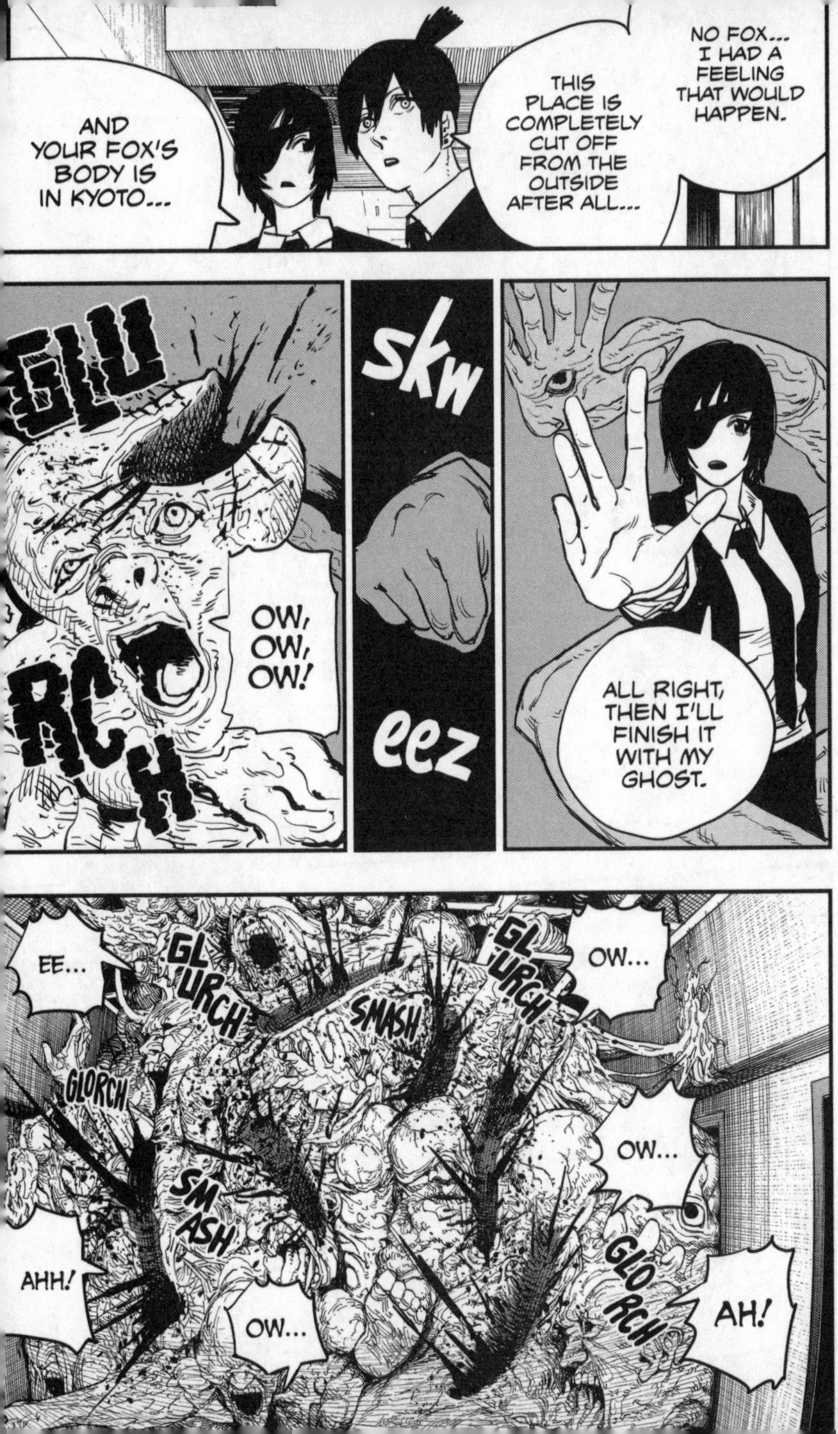
NO FOX... I HAD A FEELING THAT WOULD HAPPEN.
THIS PLACE IS COMPLETELY CUT OFF FROM THE OUTSIDE AFTER ALL...
AND YOUR FOX'S BODY IS IN KYOTO...
ALL RIGHT, THEN I'LL FINISH IT WITH MY GHOST.
SKWEEZ
OW, OW, OW!
GLURCH
OW...
GLURCH
EE...
SMASH
GLORCH
OW...
AH!
GLORCH
SMASH
OW...
AHH!

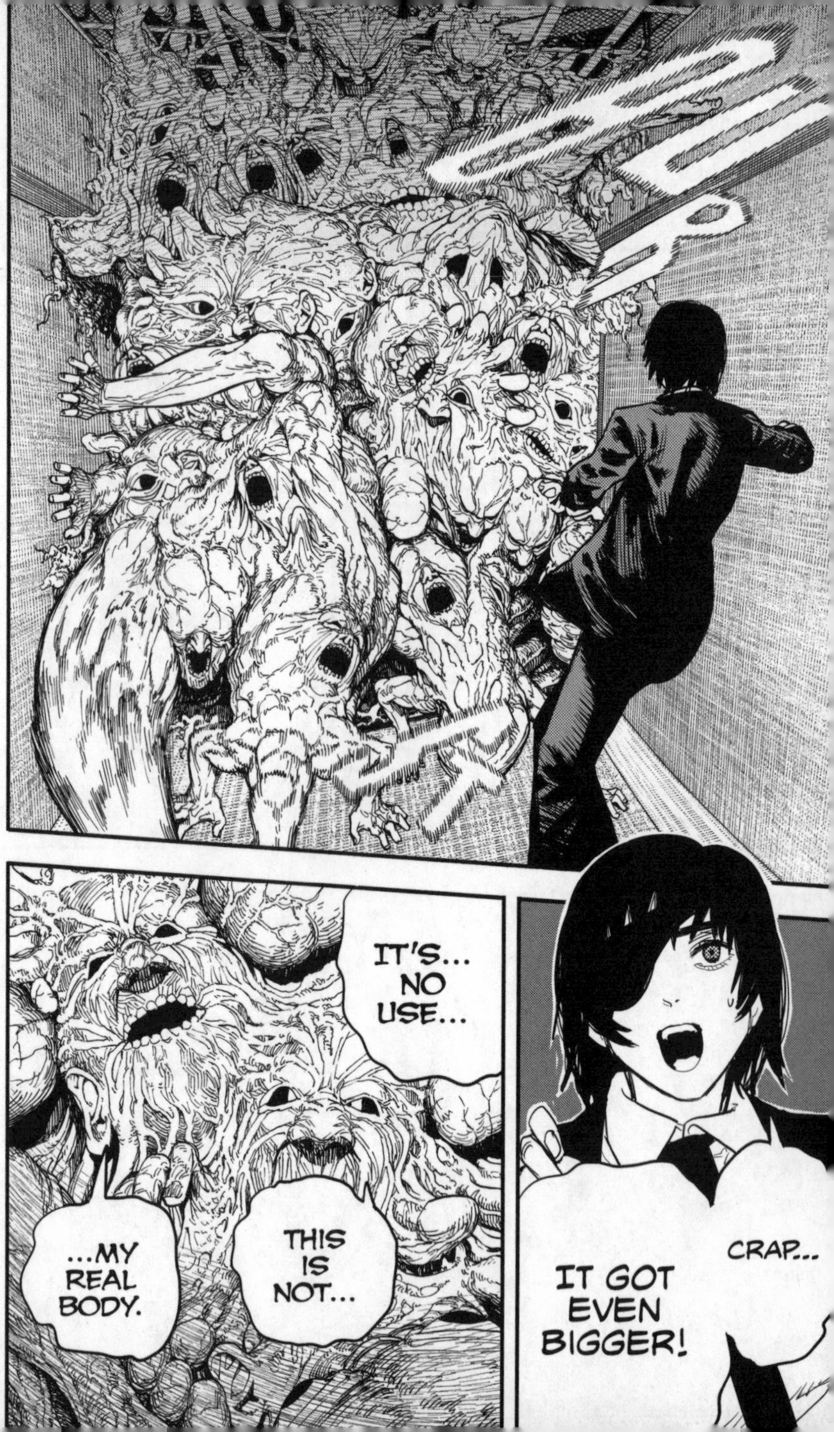
CRAP...
IT GOT EVEN BIGGER!
IT'S... NO USE...
THIS IS NOT...
...MY REAL BODY.

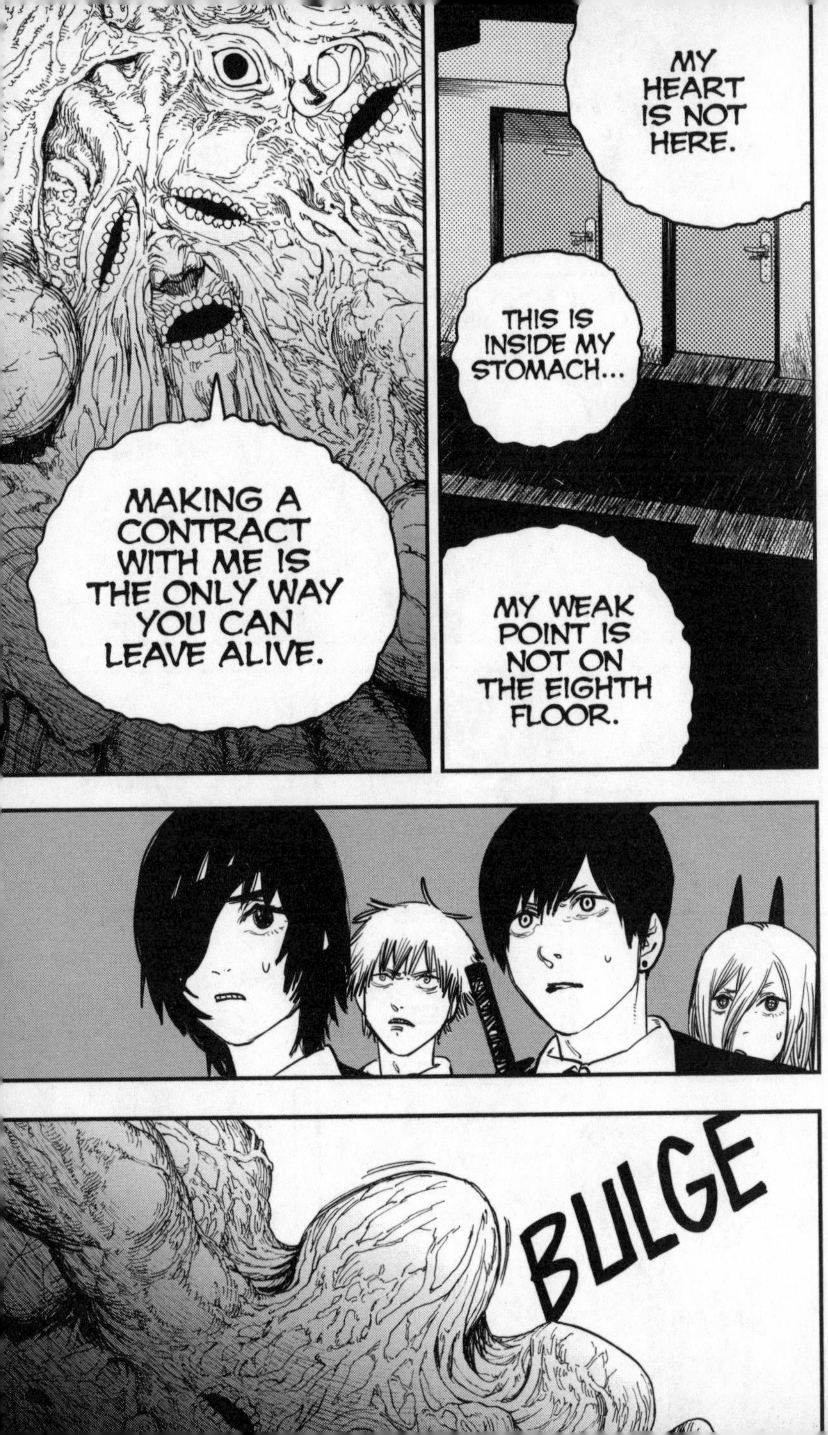
MY HEART IS NOT HERE.
THIS IS INSIDE MY STOMACH...
MY WEAK POINT IS NOT ON THE EIGHTH FLOOR.
MAKING A CONTRACT WITH ME IS THE ONLY WAY YOU CAN LEAVE ALIVE.
BULGE

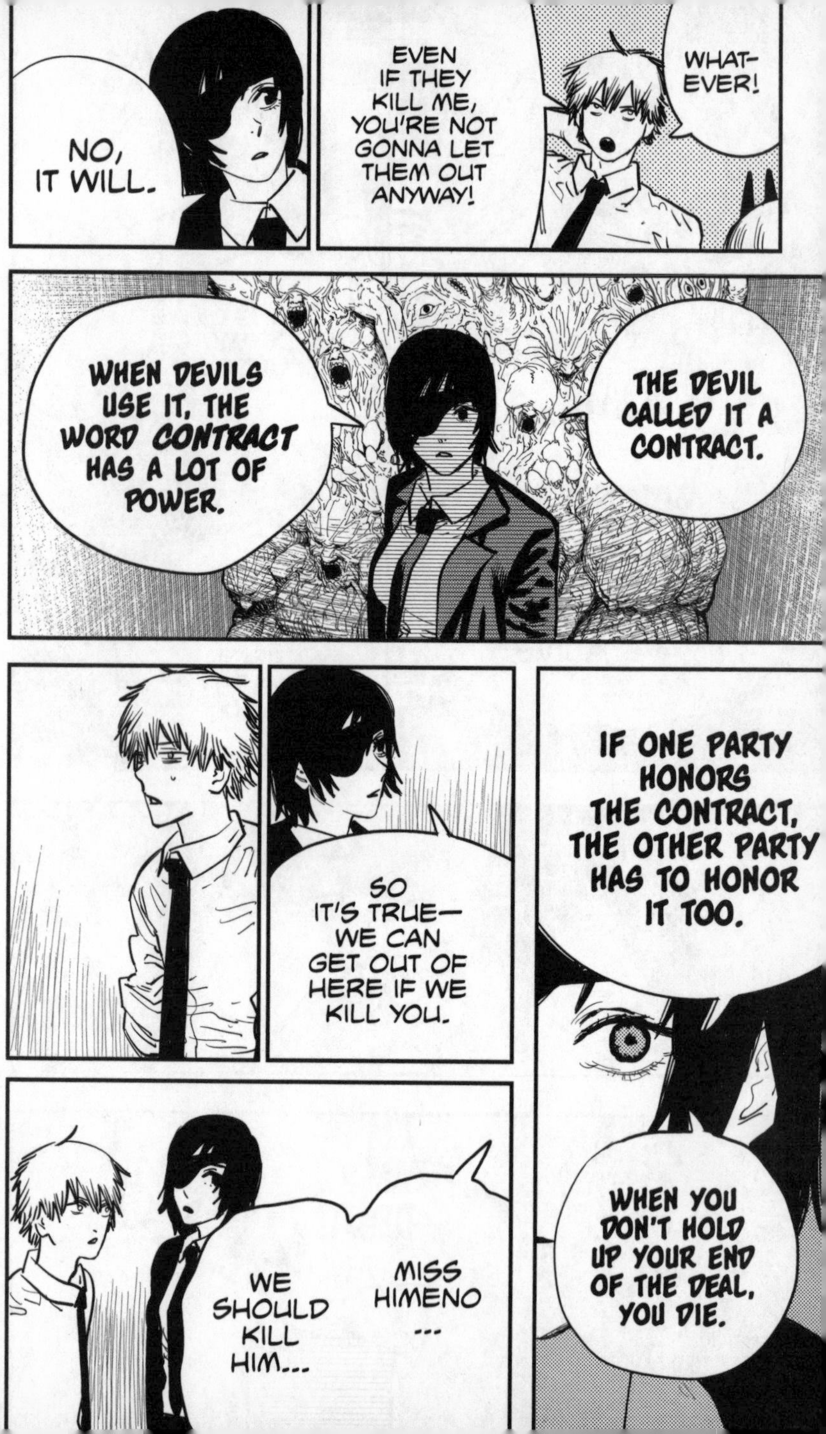
WHAT-EVER!
EVEN IF THEY KILL ME, YOU'RE NOT GONNA LET THEM OUT ANYWAY!
NO, IT WILL.
THE DEVIL CALLED IT A CONTRACT.
WHEN DEVILS USE IT, THE WORD CONTRACT HAS A LOT OF POWER.
IF ONE PARTY HONORS THE CONTRACT, THE OTHER PARTY HAS TO HONOR IT TOO.
WHEN YOU DON'T HOLD UP YOUR END OF THE DEAL, YOU DIE.
SO IT'S TRUE— WE CAN GET OUT OF HERE IF WE KILL YOU.
MISS HIMENO...
WE SHOULD KILL HIM...

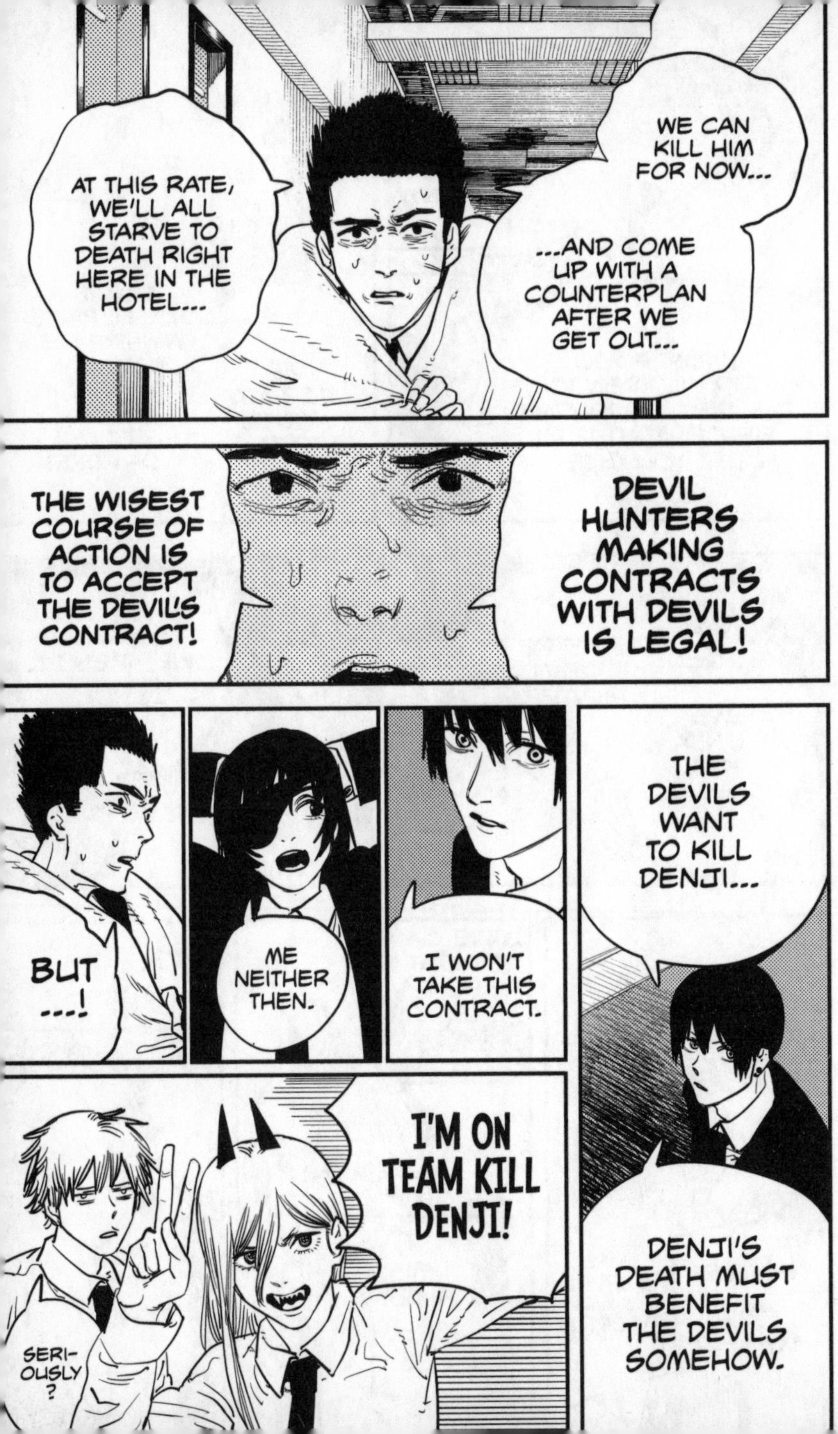
WE CAN KILL HIM FOR NOW...
...AND COME UP WITH A COUNTERPLAN AFTER WE GET OUT...
AT THIS RATE, WE'LL ALL STARVE TO DEATH RIGHT HERE IN THE HOTEL...
DEVIL HUNTERS MAKING CONTRACTS WITH DEVILS IS LEGAL!
THE WISEST COURSE OF ACTION IS TO ACCEPT THE DEVIL'S CONTRACT!
THE DEVILS WANT TO KILL DENJI...
DENJI'S DEATH MUST BENEFIT THE DEVILS SOMEHOW.
I WON'T TAKE THIS CONTRACT.
ME NEITHER THEN.
BUT ...!
I'M ON TEAM KILL DENJI!
SERI-OUSLY?

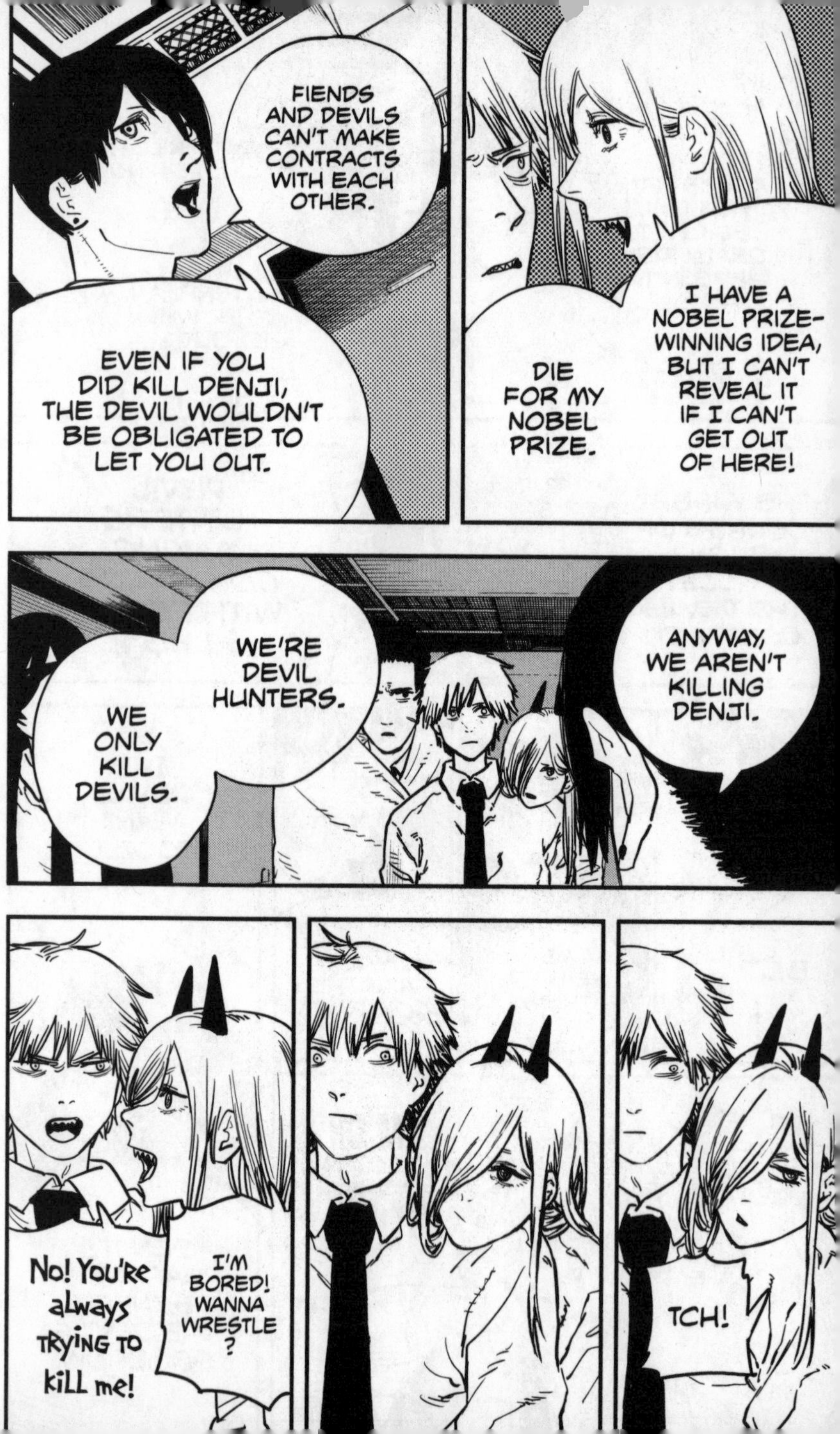
I HAVE A NOBEL PRIZE-WINNING IDEA, BUT I CAN'T REVEAL IT IF I CAN'T GET OUT OF HERE!
DIE FOR MY NOBEL PRIZE.
FIENDS AND DEVILS CAN'T MAKE CONTRACTS WITH EACH OTHER.
EVEN IF YOU DID KILL DENJI, THE DEVIL WOULDN'T BE OBLIGATED TO LET YOU OUT.
ANYWAY, WE AREN'T KILLING DENJI.
WE'RE DEVIL HUNTERS.
WE ONLY KILL DEVILS.
TCH!
I'M BORED! WANNA WRESTLE?
No! You're always trying to kill me!

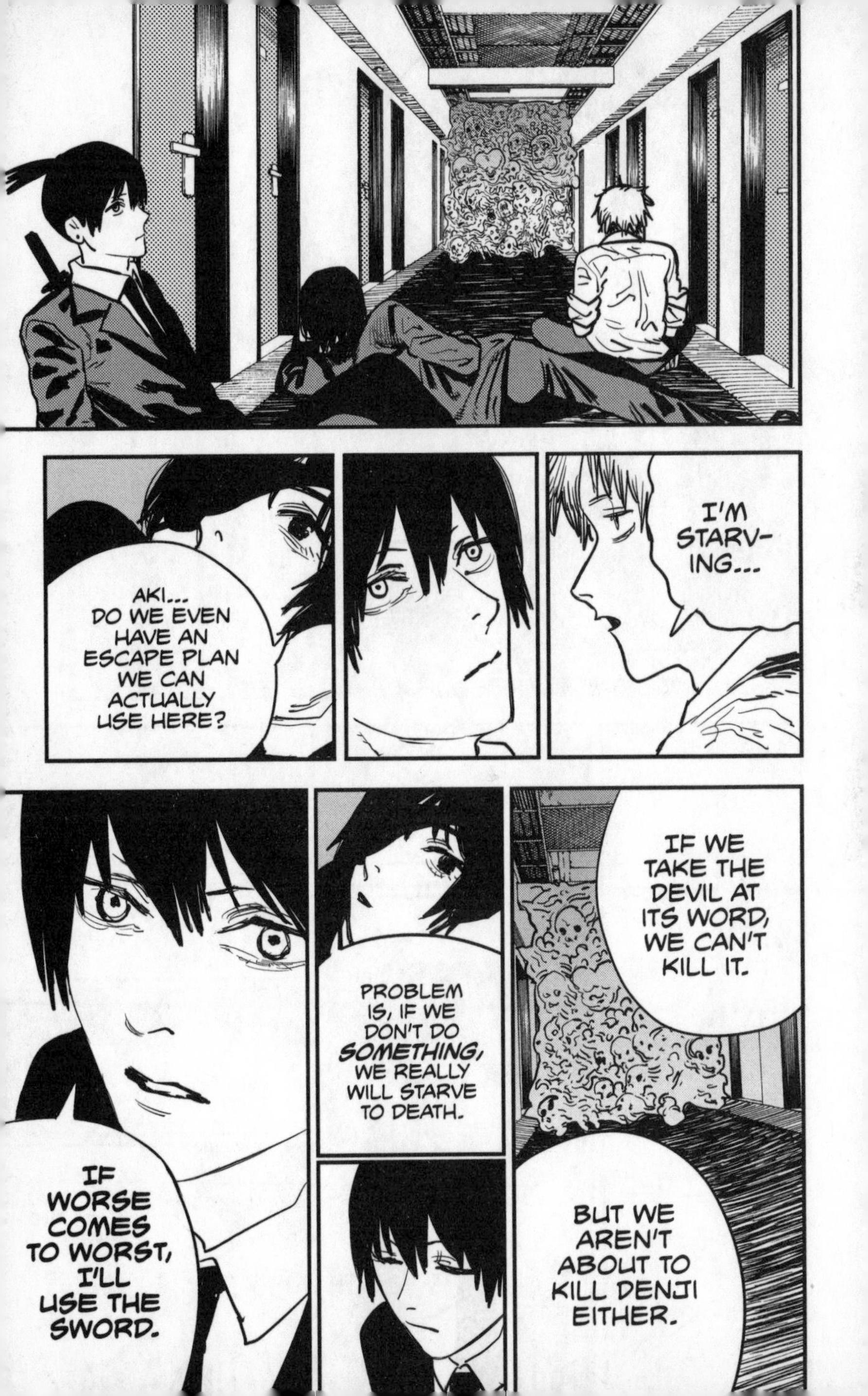

I'M STARV-ING...
AKI... DO WE EVEN HAVE AN ESCAPE PLAN WE CAN ACTUALLY USE HERE?
IF WE TAKE THE DEVIL AT ITS WORD, WE CAN'T KILL IT.
BUT WE AREN'T ABOUT TO KILL DENJI EITHER.
PROBLEM IS, IF WE DON'T DO *SOMETHING,* WE REALLY WILL STARVE TO DEATH.
IF WORSE COMES TO WORST, I'LL USE THE SWORD.

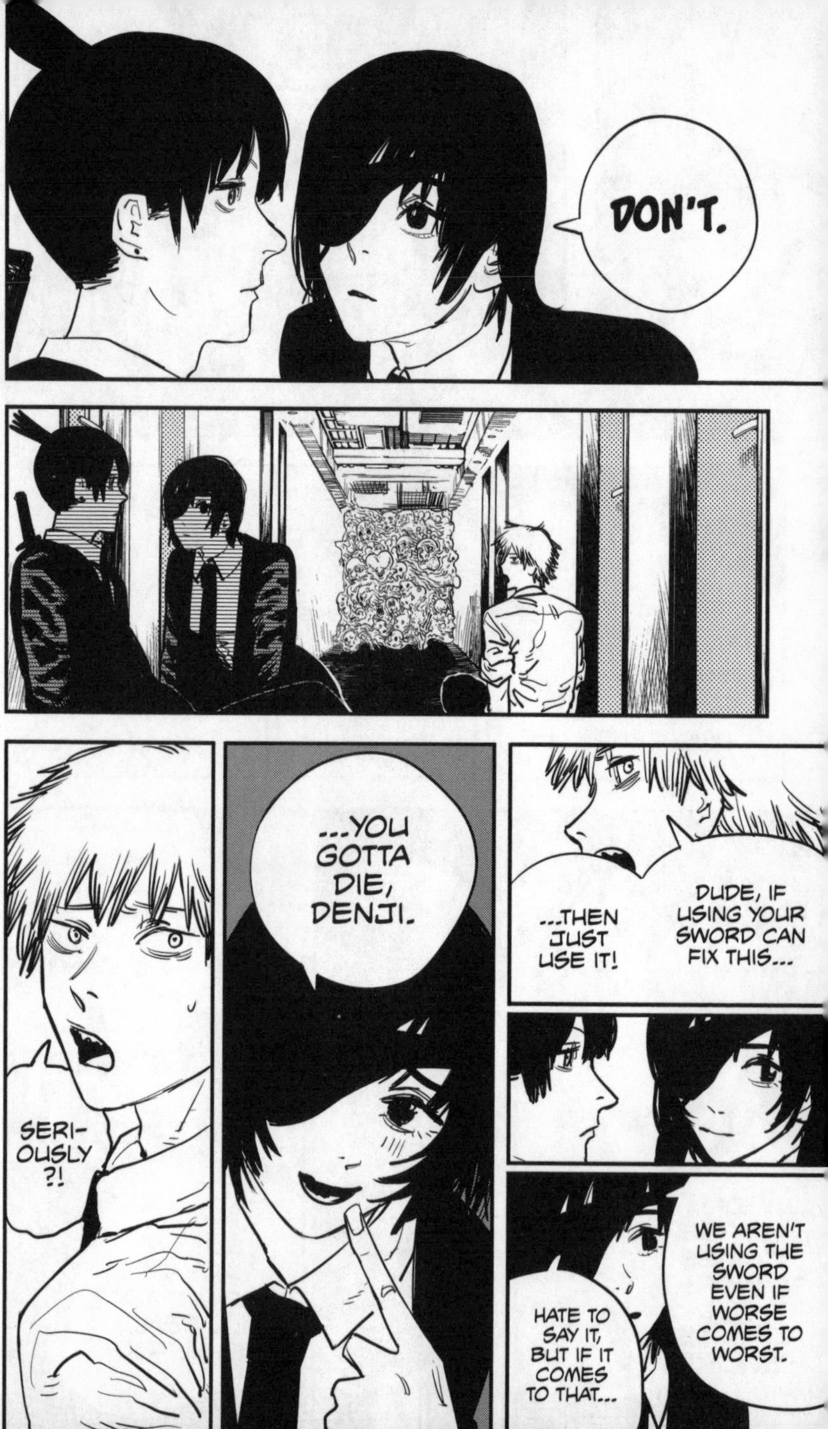
DON'T.
DUDE, IF USING YOUR SWORD CAN FIX THIS...
...THEN JUST USE IT!
WE AREN'T USING THE SWORD EVEN IF WORSE COMES TO WORST.
HATE TO SAY IT, BUT IF IT COMES TO THAT...
...YOU GOTTA DIE, DENJI.
SERI-OUSLY?!

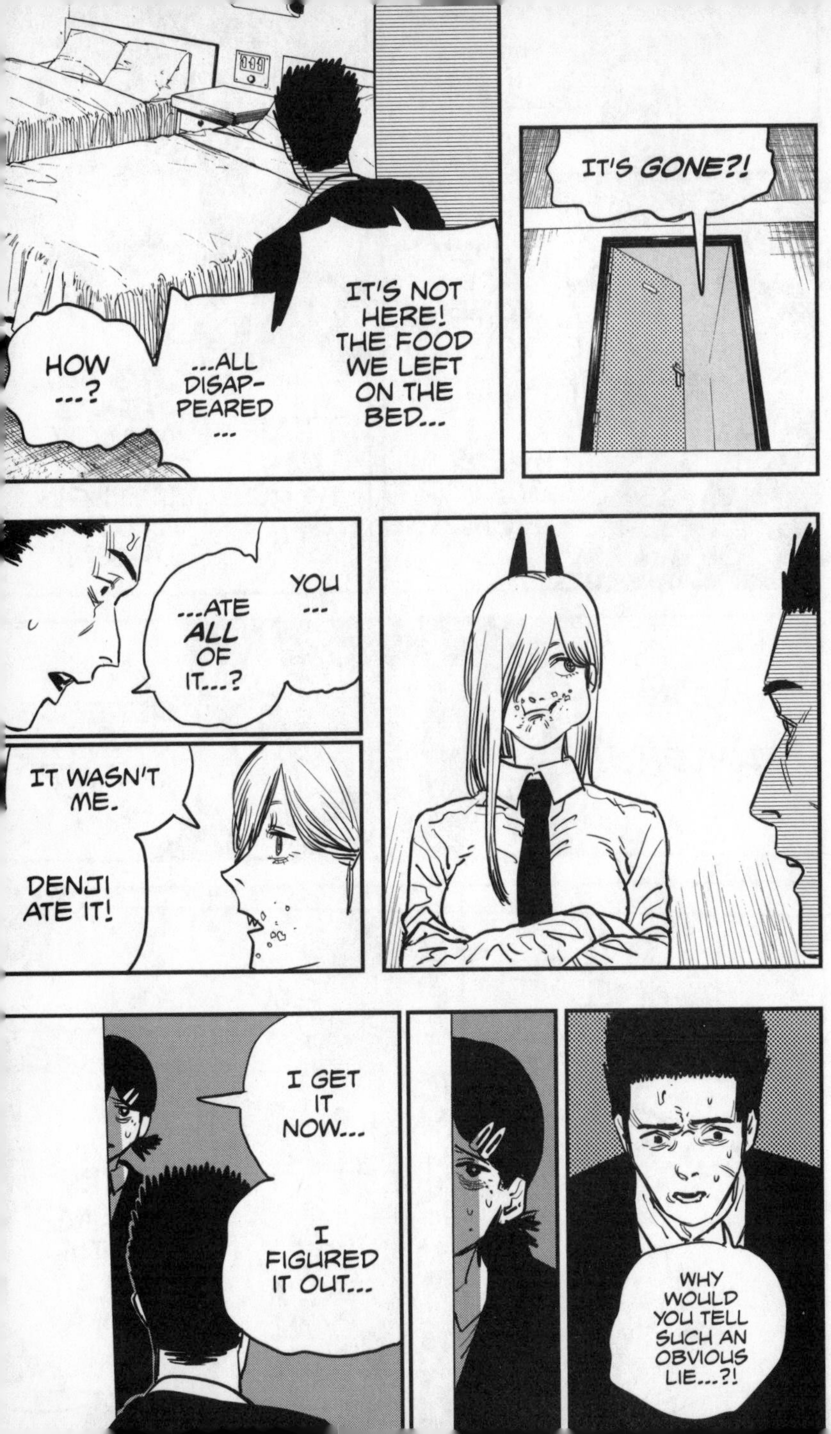
IT'S GONE?!
IT'S NOT HERE! THE FOOD WE LEFT ON THE BED...
...ALL DISAPPEARED ...
HOW ...?
YOU ...
...ATE ALL OF IT...?
IT WASN'T ME.
DENJI ATE IT!
WHY WOULD YOU TELL SUCH AN OBVIOUS LIE...?!
I GET IT NOW...
I FIGURED IT OUT...

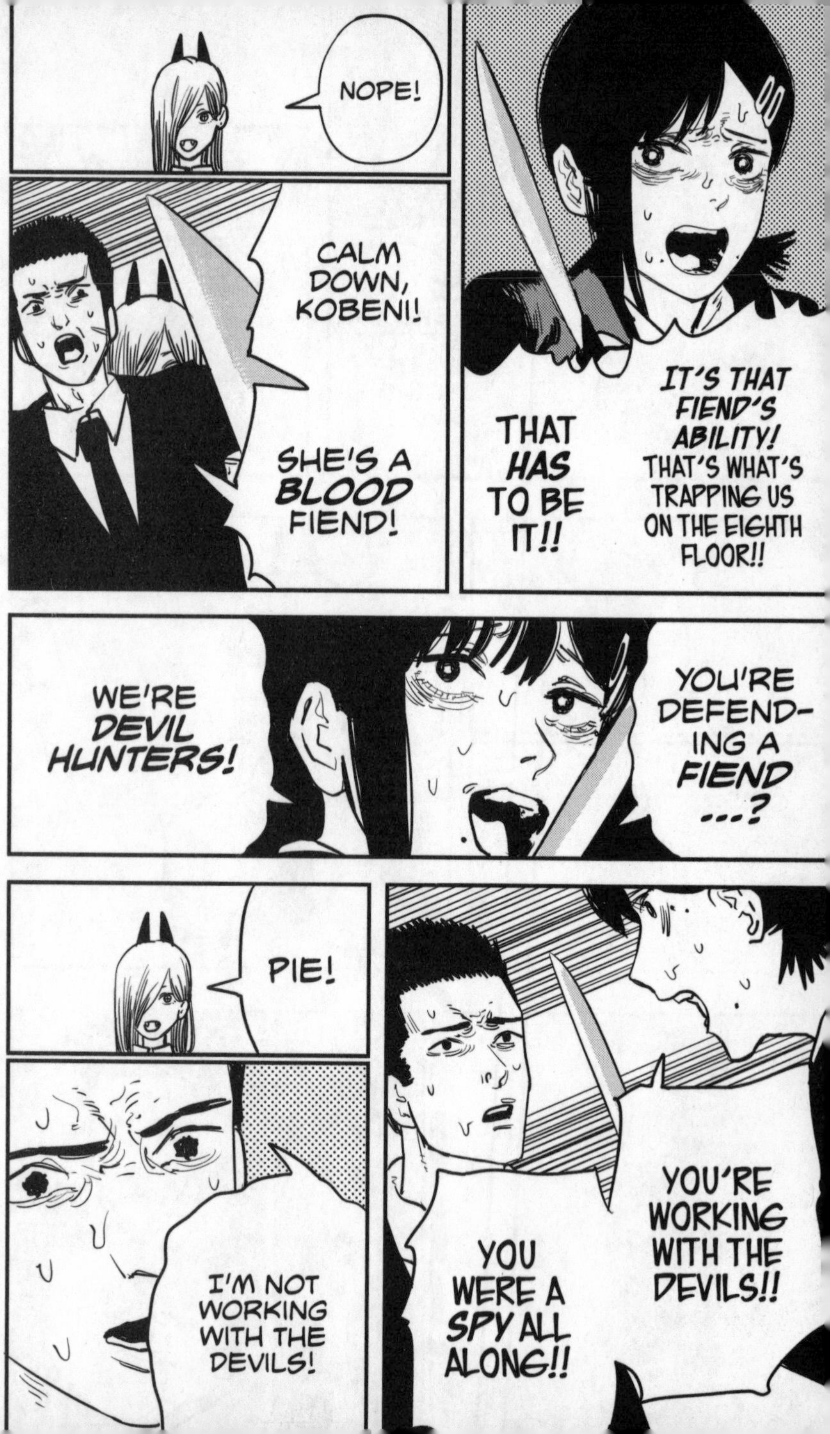
IT'S THAT FIEND'S ABILITY! THAT'S WHAT'S TRAPPING US ON THE EIGHTH FLOOR!!
THAT HAS TO BE IT!!
NOPE!
CALM DOWN, KOBENI!
SHE'S A BLOOD FIEND!
YOU'RE DEFENDING A FIEND...?
WE'RE DEVIL HUNTERS!
YOU'RE WORKING WITH THE DEVILS!!
YOU WERE A SPY ALL ALONG!!
PIE!
I'M NOT WORKING WITH THE DEVILS!

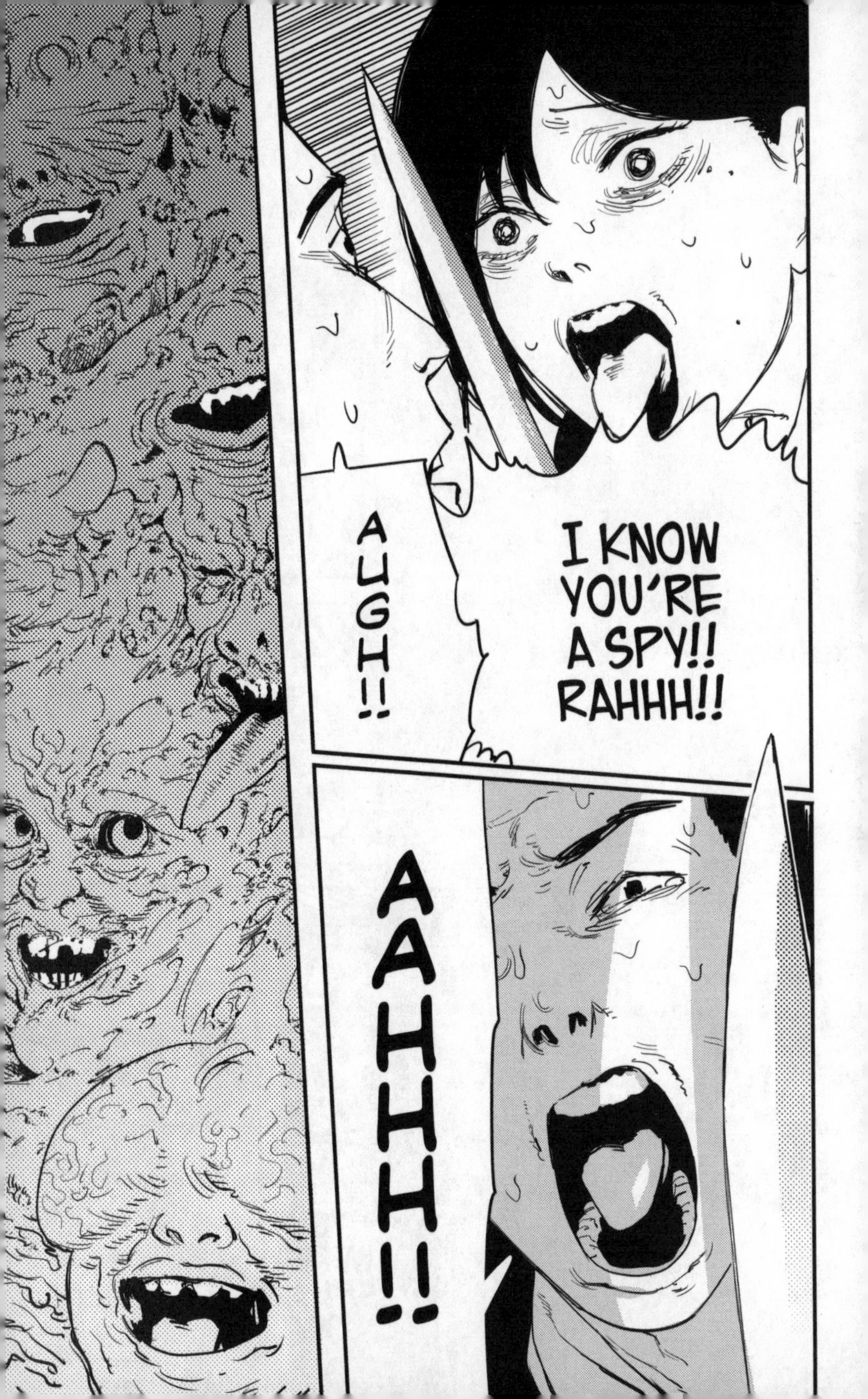
I KNOW YOU'RE A SPY!! RAHHH!!
AUGH!!
AAHHH!!

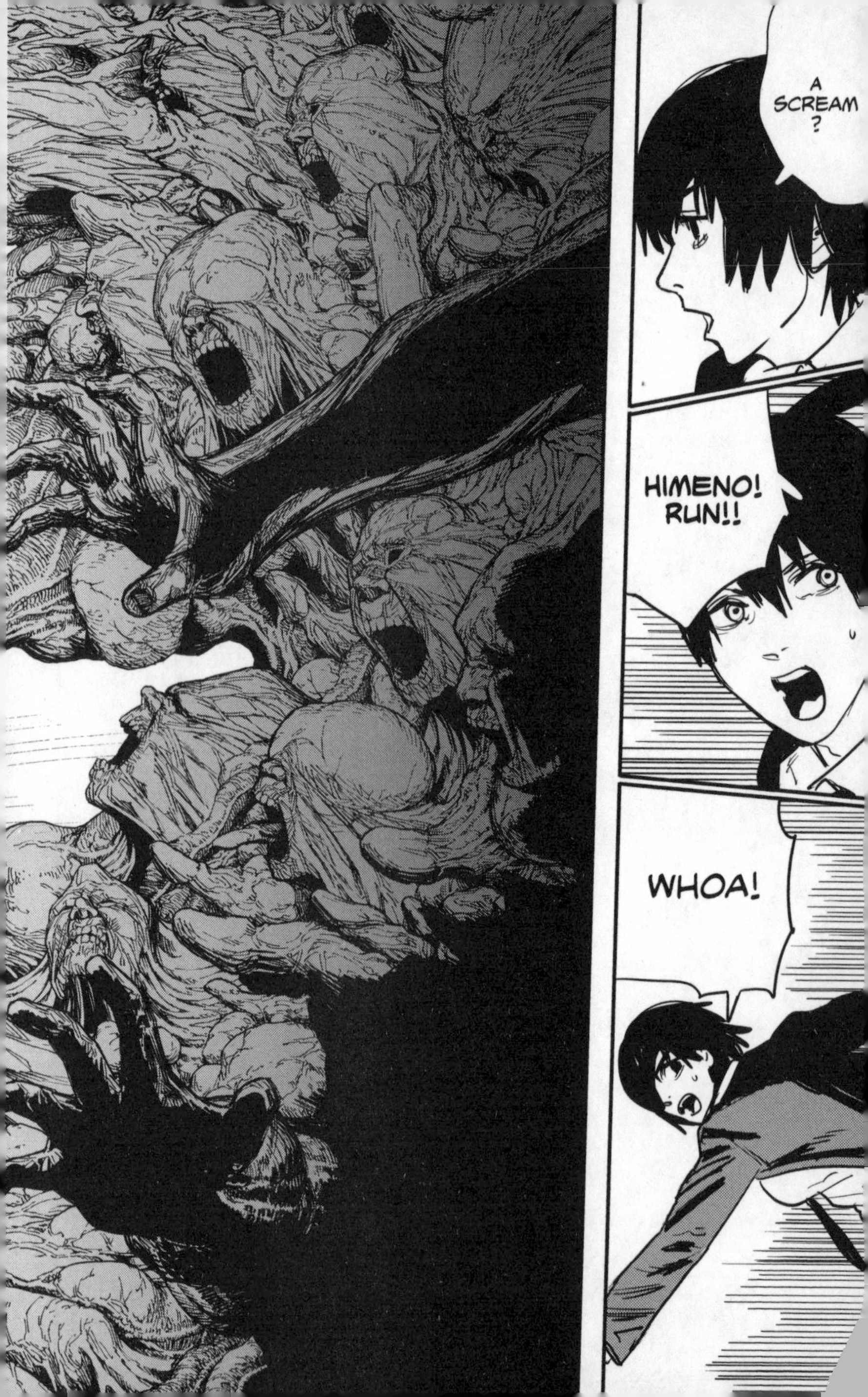
A SCREAM?
HIMENO! RUN!!
WHOA!

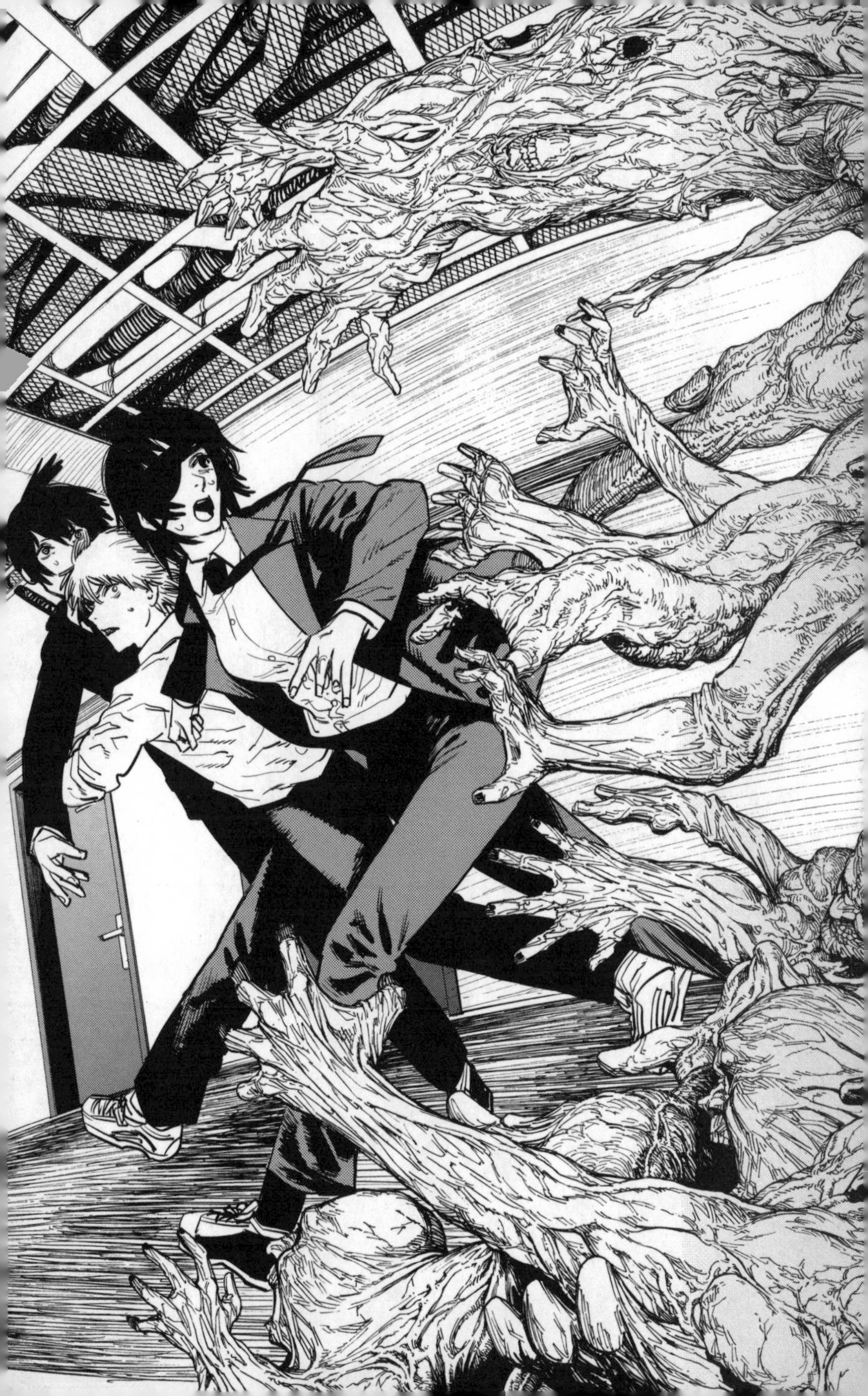

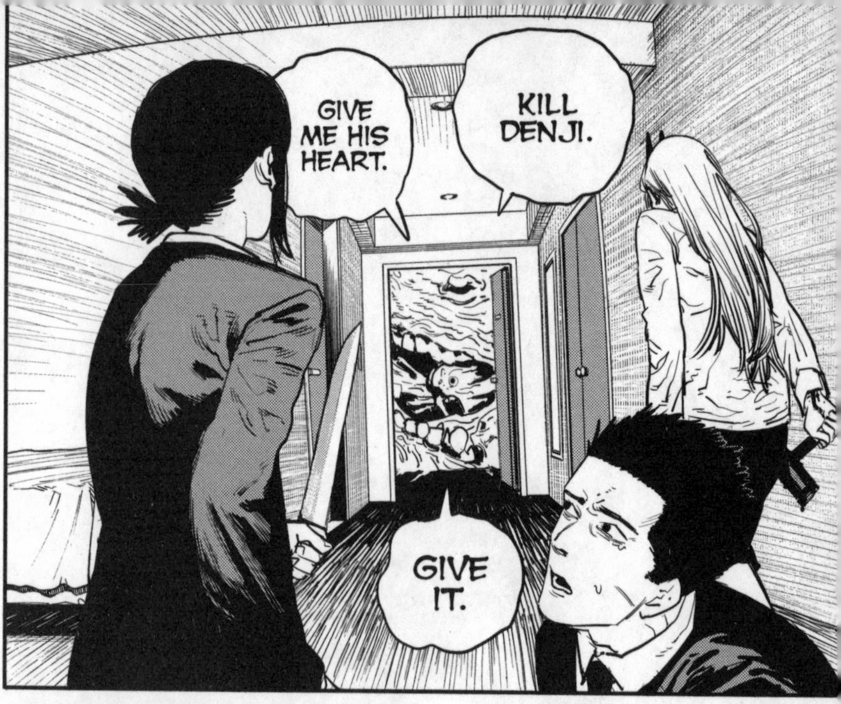
KILL DENJI.
GIVE ME HIS HEART.
GIVE IT.

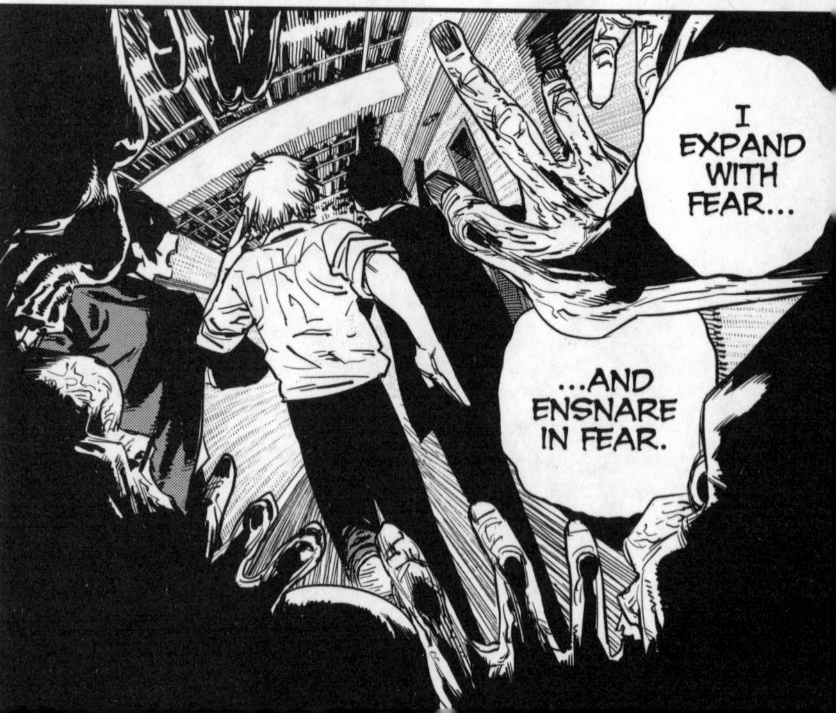
I EXPAND WITH FEAR...
...AND ENSNARE IN FEAR.

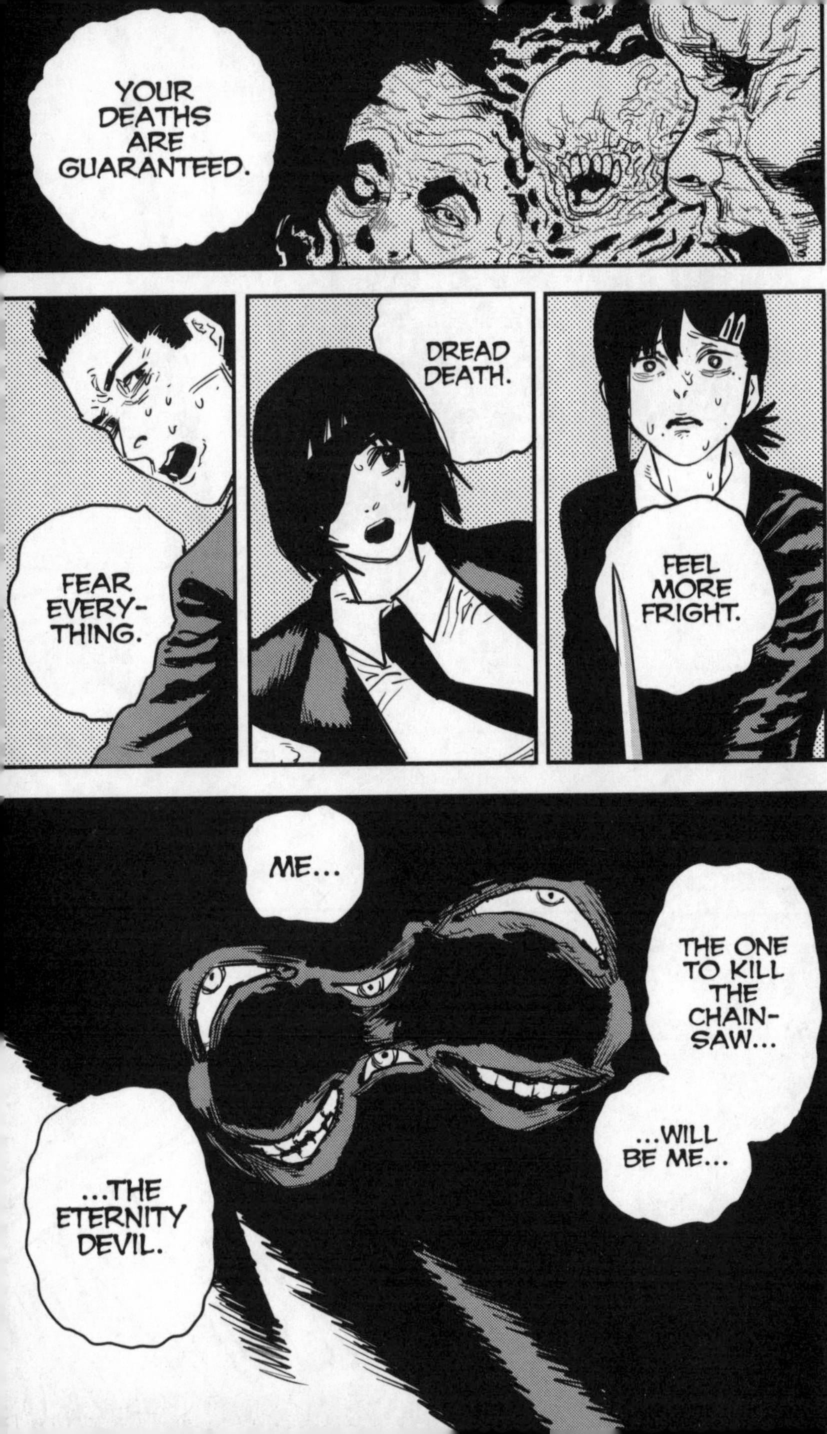
YOUR DEATHS ARE GUARANTEED.
FEEL MORE FRIGHT.
DREAD DEATH.
FEAR EVERY-THING.
ME...
THE ONE TO KILL THE CHAIN-SAW...
...WILL BE ME...
...THE ETERNITY DEVIL.

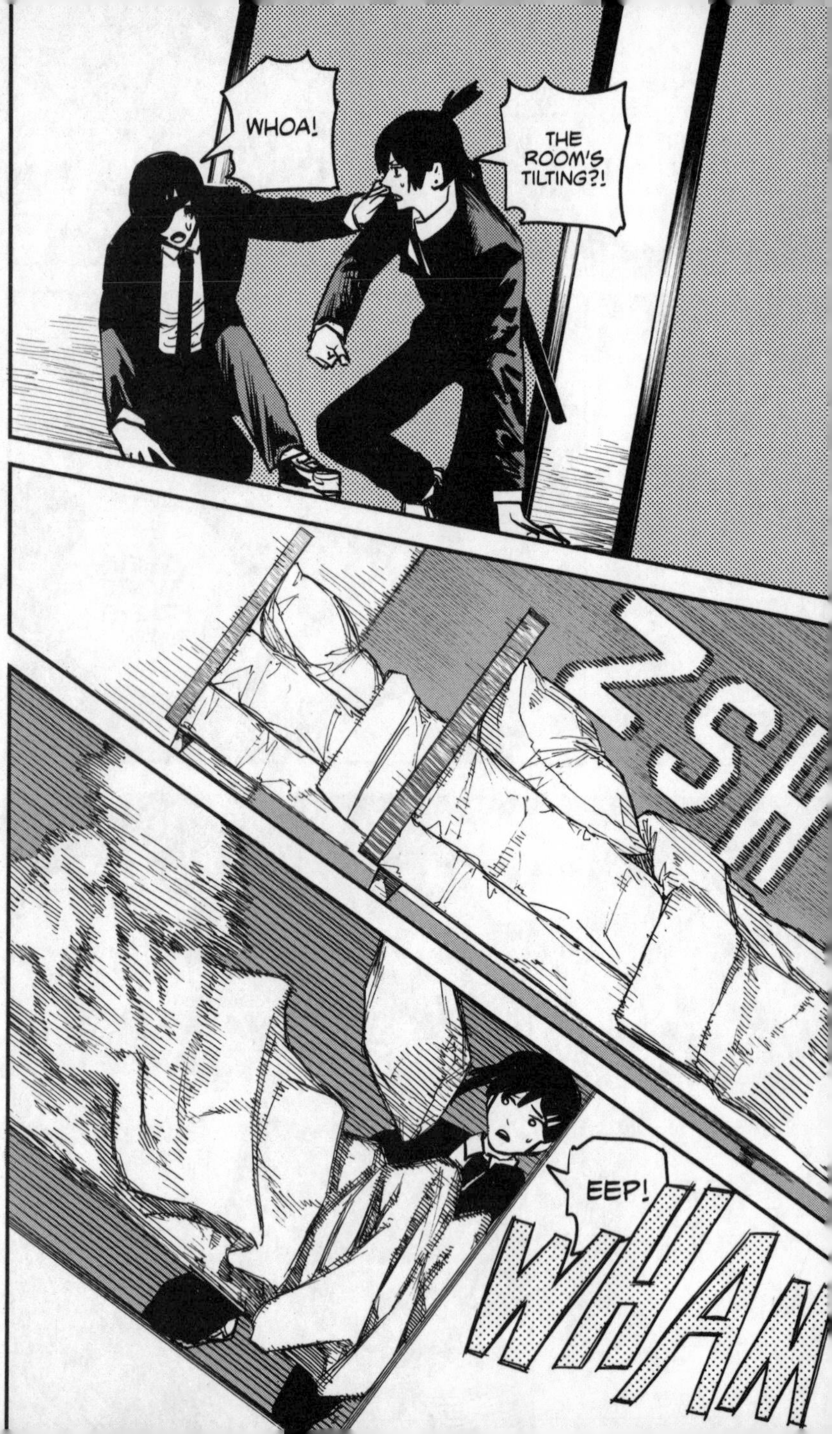
THE ROOM'S TILTING?!
WHOA!
ZSH
EEP!
WHAM

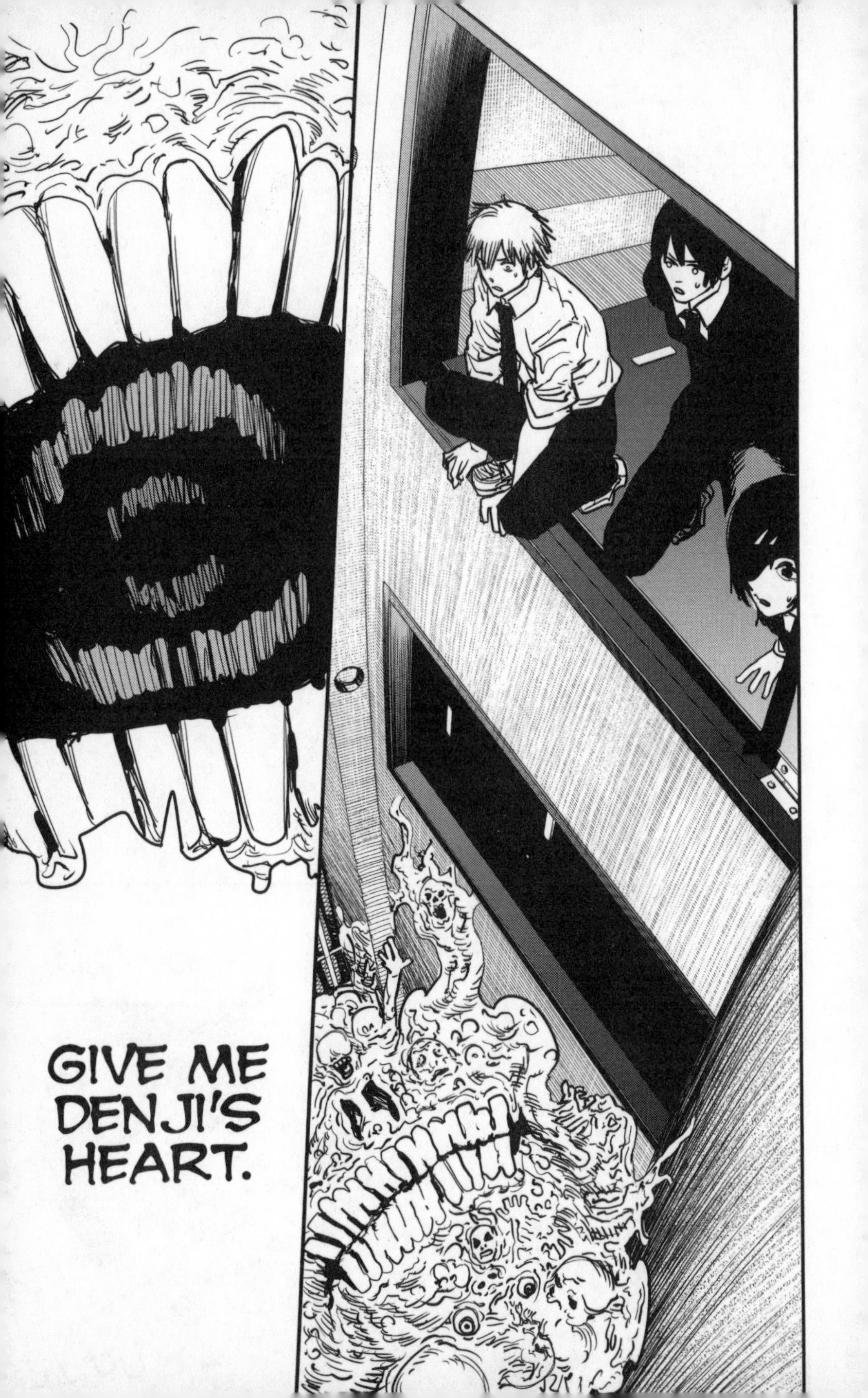
GIVE ME DENJI'S HEART.

Chain saw man

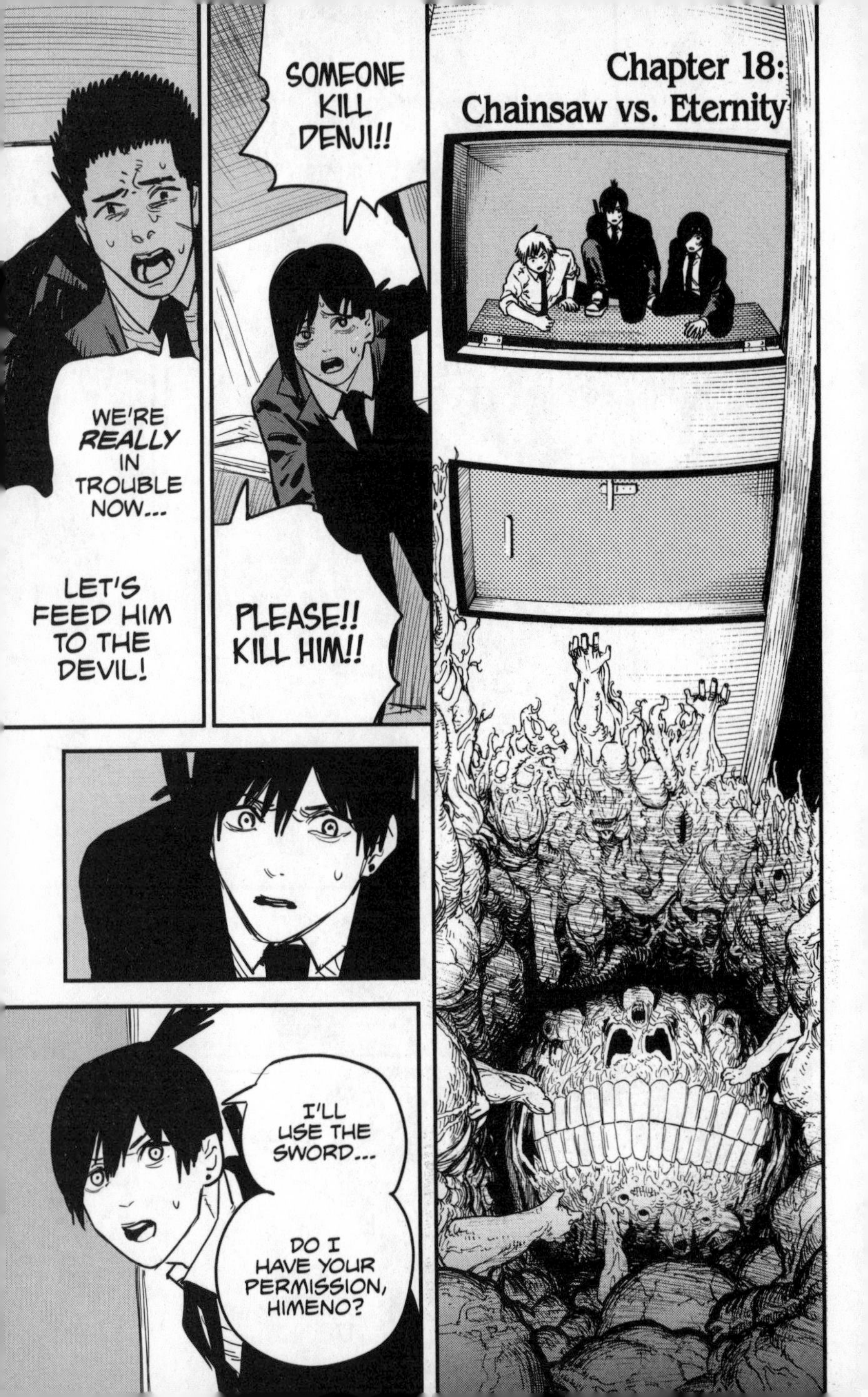
Chapter 18: Chainsaw vs. Eternity
SOMEONE KILL DENJI!!
PLEASE!! KILL HIM!!
WE'RE REALLY IN TROUBLE NOW...
LET'S FEED HIM TO THE DEVIL!
I'LL USE THE SWORD...
DO I HAVE YOUR PERMISSION, HIMENO?

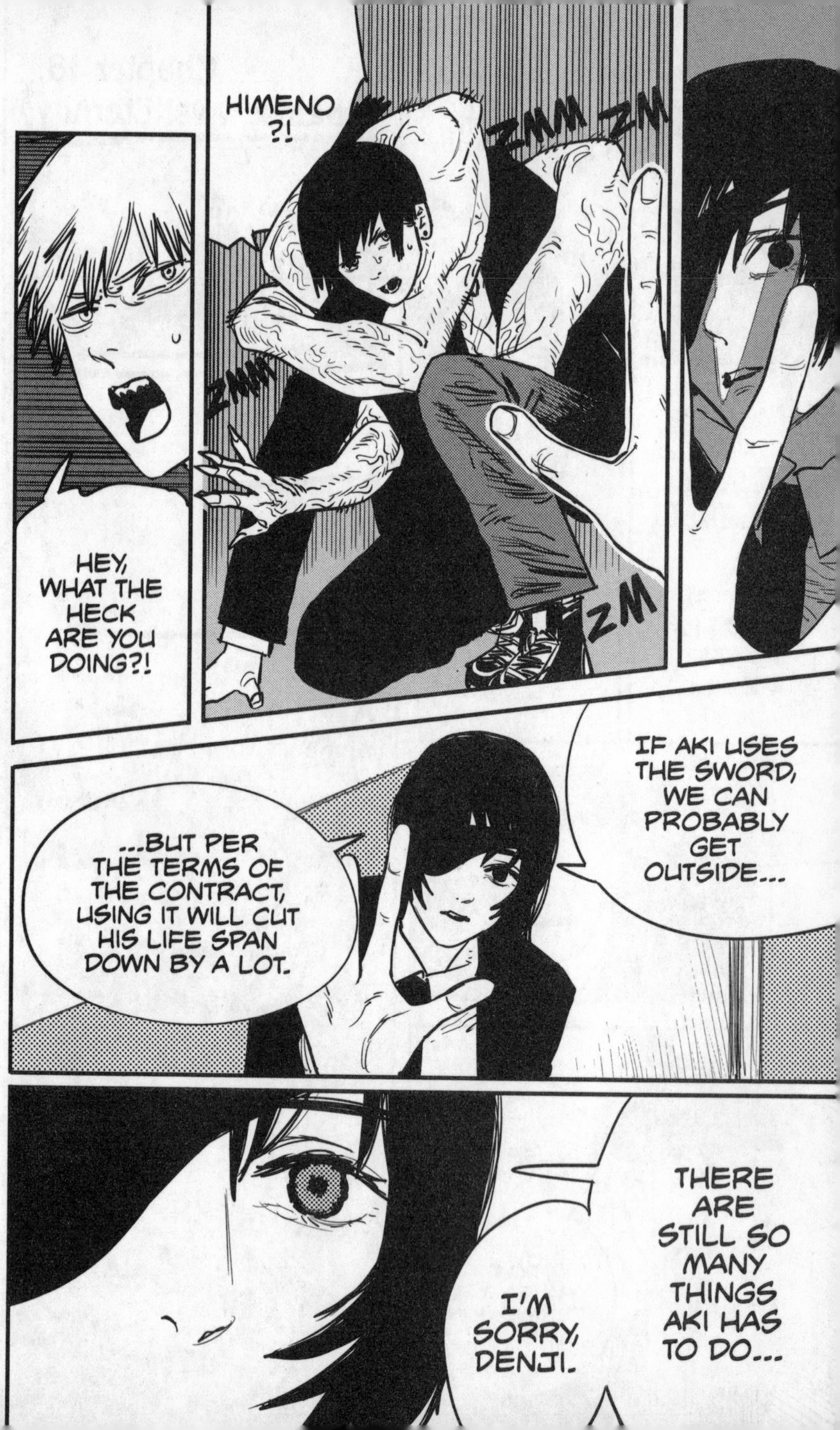
HIMENO ?!
ZMM ZM
ZMM
ZM
HEY, WHAT THE HECK ARE YOU DOING?!
IF AKI USES THE SWORD, WE CAN PROBABLY GET OUTSIDE...
...BUT PER THE TERMS OF THE CONTRACT, USING IT WILL CUT HIS LIFE SPAN DOWN BY A LOT.
THERE ARE STILL SO MANY THINGS AKI HAS TO DO...
I'M SORRY, DENJI.

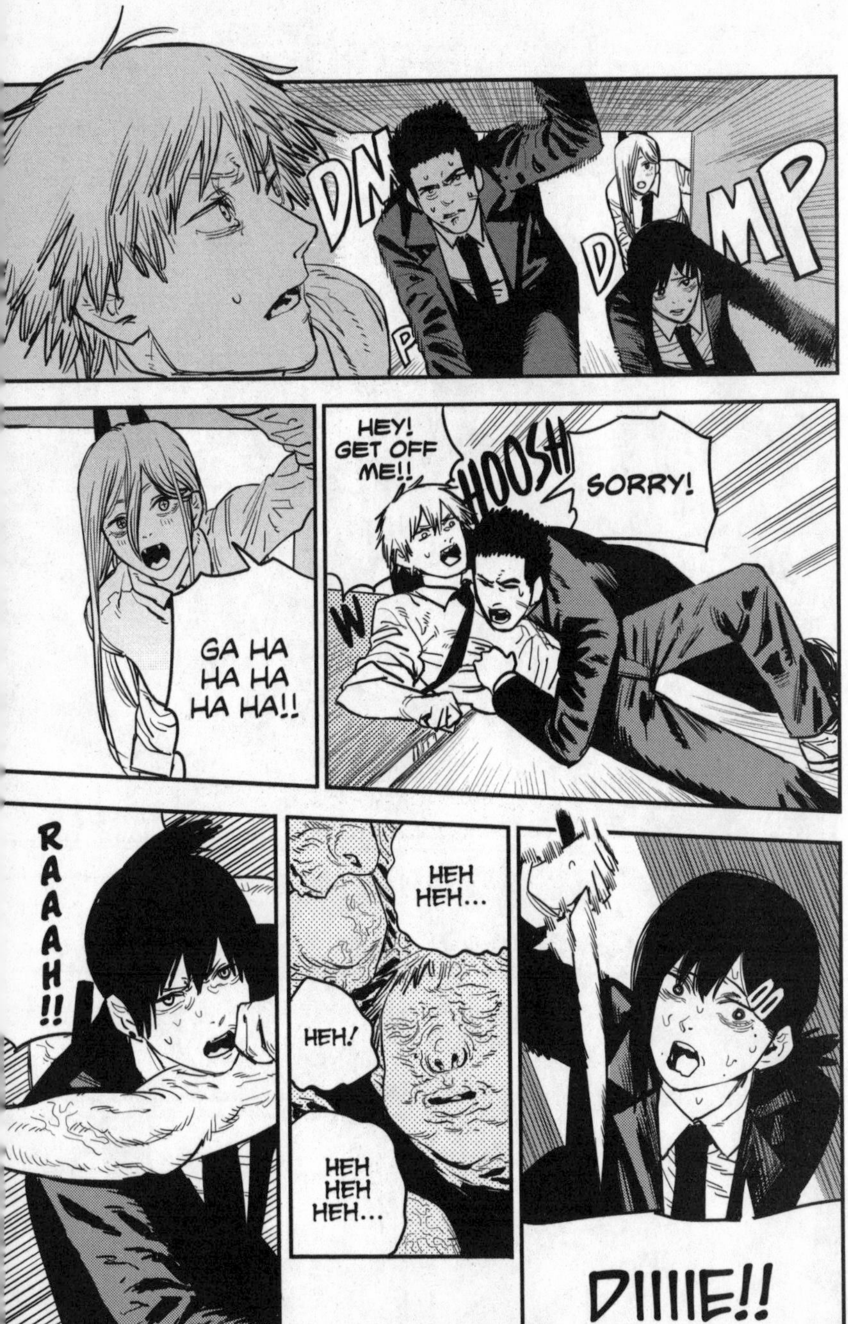
D
MP
DN
P
HEY! GET OFF ME!!
HOOSH
SORRY!
W
GA HA HA HA HA HA!!
DIIIIE!!
HEH HEH...
HEH!
HEH HEH HEH...
RAAAAH!!

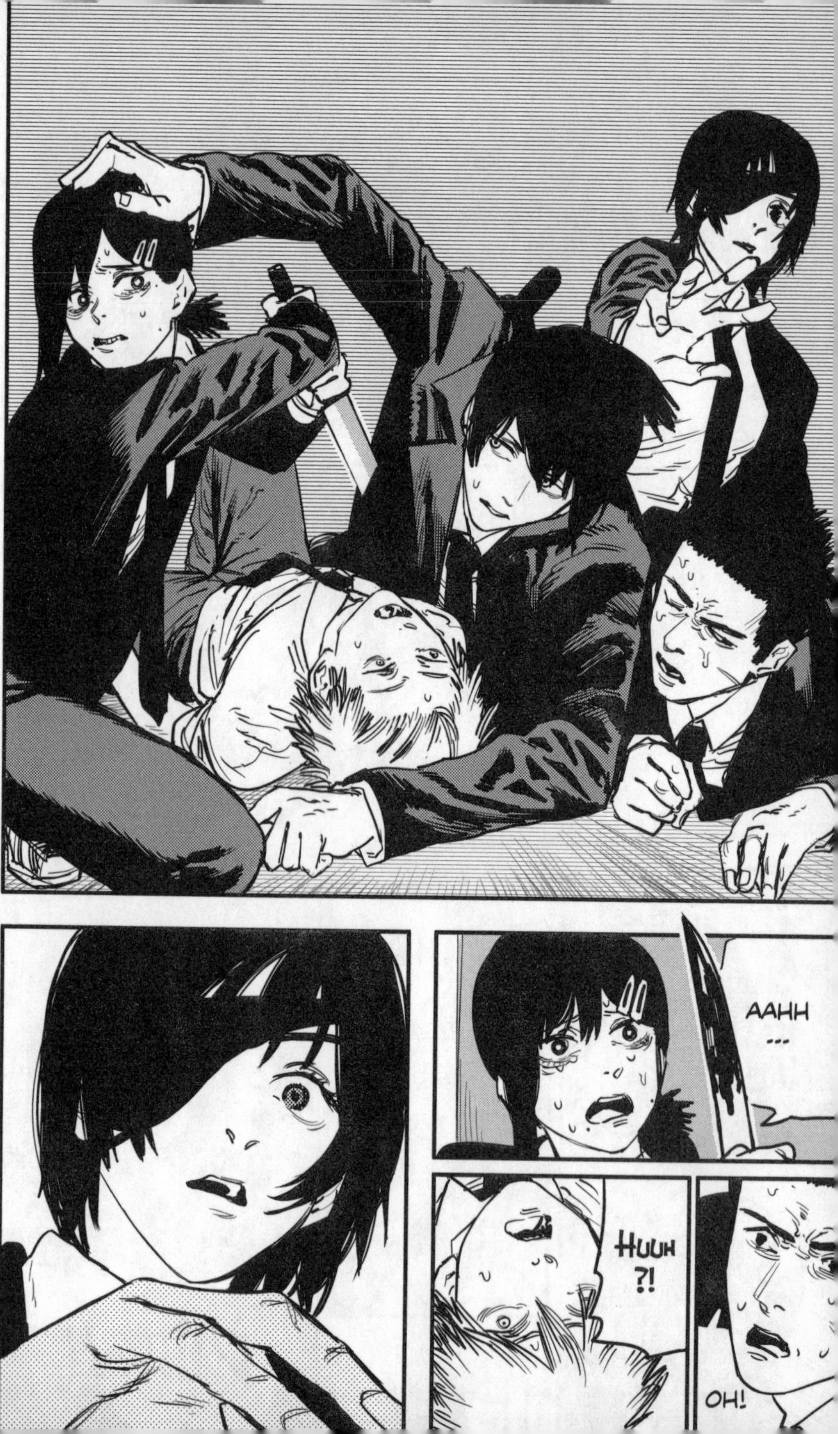
AAHH
...
HUUH
?!
OH!

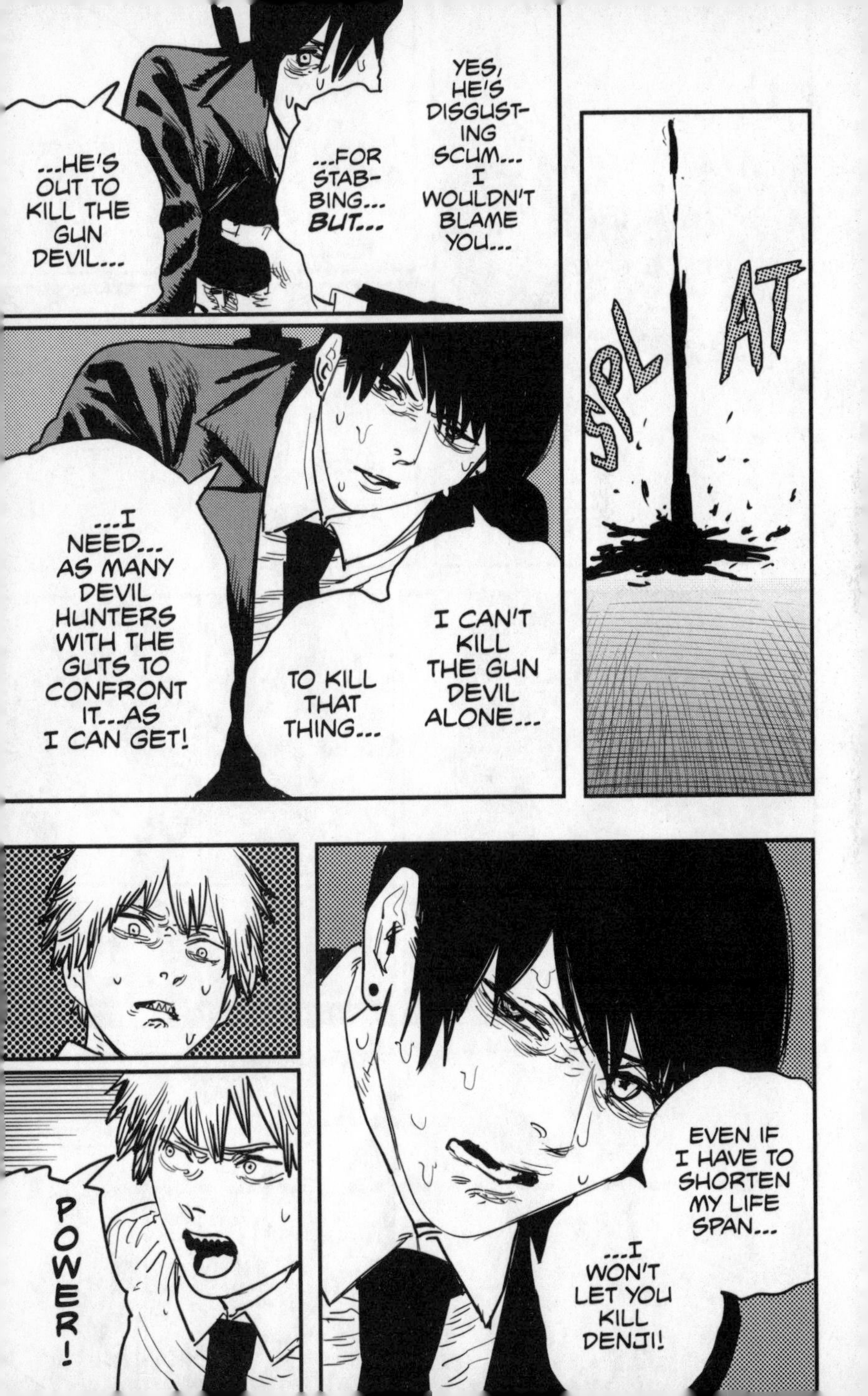
YES, HE'S DISGUSTING SCUM... I WOULDN'T BLAME YOU...
...FOR STABBING... *BUT...*
...HE'S OUT TO KILL THE GUN DEVIL...
SPLAT
I CAN'T KILL THE GUN DEVIL ALONE...
TO KILL THAT THING...
...I NEED... AS MANY DEVIL HUNTERS WITH THE GUTS TO CONFRONT IT...AS I CAN GET!
EVEN IF I HAVE TO SHORTEN MY LIFE SPAN...
...I WON'T LET YOU KILL DENJI!
POWER!

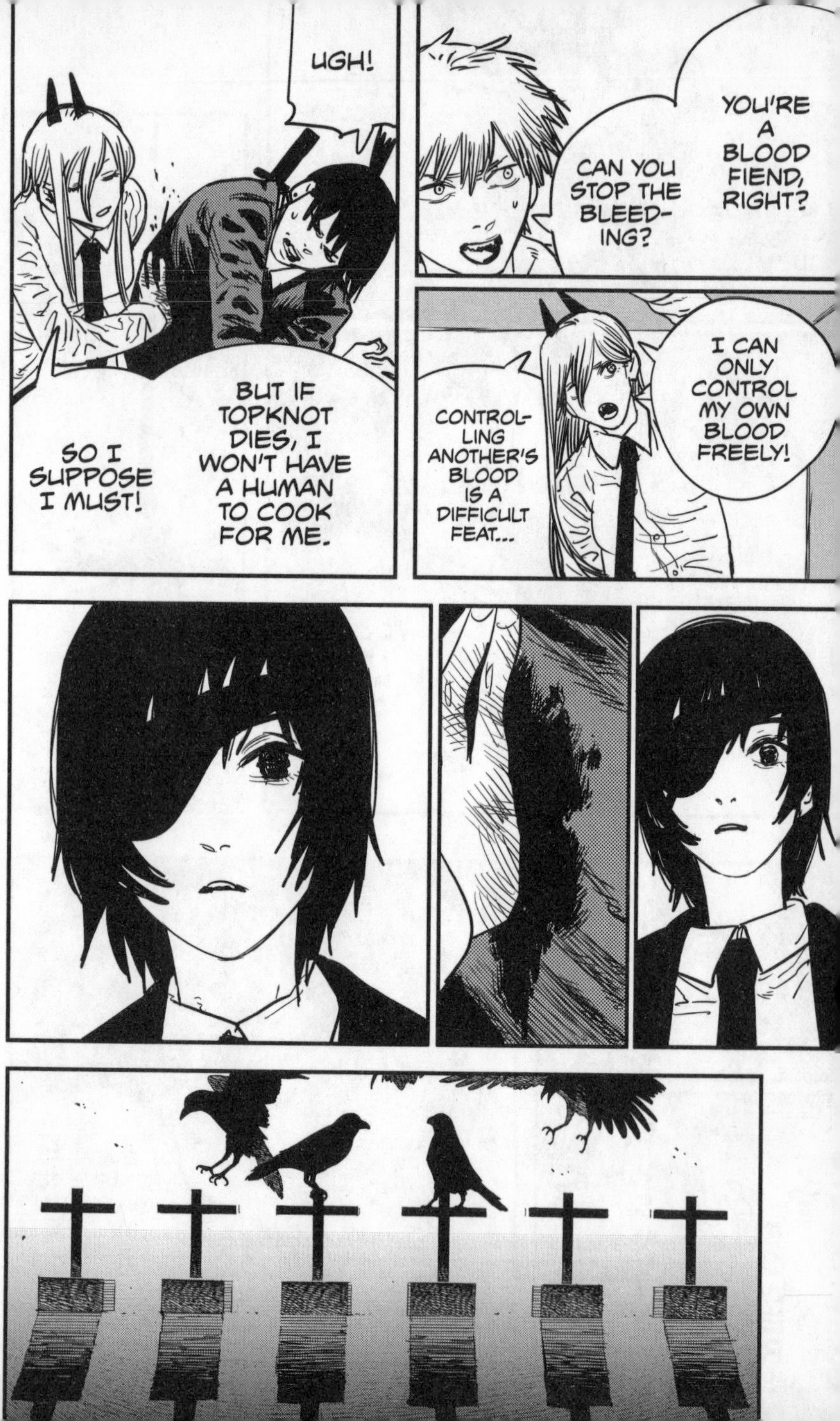
YOU'RE A BLOOD FIEND, RIGHT?
CAN YOU STOP THE BLEED-ING?
I CAN ONLY CONTROL MY OWN BLOOD FREELY!
CONTROL-LING ANOTHER'S BLOOD IS A DIFFICULT FEAT...
UGH!
BUT IF TOPKNOT DIES, I WON'T HAVE A HUMAN TO COOK FOR ME.
SO I SUPPOSE I MUST!

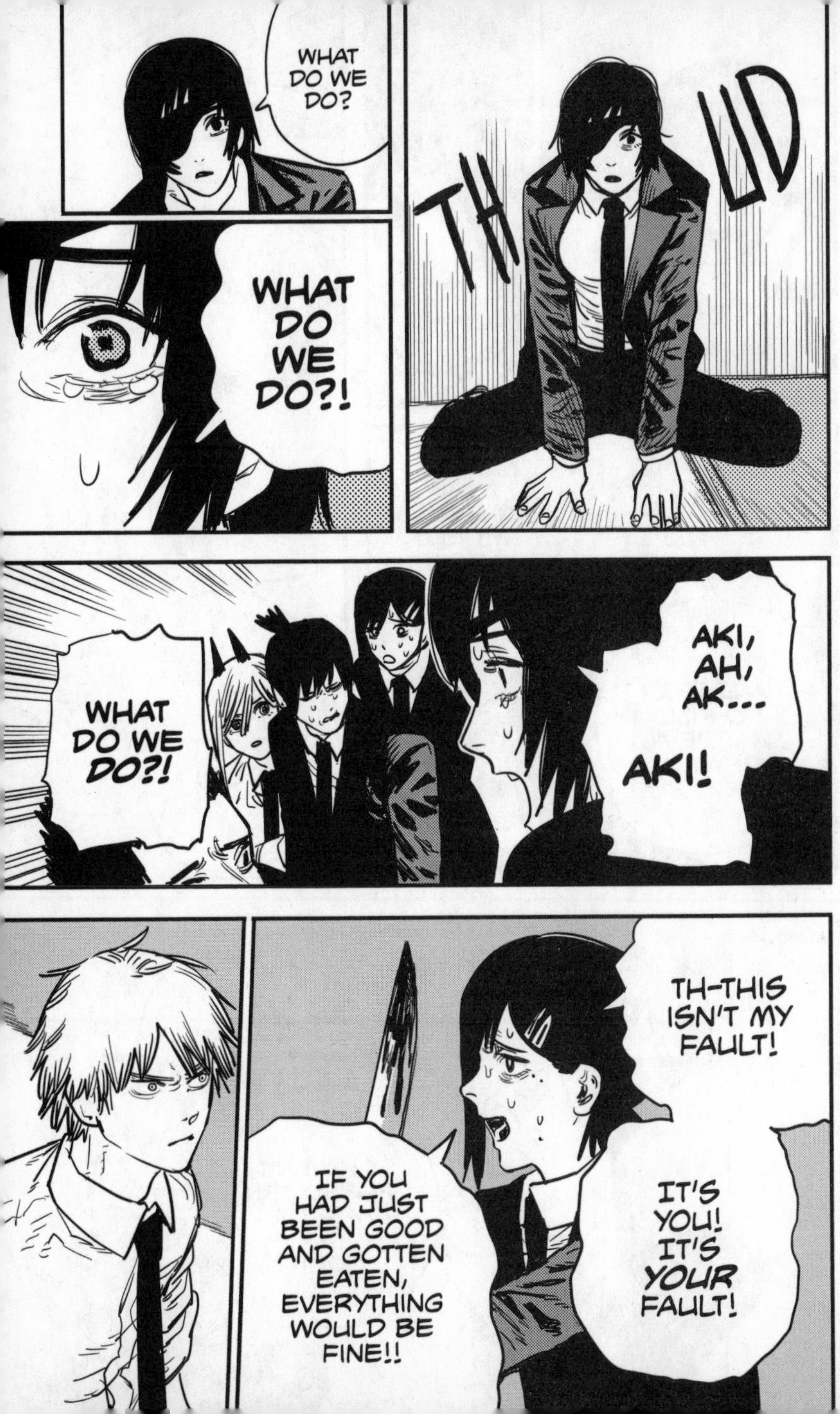
THUD
WHAT DO WE DO?
WHAT DO WE DO?!
AKI, AH, AK...
AKI!
WHAT DO WE DO?!
TH-THIS ISN'T MY FAULT!
IT'S YOU! IT'S *YOUR* FAULT!
IF YOU HAD JUST BEEN GOOD AND GOTTEN EATEN, EVERYTHING WOULD BE FINE!!

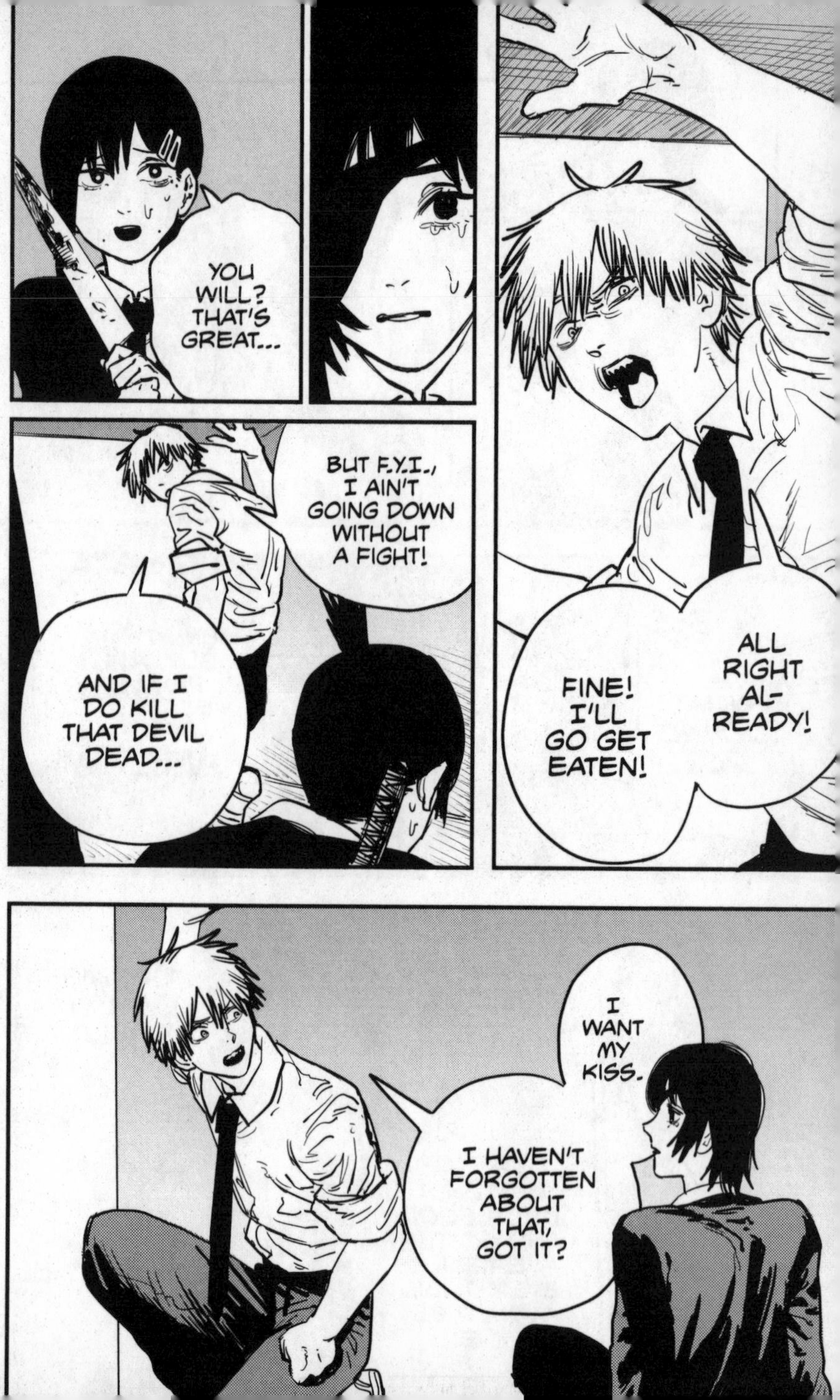
ALL RIGHT AL-READY!
FINE! I'LL GO GET EATEN!
YOU WILL? THAT'S GREAT...
BUT F.Y.I., I AIN'T GOING DOWN WITHOUT A FIGHT!
AND IF I DO KILL THAT DEVIL DEAD...
I WANT MY KISS.
I HAVEN'T FORGOTTEN ABOUT THAT, GOT IT?

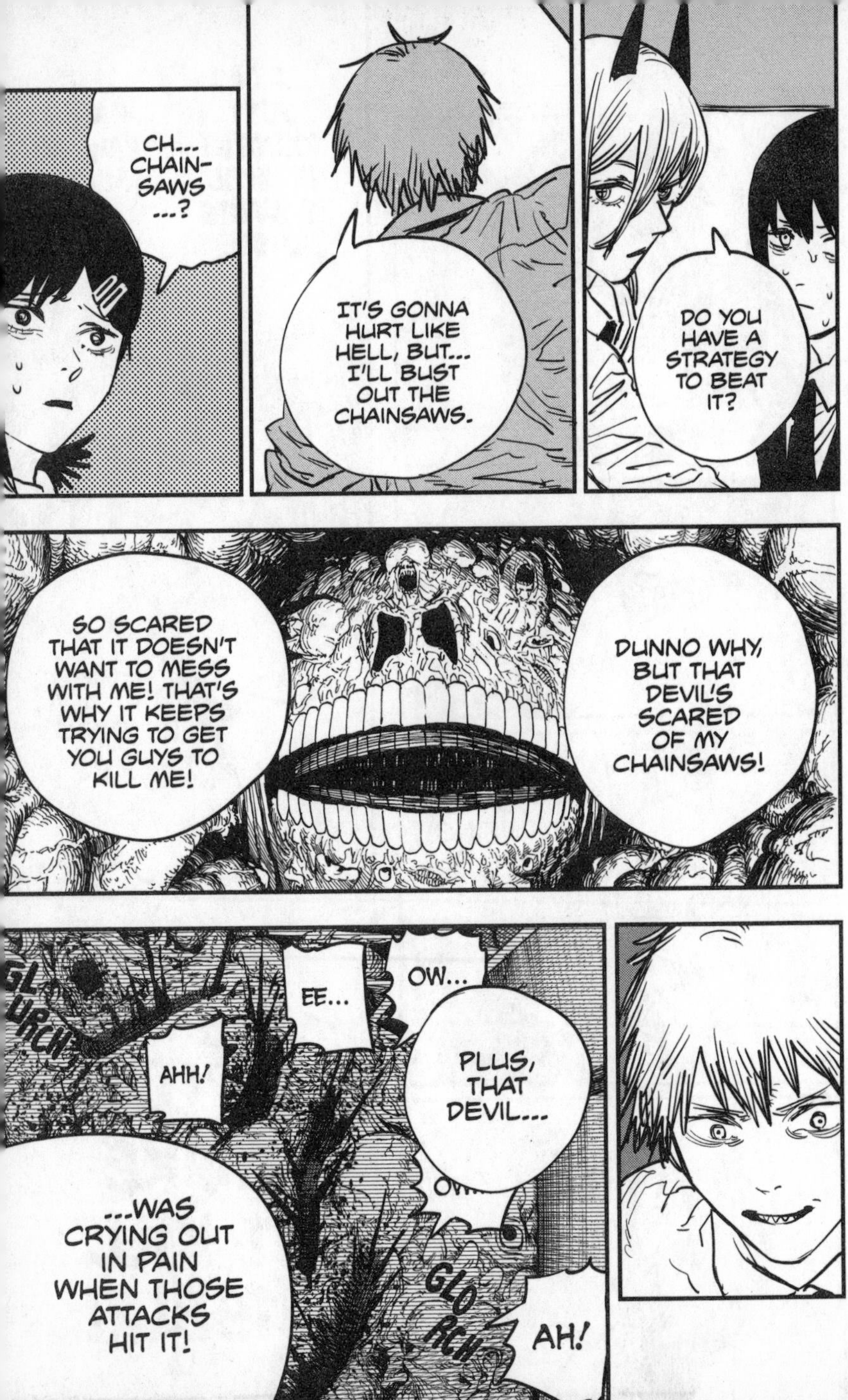
DO YOU HAVE A STRATEGY TO BEAT IT?
IT'S GONNA HURT LIKE HELL, BUT... I'LL BUST OUT THE CHAINSAWS.
CH... CHAIN-SAWS ...?
DUNNO WHY, BUT THAT DEVIL'S SCARED OF MY CHAINSAWS!
SO SCARED THAT IT DOESN'T WANT TO MESS WITH ME! THAT'S WHY IT KEEPS TRYING TO GET YOU GUYS TO KILL ME!
OW...
EE...
PLUS, THAT DEVIL...
GLURCH
AHH!
...WAS CRYING OUT IN PAIN WHEN THOSE ATTACKS HIT IT!
GLORCH
AH!

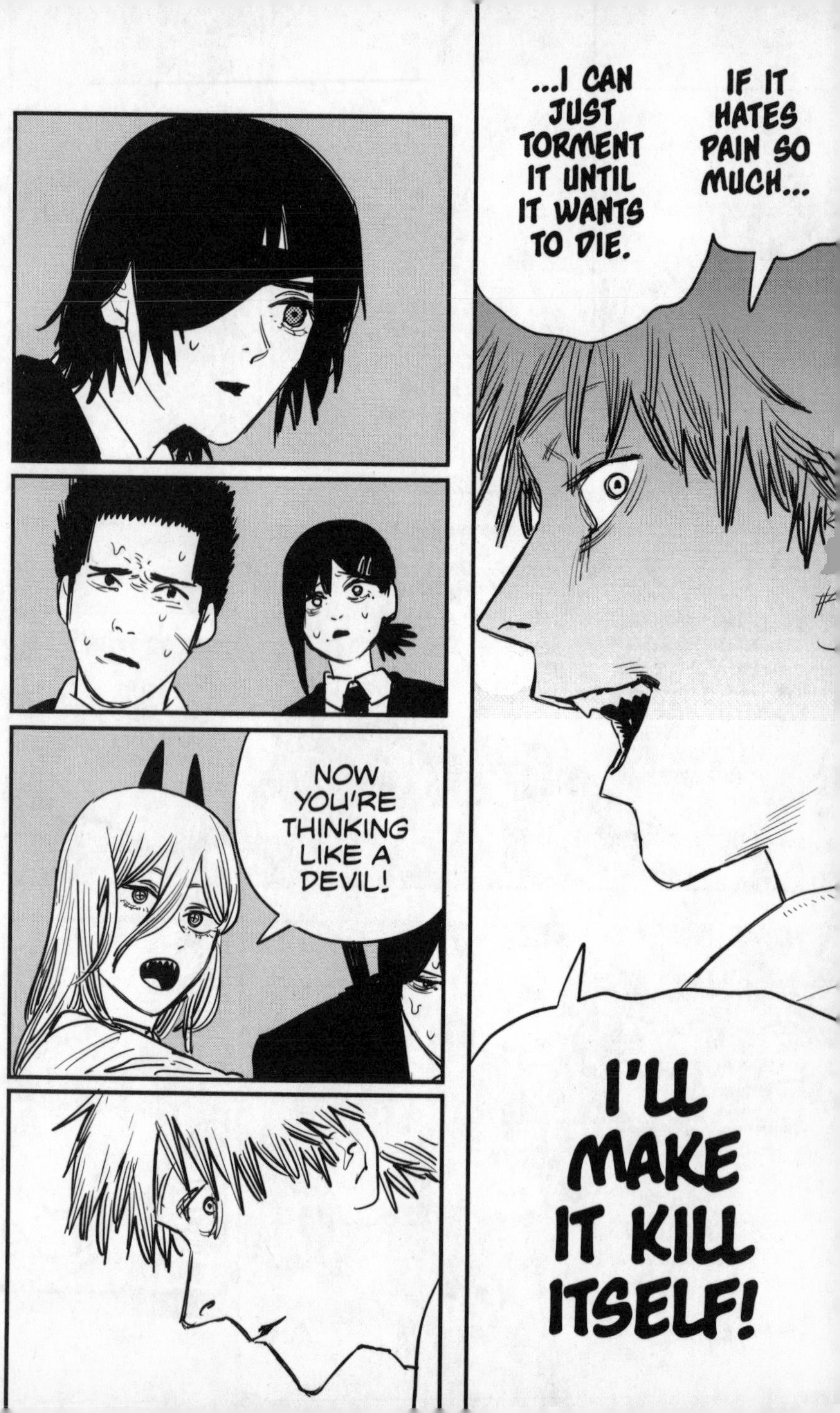
IF IT HATES PAIN SO MUCH...
...I CAN JUST TORMENT IT UNTIL IT WANTS TO DIE.
I'LL MAKE IT KILL ITSELF!
NOW YOU'RE THINKING LIKE A DEVIL!

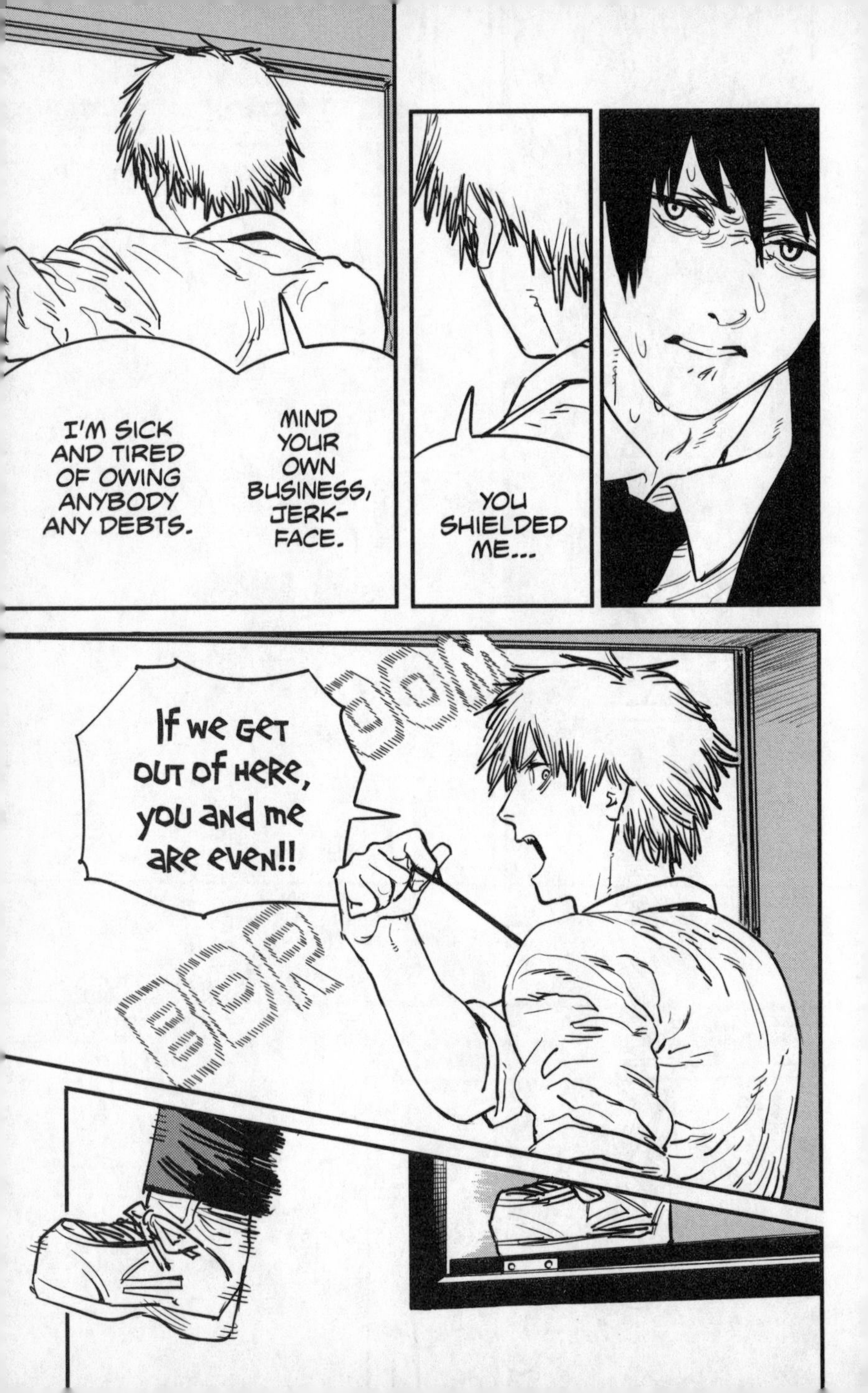
YOU SHIELDED ME...
MIND YOUR OWN BUSINESS, JERK-FACE.
I'M SICK AND TIRED OF OWING ANYBODY ANY DEBTS.
If we get out of here, you and me are even!!

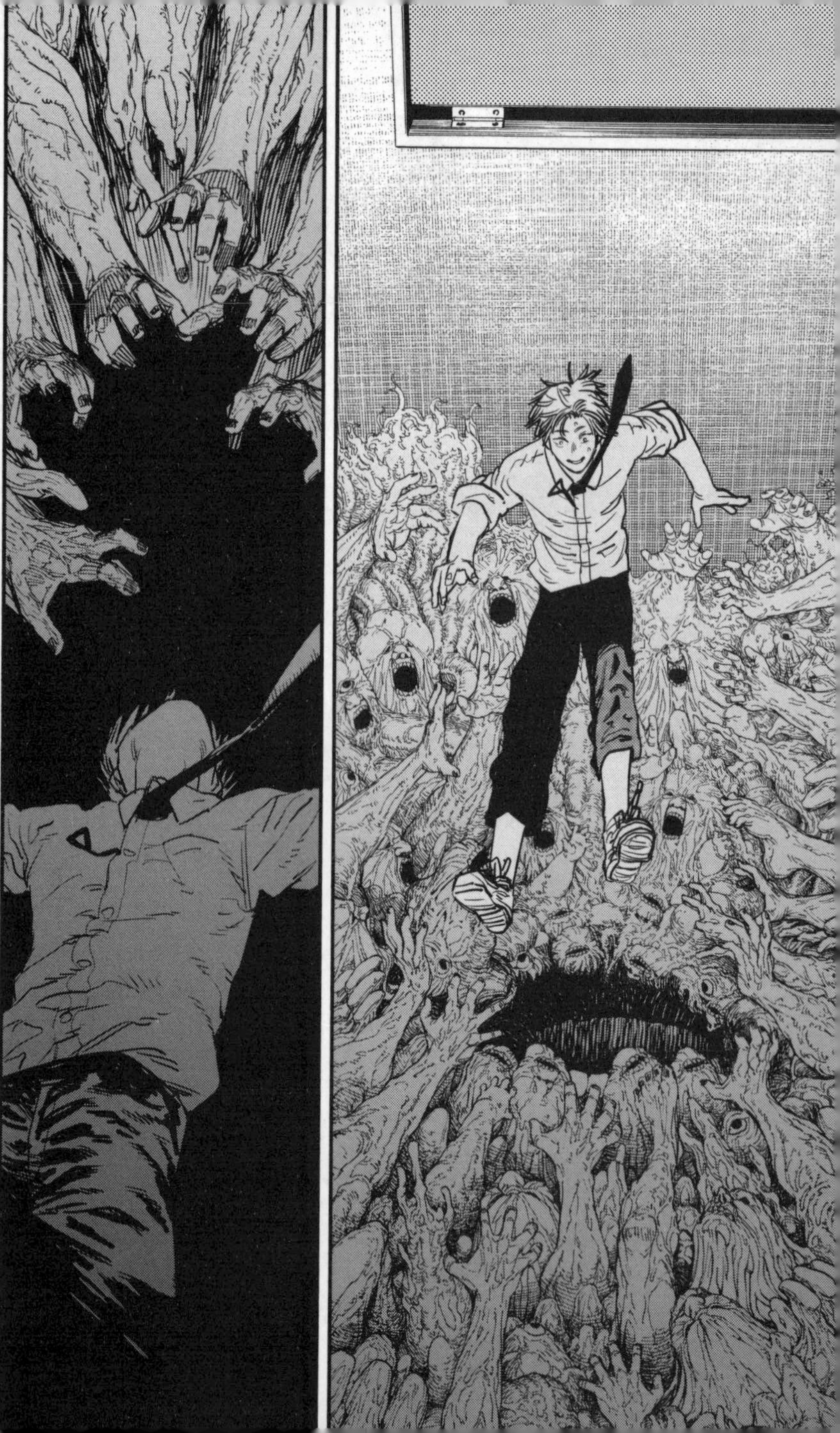

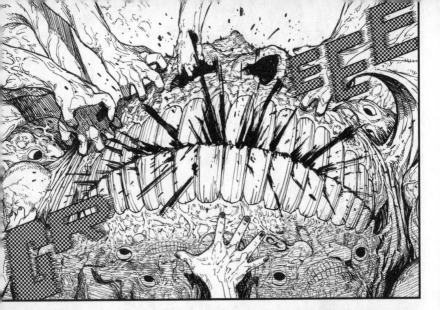

HE
DID
IT...

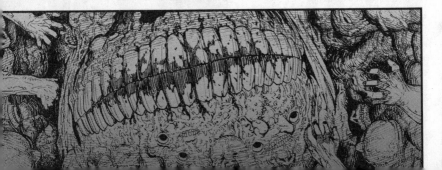

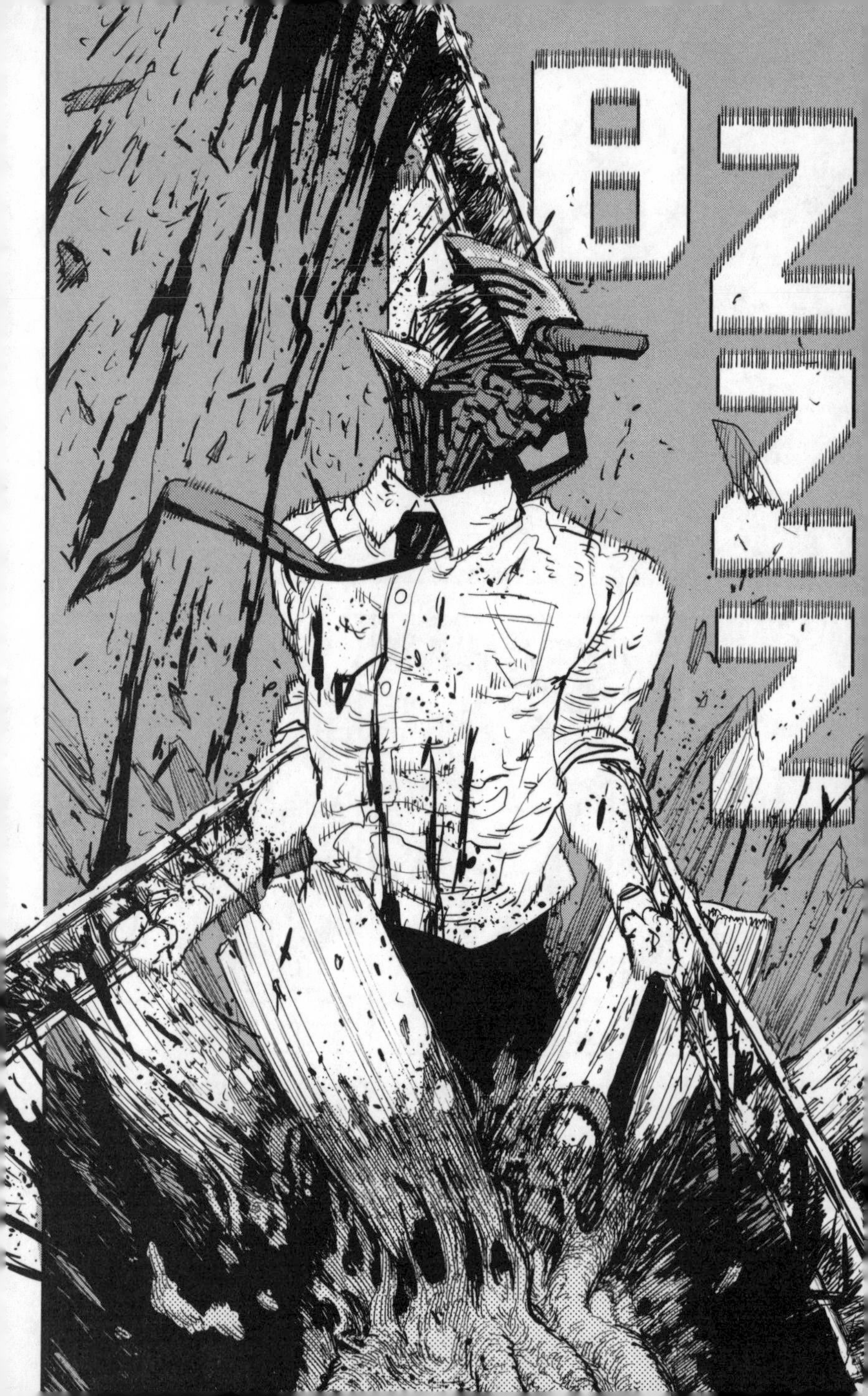
BZZZZ

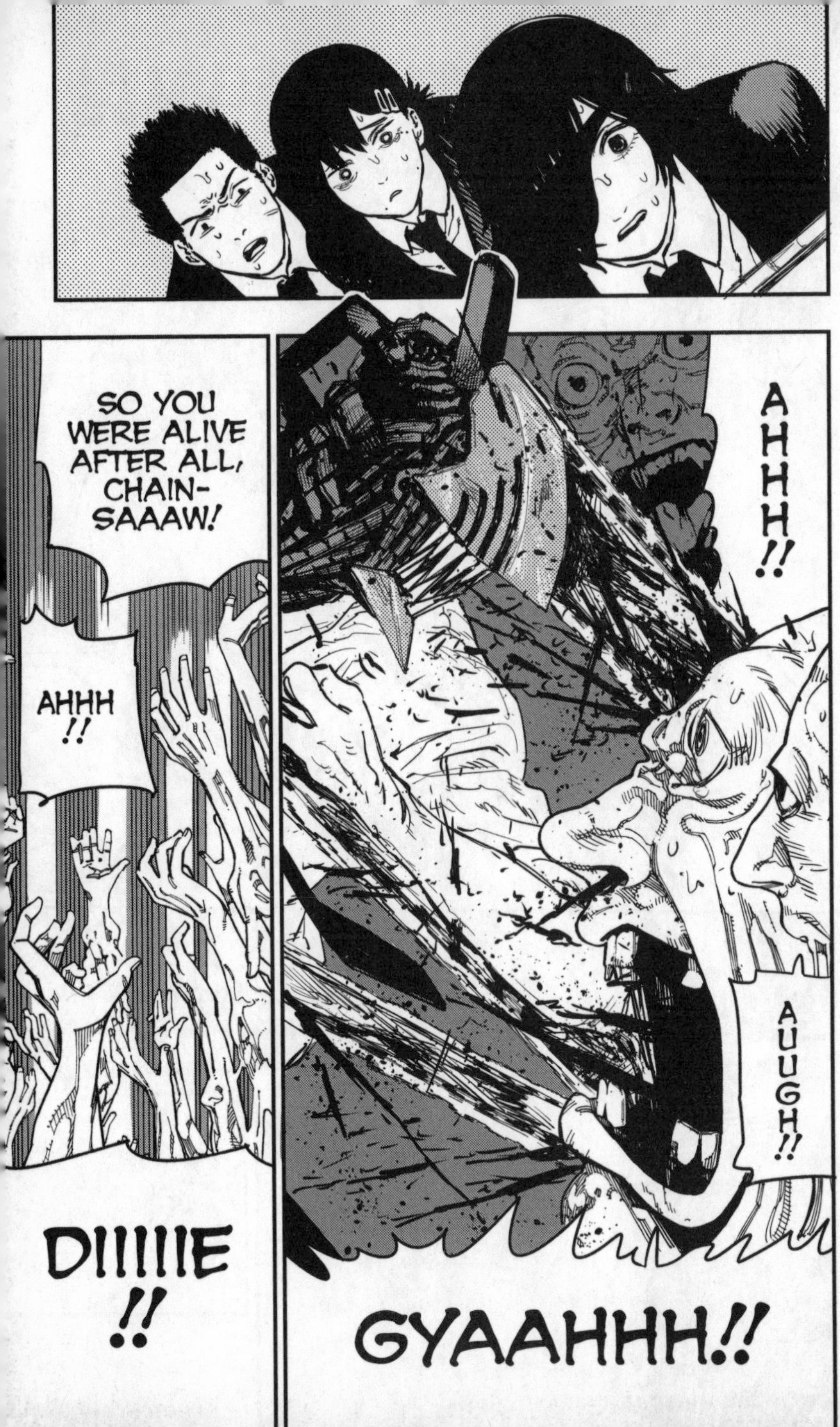
AHHH!!
AUUGH!!
GYAAHHH!!
SO YOU WERE ALIVE AFTER ALL, CHAIN-SAAAW!
AHHH!!
DIIIIIE!!

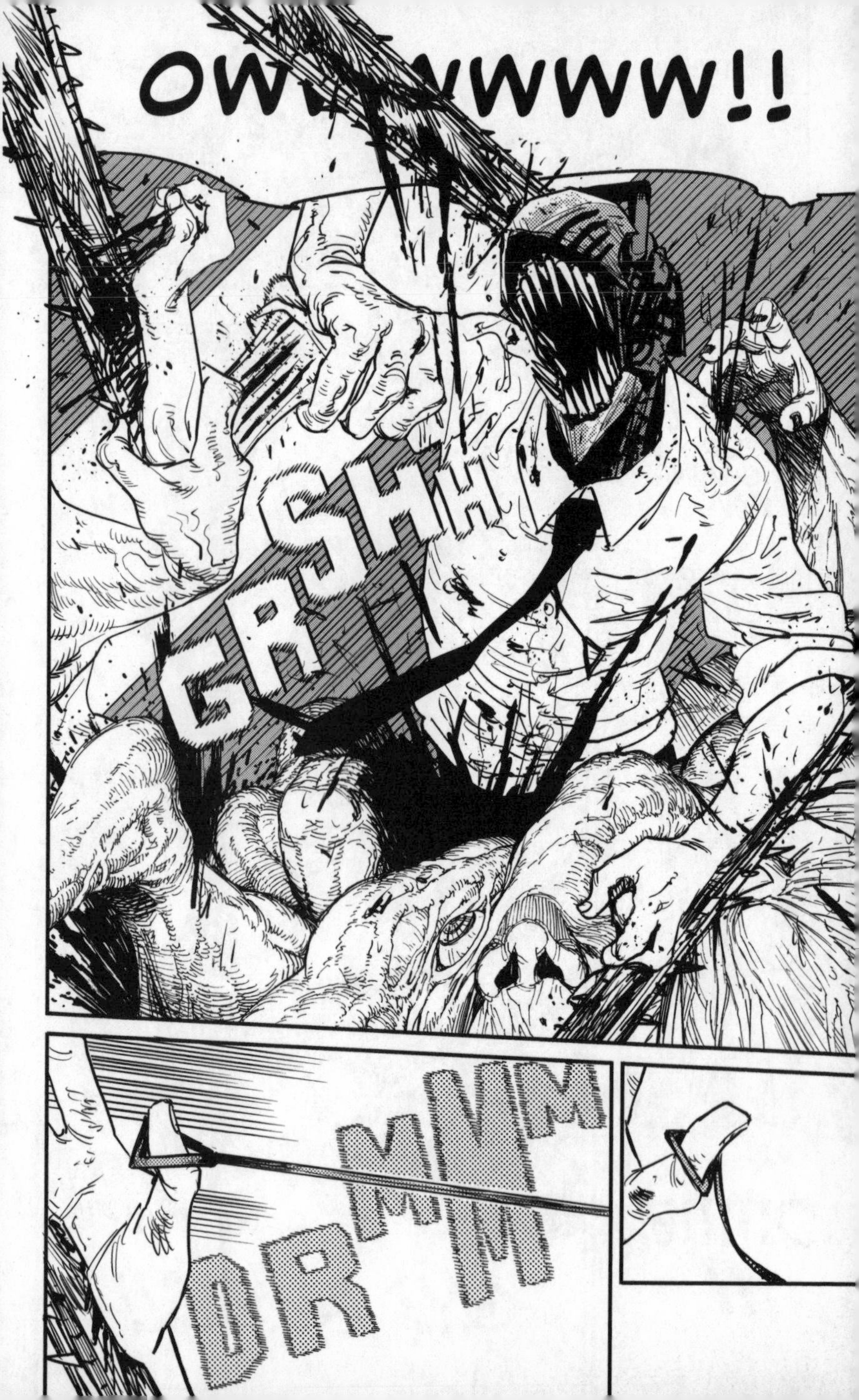
OWWWWWW!!
GRSHH
DRMMMM

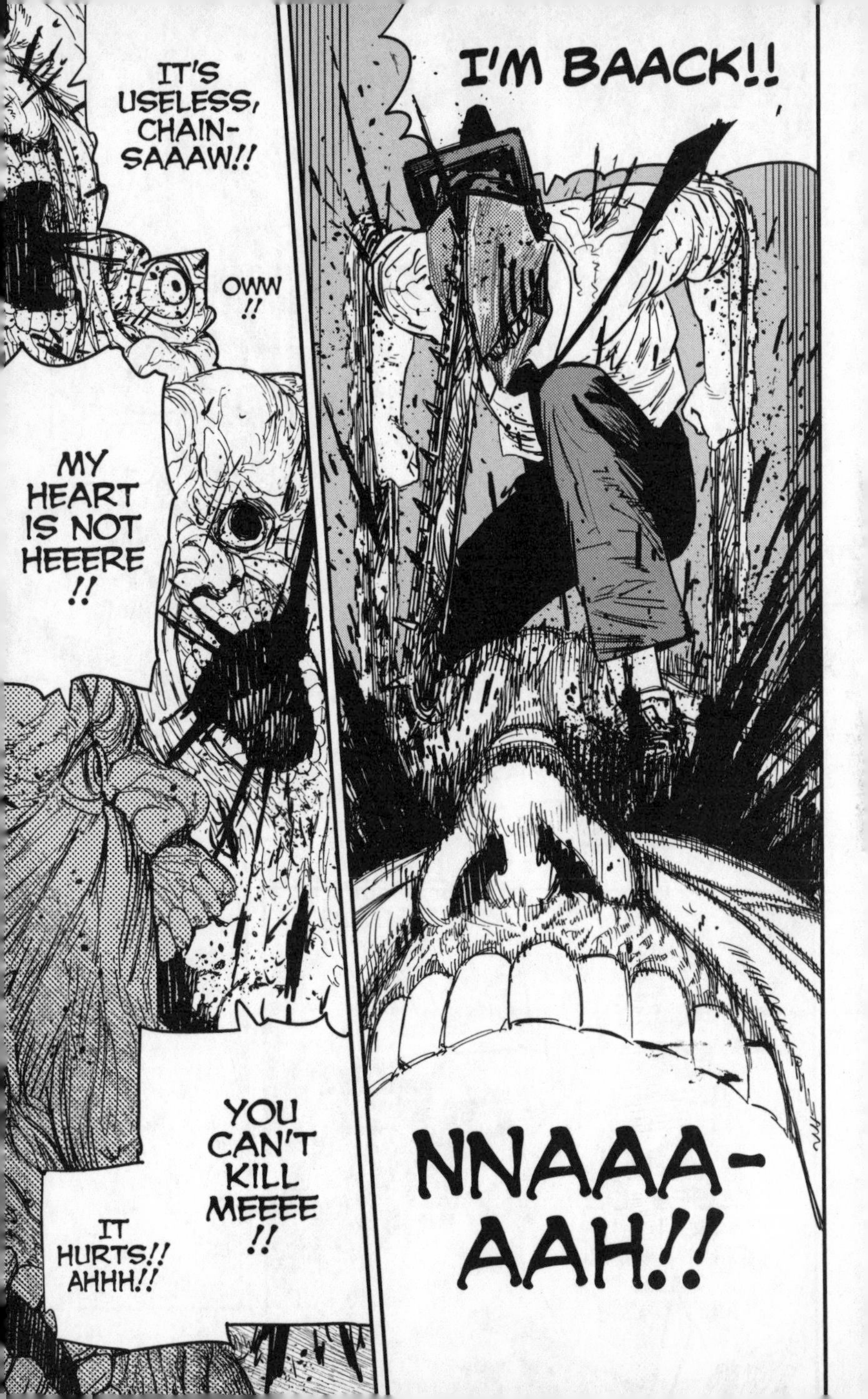
I'M BAACK!!
NNAAA-AAH!!
IT'S USELESS, CHAIN-SAAAW!!
OWW!!
MY HEART IS NOT HEEERE!!
YOU CAN'T KILL MEEEE!!
IT HURTS!! AHHH!!

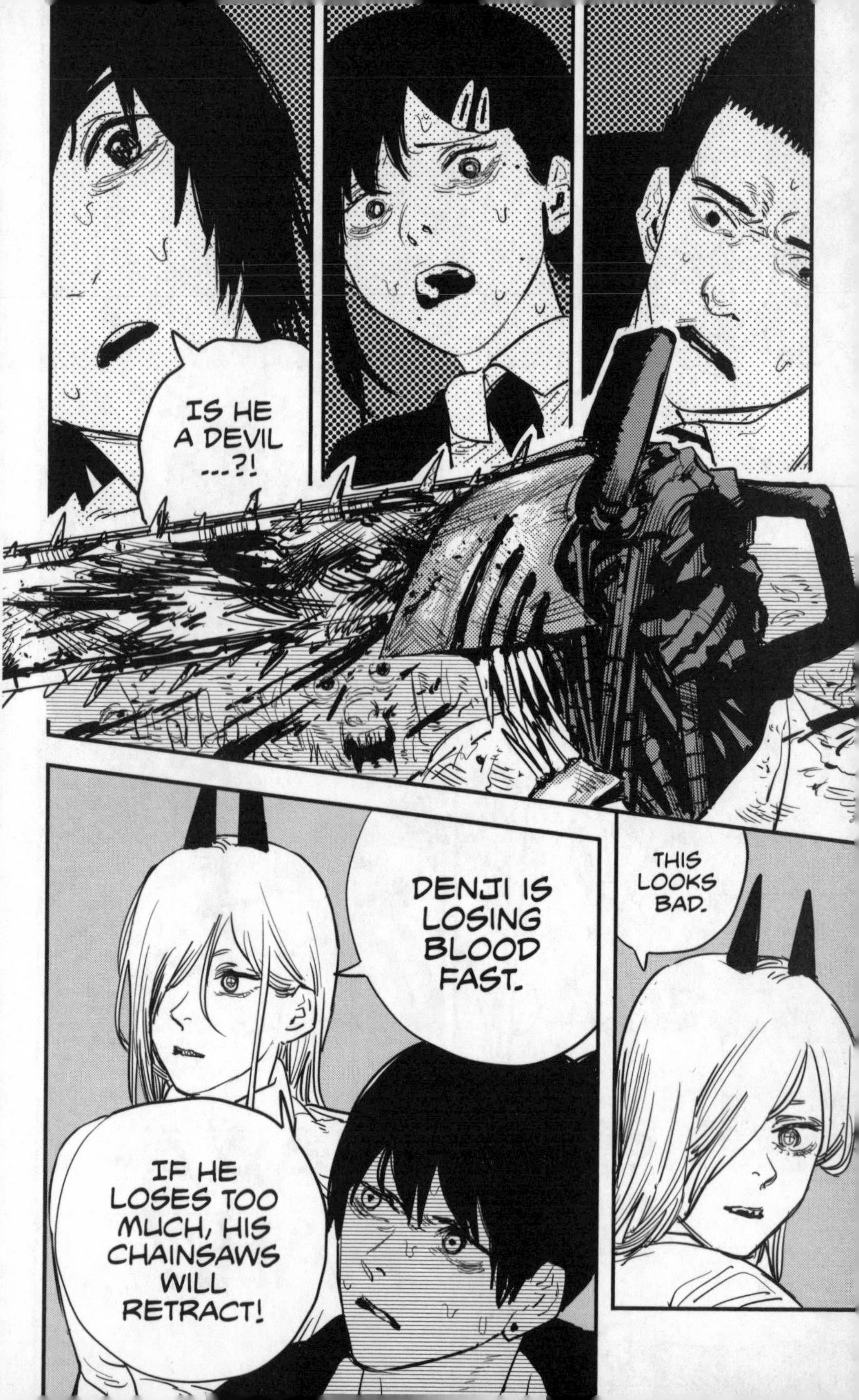
IS HE A DEVIL ---?!
THIS LOOKS BAD.
DENJI IS LOSING BLOOD FAST.
IF HE LOSES TOO MUCH, HIS CHAINSAWS WILL RETRACT!

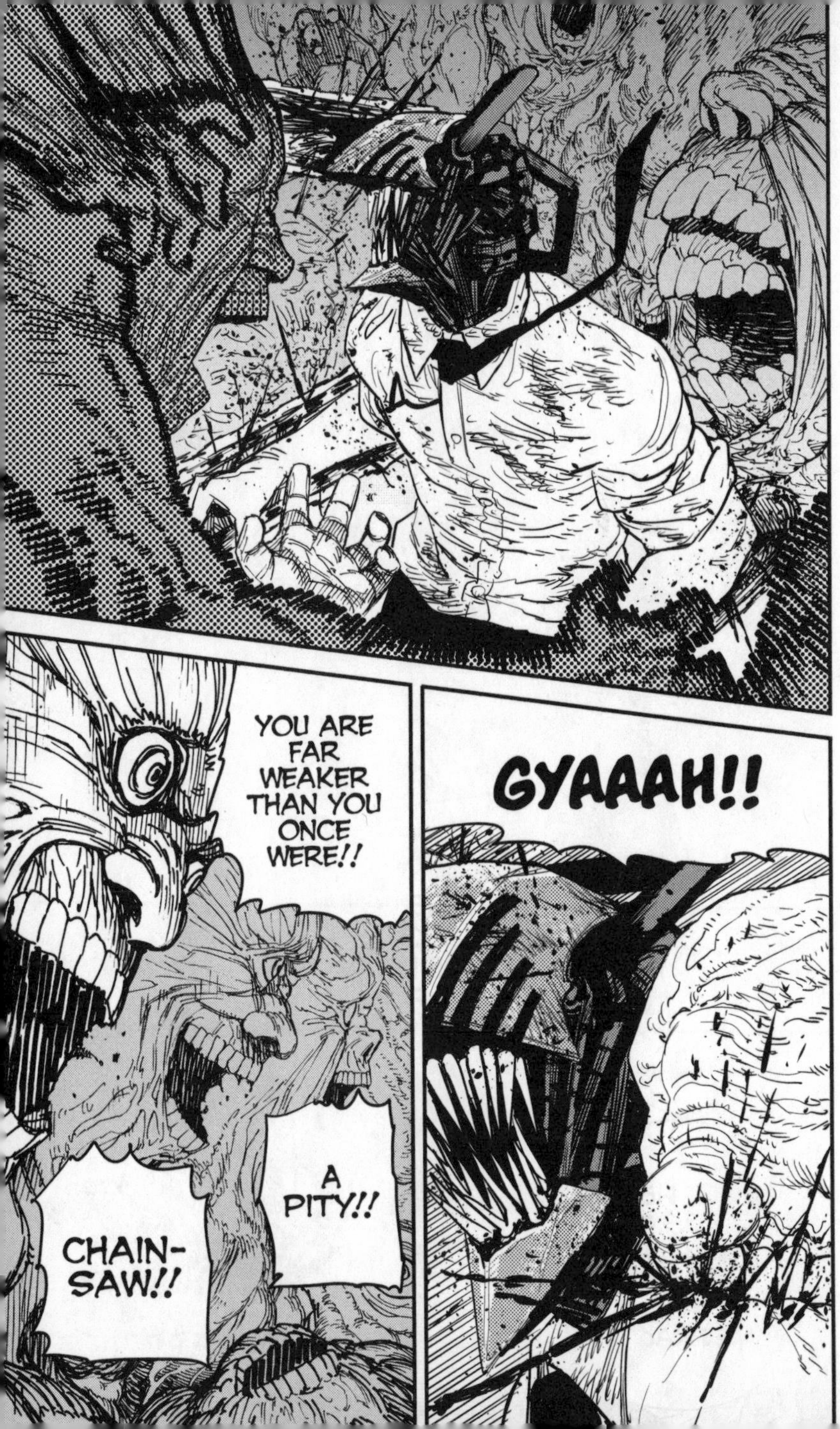
GYAAAH!!
YOU ARE FAR WEAKER THAN YOU ONCE WERE!!
A PITY!!
CHAIN-SAW!!

*Chain
saw man*

Chapter 19: Nobel Prize

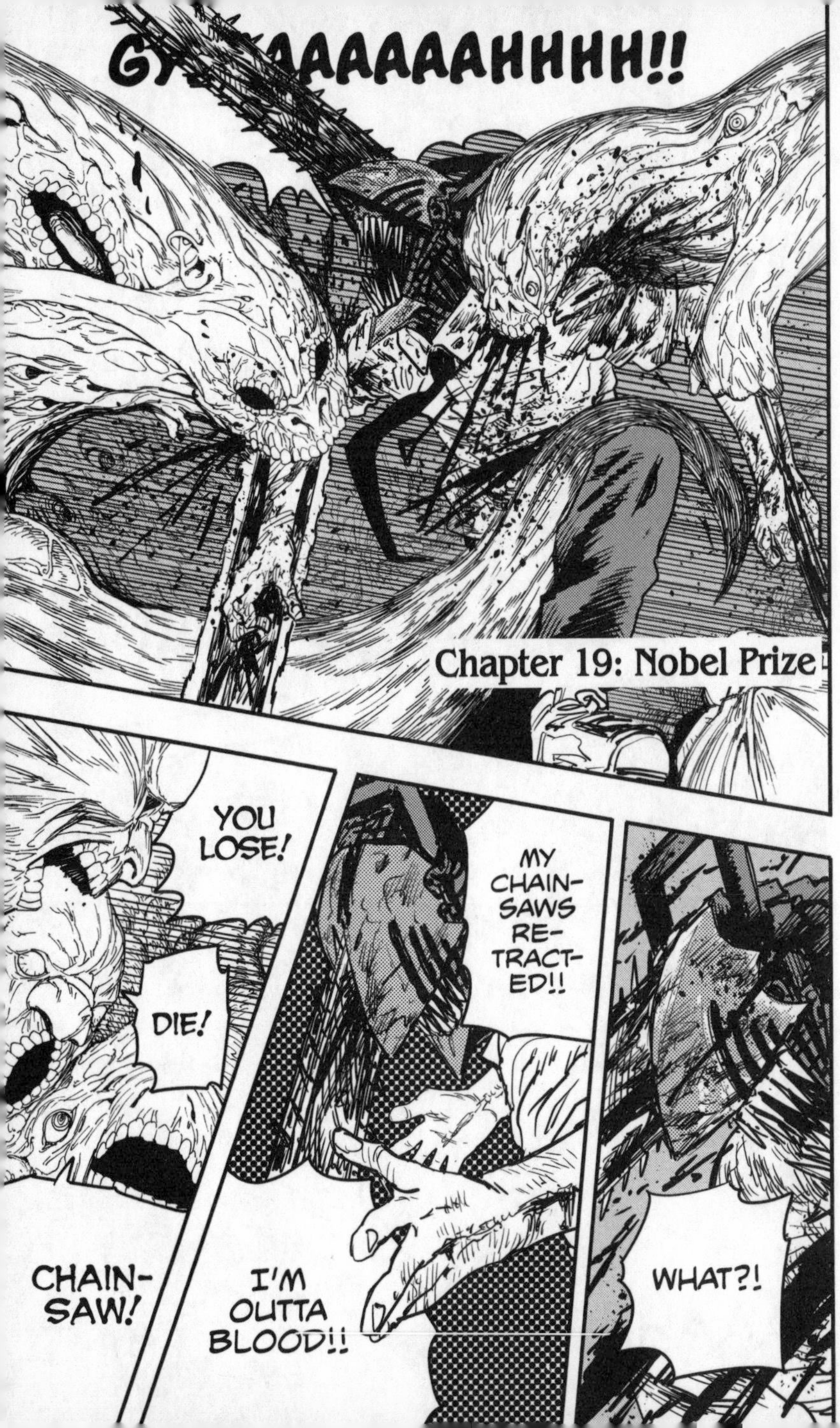
GYAAAAAAAHHHH!!
WHAT?!
MY CHAIN-SAWS RE-TRACT-ED!!
I'M OUTTA BLOOD!!
YOU LOSE!
DIE!
CHAIN-SAW!

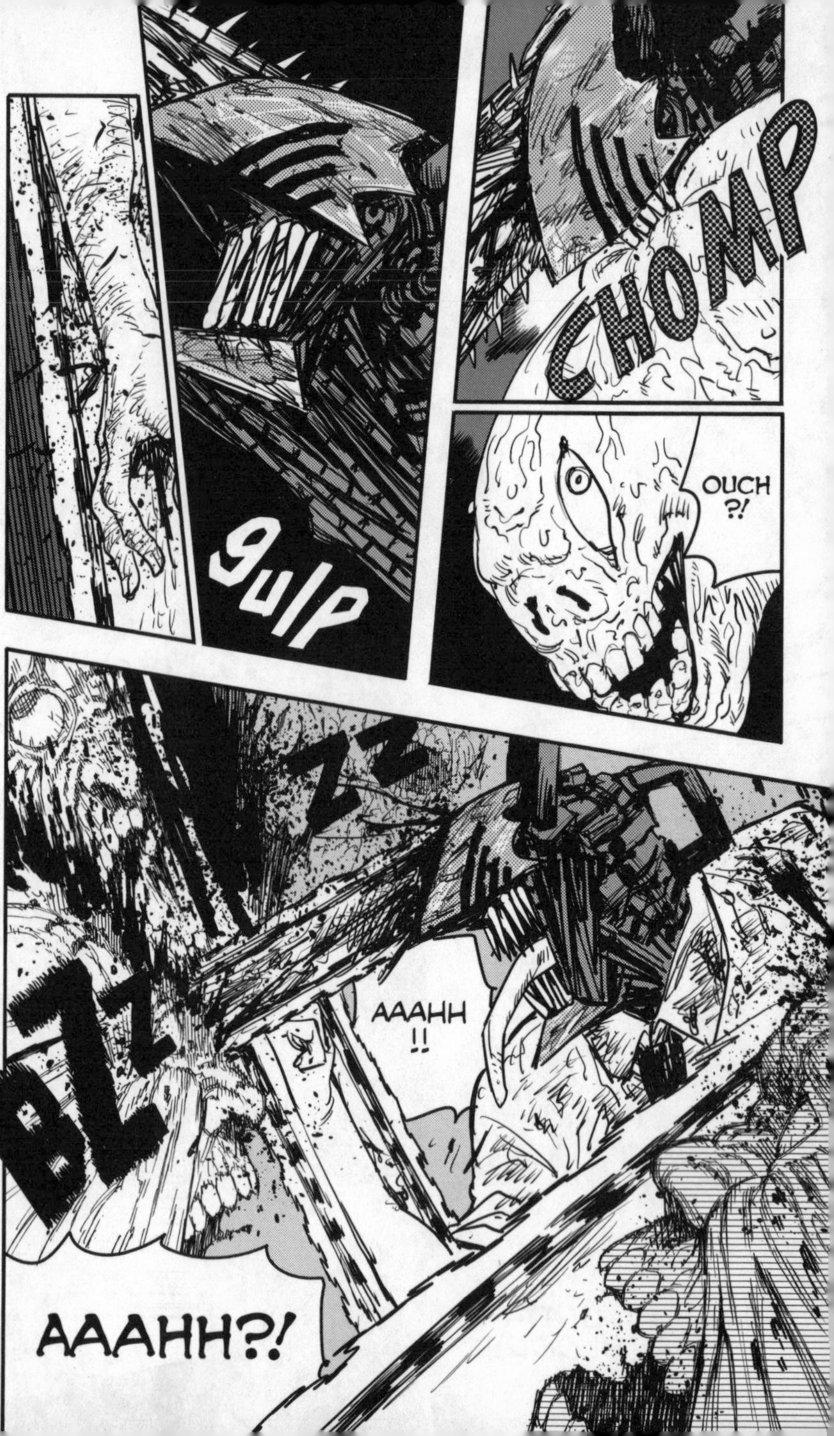
CHOMP
OUCH ?!
gulp
BZZZ
AAAHH !!
AAAHH?!

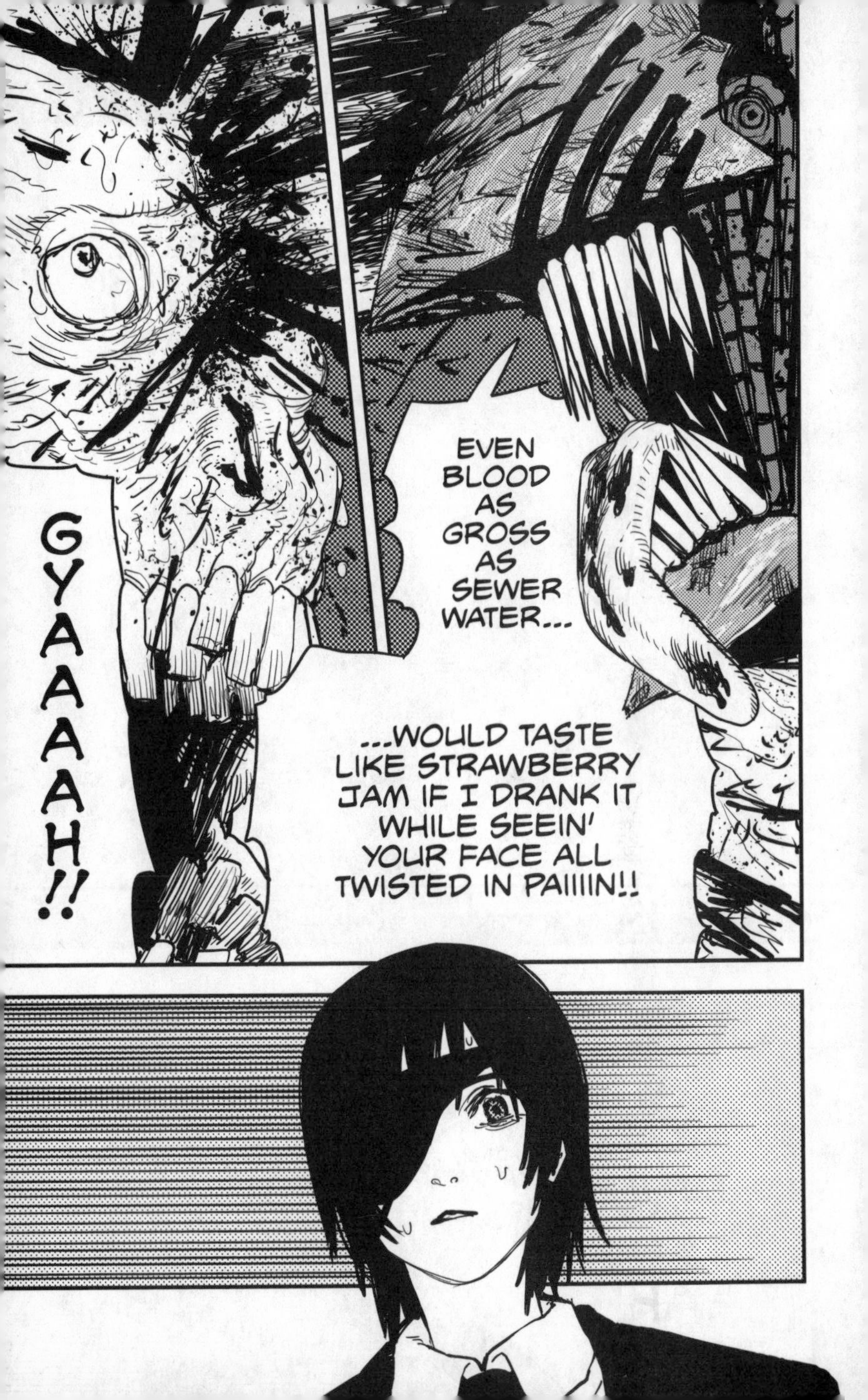
EVEN BLOOD AS GROSS AS SEWER WATER...
...WOULD TASTE LIKE STRAWBERRY JAM IF I DRANK IT WHILE SEEIN' YOUR FACE ALL TWISTED IN PAIIIIIN!!
GYAAAAH!!

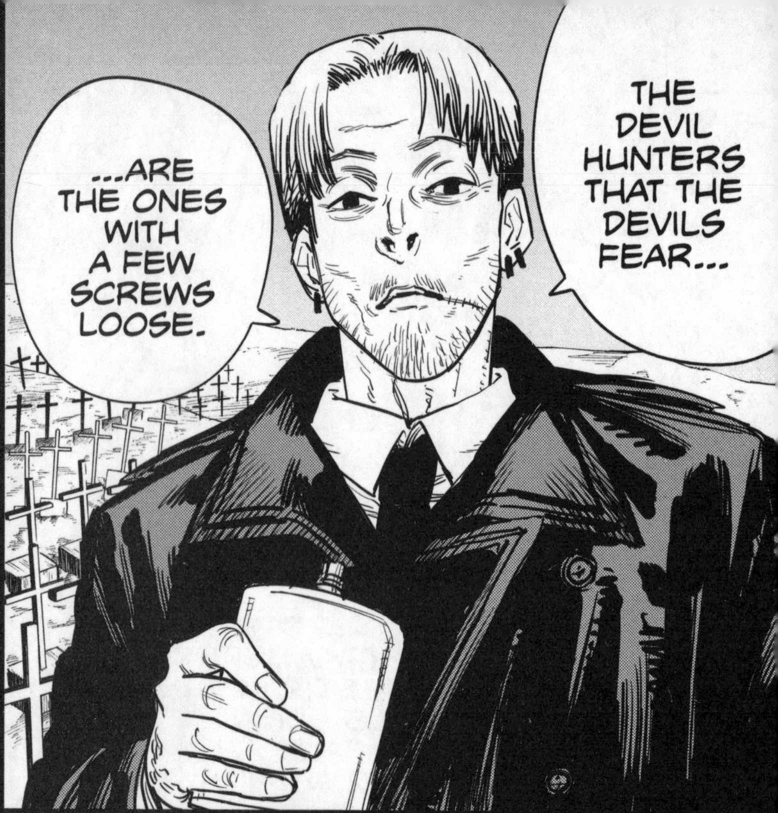
THE DEVIL HUNTERS THAT THE DEVILS FEAR...
...ARE THE ONES WITH A FEW SCREWS LOOSE.
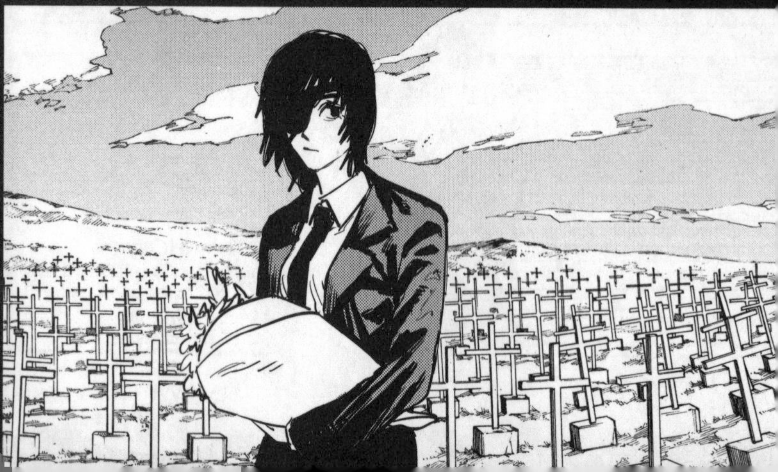

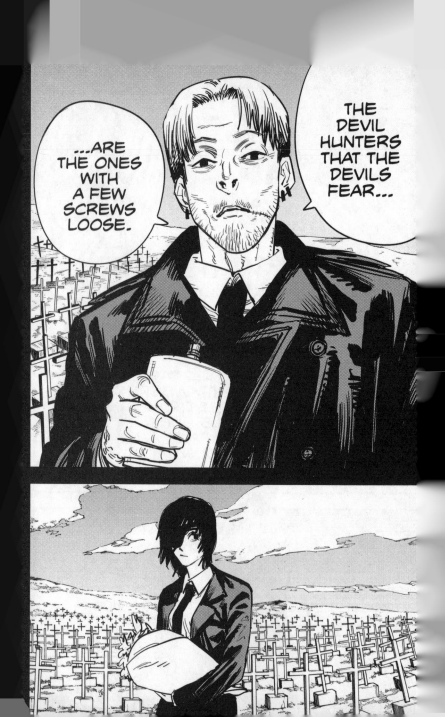

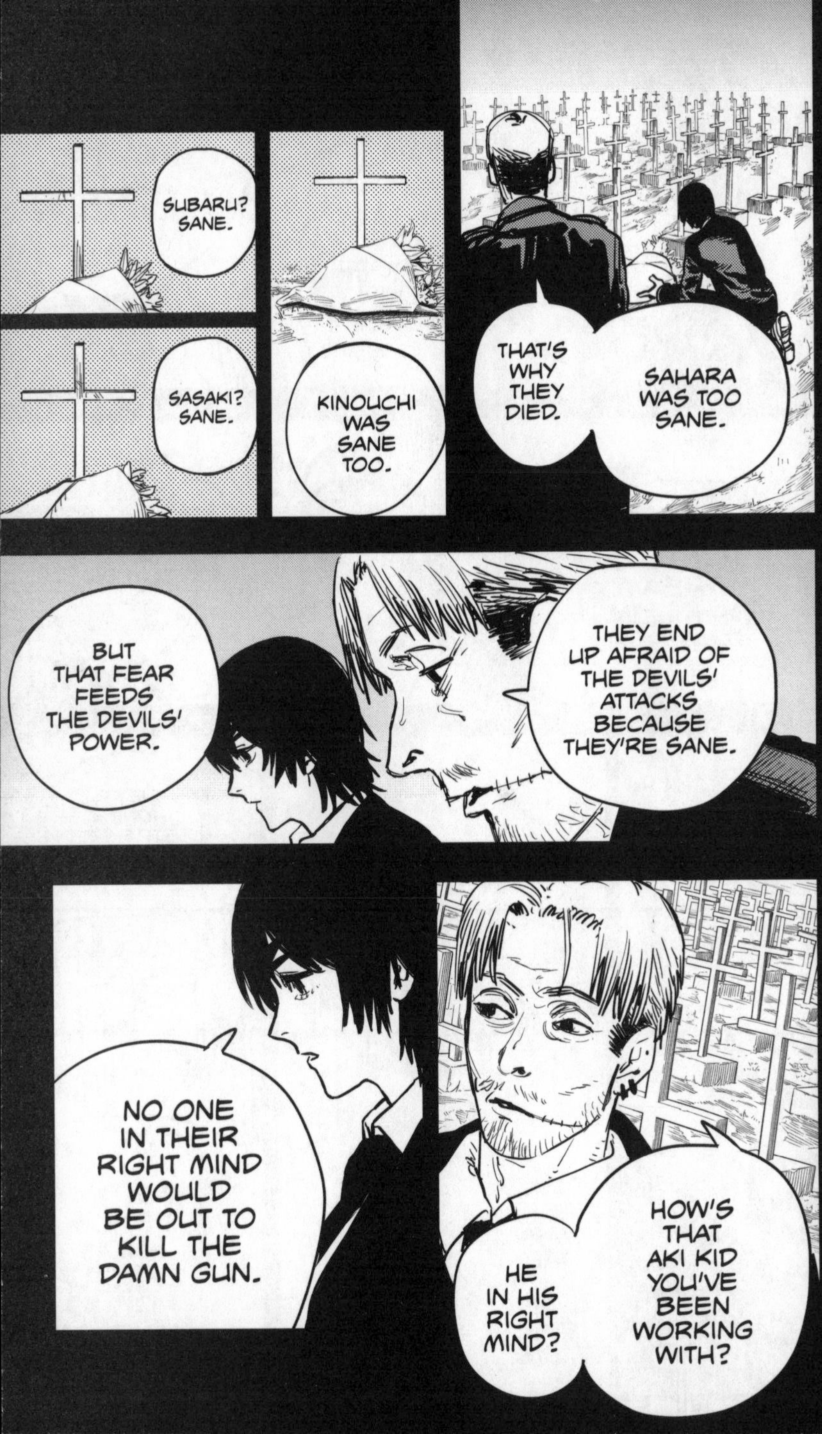
SAHARA WAS TOO SANE.
THAT'S WHY THEY DIED.
KINOUCHI WAS SANE TOO.
SUBARU? SANE.
SASAKI? SANE.
THEY END UP AFRAID OF THE DEVILS' ATTACKS BECAUSE THEY'RE SANE.
BUT THAT FEAR FEEDS THE DEVILS' POWER.
HOW'S THAT AKI KID YOU'VE BEEN WORKING WITH?
HE IN HIS RIGHT MIND?
NO ONE IN THEIR RIGHT MIND WOULD BE OUT TO KILL THE DAMN GUN.

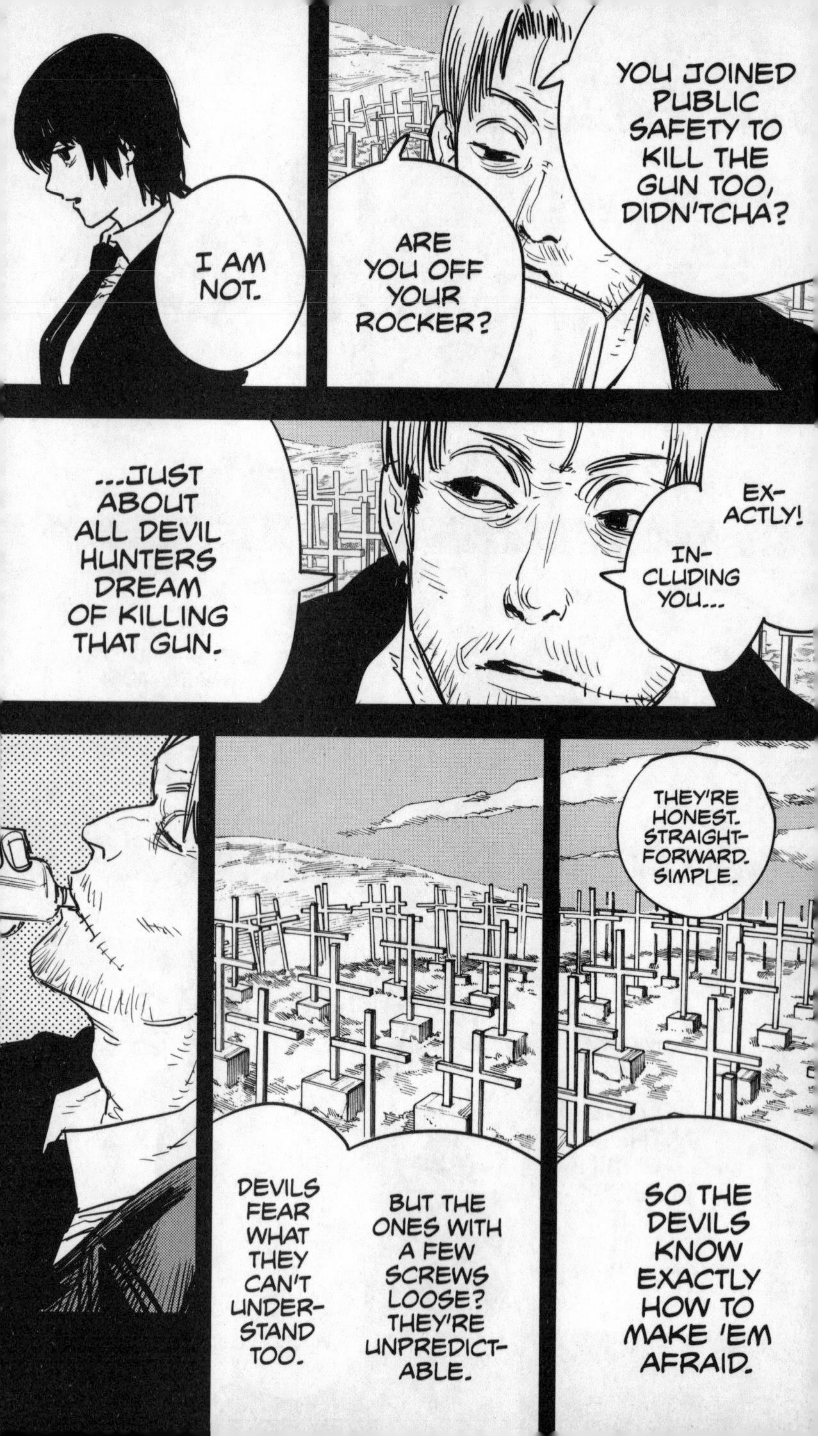
YOU JOINED PUBLIC SAFETY TO KILL THE GUN TOO, DIDN'TCHA?
ARE YOU OFF YOUR ROCKER?
I AM NOT.
...JUST ABOUT ALL DEVIL HUNTERS DREAM OF KILLING THAT GUN.
EX-ACTLY!
IN-CLUDING YOU...
THEY'RE HONEST. STRAIGHT-FORWARD. SIMPLE.
SO THE DEVILS KNOW EXACTLY HOW TO MAKE 'EM AFRAID.
BUT THE ONES WITH A FEW SCREWS LOOSE? THEY'RE UNPREDICT-ABLE.
DEVILS FEAR WHAT THEY CAN'T UNDER-STAND TOO.

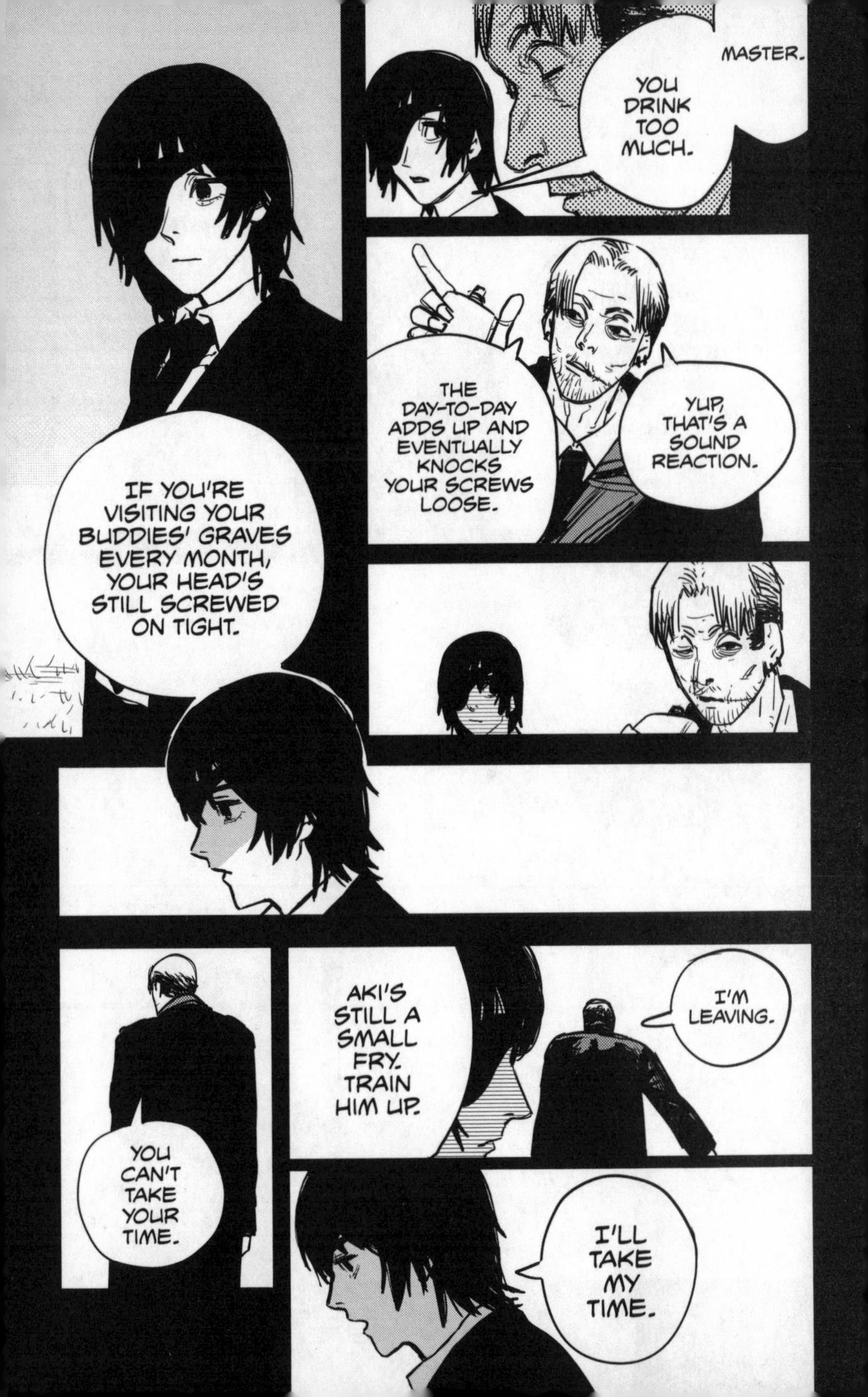
MASTER.
YOU DRINK TOO MUCH.
YUP, THAT'S A SOUND REACTION.
THE DAY-TO-DAY ADDS UP AND EVENTUALLY KNOCKS YOUR SCREWS LOOSE.
IF YOU'RE VISITING YOUR BUDDIES' GRAVES EVERY MONTH, YOUR HEAD'S STILL SCREWED ON TIGHT.
I'M LEAVING.
AKI'S STILL A SMALL FRY. TRAIN HIM UP.
YOU CAN'T TAKE YOUR TIME.
I'LL TAKE MY TIME.

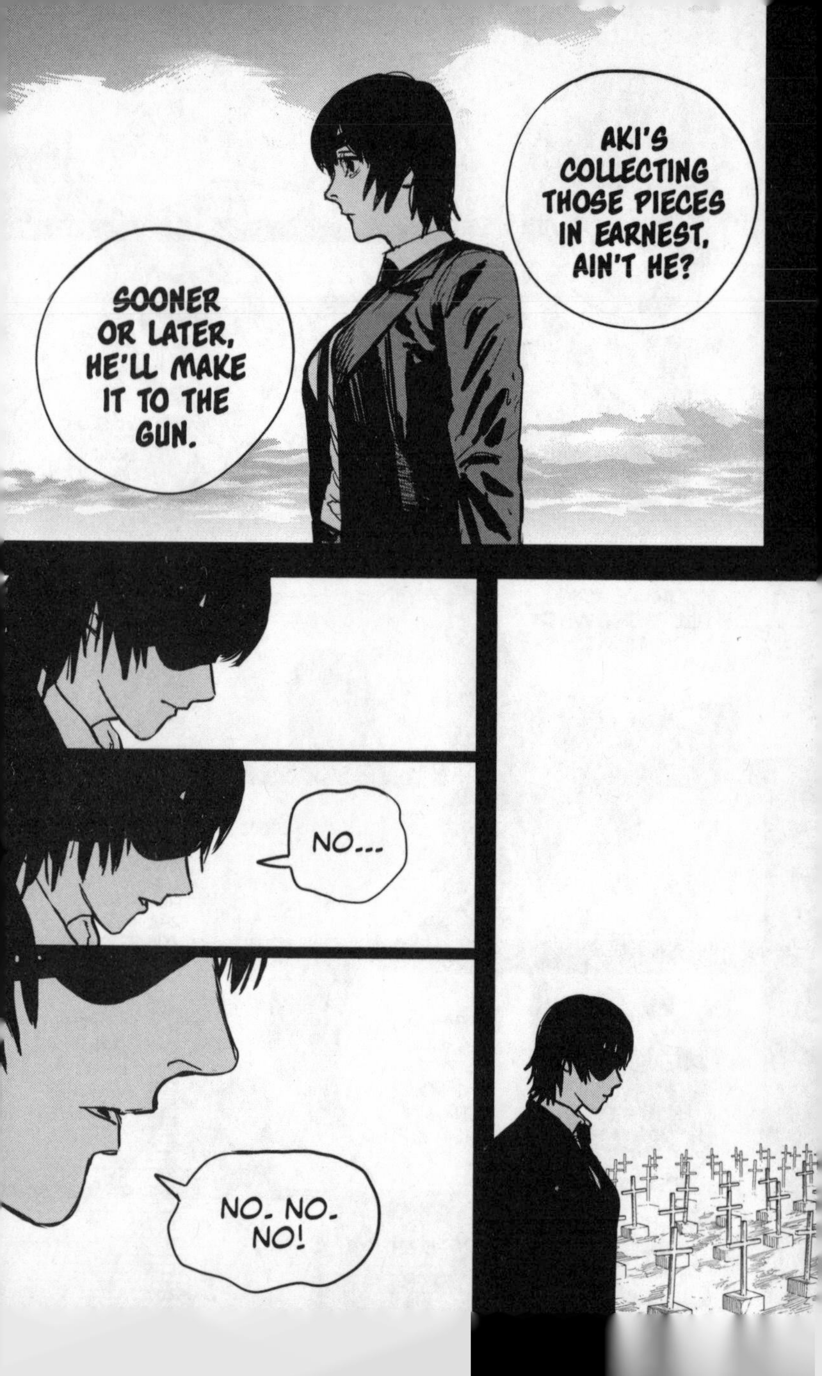
AKI'S COLLECTING THOSE PIECES IN EARNEST, AIN'T HE?
SOONER OR LATER, HE'LL MAKE IT TO THE GUN.
NO...
NO, NO, NO!

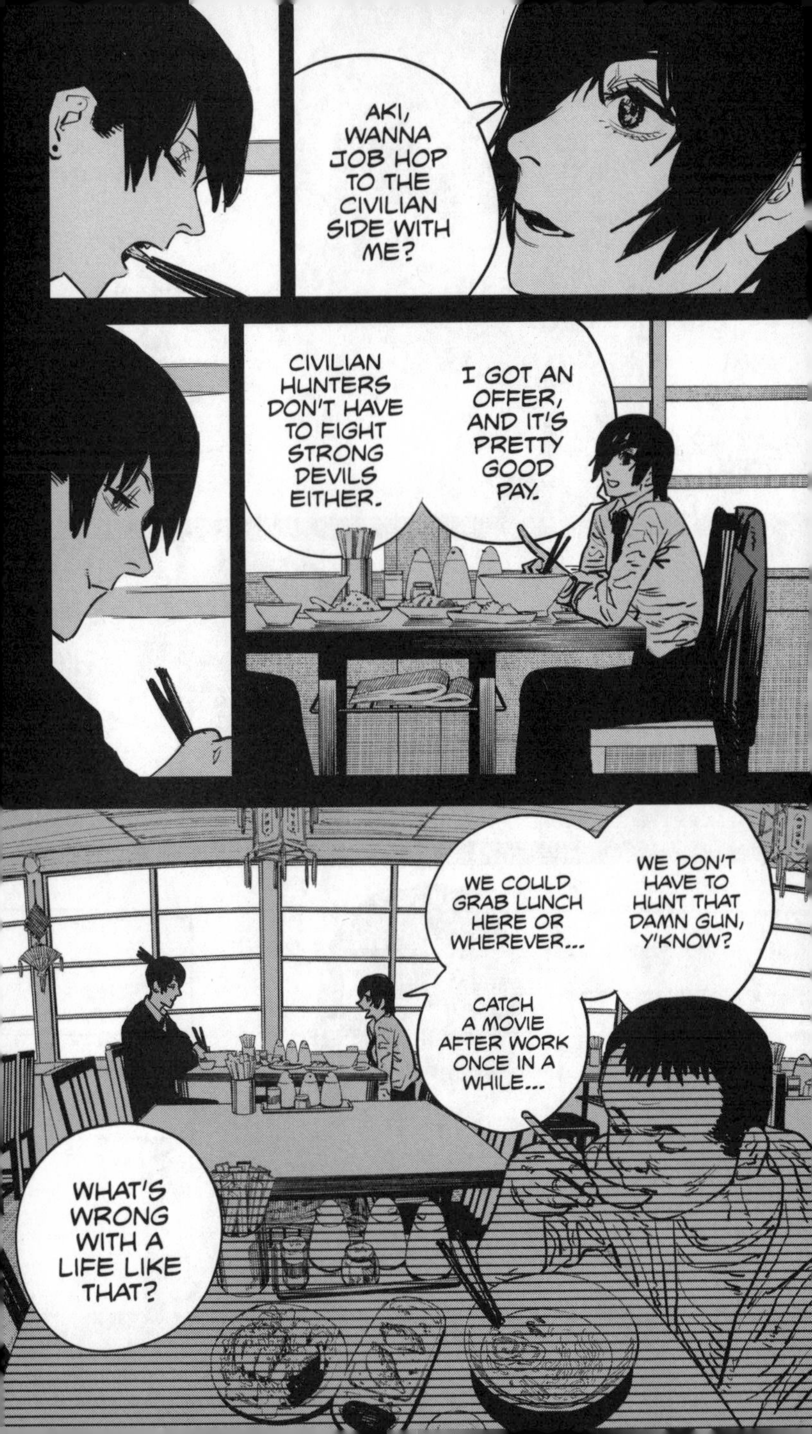
AKI, WANNA JOB HOP TO THE CIVILIAN SIDE WITH ME?
I GOT AN OFFER, AND IT'S PRETTY GOOD PAY.
CIVILIAN HUNTERS DON'T HAVE TO FIGHT STRONG DEVILS EITHER.
WE DON'T HAVE TO HUNT THAT DAMN GUN, Y'KNOW?
WE COULD GRAB LUNCH HERE OR WHEREVER...
CATCH A MOVIE AFTER WORK ONCE IN A WHILE...
WHAT'S WRONG WITH A LIFE LIKE THAT?

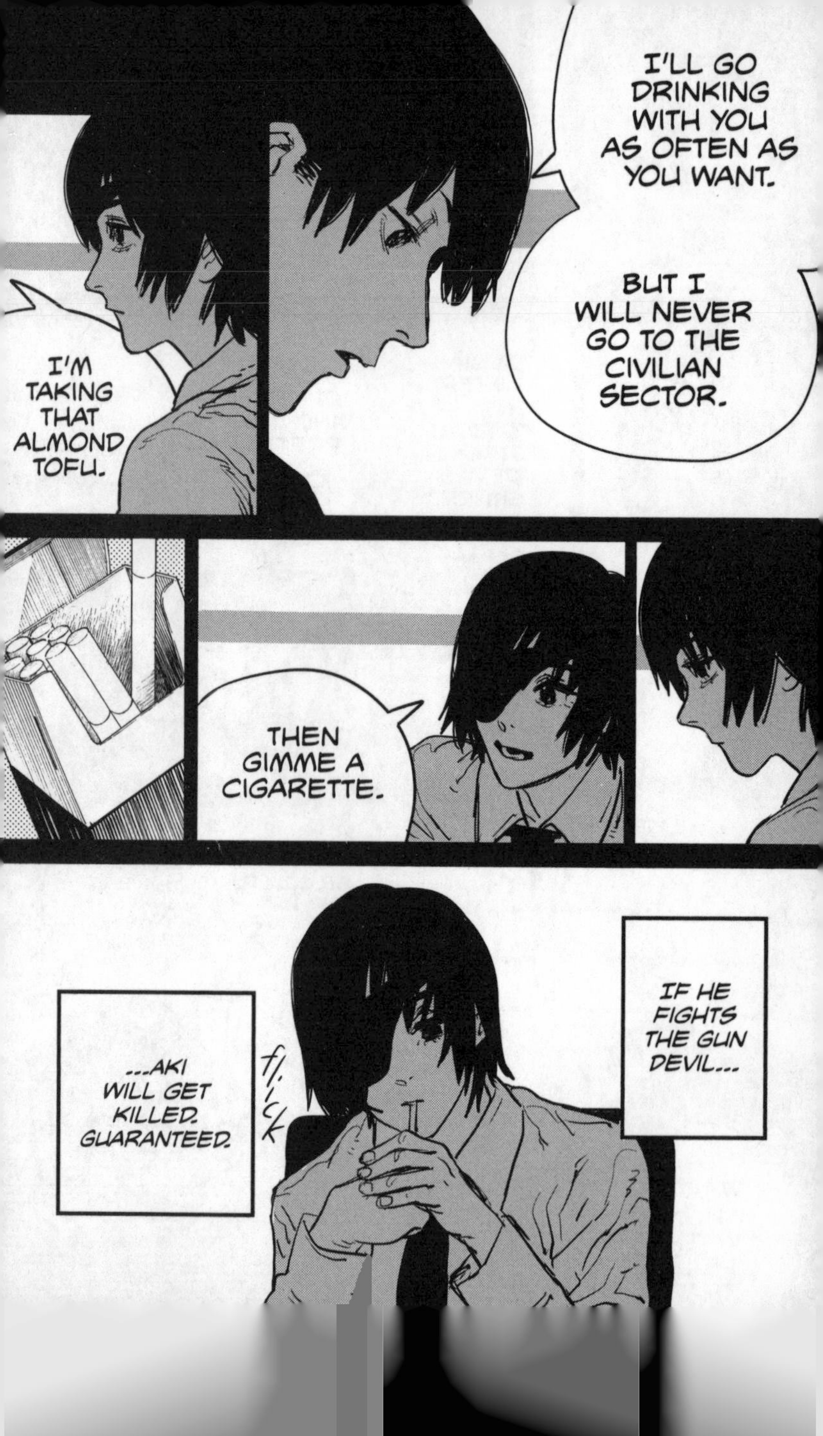
I'LL GO DRINKING WITH YOU AS OFTEN AS YOU WANT.
BUT I WILL NEVER GO TO THE CIVILIAN SECTOR.
I'M TAKING THAT ALMOND TOFU.
THEN GIMME A CIGARETTE.
IF HE FIGHTS THE GUN DEVIL...
flick
...AKI WILL GET KILLED. GUARANTEED.

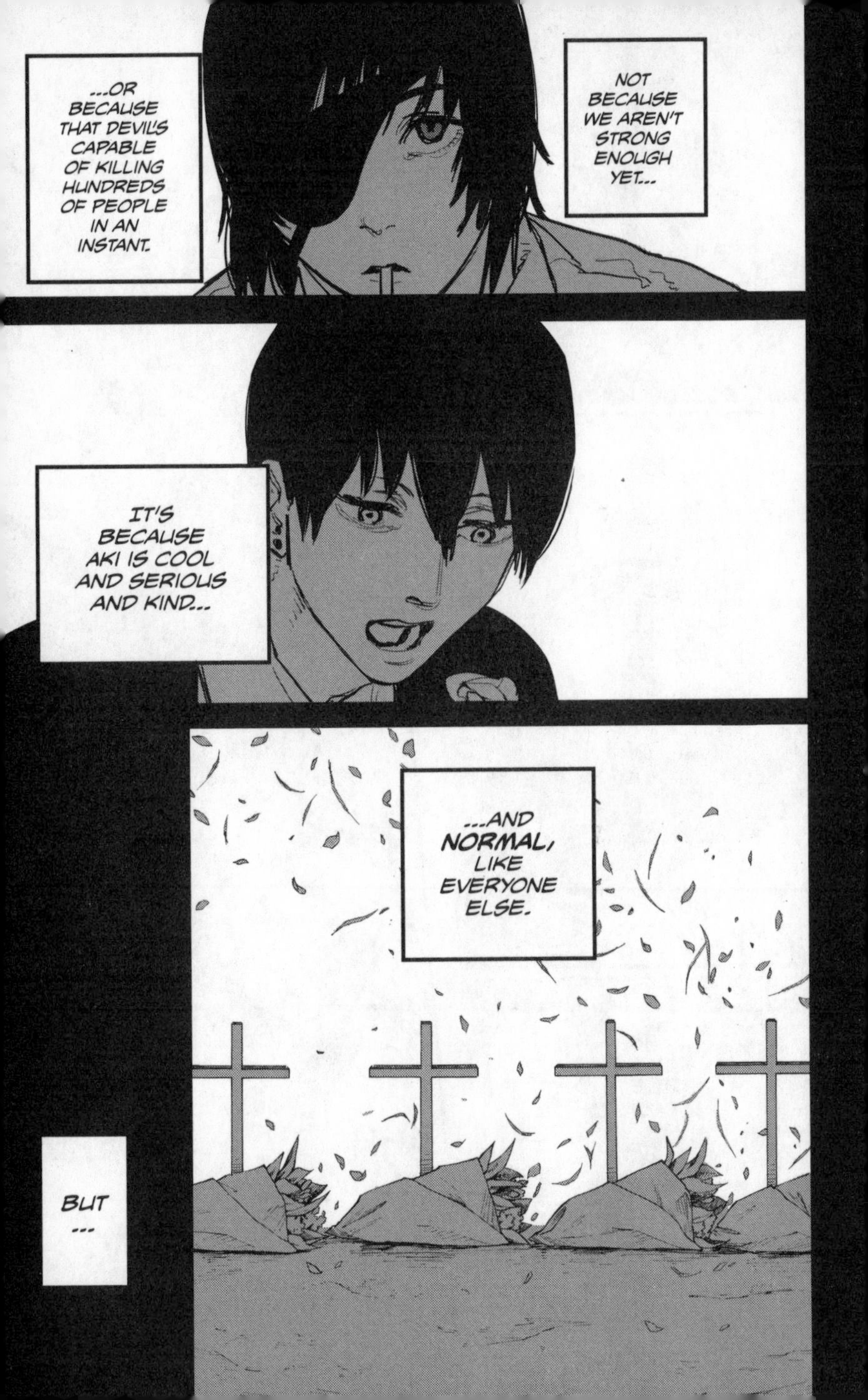
NOT BECAUSE WE AREN'T STRONG ENOUGH YET...
...OR BECAUSE THAT DEVIL'S CAPABLE OF KILLING HUNDREDS OF PEOPLE IN AN INSTANT.
IT'S BECAUSE AKI IS COOL AND SERIOUS AND KIND...
...AND **NORMAL,** LIKE EVERYONE ELSE.
BUT ...

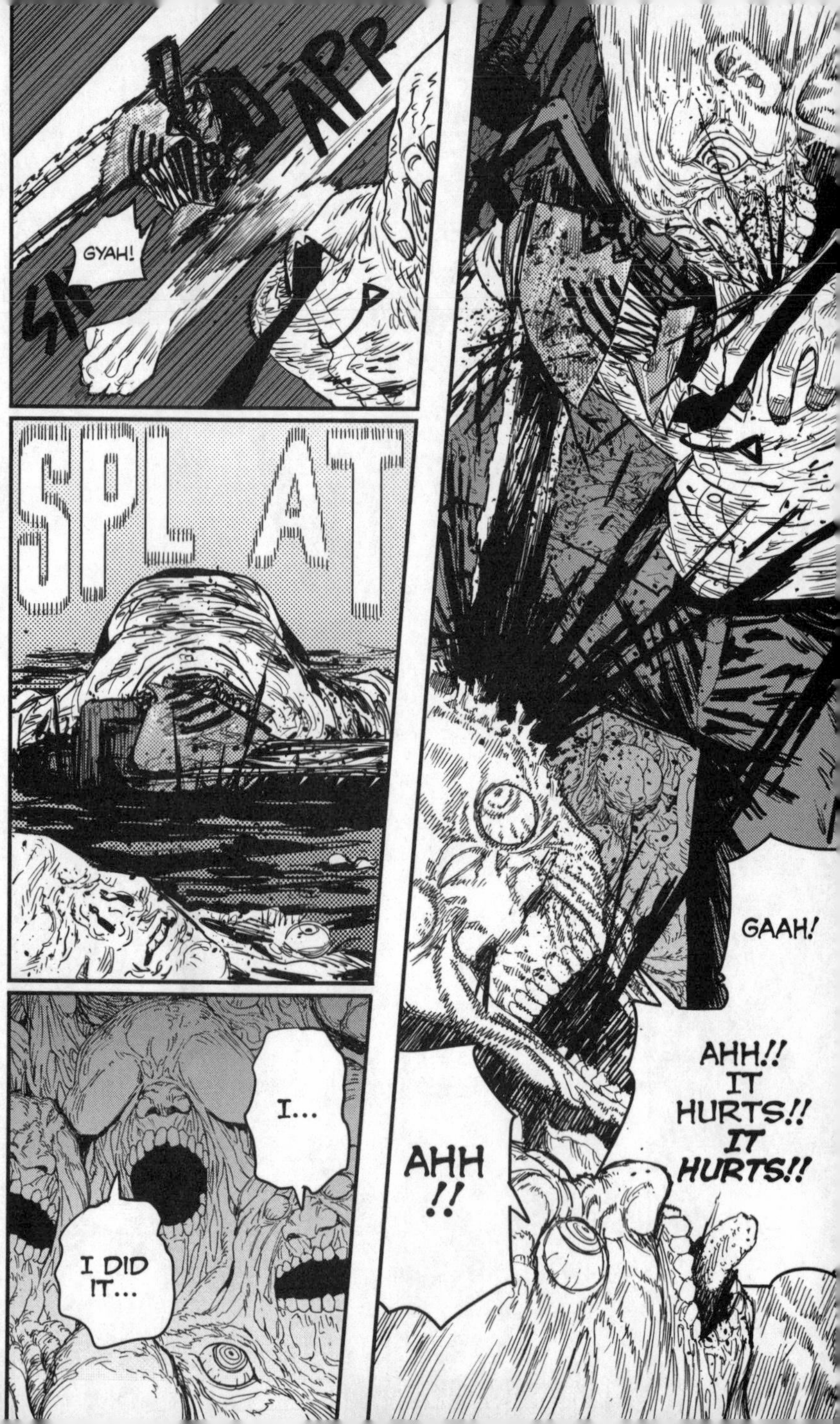
GAAH!
AHH!! IT HURTS!! IT HURTS!!
AHH !!
DAPP
GYAH!
SK
SPLAT
I...
I DID IT...

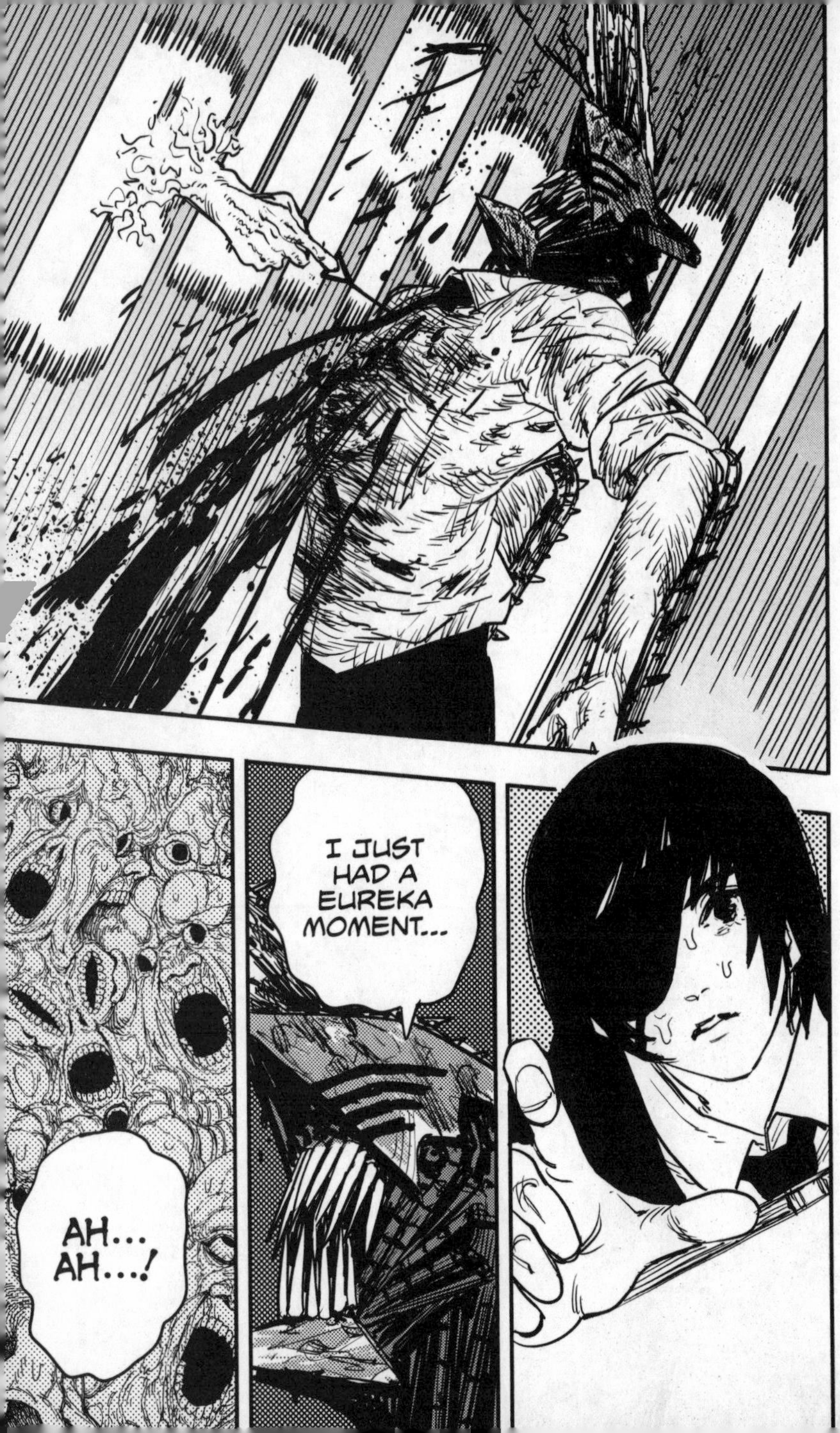
I JUST HAD A EUREKA MOMENT...
AH... AH...!

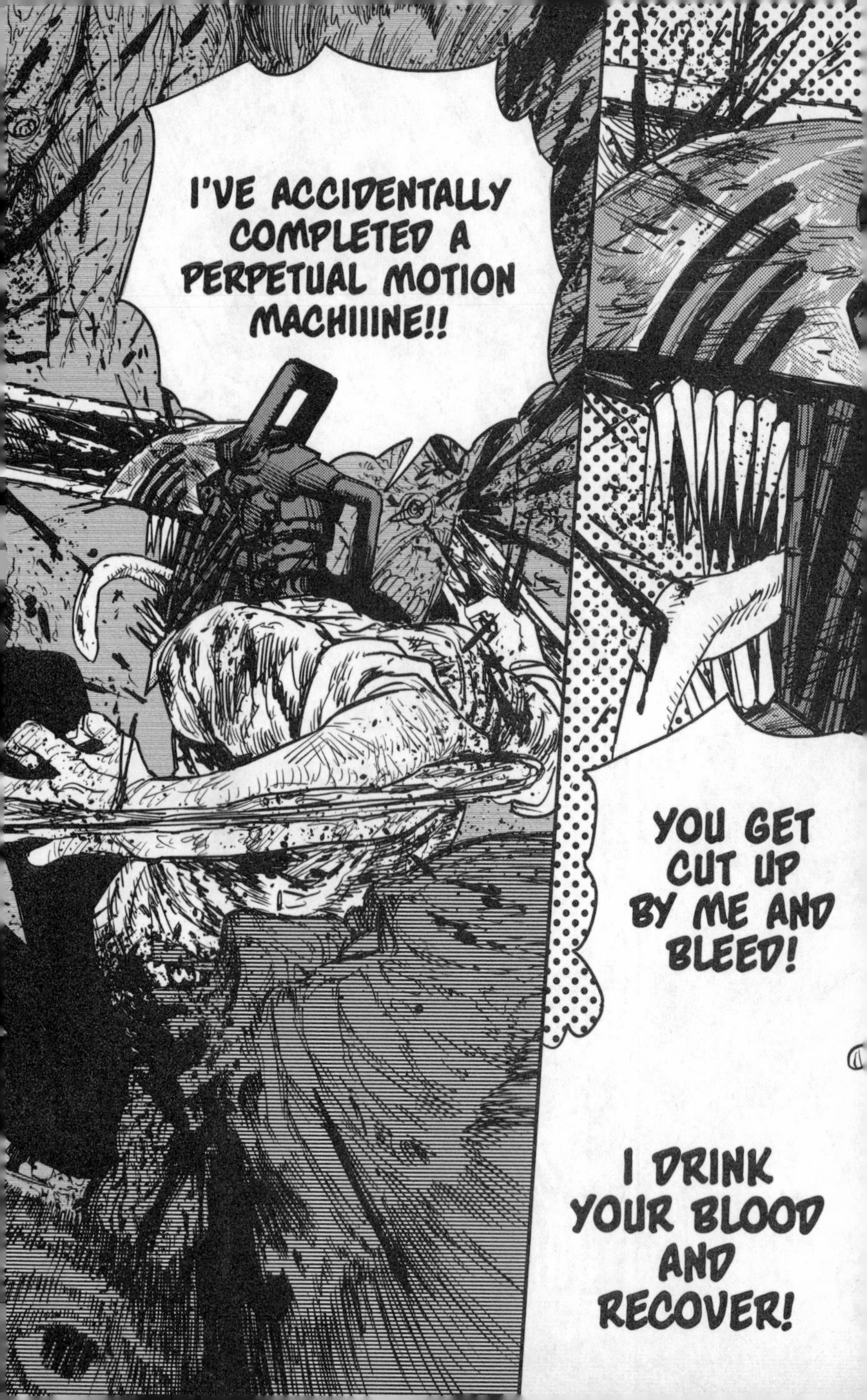
YOU GET CUT UP BY ME AND BLEED!
I DRINK YOUR BLOOD AND RECOVER!
I'VE ACCIDENTALLY COMPLETED A PERPETUAL MOTION MACHIIINE!!

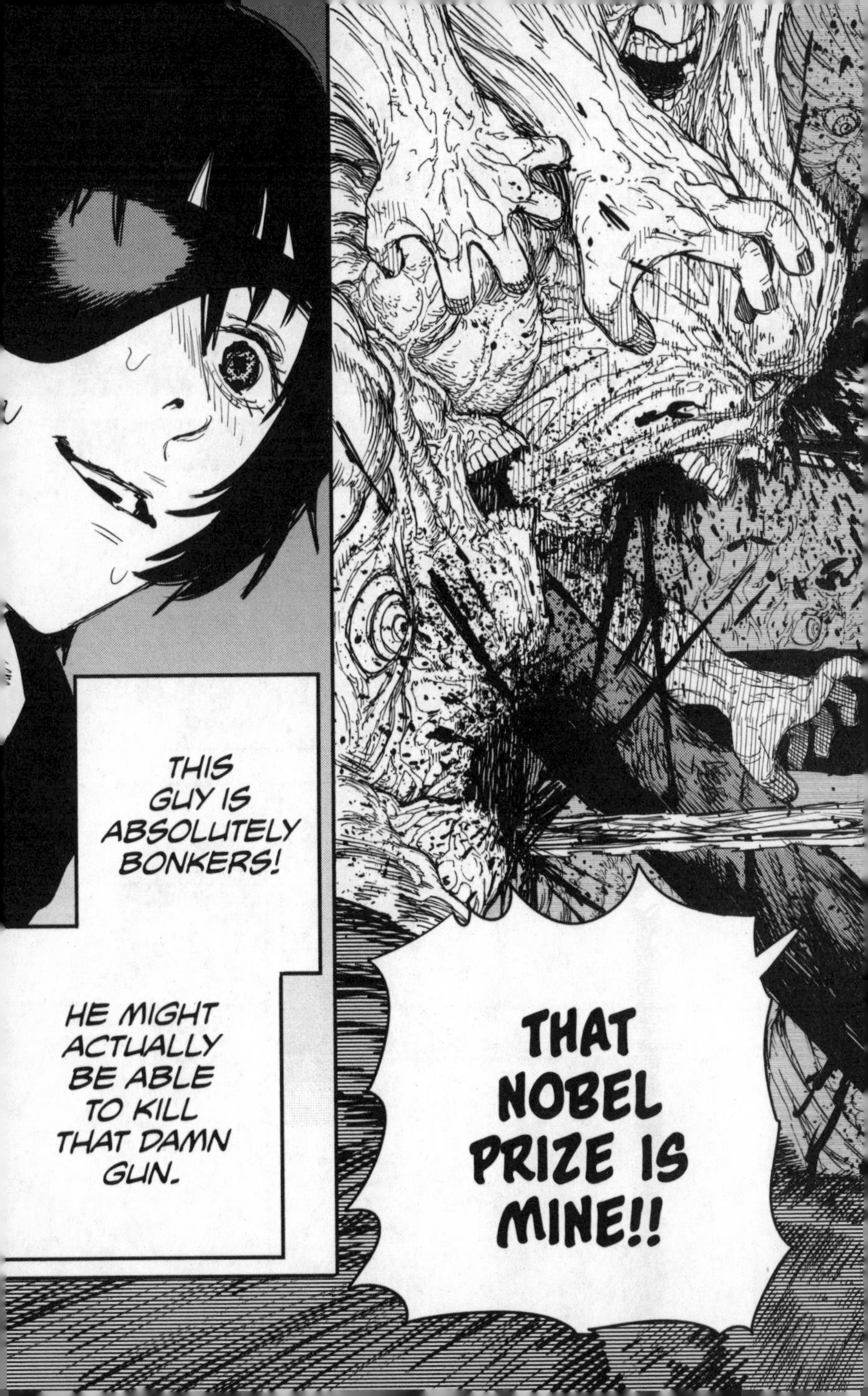
THAT NOBEL PRIZE IS MINE!!
THIS GUY IS ABSOLUTELY BONKERS!
HE MIGHT ACTUALLY BE ABLE TO KILL THAT DAMN GUN.

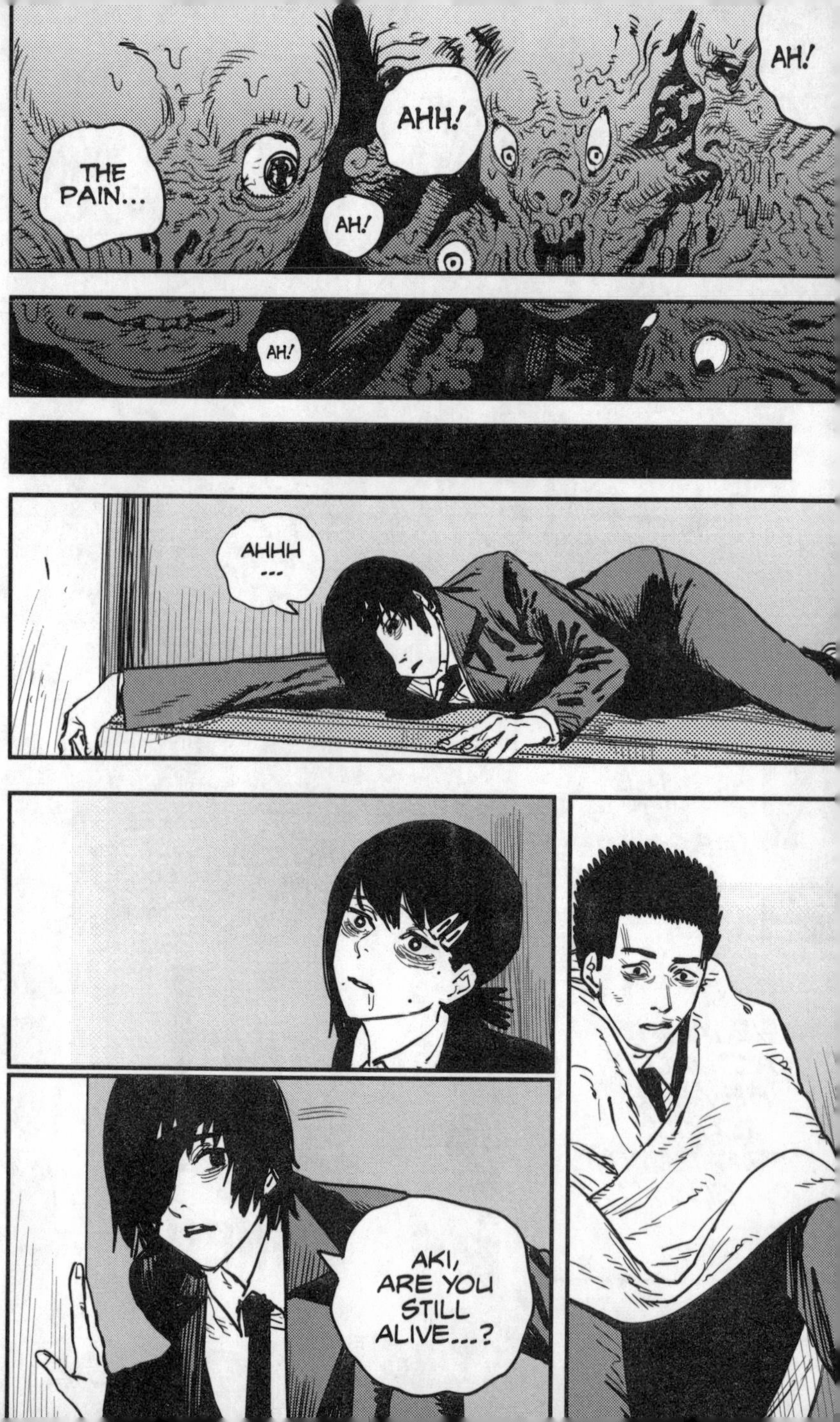
AH!
AHH!
THE PAIN...
AH!
AH!
AHHH ---
AKI, ARE YOU STILL ALIVE...?

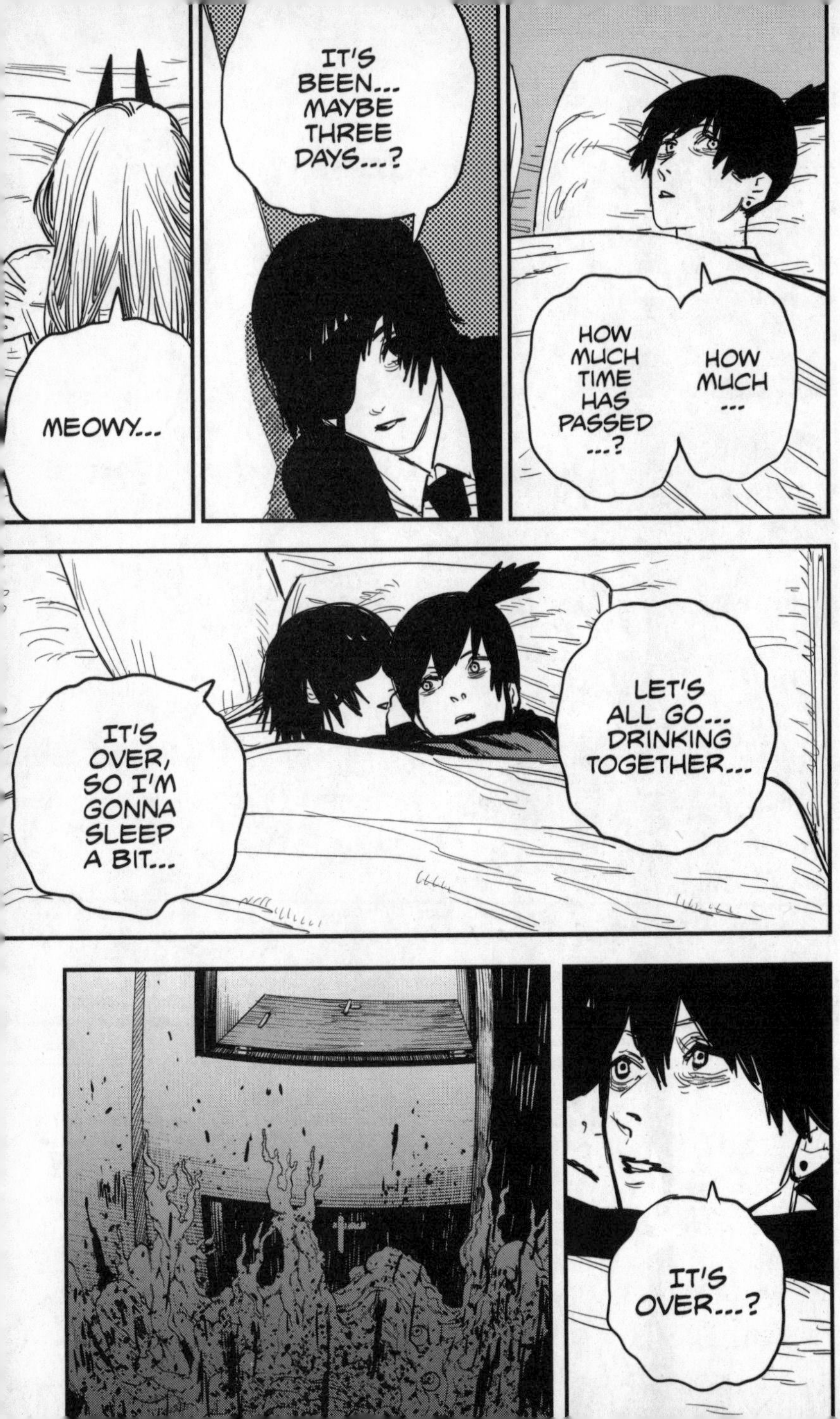
HOW MUCH ...
HOW MUCH TIME HAS PASSED ...?
IT'S BEEN... MAYBE THREE DAYS...?
MEOWY...
LET'S ALL GO... DRINKING TOGETHER...
IT'S OVER, SO I'M GONNA SLEEP A BIT...
IT'S OVER...?

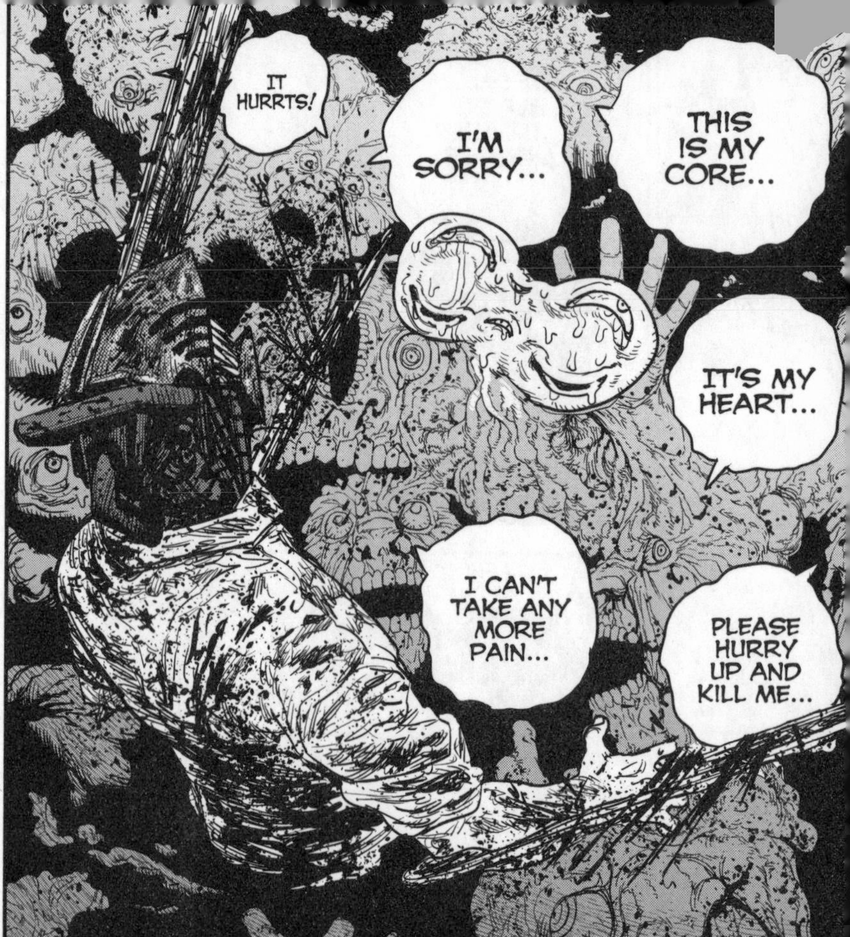
THIS IS MY CORE...
IT'S MY HEART...
I'M SORRY...
IT HURRTS!
PLEASE HURRY UP AND KILL ME...
I CAN'T TAKE ANY MORE PAIN...
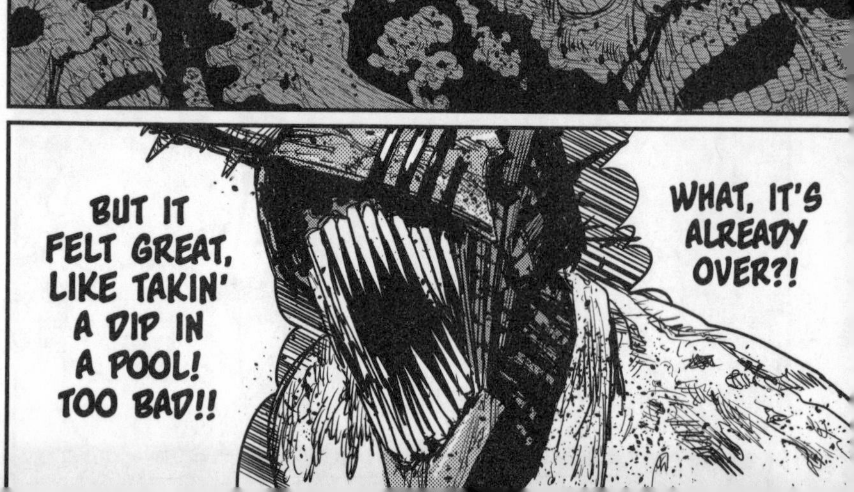
WHAT, IT'S ALREADY OVER?!
BUT IT FELT GREAT, LIKE TAKIN' A DIP IN A POOL! TOO BAD!!

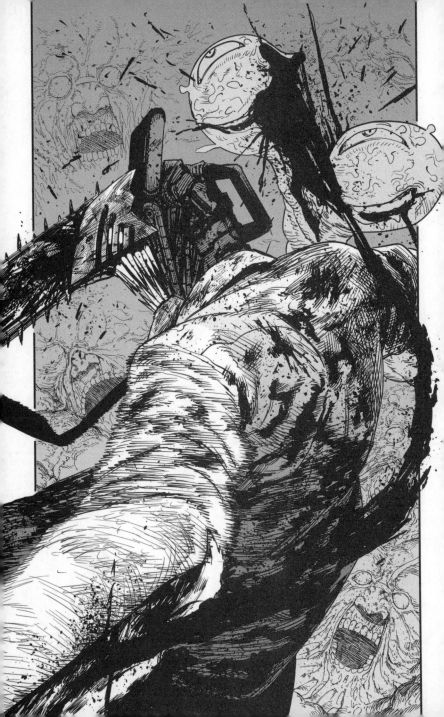

chain saw man

Chapter 20: Drinking

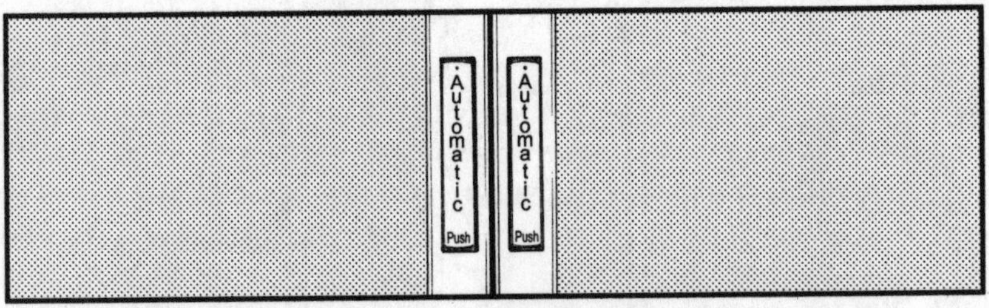
Automatic
Push
Automatic
Push

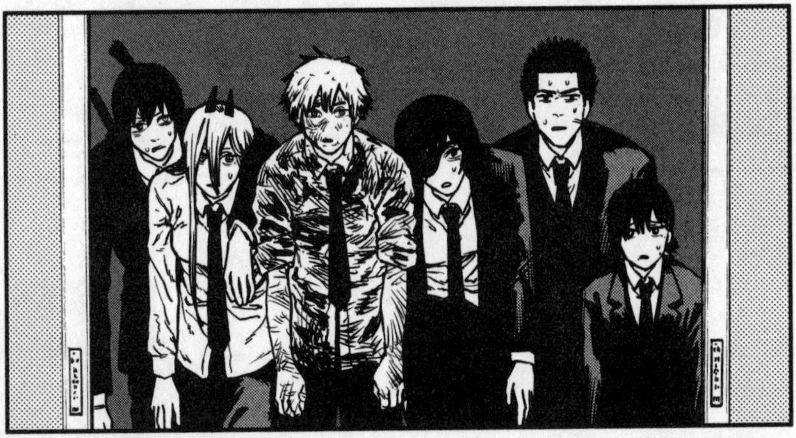

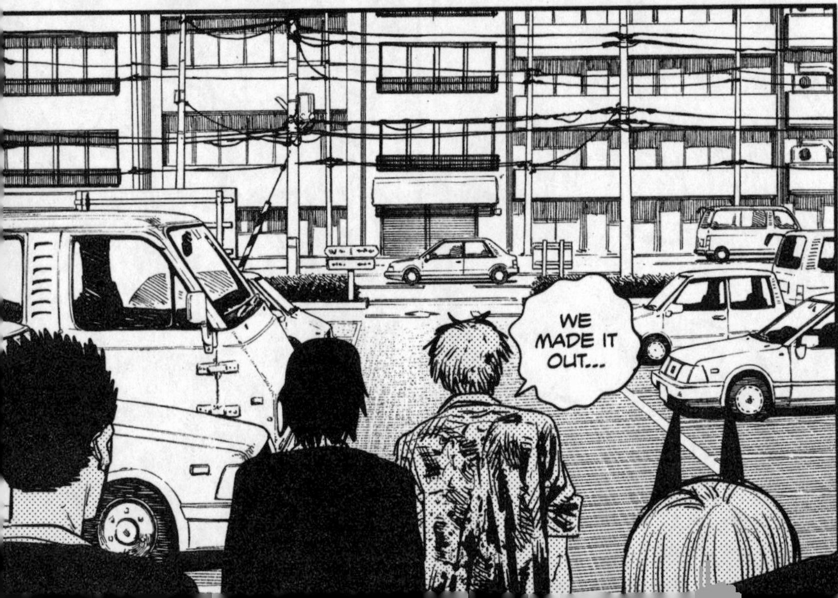
WE MADE IT OUT...

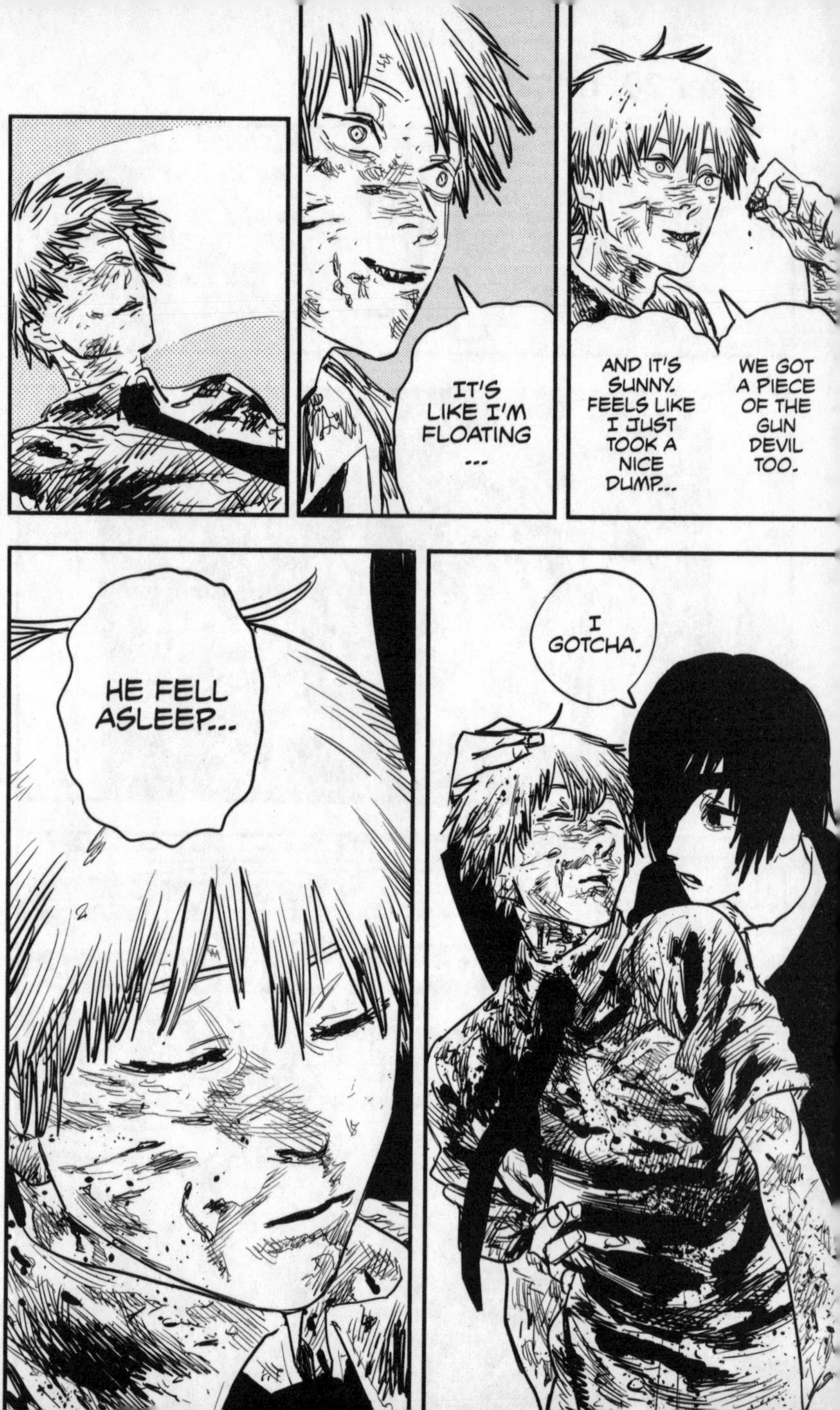
WE GOT A PIECE OF THE GUN DEVIL TOO.
AND IT'S SUNNY. FEELS LIKE I JUST TOOK A NICE DUMP...
IT'S LIKE I'M FLOATING ...
I GOTCHA.
HE FELL ASLEEP...

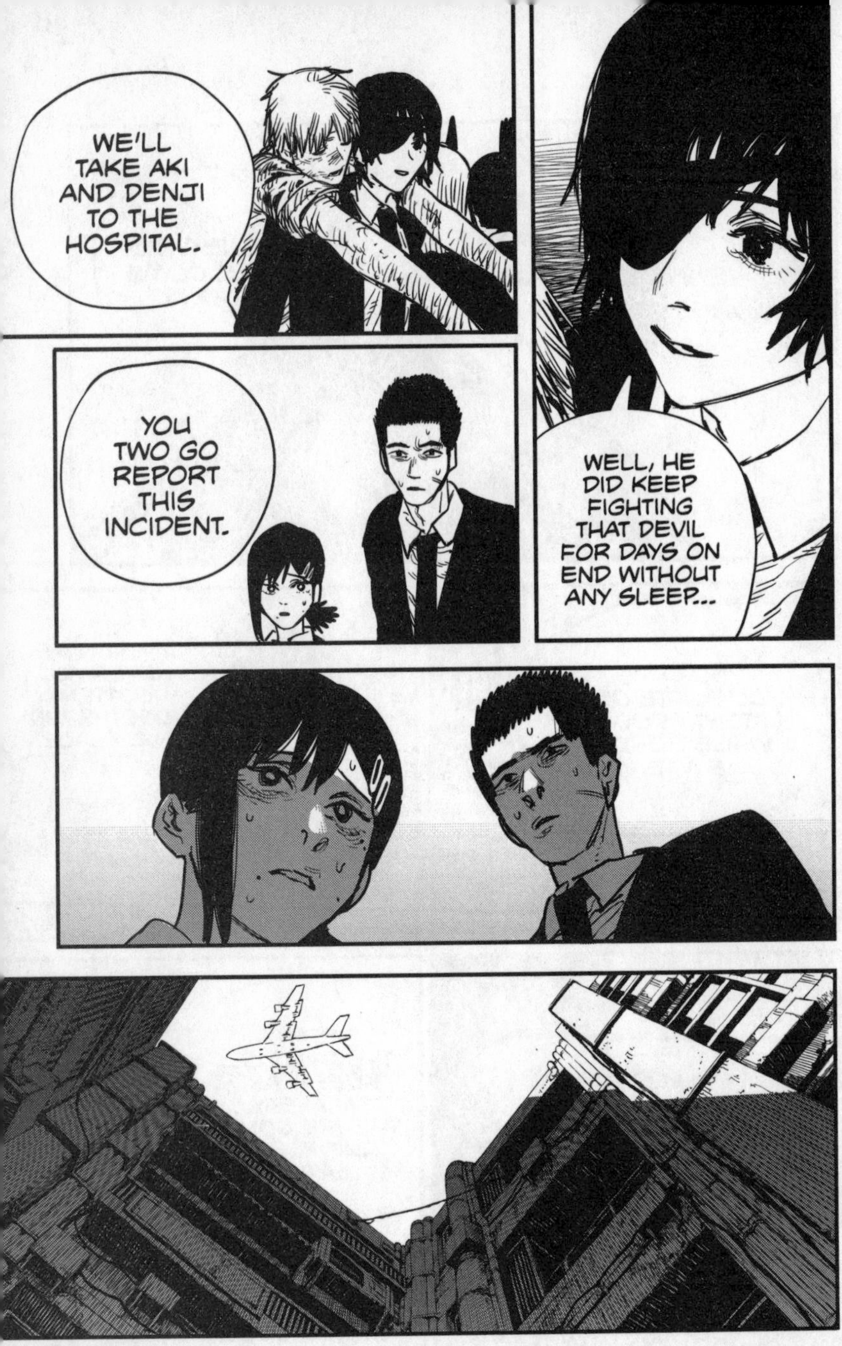
WELL, HE DID KEEP FIGHTING THAT DEVIL FOR DAYS ON END WITHOUT ANY SLEEP...
WE'LL TAKE AKI AND DENJI TO THE HOSPITAL.
YOU TWO GO REPORT THIS INCIDENT.

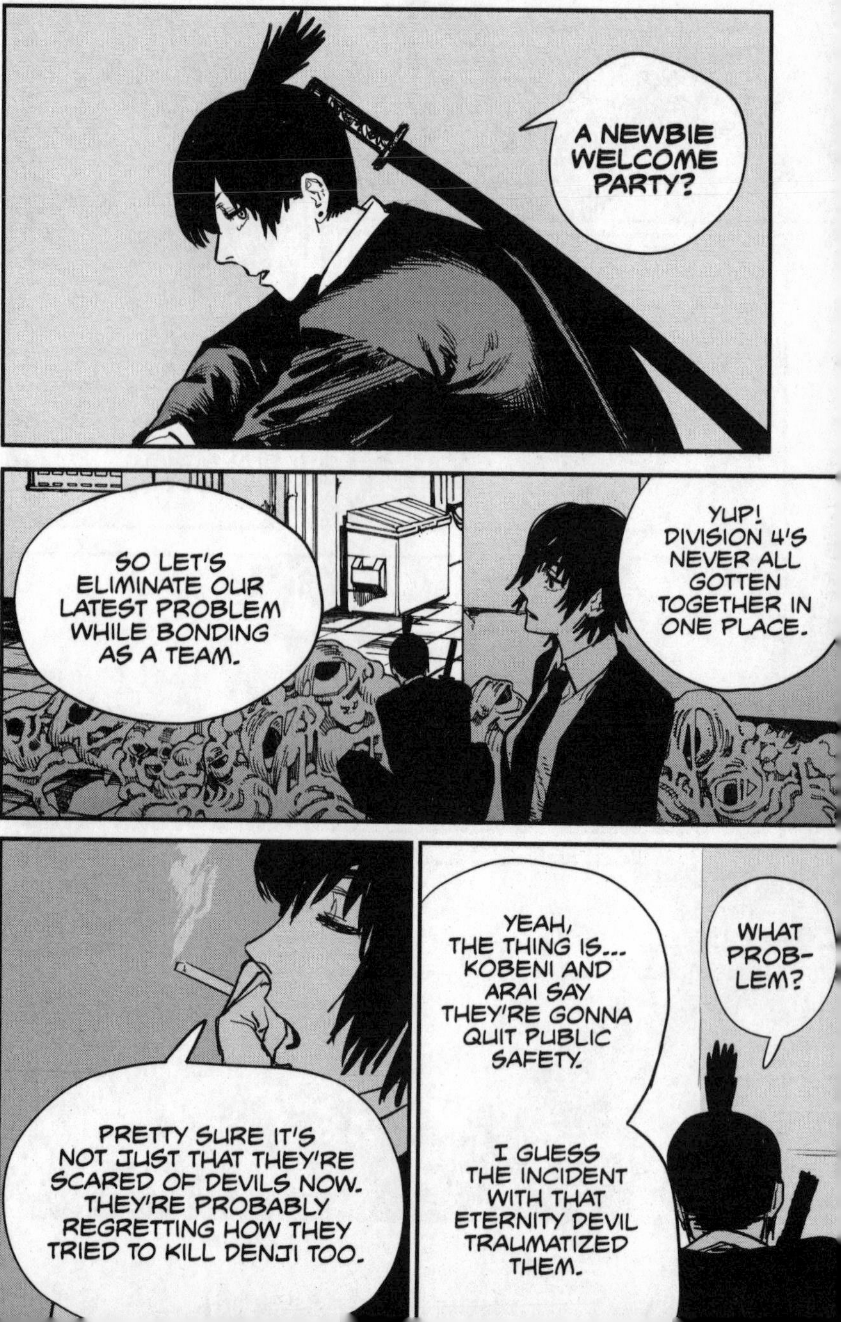
A NEWBIE WELCOME PARTY?
YUP! DIVISION 4'S NEVER ALL GOTTEN TOGETHER IN ONE PLACE.
SO LET'S ELIMINATE OUR LATEST PROBLEM WHILE BONDING AS A TEAM.
WHAT PROB-LEM?
YEAH, THE THING IS... KOBENI AND ARAI SAY THEY'RE GONNA QUIT PUBLIC SAFETY.
I GUESS THE INCIDENT WITH THAT ETERNITY DEVIL TRAUMATIZED THEM.
PRETTY SURE IT'S NOT JUST THAT THEY'RE SCARED OF DEVILS NOW. THEY'RE PROBABLY REGRETTING HOW THEY TRIED TO KILL DENJI TOO.

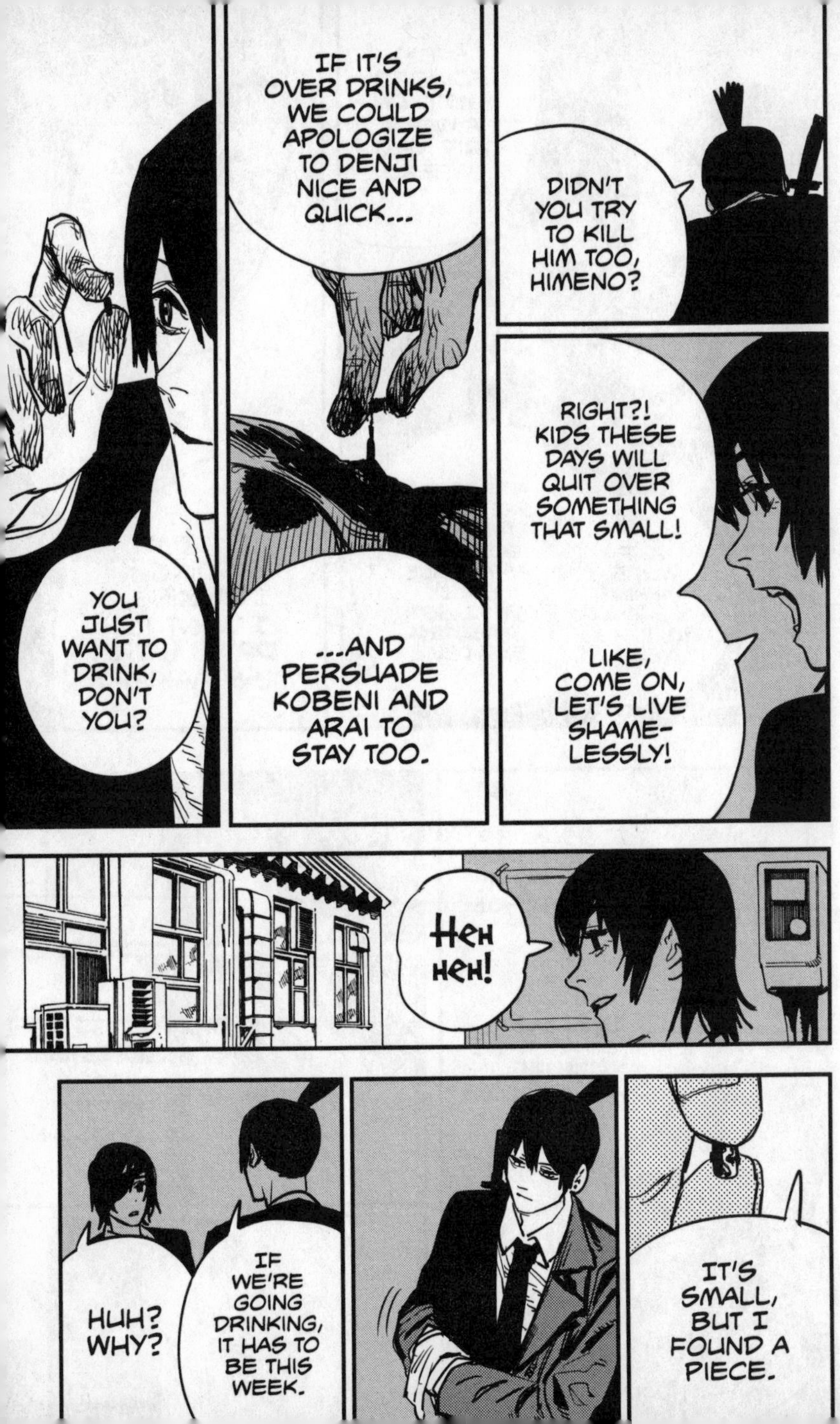
DIDN'T YOU TRY TO KILL HIM TOO, HIMENO?
RIGHT?! KIDS THESE DAYS WILL QUIT OVER SOMETHING THAT SMALL!
LIKE, COME ON, LET'S LIVE SHAME-LESSLY!
IF IT'S OVER DRINKS, WE COULD APOLOGIZE TO DENJI NICE AND QUICK...
...AND PERSUADE KOBENI AND ARAI TO STAY TOO.
YOU JUST WANT TO DRINK, DON'T YOU?
HEH HEH!
IT'S SMALL, BUT I FOUND A PIECE.
IF WE'RE GOING DRINKING, IT HAS TO BE THIS WEEK.
HUH? WHY?

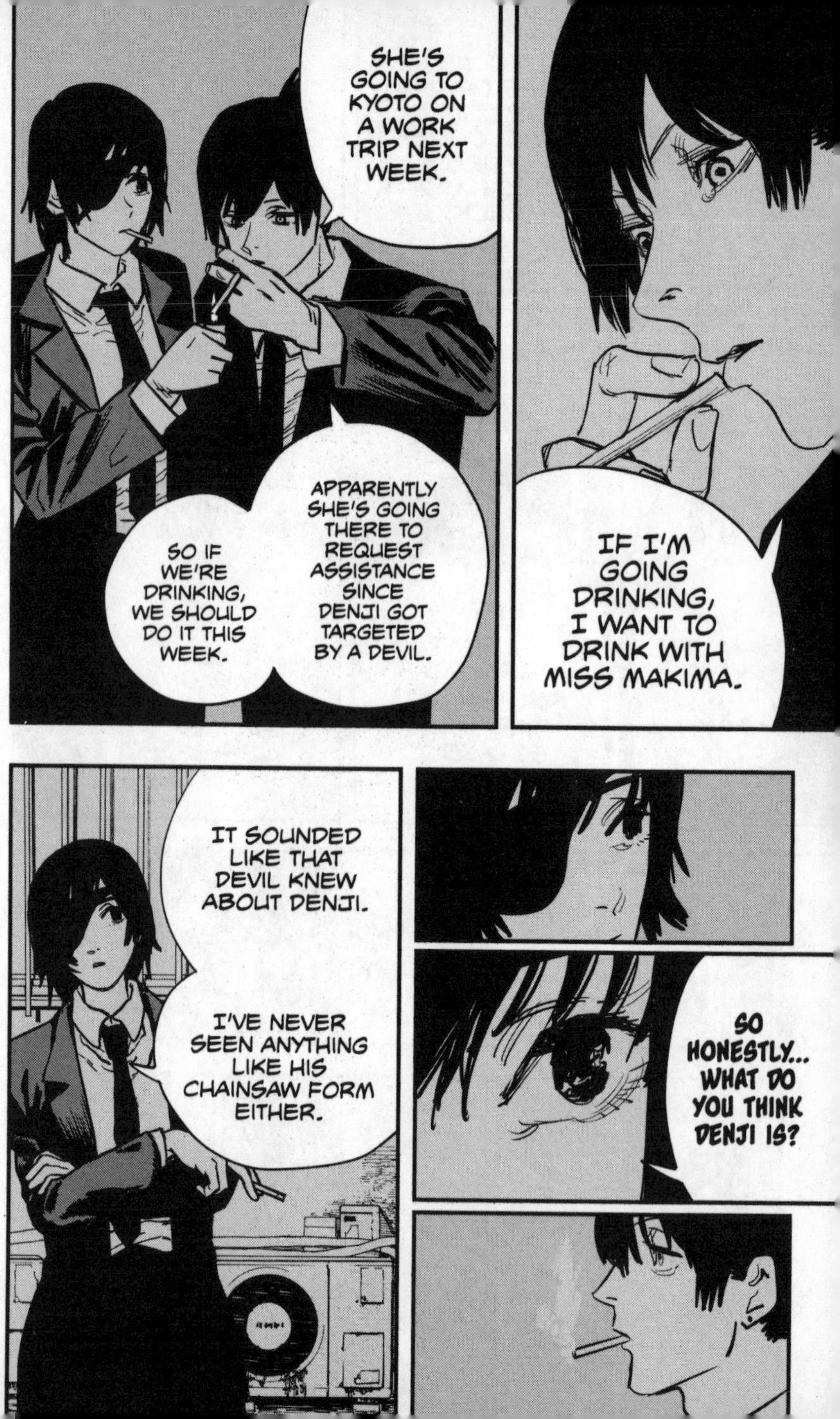
IF I'M GOING DRINKING, I WANT TO DRINK WITH MISS MAKIMA.
SHE'S GOING TO KYOTO ON A WORK TRIP NEXT WEEK.
APPARENTLY SHE'S GOING THERE TO REQUEST ASSISTANCE SINCE DENJI GOT TARGETED BY A DEVIL.
SO IF WE'RE DRINKING, WE SHOULD DO IT THIS WEEK.
SO HONESTLY... WHAT DO YOU THINK DENJI IS?
IT SOUNDED LIKE THAT DEVIL KNEW ABOUT DENJI.
I'VE NEVER SEEN ANYTHING LIKE HIS CHAINSAW FORM EITHER.

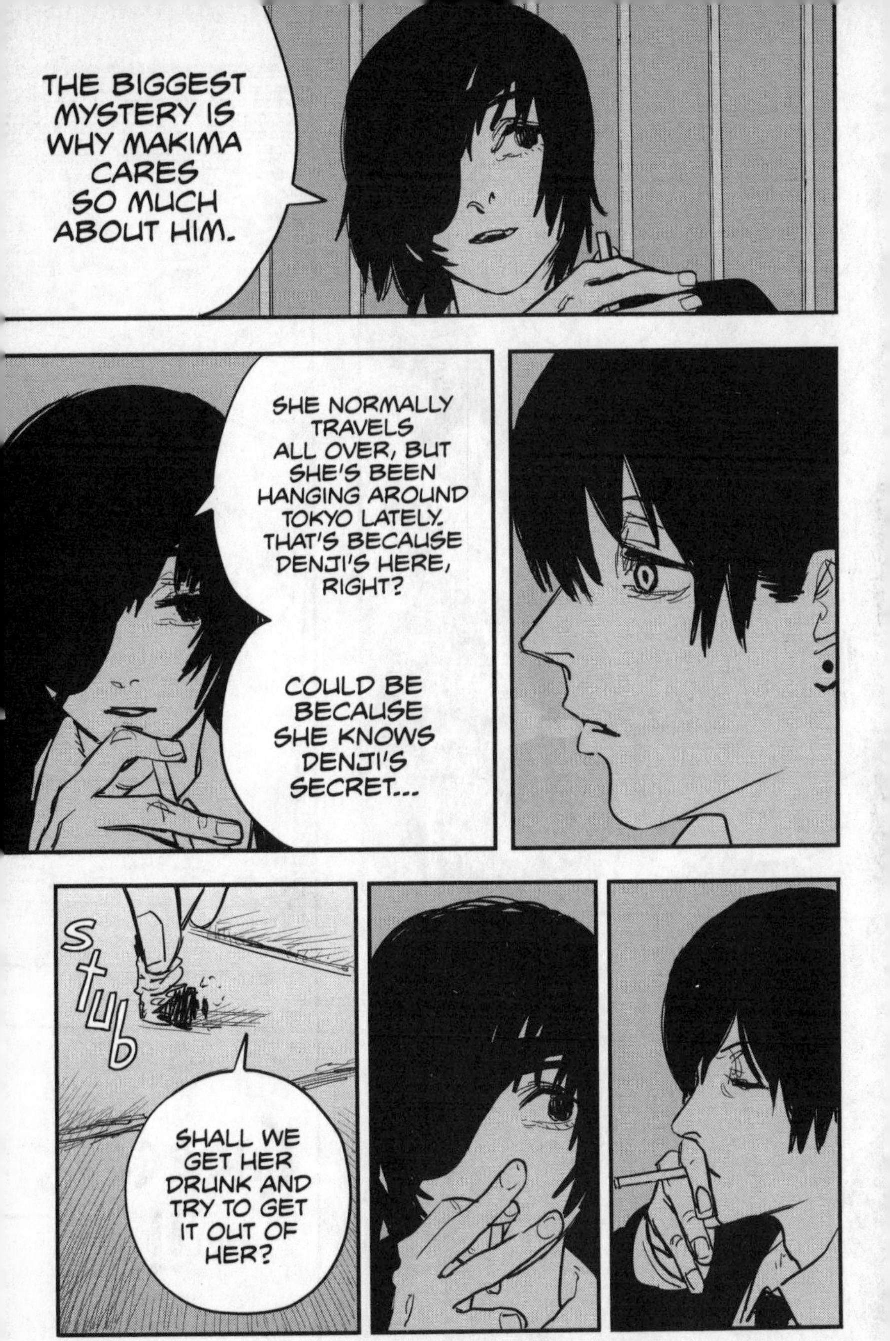
THE BIGGEST MYSTERY IS WHY MAKIMA CARES SO MUCH ABOUT HIM.
SHE NORMALLY TRAVELS ALL OVER, BUT SHE'S BEEN HANGING AROUND TOKYO LATELY. THAT'S BECAUSE DENJI'S HERE, RIGHT?
COULD BE BECAUSE SHE KNOWS DENJI'S SECRET...
stub
SHALL WE GET HER DRUNK AND TRY TO GET IT OUT OF HER?

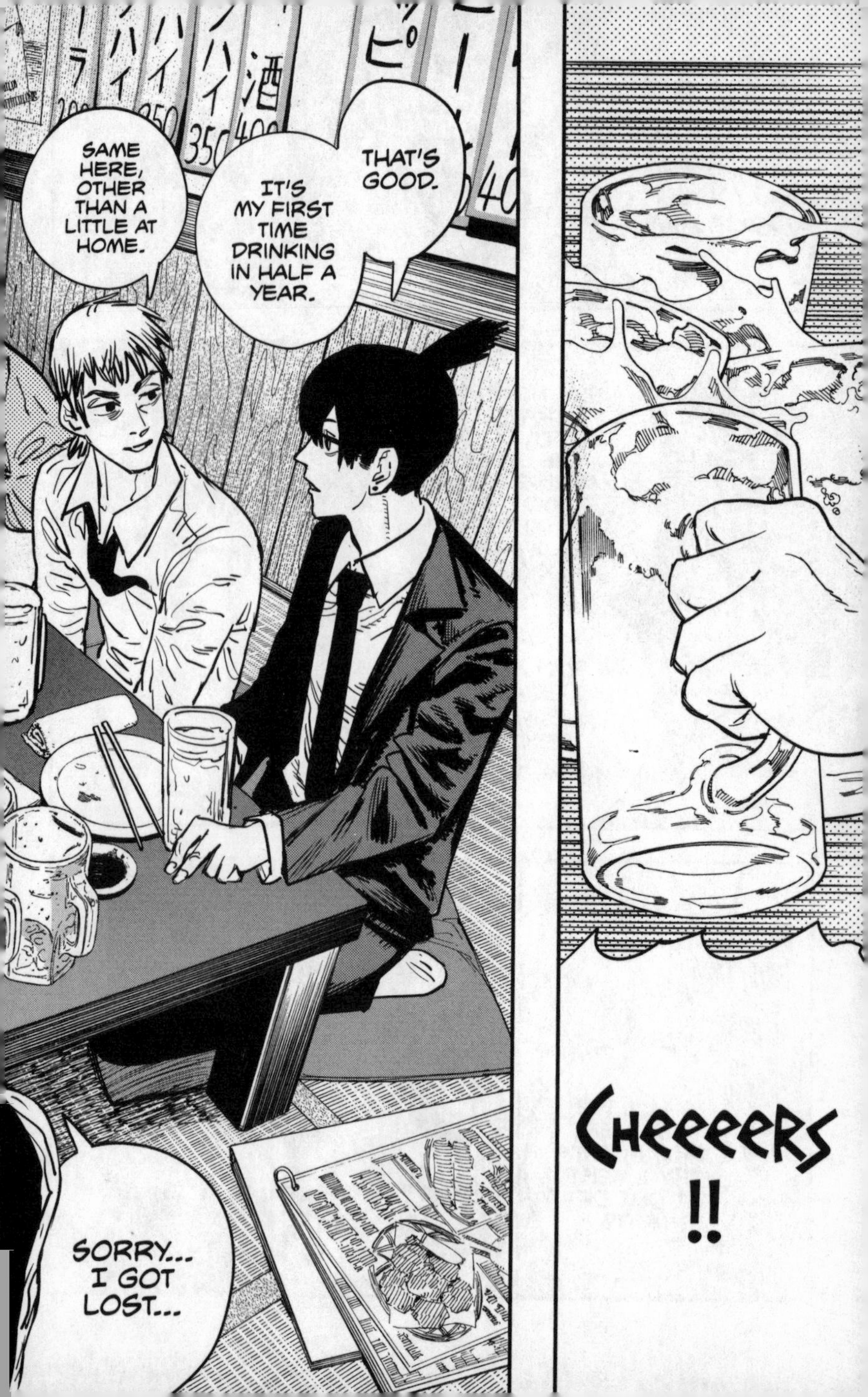
CHEEEERS!!
THAT'S GOOD.
IT'S MY FIRST TIME DRINKING IN HALF A YEAR.
SAME HERE, OTHER THAN A LITTLE AT HOME.
SORRY... I GOT LOST...

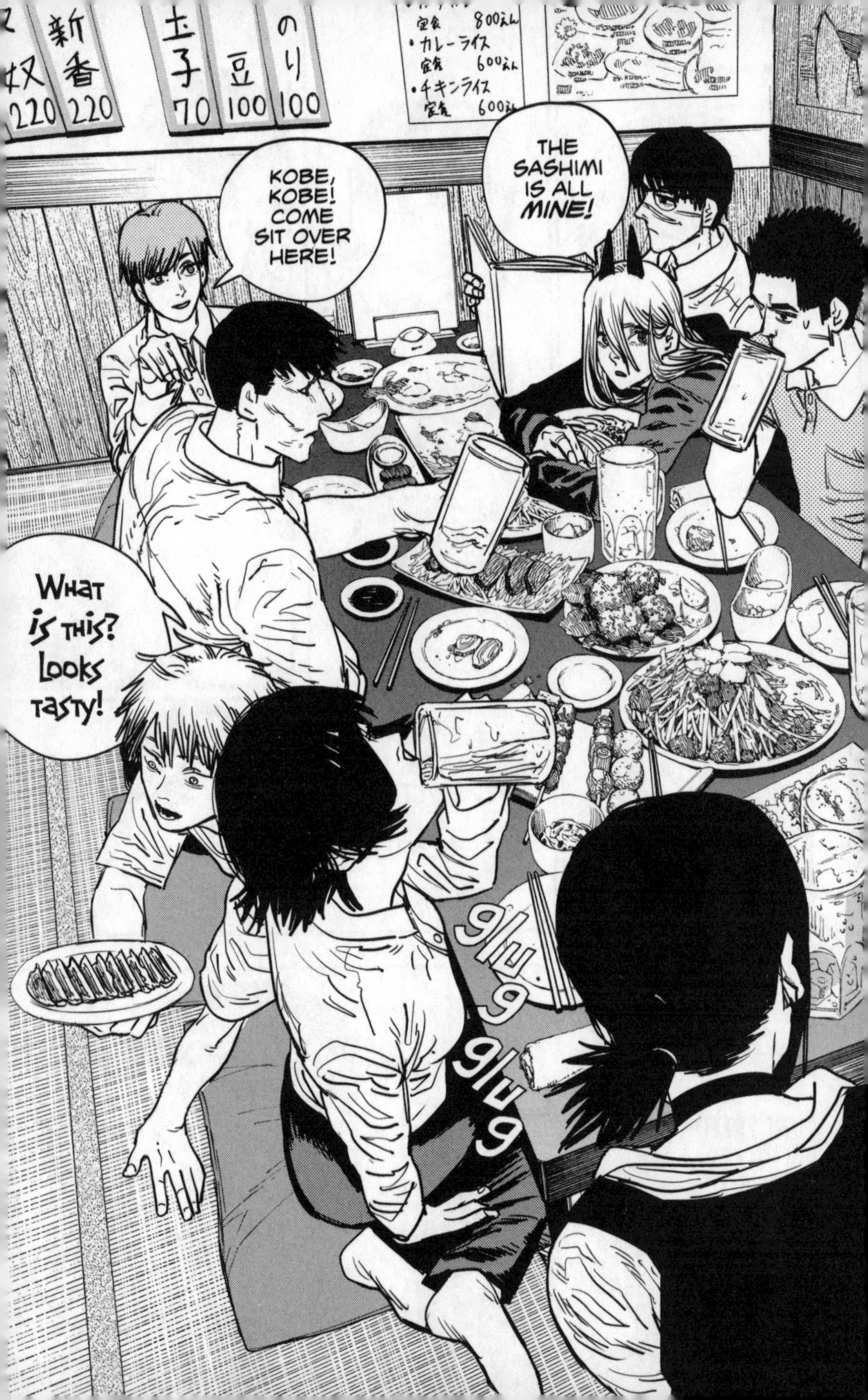
定食 800えん
・カレーライス 定食 600えん
・チキンライス 定食 600えん
のり 100
豆 100
玉子 70
新香 220
奴 220
THE SASHIMI IS ALL MINE!
KOBE, KOBE! COME SIT OVER HERE!
WHAT is THIS? LOOKS TASTY!
glug
glug

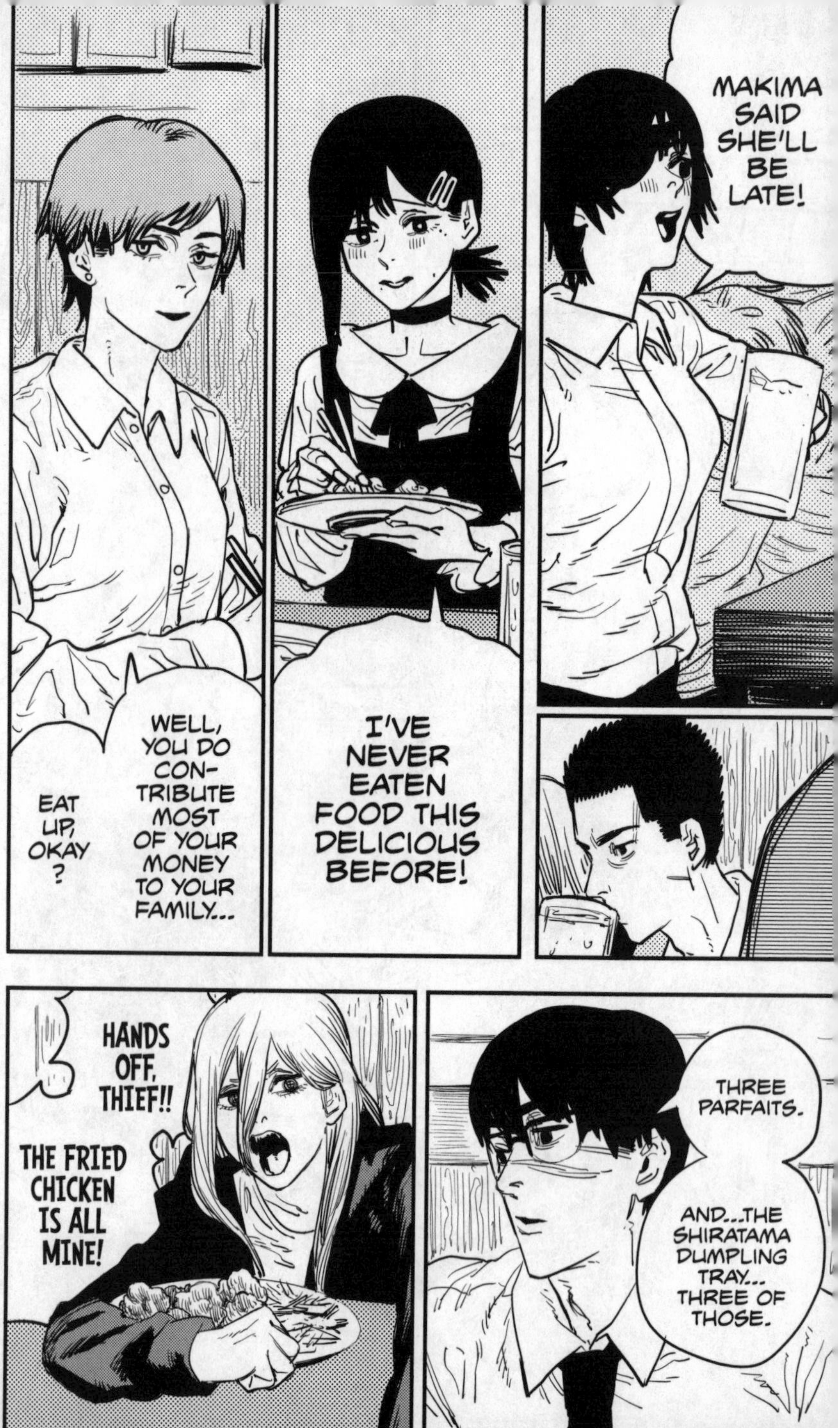
MAKIMA SAID SHE'LL BE LATE!
I'VE NEVER EATEN FOOD THIS DELICIOUS BEFORE!
WELL, YOU DO CON-TRIBUTE MOST OF YOUR MONEY TO YOUR FAMILY...
EAT UP, OKAY?
THREE PARFAITS.
AND...THE SHIRATAMA DUMPLING TRAY... THREE OF THOSE.
HANDS OFF, THIEF!!
THE FRIED CHICKEN IS ALL MINE!

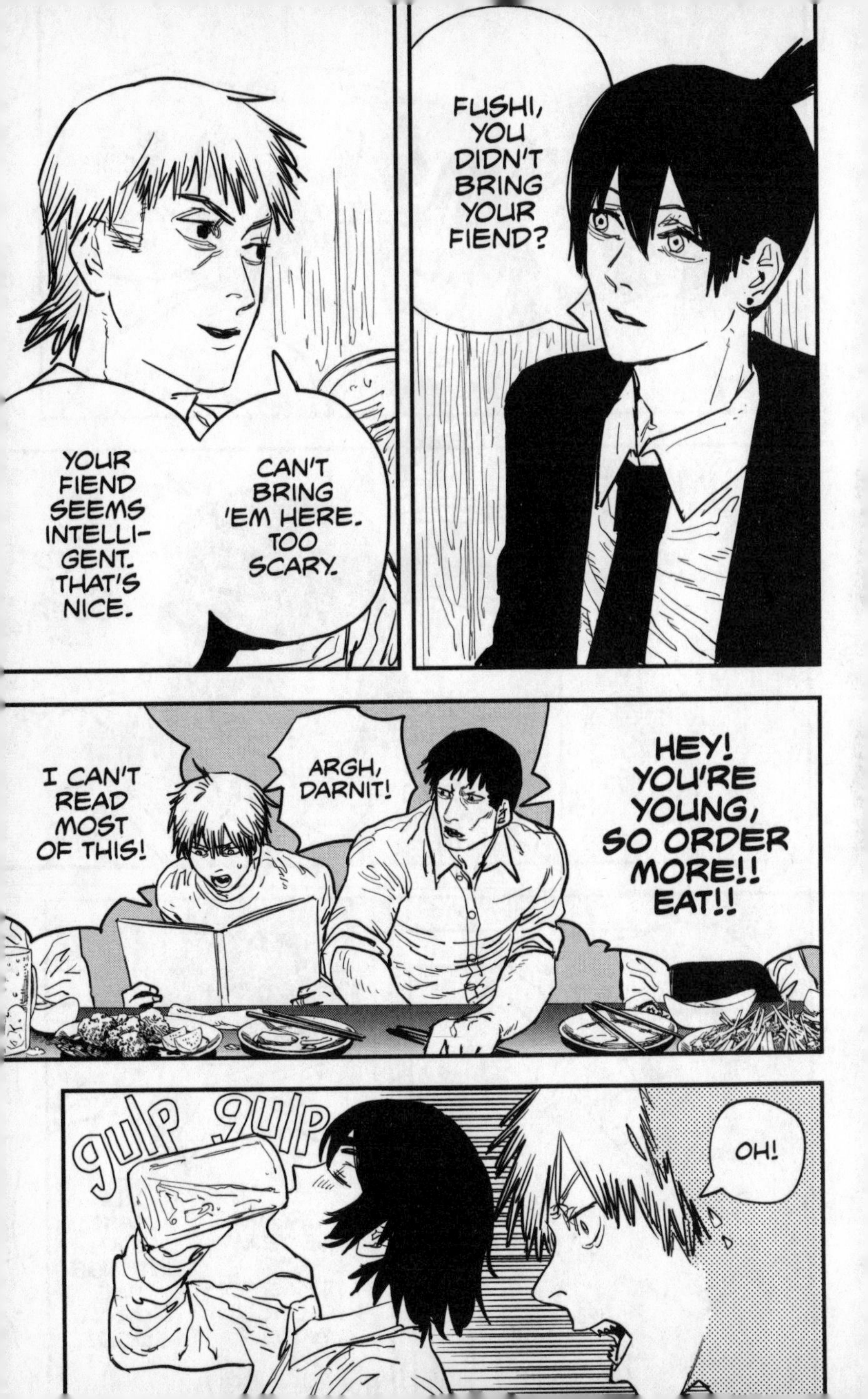
FUSHI, YOU DIDN'T BRING YOUR FIEND?
CAN'T BRING 'EM HERE. TOO SCARY.
YOUR FIEND SEEMS INTELLI- GENT. THAT'S NICE.
HEY! YOU'RE YOUNG, SO ORDER MORE!! EAT!!
ARGH, DARNIT!
I CAN'T READ MOST OF THIS!
OH!
gulp gulp

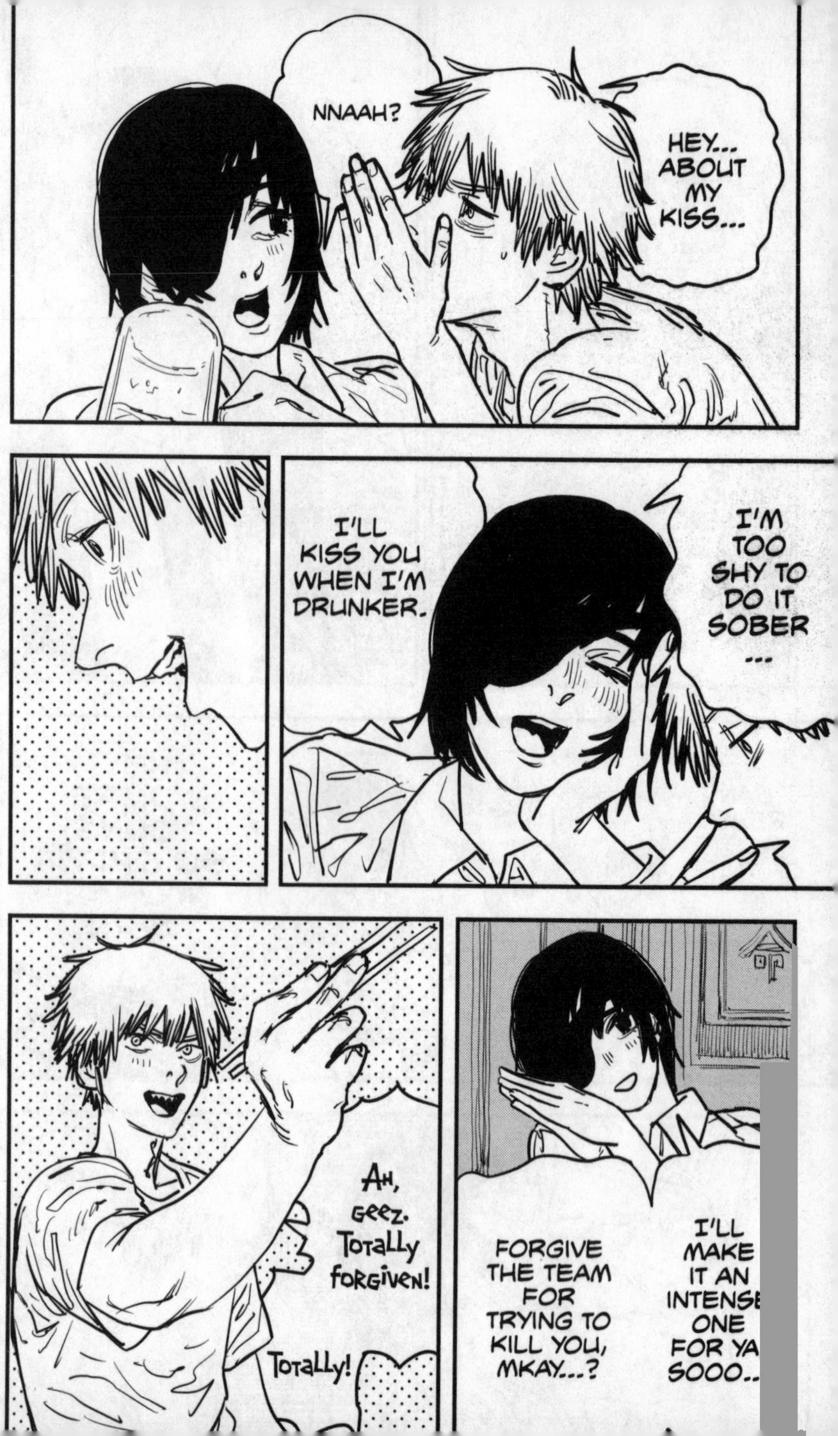
HEY... ABOUT MY KISS...
NNAAH?
I'M TOO SHY TO DO IT SOBER ...
I'LL KISS YOU WHEN I'M DRUNKER.
I'LL MAKE IT AN INTENSE ONE FOR YA SOOO...
FORGIVE THE TEAM FOR TRYING TO KILL YOU, MKAY...?
Ah, geez. Totally forgiven!
Totally!

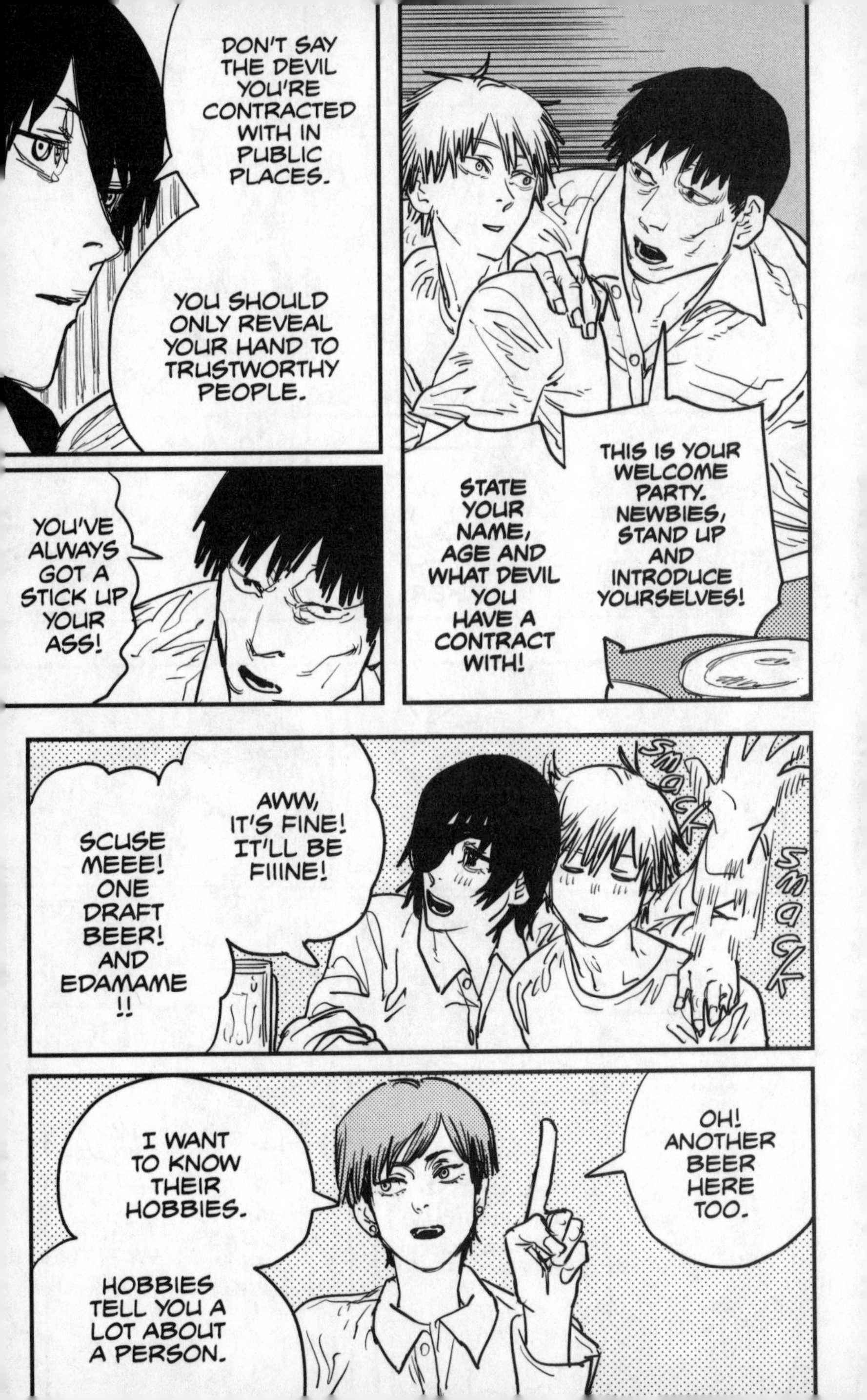

THIS IS YOUR WELCOME PARTY. NEWBIES, STAND UP AND INTRODUCE YOURSELVES!
STATE YOUR NAME, AGE AND WHAT DEVIL YOU HAVE A CONTRACT WITH!
DON'T SAY THE DEVIL YOU'RE CONTRACTED WITH IN PUBLIC PLACES.
YOU SHOULD ONLY REVEAL YOUR HAND TO TRUSTWORTHY PEOPLE.
YOU'VE ALWAYS GOT A STICK UP YOUR ASS!
SMACK
SMACK
AWW, IT'S FINE! IT'LL BE FIIINE!
SCUSE MEEE! ONE DRAFT BEER! AND EDAMAME !!
OH! ANOTHER BEER HERE TOO.
I WANT TO KNOW THEIR HOBBIES.
HOBBIES TELL YOU A LOT ABOUT A PERSON.

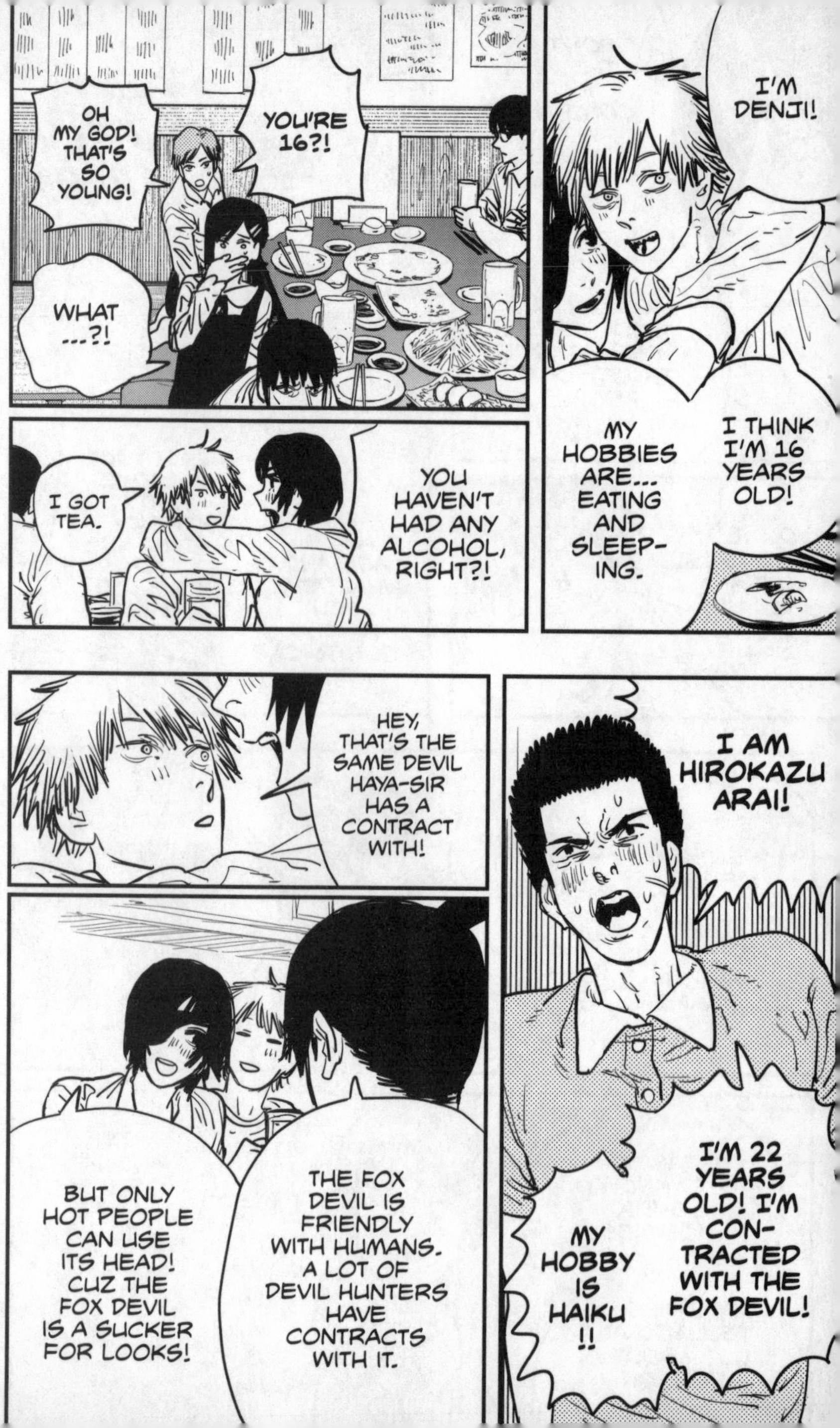
I'M DENJI!
I THINK I'M 16 YEARS OLD!
MY HOBBIES ARE... EATING AND SLEEPING.
YOU'RE 16?!
OH MY GOD! THAT'S SO YOUNG!
WHAT ...?!
YOU HAVEN'T HAD ANY ALCOHOL, RIGHT?!
I GOT TEA.
I AM HIROKAZU ARAI!
I'M 22 YEARS OLD! I'M CONTRACTED WITH THE FOX DEVIL!
MY HOBBY IS HAIKU!!
HEY, THAT'S THE SAME DEVIL HAYA-SIR HAS A CONTRACT WITH!
THE FOX DEVIL IS FRIENDLY WITH HUMANS. A LOT OF DEVIL HUNTERS HAVE CONTRACTS WITH IT.
BUT ONLY HOT PEOPLE CAN USE ITS HEAD! CUZ THE FOX DEVIL IS A SUCKER FOR LOOKS!

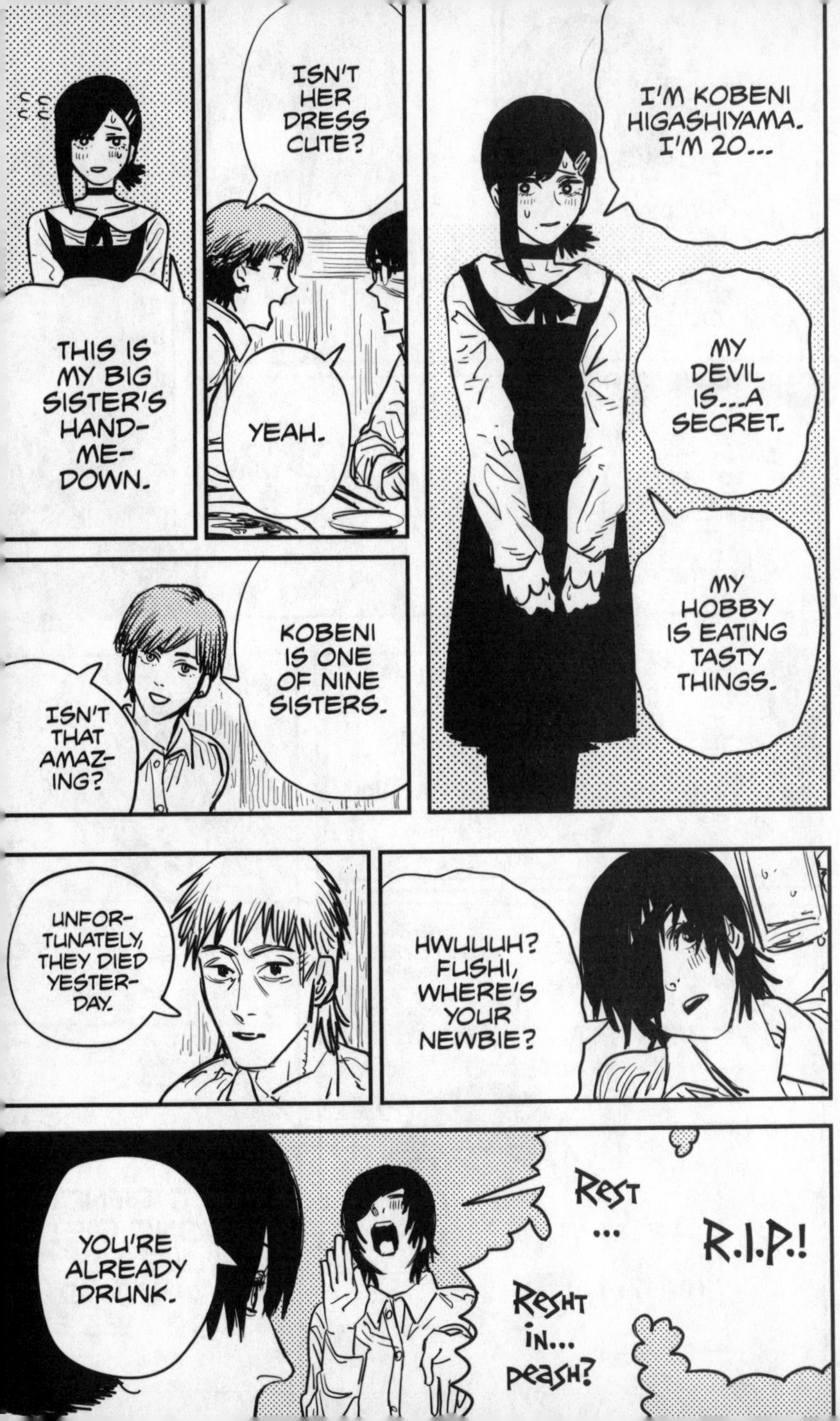
I'M KOBENI HIGASHIYAMA. I'M 20...
MY DEVIL IS...A SECRET.
MY HOBBY IS EATING TASTY THINGS.
ISN'T HER DRESS CUTE?
YEAH.
THIS IS MY BIG SISTER'S HAND-ME-DOWN.
KOBENI IS ONE OF NINE SISTERS.
ISN'T THAT AMAZING?
HWUUUH? FUSHI, WHERE'S YOUR NEWBIE?
UNFORTUNATELY, THEY DIED YESTERDAY.
R.I.P.!
Rest ...
Resht in... peash?
YOU'RE ALREADY DRUNK.

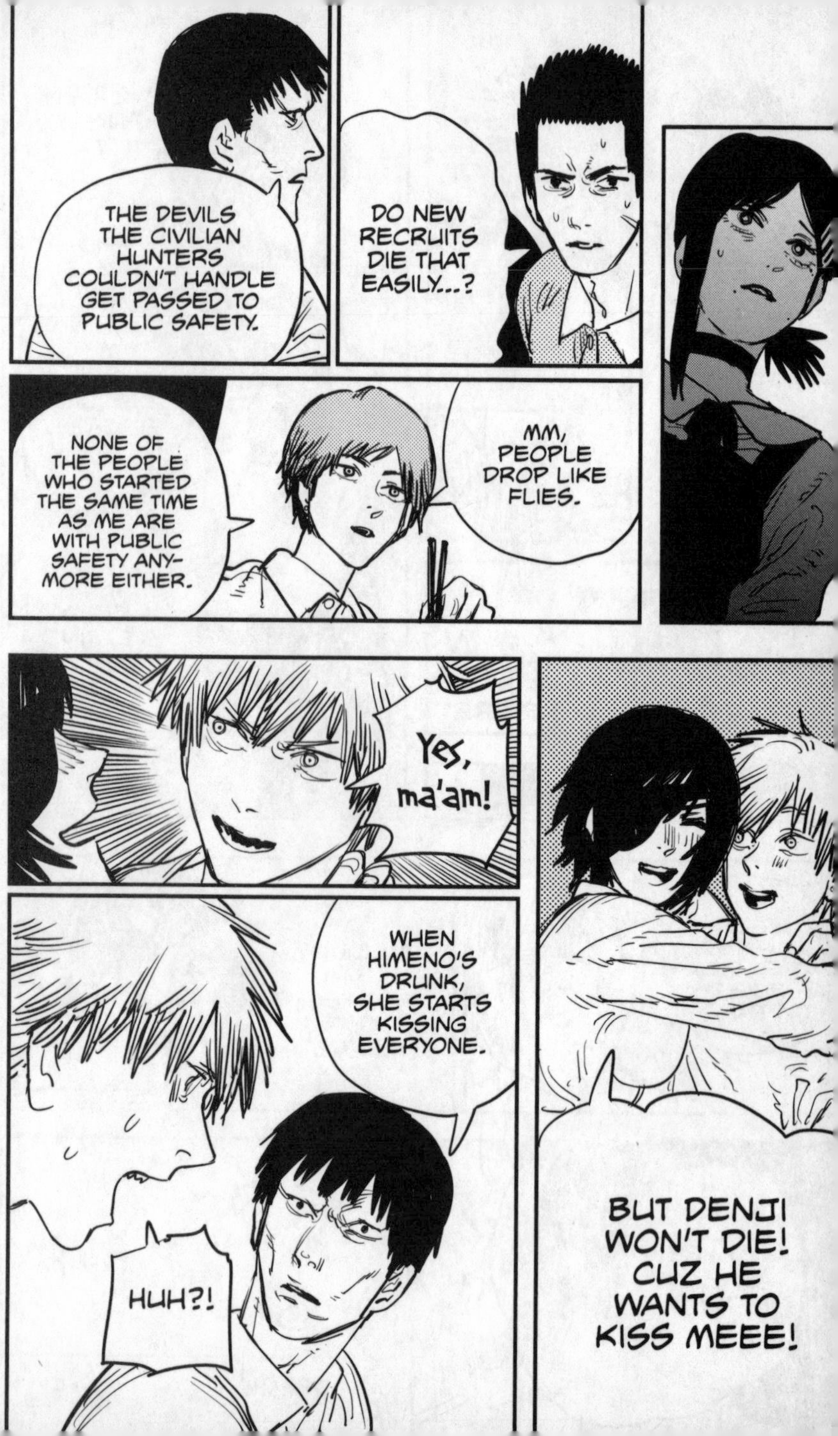
DO NEW RECRUITS DIE THAT EASILY...?
THE DEVILS THE CIVILIAN HUNTERS COULDN'T HANDLE GET PASSED TO PUBLIC SAFETY.
MM, PEOPLE DROP LIKE FLIES.
NONE OF THE PEOPLE WHO STARTED THE SAME TIME AS ME ARE WITH PUBLIC SAFETY ANY-MORE EITHER.
BUT DENJI WON'T DIE! CUZ HE WANTS TO KISS MEEE!
Yes, ma'am!
WHEN HIMENO'S DRUNK, SHE STARTS KISSING EVERYONE.
HUH?!

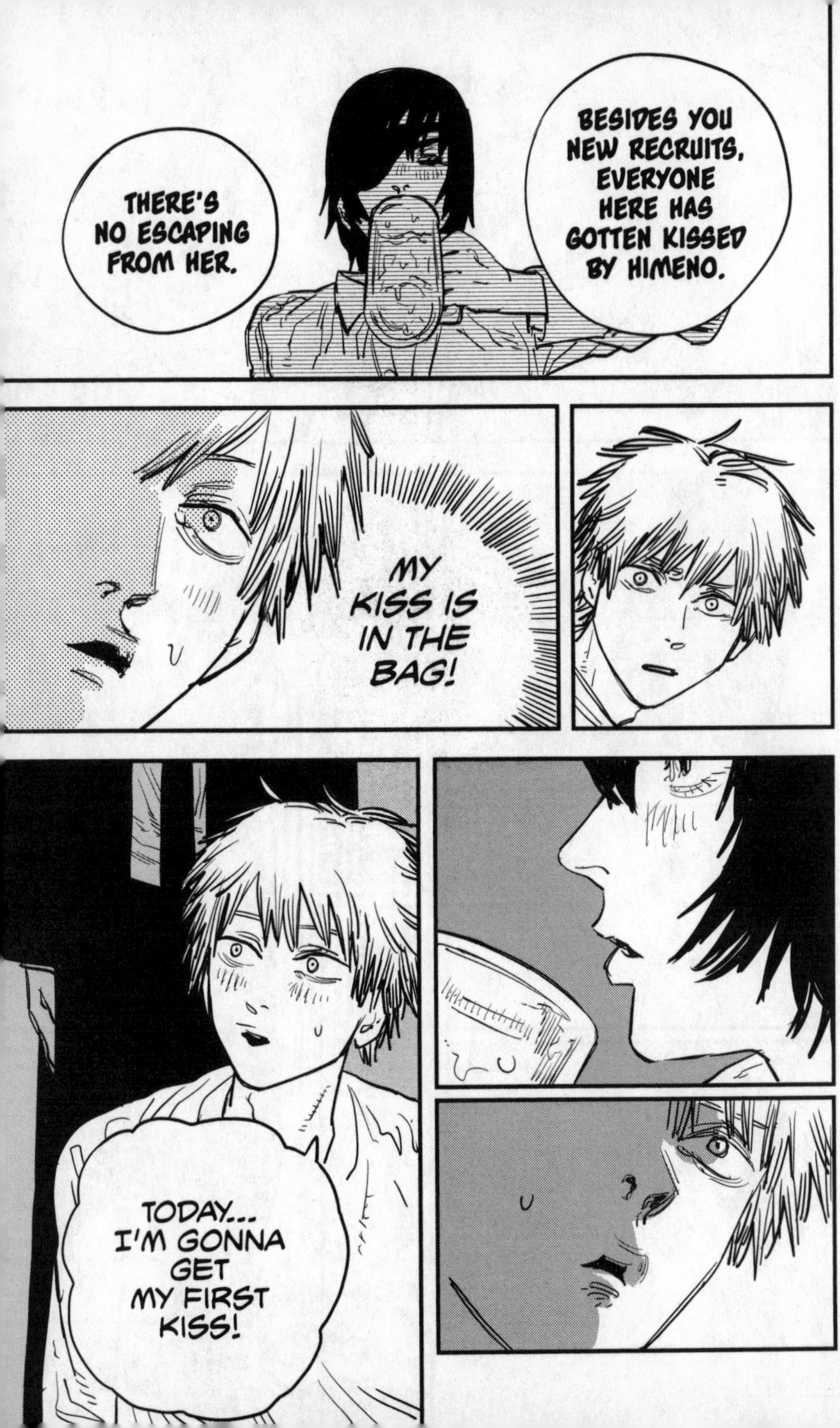
BESIDES YOU NEW RECRUITS, EVERYONE HERE HAS GOTTEN KISSED BY HIMENO.
THERE'S NO ESCAPING FROM HER.
MY KISS IS IN THE BAG!
TODAY... I'M GONNA GET MY FIRST KISS!

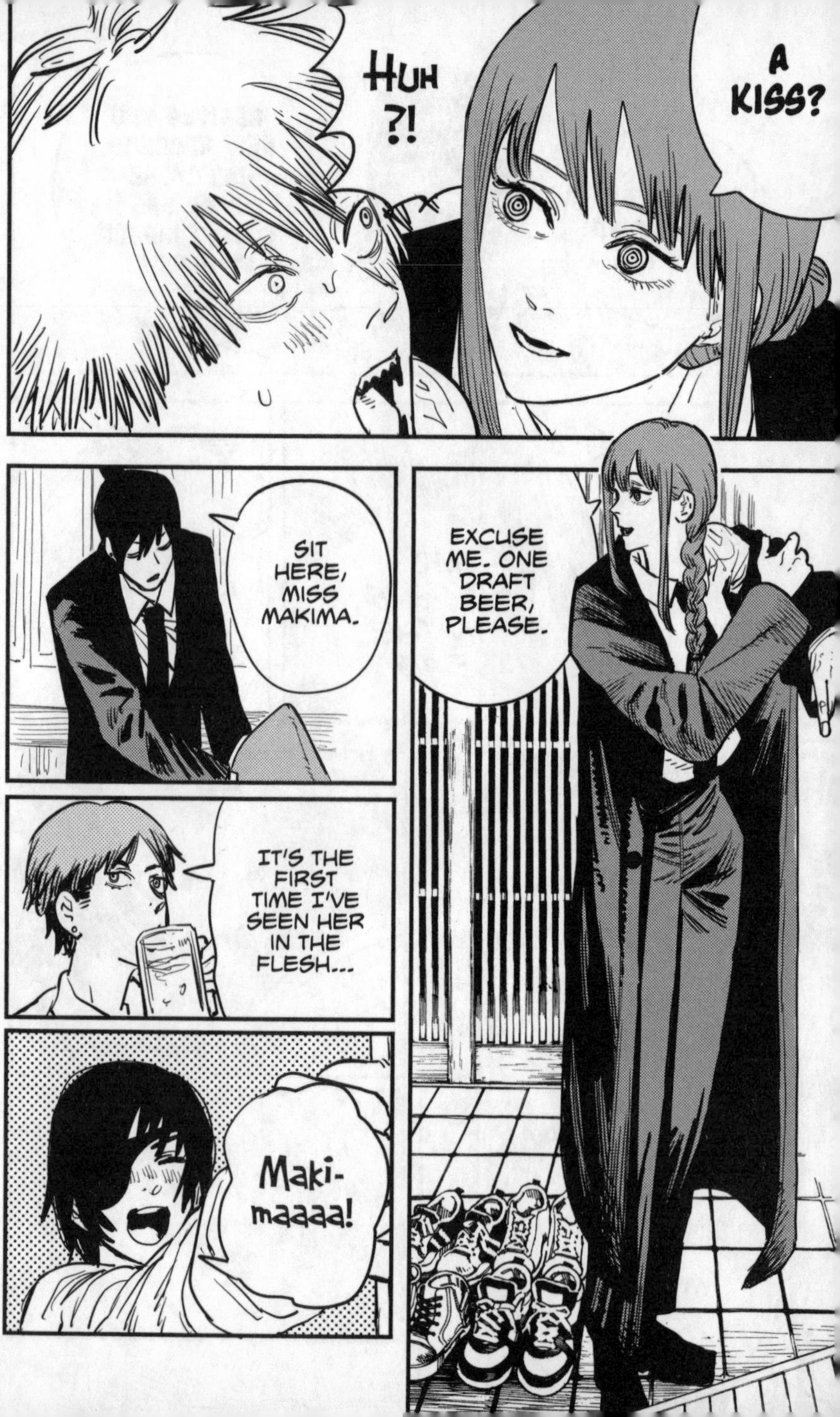
A KISS?
HUH ?!
EXCUSE ME. ONE DRAFT BEER, PLEASE.
SIT HERE, MISS MAKIMA.
IT'S THE FIRST TIME I'VE SEEN HER IN THE FLESH...
Maki-maaaa!

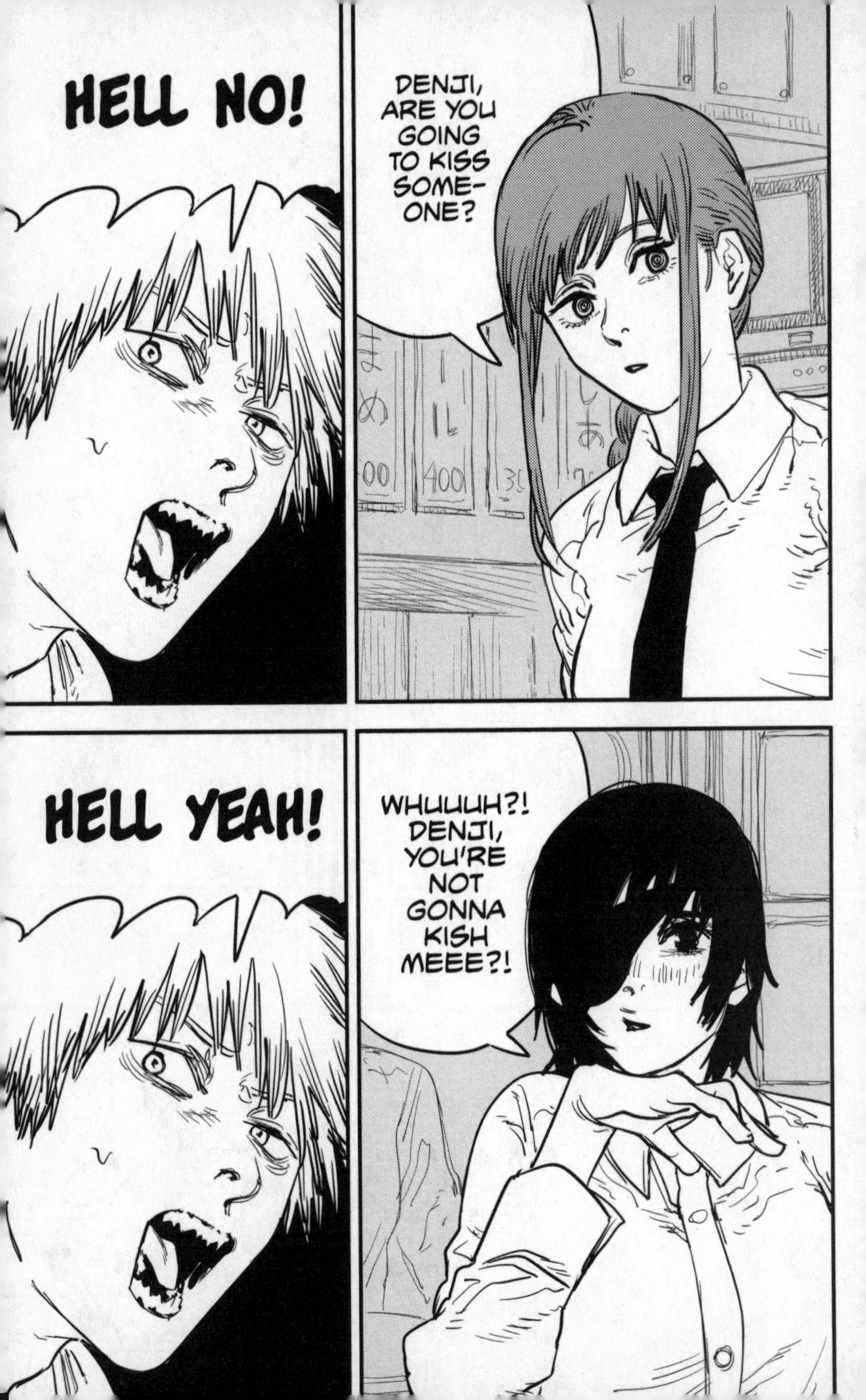
DENJI, ARE YOU GOING TO KISS SOME-ONE?
HELL NO!
WHUUUH?! DENJI, YOU'RE NOT GONNA KISH MEEE?!
HELL YEAH!

Chain
saw
man

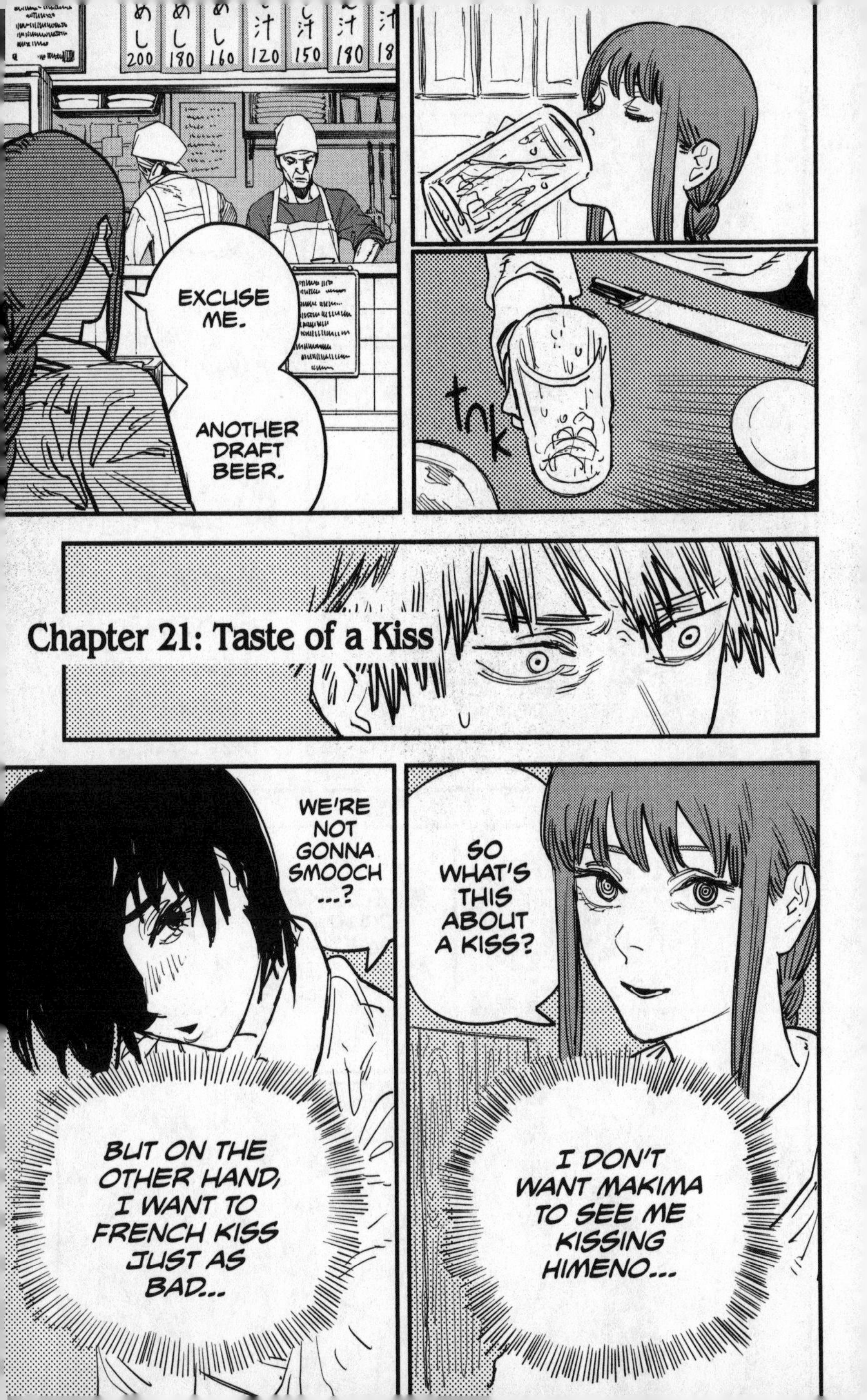
tnk
EXCUSE ME.
ANOTHER DRAFT BEER.
Chapter 21: Taste of a Kiss
SO WHAT'S THIS ABOUT A KISS?
I DON'T WANT MAKIMA TO SEE ME KISSING HIMENO...
WE'RE NOT GONNA SMOOCH ...?
BUT ON THE OTHER HAND, I WANT TO FRENCH KISS JUST AS BAD...

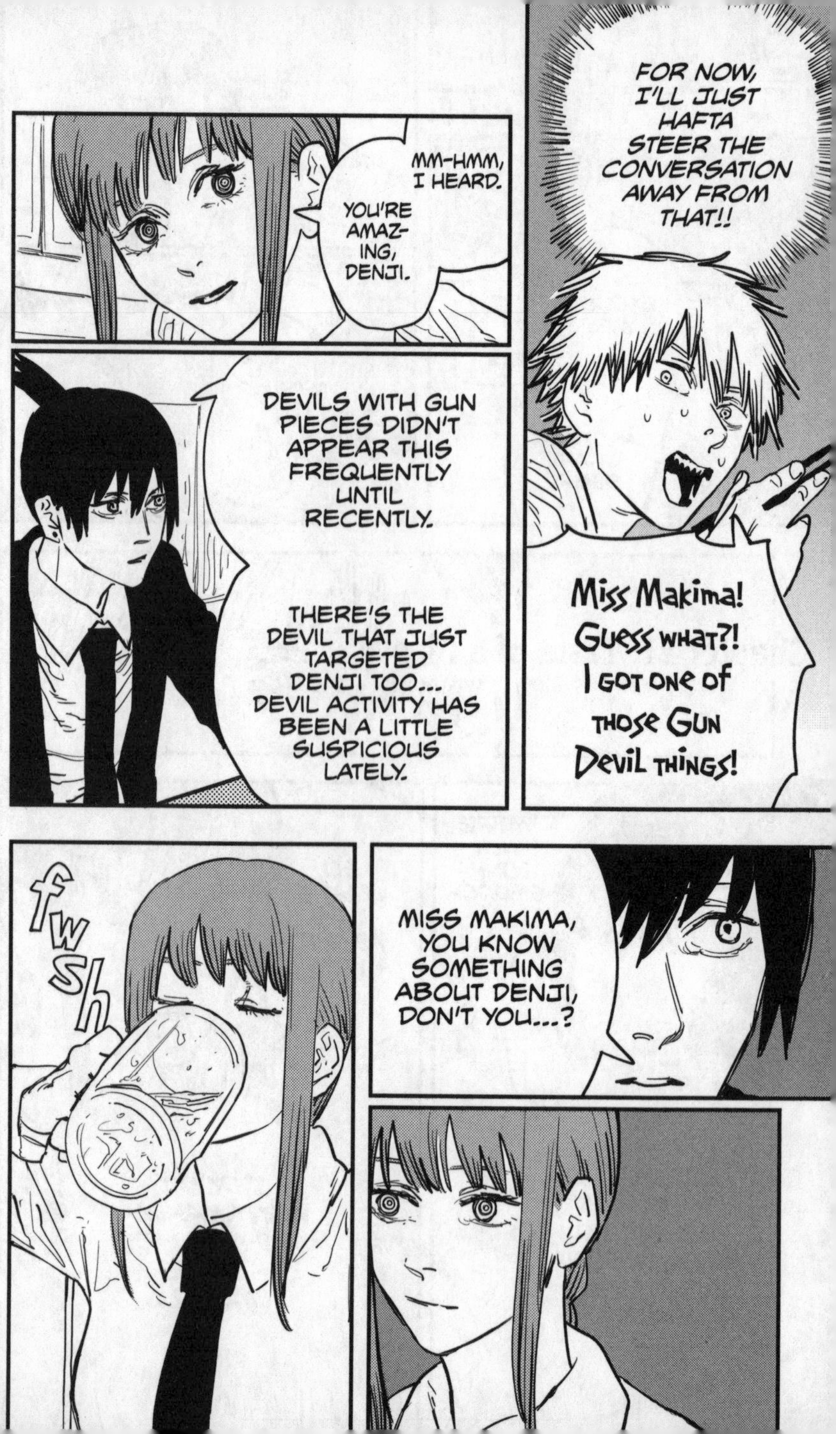
FOR NOW, I'LL JUST HAFTA STEER THE CONVERSATION AWAY FROM THAT!!
Miss Makima! Guess what?! I got one of those Gun Devil things!
MM-HMM, I HEARD.
YOU'RE AMAZ-ING, DENJI.
DEVILS WITH GUN PIECES DIDN'T APPEAR THIS FREQUENTLY UNTIL RECENTLY.
THERE'S THE DEVIL THAT JUST TARGETED DENJI TOO... DEVIL ACTIVITY HAS BEEN A LITTLE SUSPICIOUS LATELY.
MISS MAKIMA, YOU KNOW SOMETHING ABOUT DENJI, DON'T YOU...?
fwsh

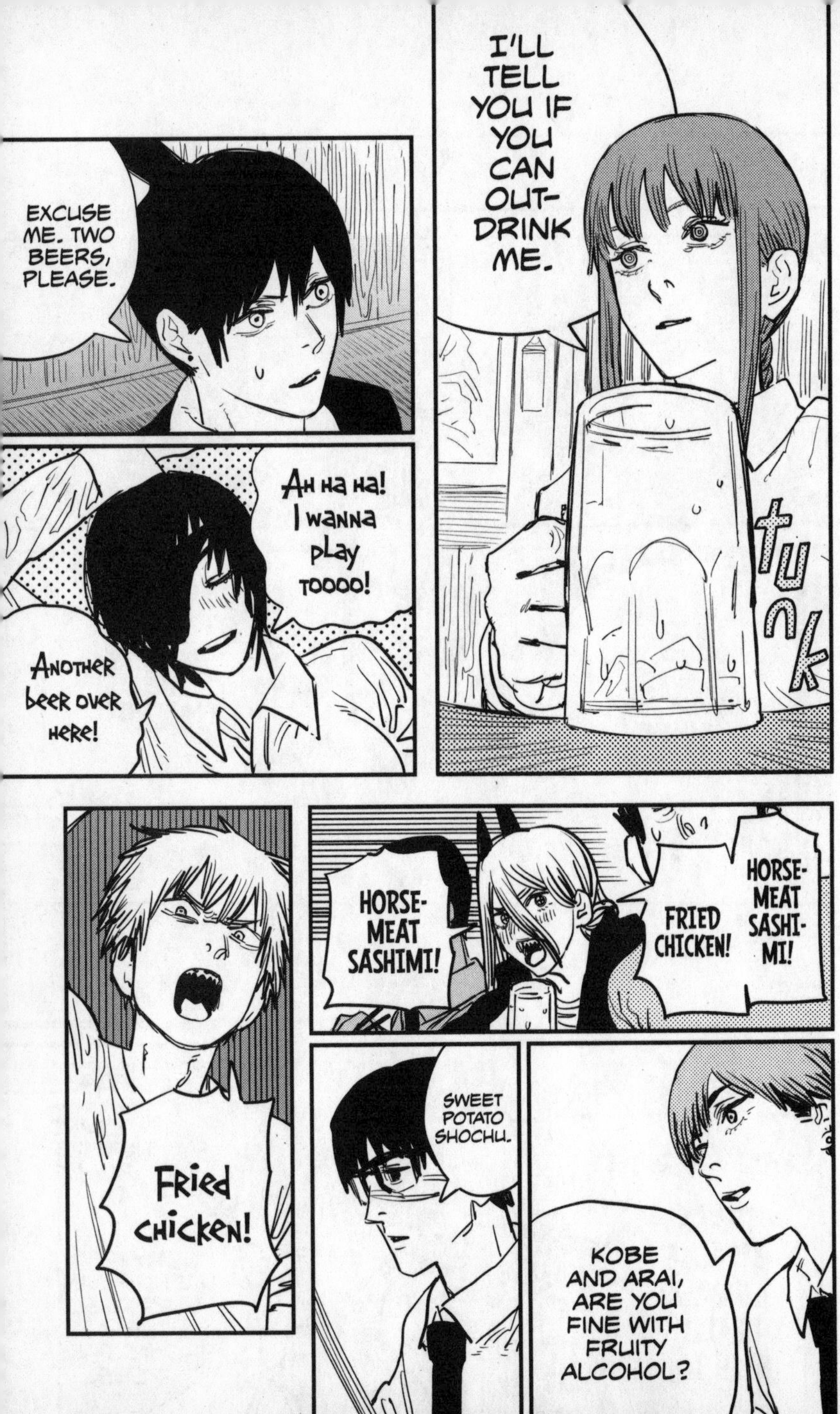
I'LL TELL YOU IF YOU CAN OUT-DRINK ME.
tunk
EXCUSE ME. TWO BEERS, PLEASE.
AH HA HA! I WANNA PLAY TOOOO!
ANOTHER BEER OVER HERE!
HORSE-MEAT SASHIMI!
FRIED CHICKEN!
HORSE-MEAT SASHIMI!
KOBE AND ARAI, ARE YOU FINE WITH FRUITY ALCOHOL?
SWEET POTATO SHOCHU.
FRIED CHICKEN!

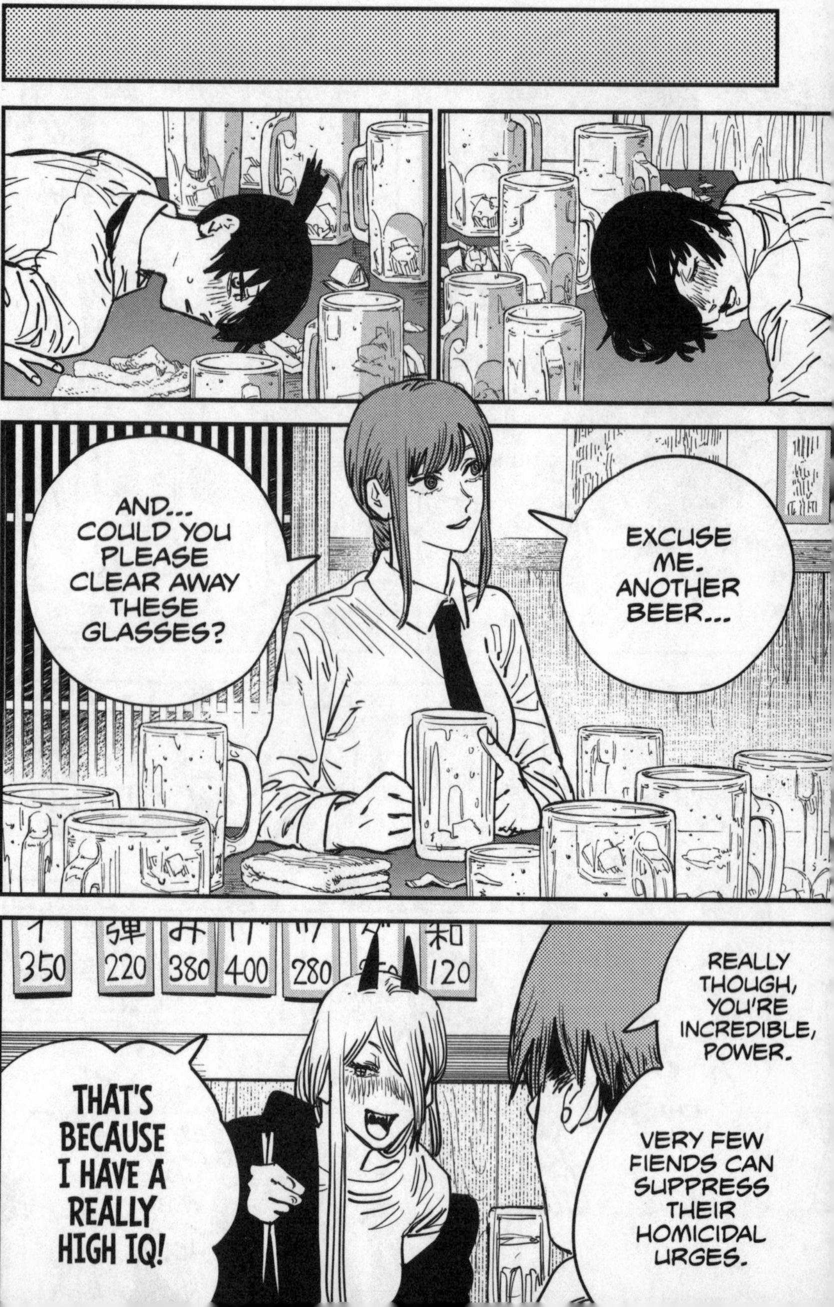
EXCUSE ME. ANOTHER BEER...
AND... COULD YOU PLEASE CLEAR AWAY THESE GLASSES?
350
220
380
400
280
120
REALLY THOUGH, YOU'RE INCREDIBLE, POWER.
VERY FEW FIENDS CAN SUPPRESS THEIR HOMICIDAL URGES.
THAT'S BECAUSE I HAVE A REALLY HIGH IQ!

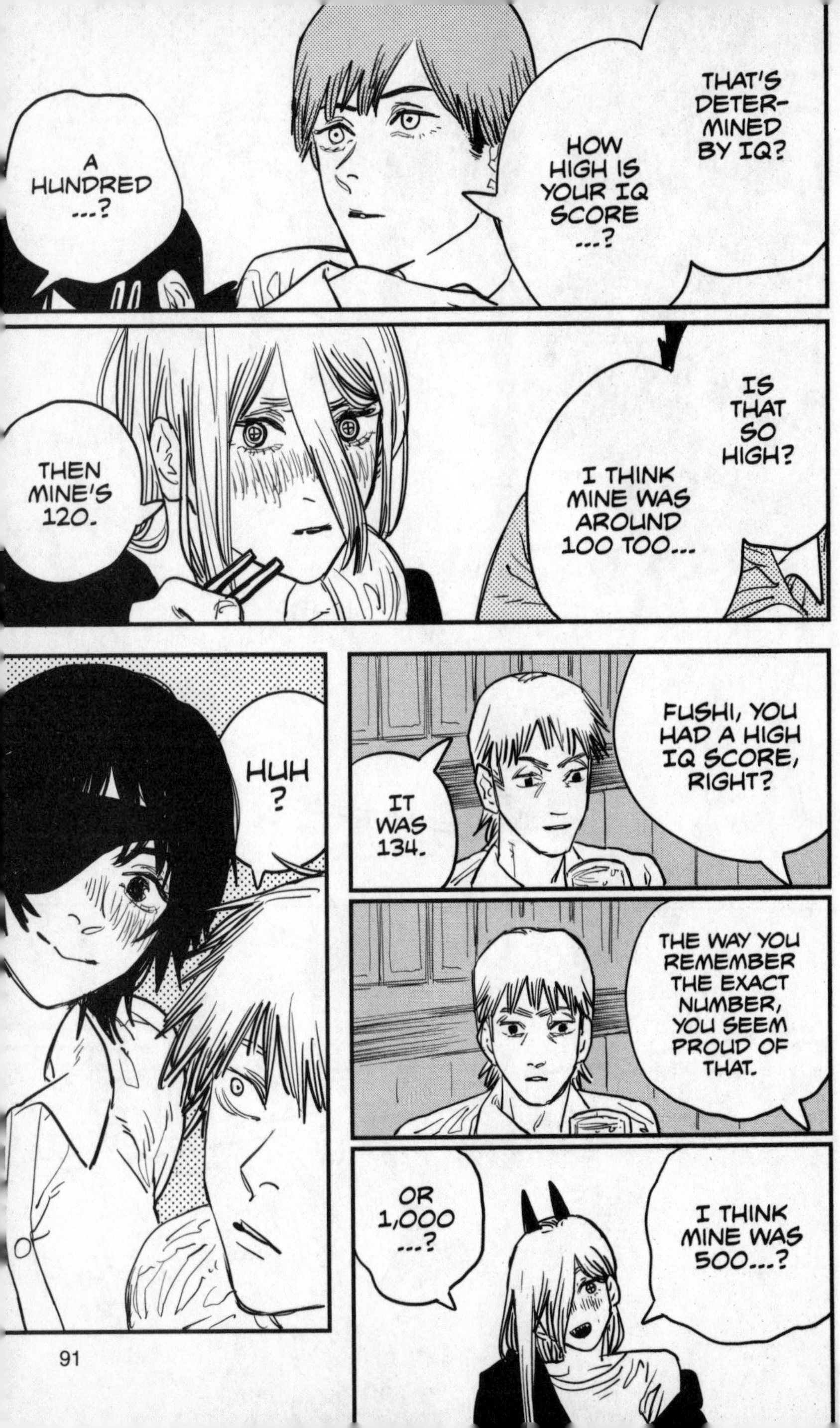
THAT'S DETER-MINED BY IQ?
HOW HIGH IS YOUR IQ SCORE ...?
A HUNDRED ...?
IS THAT SO HIGH?
I THINK MINE WAS AROUND 100 TOO...
THEN MINE'S 120.
FUSHI, YOU HAD A HIGH IQ SCORE, RIGHT?
IT WAS 134.
THE WAY YOU REMEMBER THE EXACT NUMBER, YOU SEEM PROUD OF THAT.
I THINK MINE WAS 500...?
OR 1,000 ...?
HUH ?

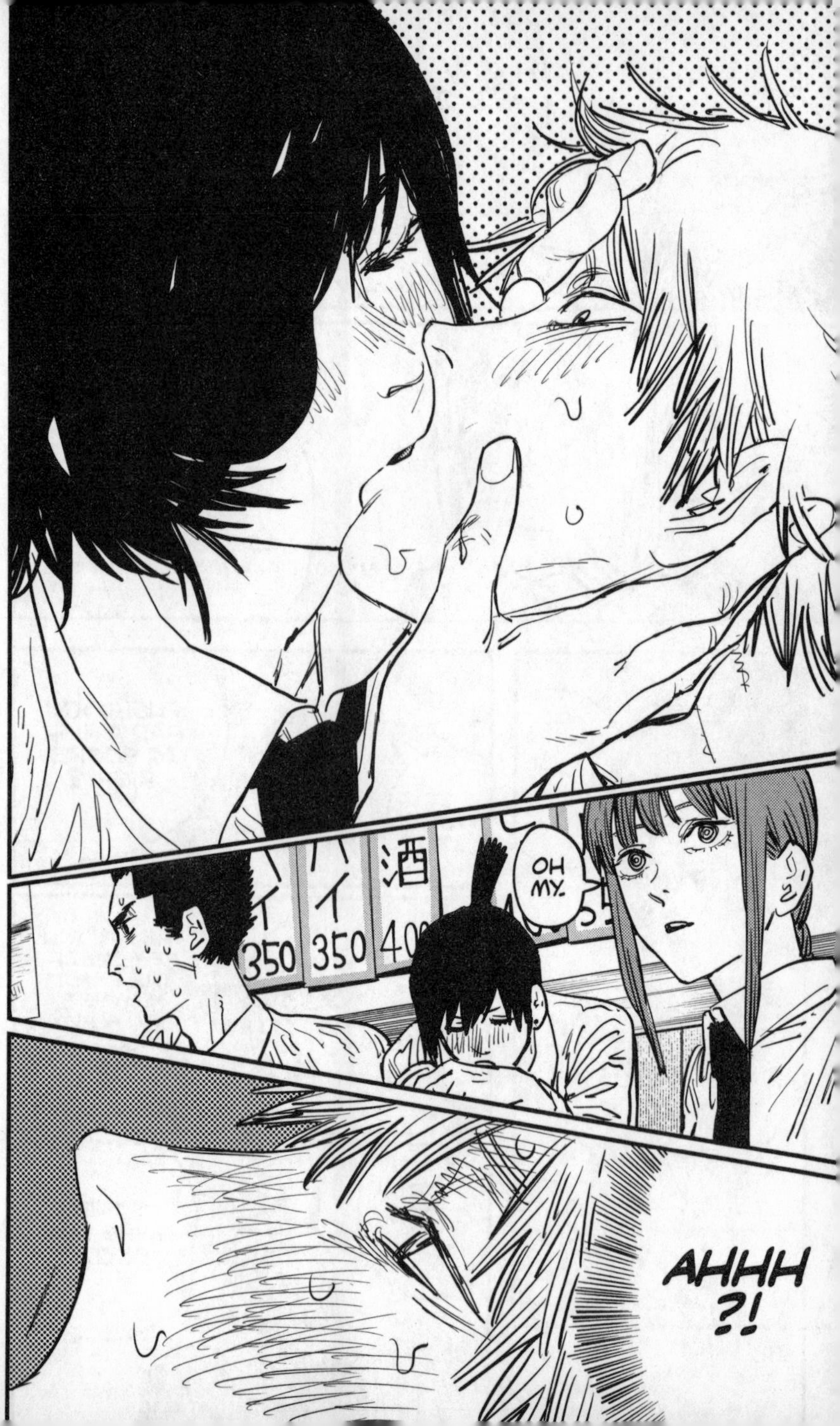

OH MY.
酒
350
350
400
AHHH ?!

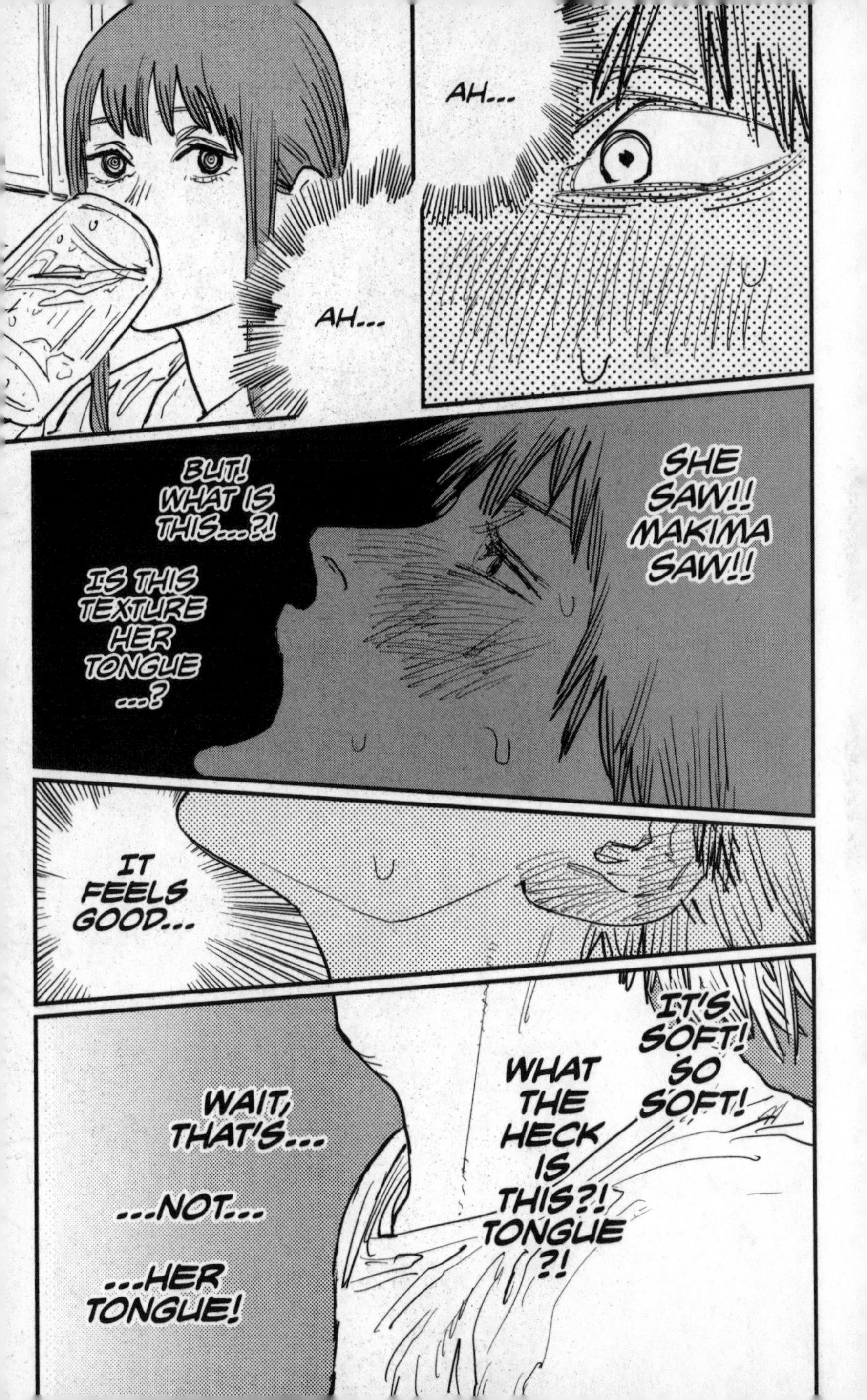
AH...
AH...
SHE SAW!! MAKIMA SAW!!
BUT! WHAT IS THIS...?!
IS THIS TEXTURE HER TONGUE ...?
IT FEELS GOOD...
IT'S SOFT! SO SOFT!
WHAT THE HECK IS THIS?! TONGUE ?!
WAIT, THAT'S...
...NOT...
...HER TONGUE!

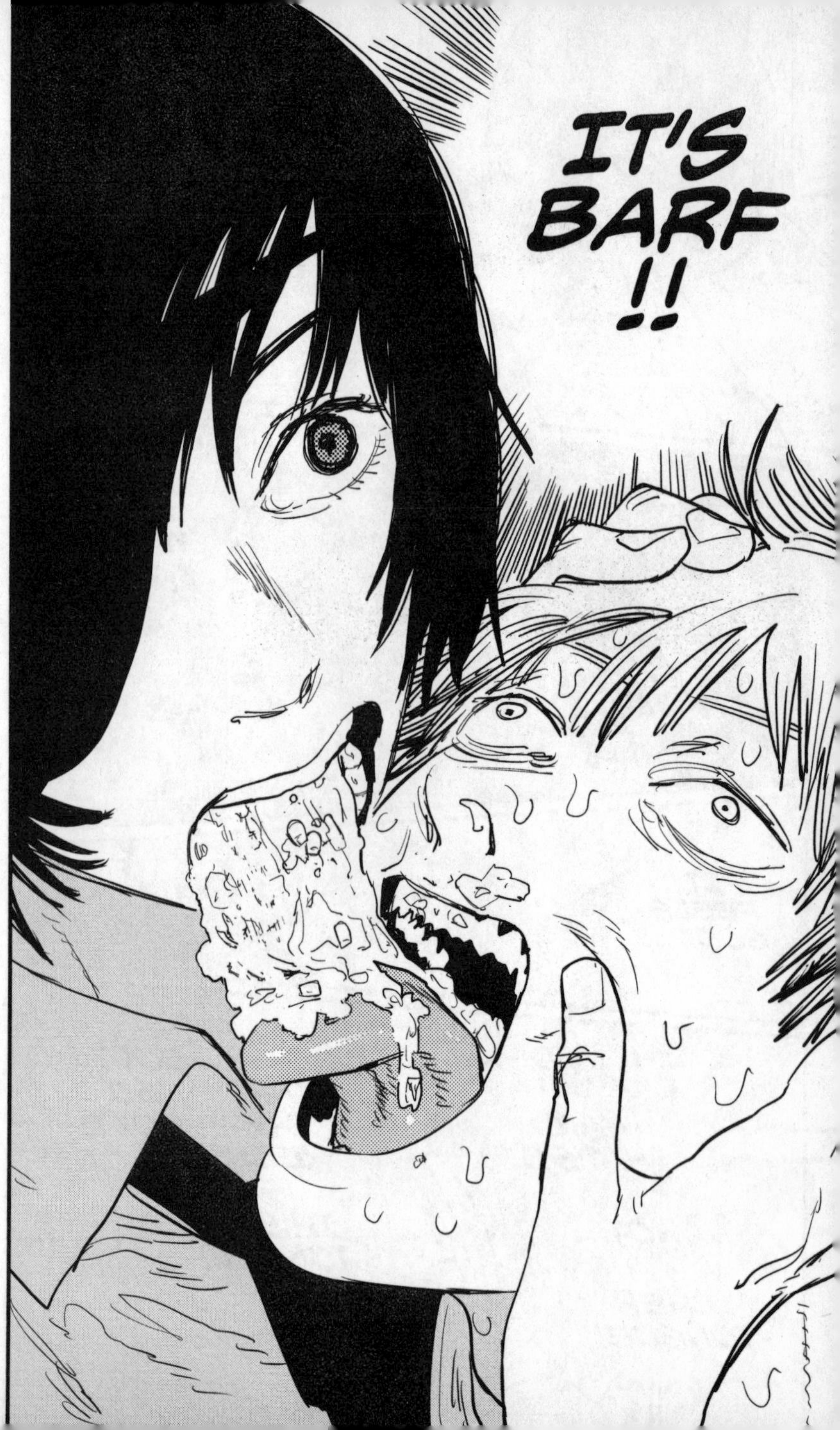
IT'S BARF !!

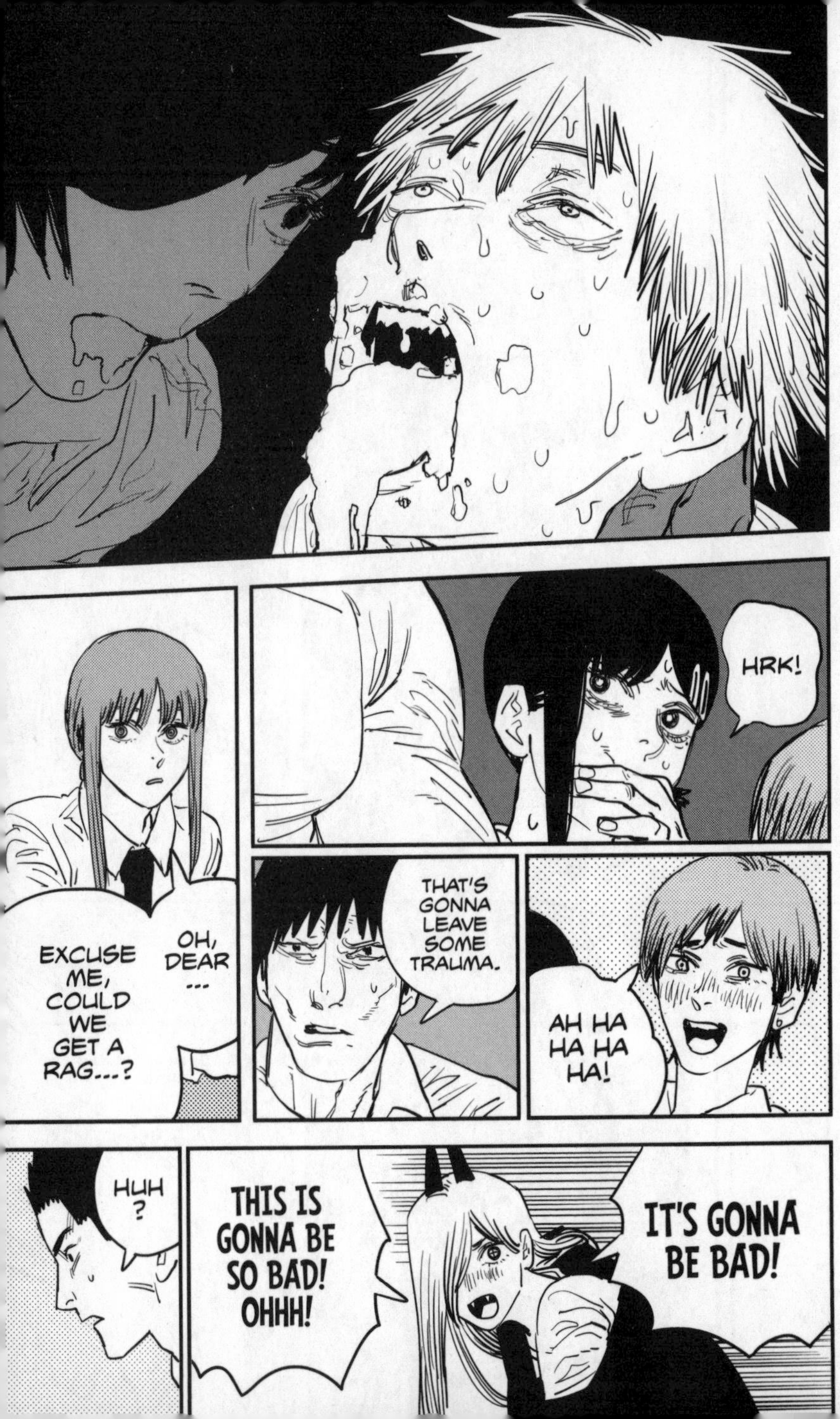
HRK!
AH HA HA HA HA!
THAT'S GONNA LEAVE SOME TRAUMA.
OH, DEAR...
EXCUSE ME, COULD WE GET A RAG...?
IT'S GONNA BE BAD!
THIS IS GONNA BE SO BAD! OHHH!
HUH?

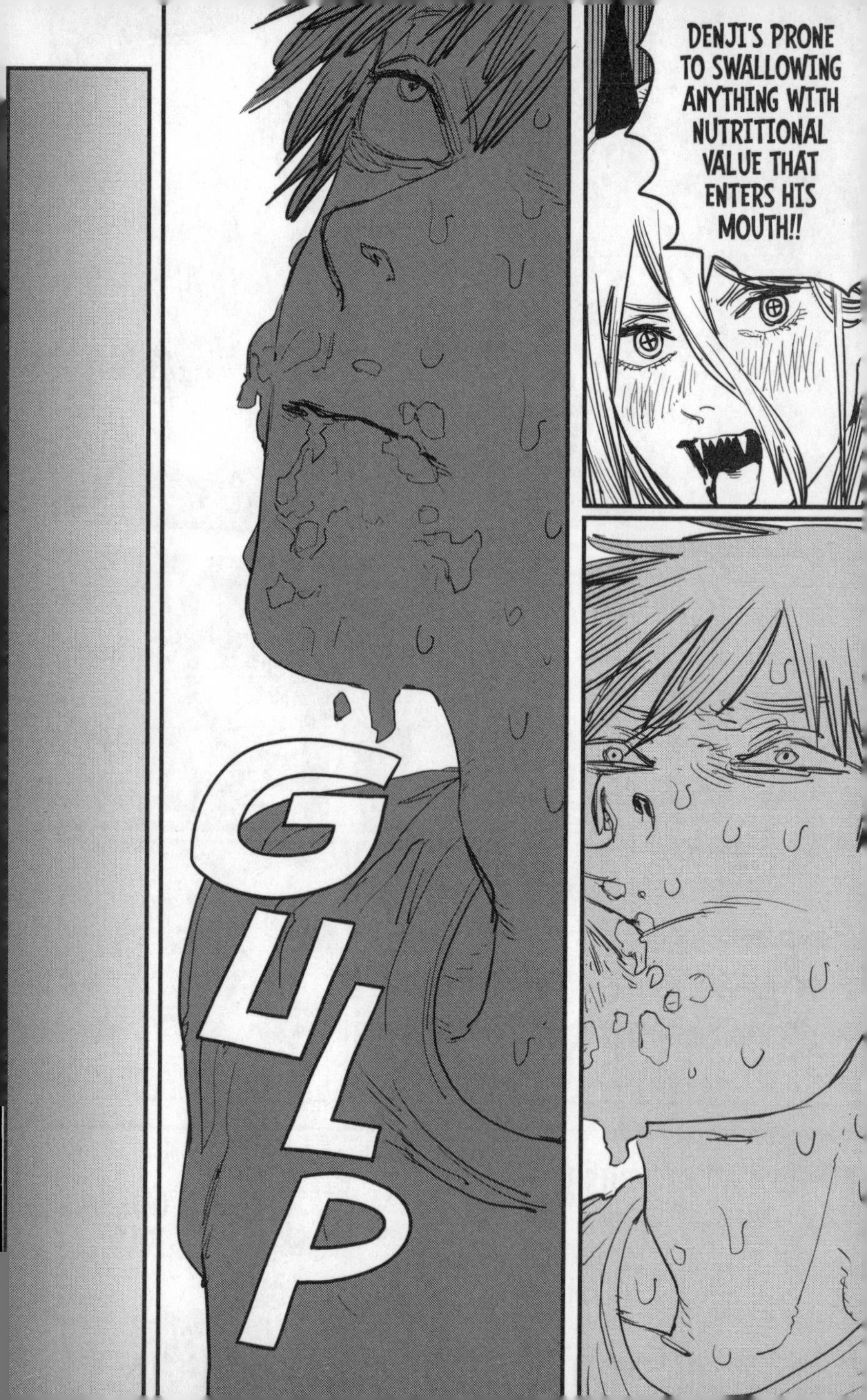
DENJI'S PRONE TO SWALLOWING ANYTHING WITH NUTRITIONAL VALUE THAT ENTERS HIS MOUTH!!
GULP

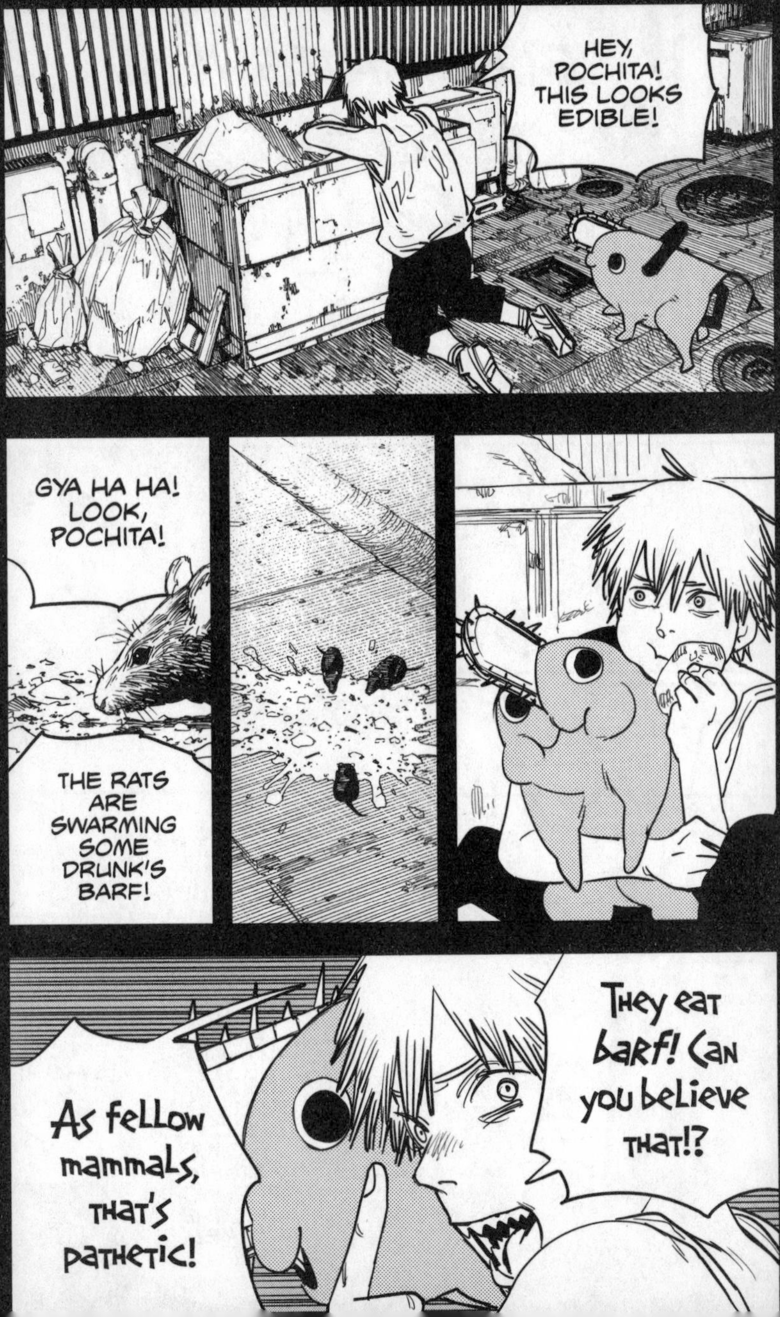
HEY, POCHITA! THIS LOOKS EDIBLE!
GYA HA HA! LOOK, POCHITA!
THE RATS ARE SWARMING SOME DRUNK'S BARF!
They eat barf! Can you believe that!?
As fellow mammals, that's pathetic!

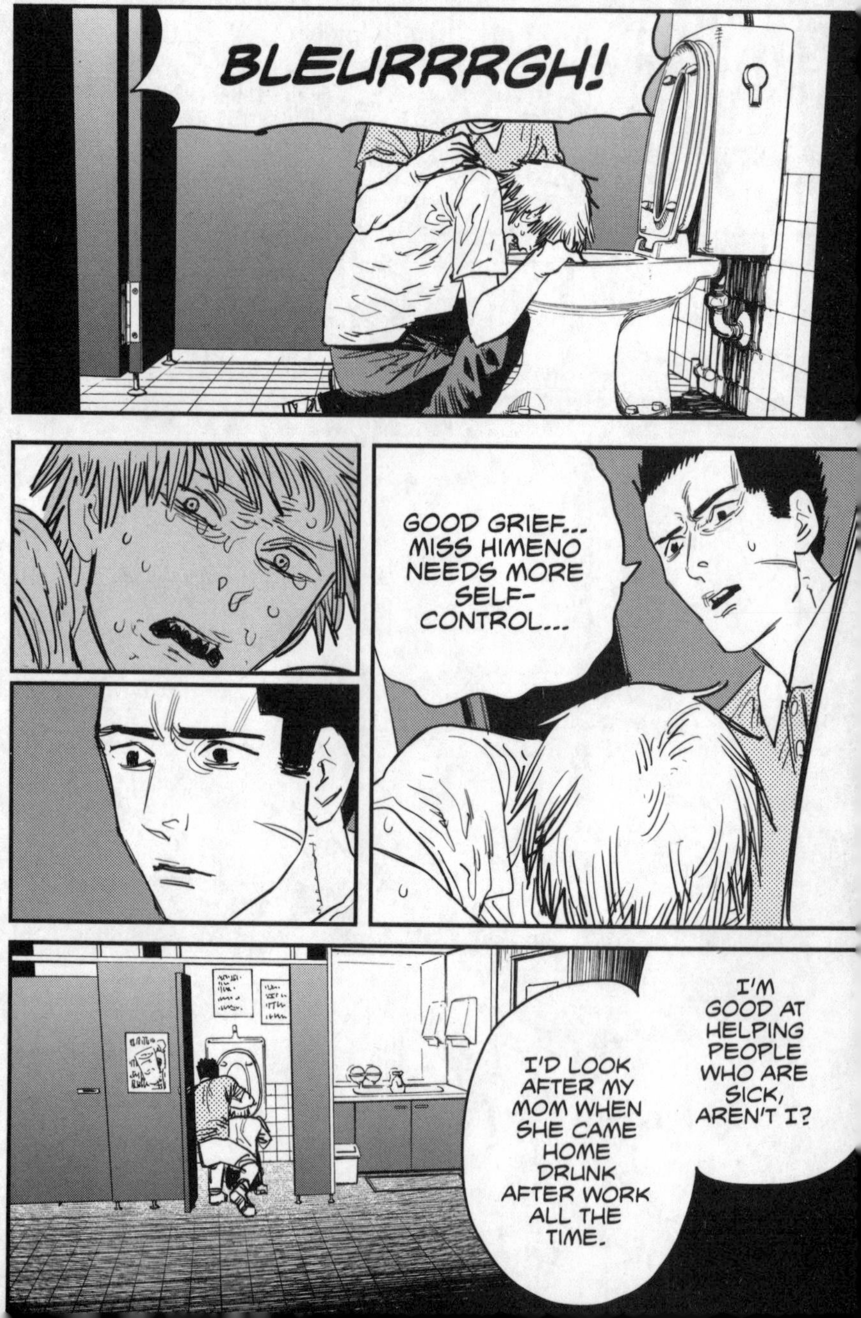
BLEURRRGH!
GOOD GRIEF... MISS HIMENO NEEDS MORE SELF-CONTROL...
I'M GOOD AT HELPING PEOPLE WHO ARE SICK, AREN'T I?
I'D LOOK AFTER MY MOM WHEN SHE CAME HOME DRUNK AFTER WORK ALL THE TIME.

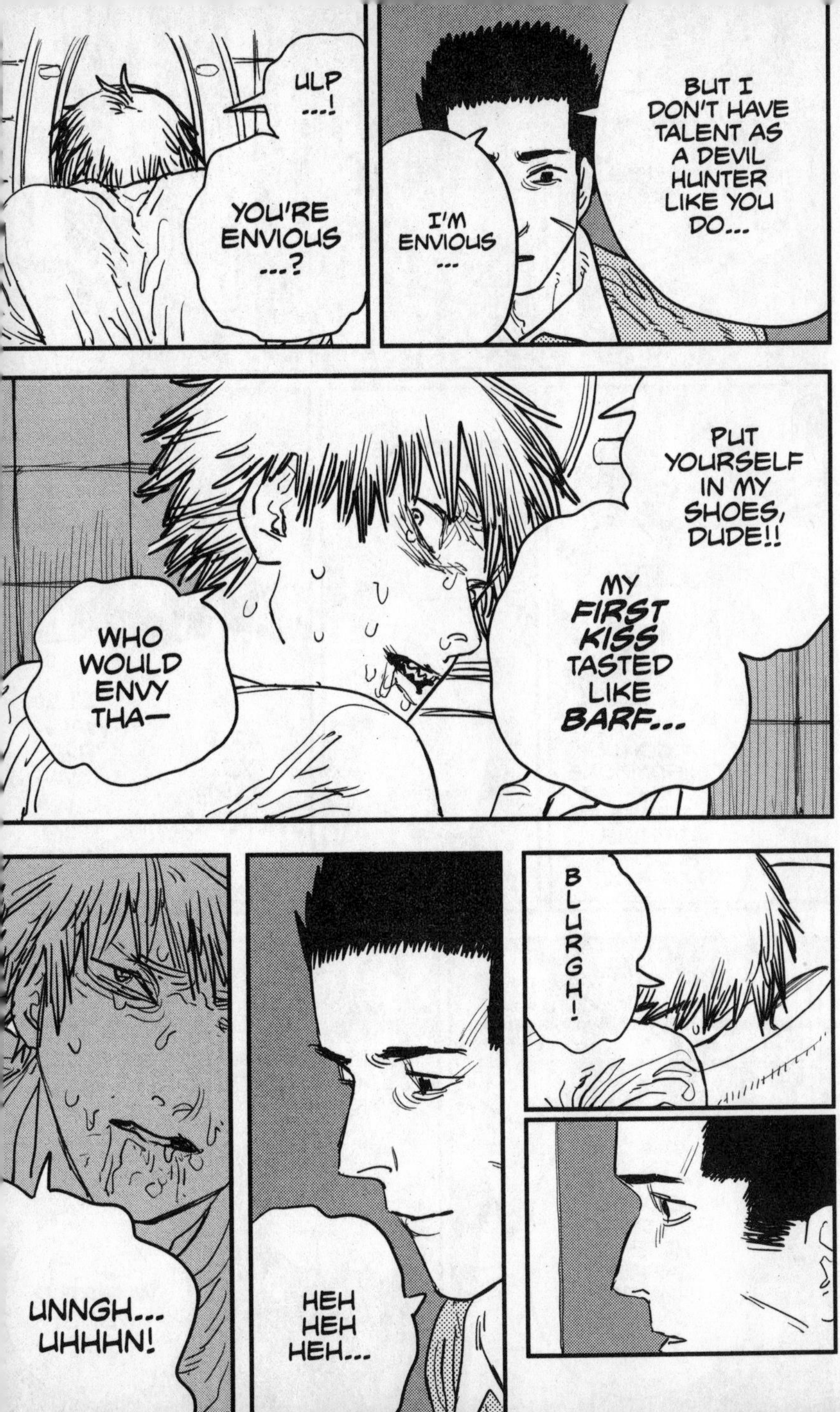
BUT I DON'T HAVE TALENT AS A DEVIL HUNTER LIKE YOU DO...
I'M ENVIOUS...
ULP...!
YOU'RE ENVIOUS...?
PUT YOURSELF IN MY SHOES, DUDE!!
MY FIRST KISS TASTED LIKE BARF...
WHO WOULD ENVY THA—
BLURGH!
HEH HEH HEH...
UNNGH... UHHHN!

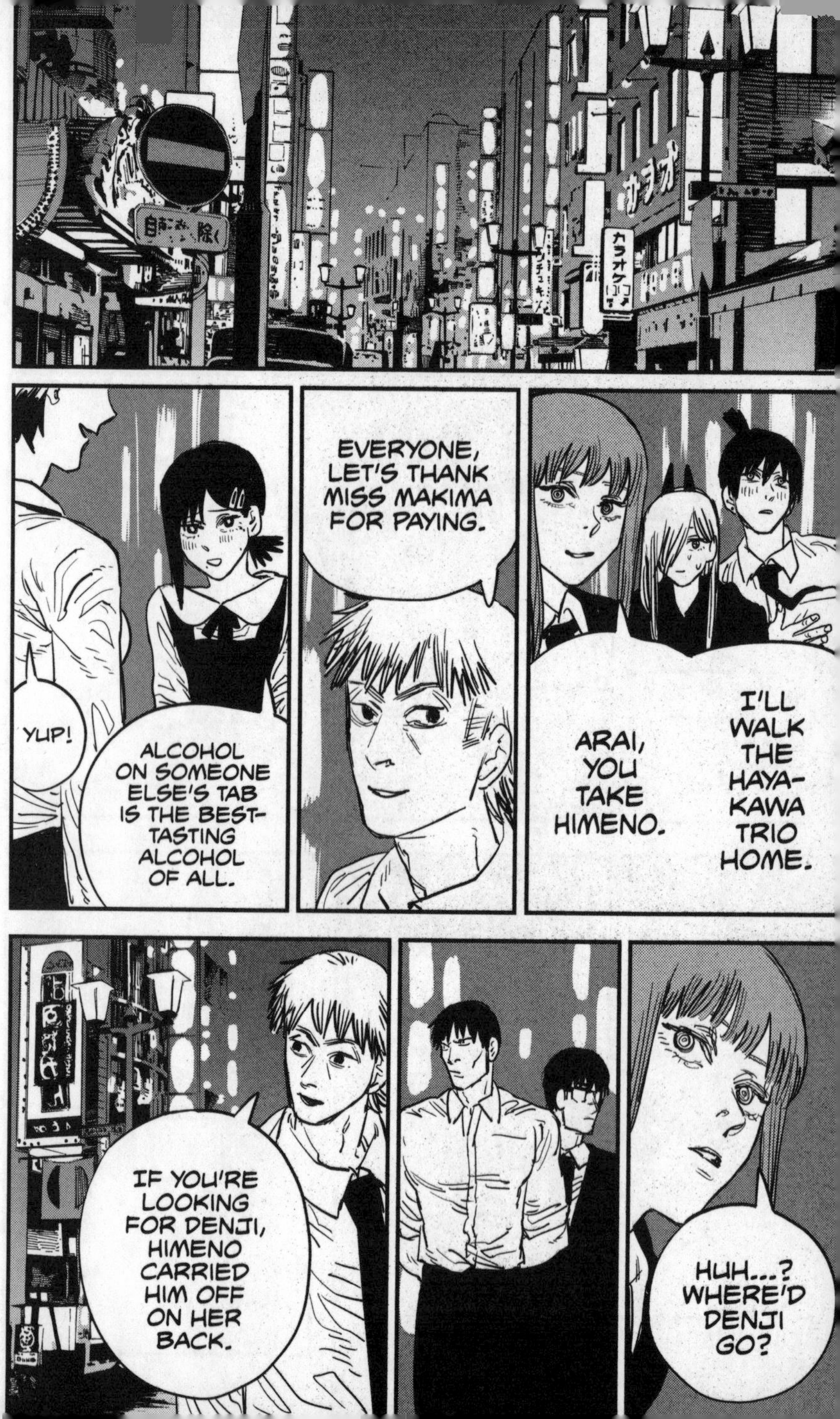
I'LL WALK THE HAYA-KAWA TRIO HOME.
ARAI, YOU TAKE HIMENO.
EVERYONE, LET'S THANK MISS MAKIMA FOR PAYING.
ALCOHOL ON SOMEONE ELSE'S TAB IS THE BEST-TASTING ALCOHOL OF ALL.
YUP!
HUH...? WHERE'D DENJI GO?
IF YOU'RE LOOKING FOR DENJI, HIMENO CARRIED HIM OFF ON HER BACK.

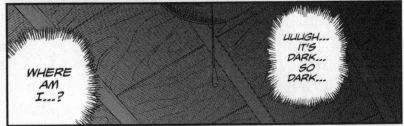

UUUGH... IT'S DARK... SO DARK...
WHERE AM I...?
WATERRR ... WATER...
WATER ...
UNGH... OH YEAH...
I GOT BARF KISSED...
...BY BARF WOMAN...
WATER ...
DAMMIIIT ...
WATER ...

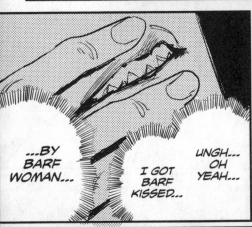

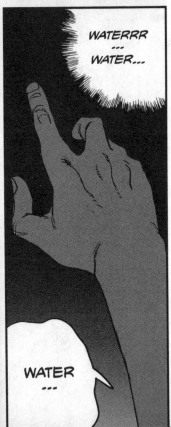

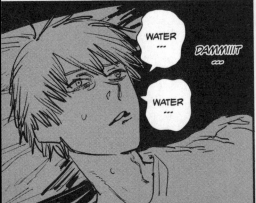

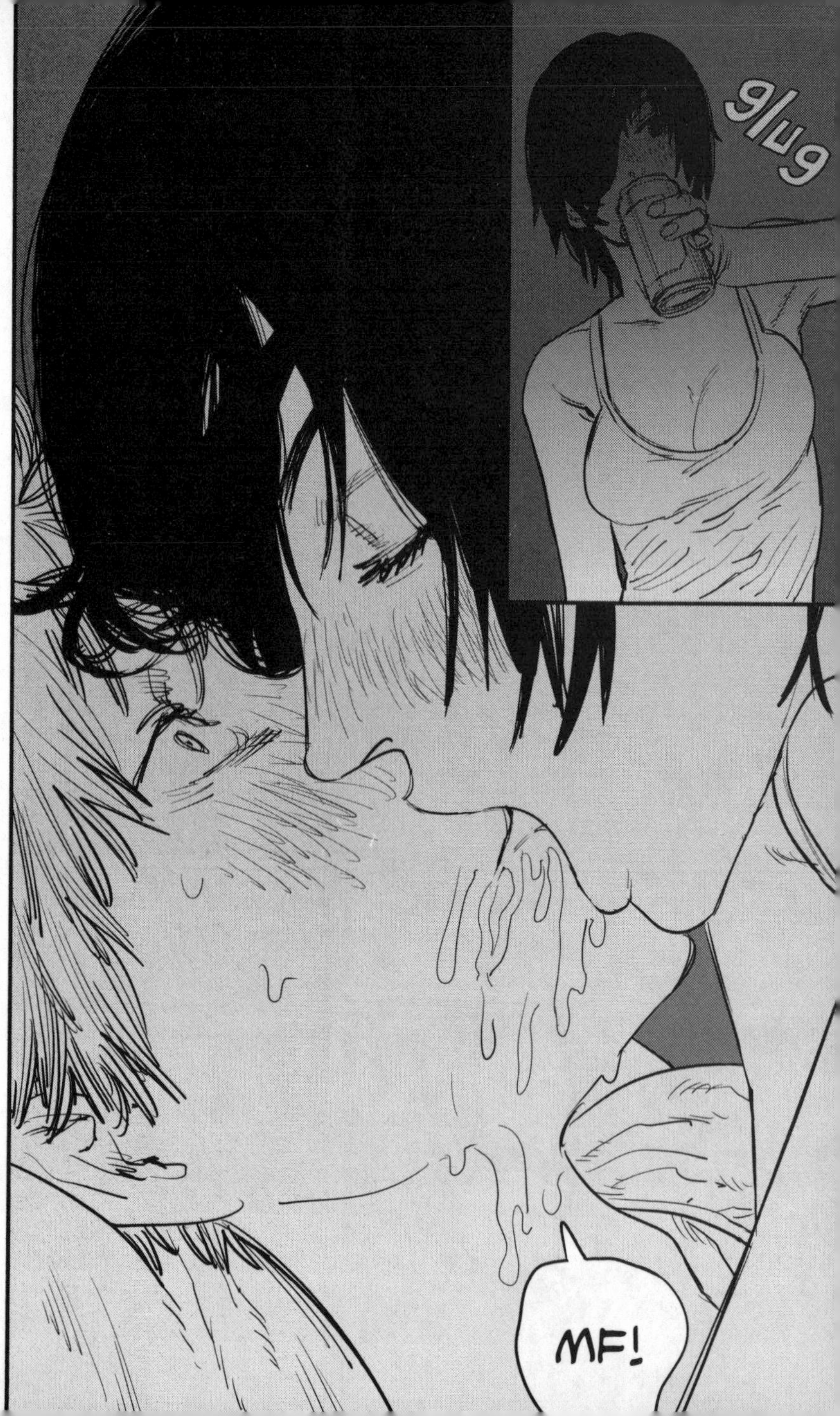
glug
MF!

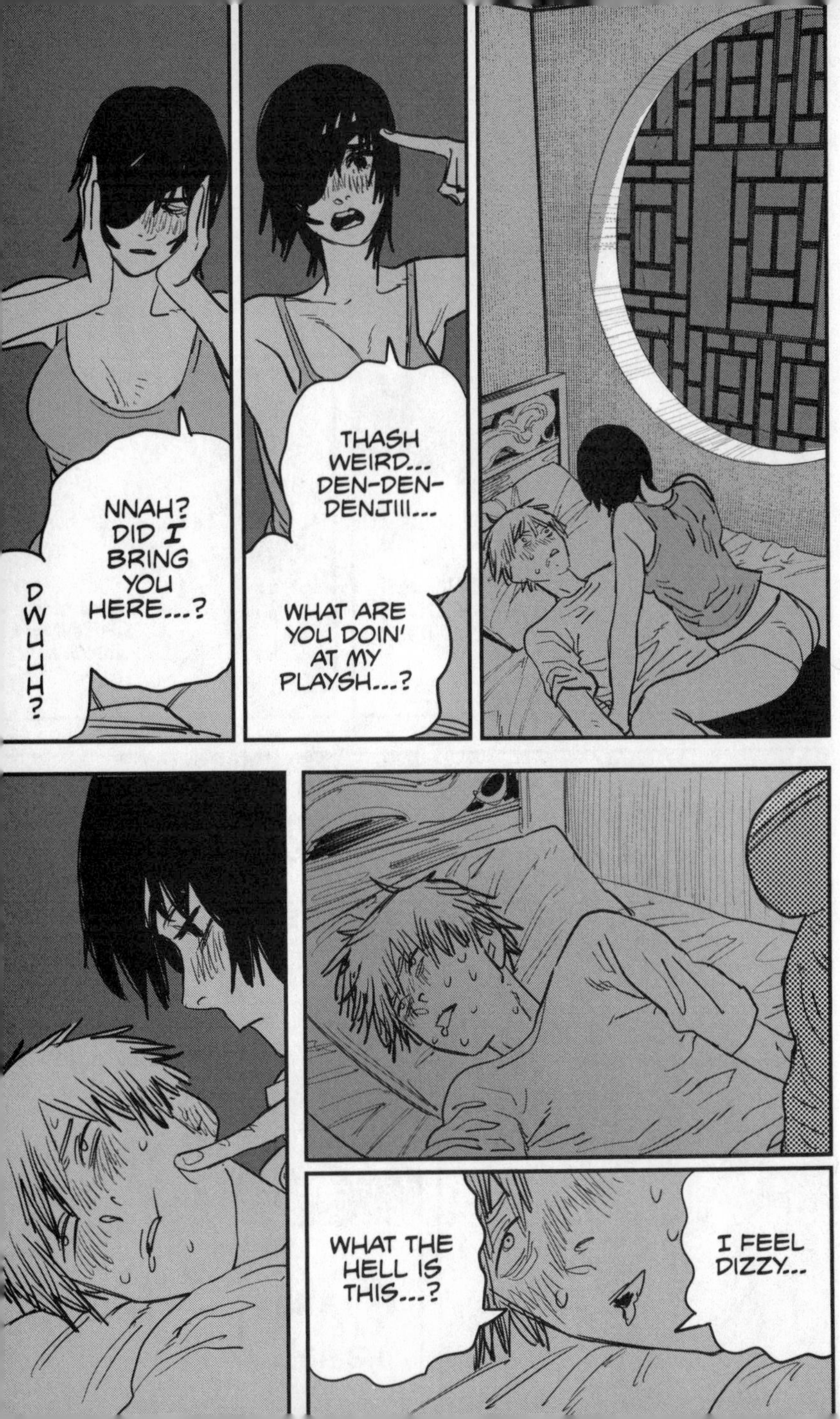
THASH WEIRD... DEN-DEN-DENJIII...
WHAT ARE YOU DOIN' AT MY PLAYSH...?
NNAH? DID I BRING YOU HERE...?
DWUUH?
I FEEL DIZZY...
WHAT THE HELL IS THIS...?

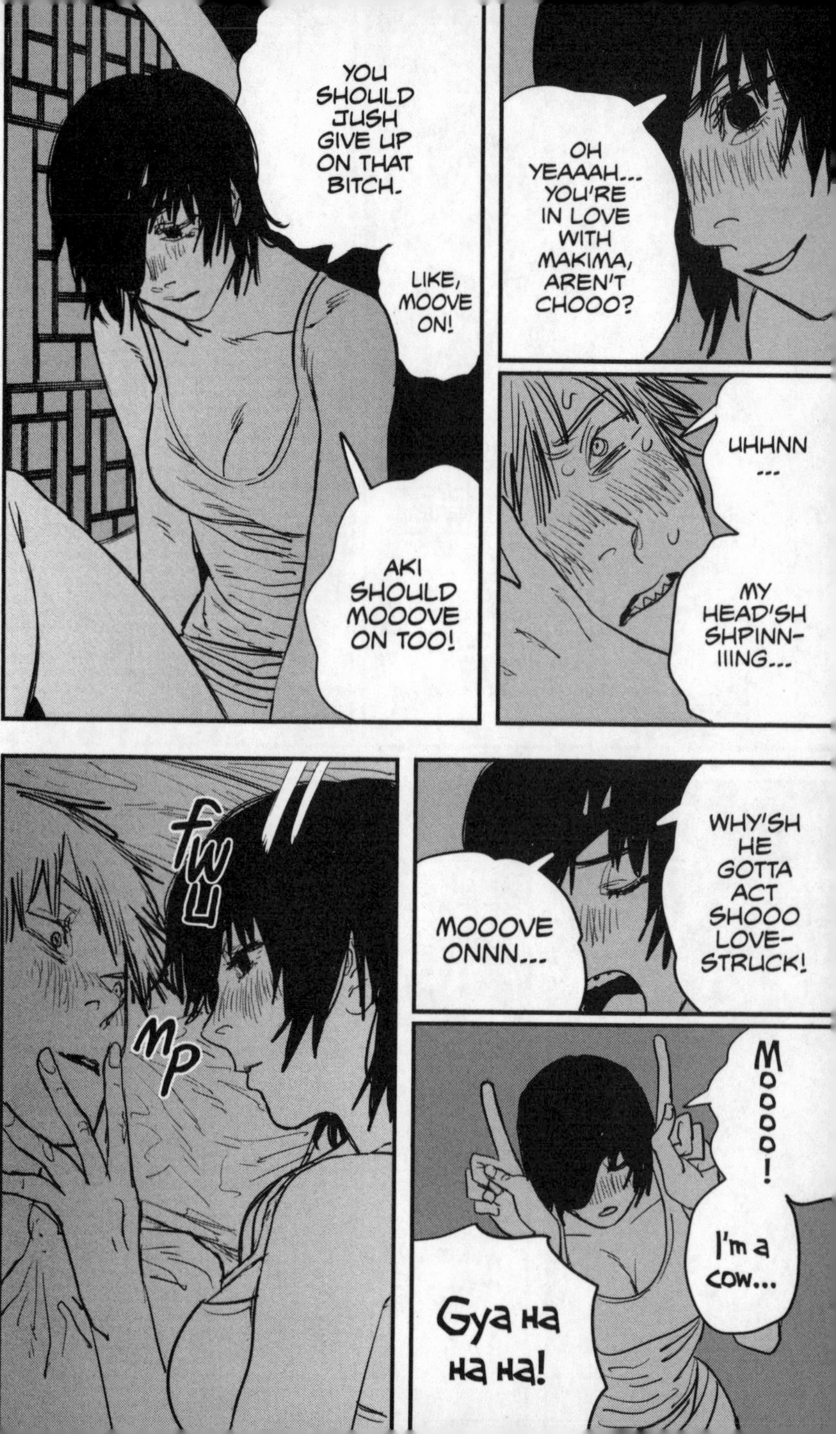
OH YEAAAH... YOU'RE IN LOVE WITH MAKIMA, AREN'T CHOOO?
UHHNN ...
MY HEAD'SH SHPINN-IIING...
YOU SHOULD JUSH GIVE UP ON THAT BITCH.
LIKE, MOOVE ON!
AKI SHOULD MOOOVE ON TOO!
WHY'SH HE GOTTA ACT SHOOO LOVE-STRUCK!
MOOOVE ONNN...
MOOOOO!
I'm a cow...
Gya ha ha ha!
fwu
mp

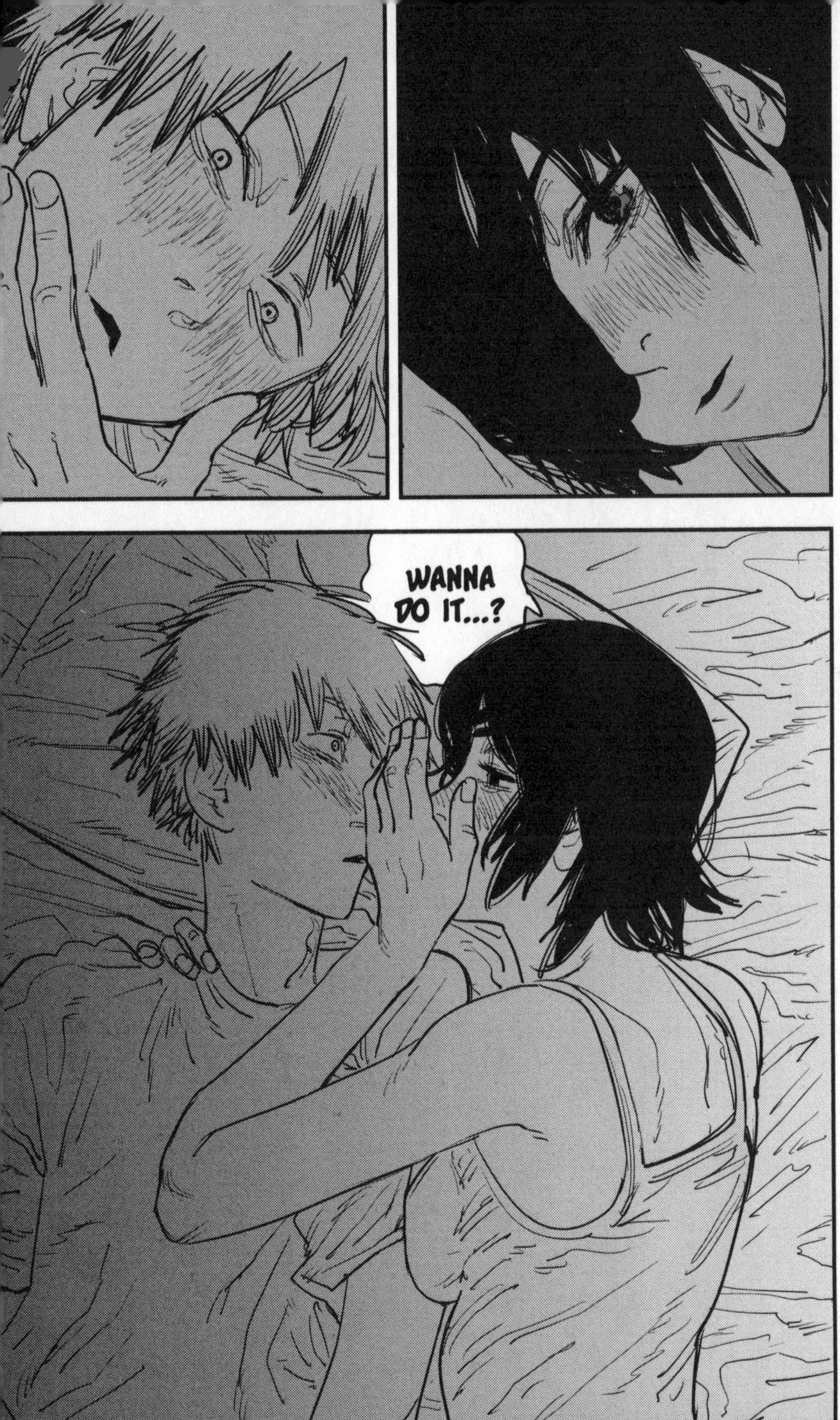
WANNA DO IT...?

Chain saw man

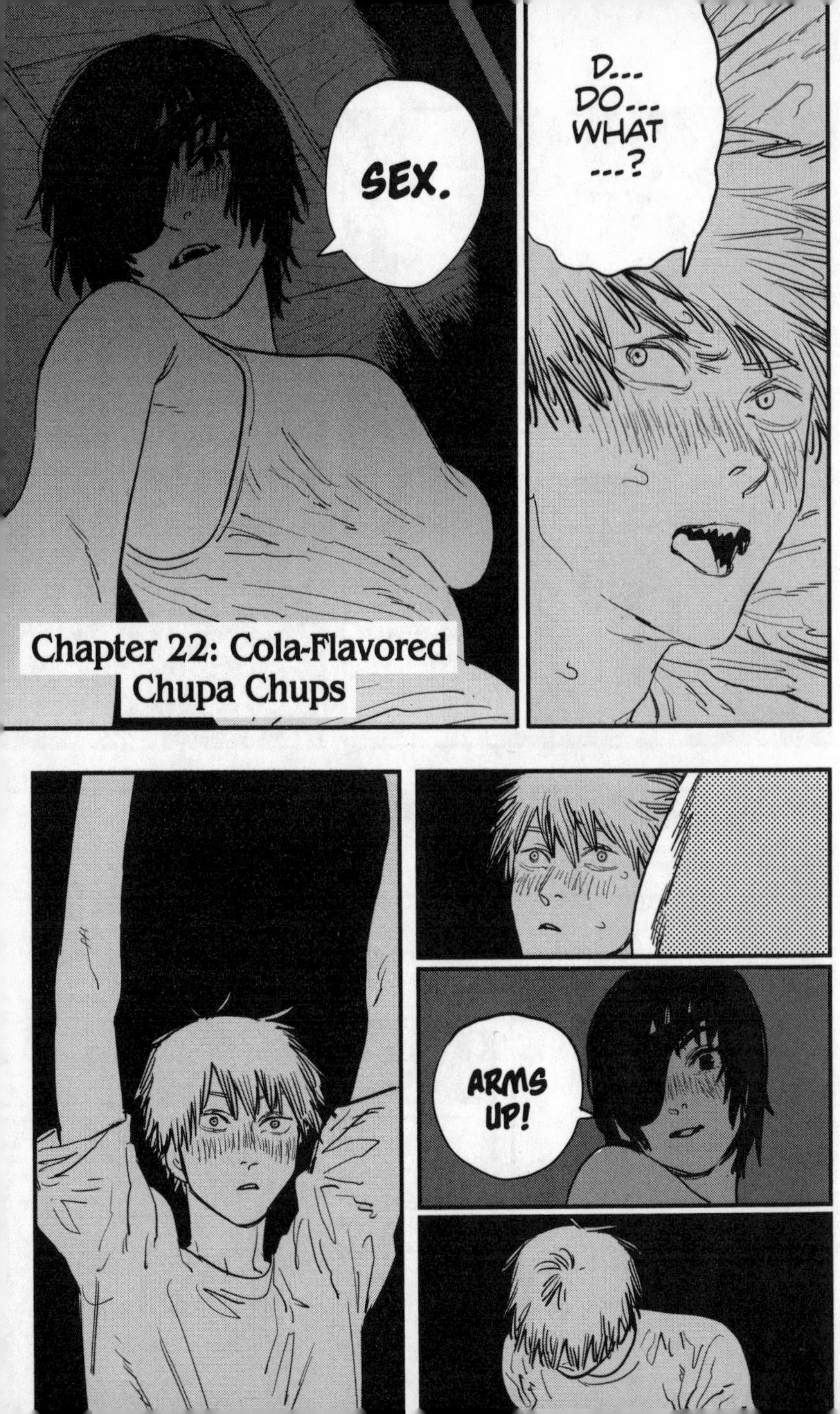
D... DO... WHAT ...?
SEX.
Chapter 22: Cola-Flavored Chupa Chups
ARMS UP!

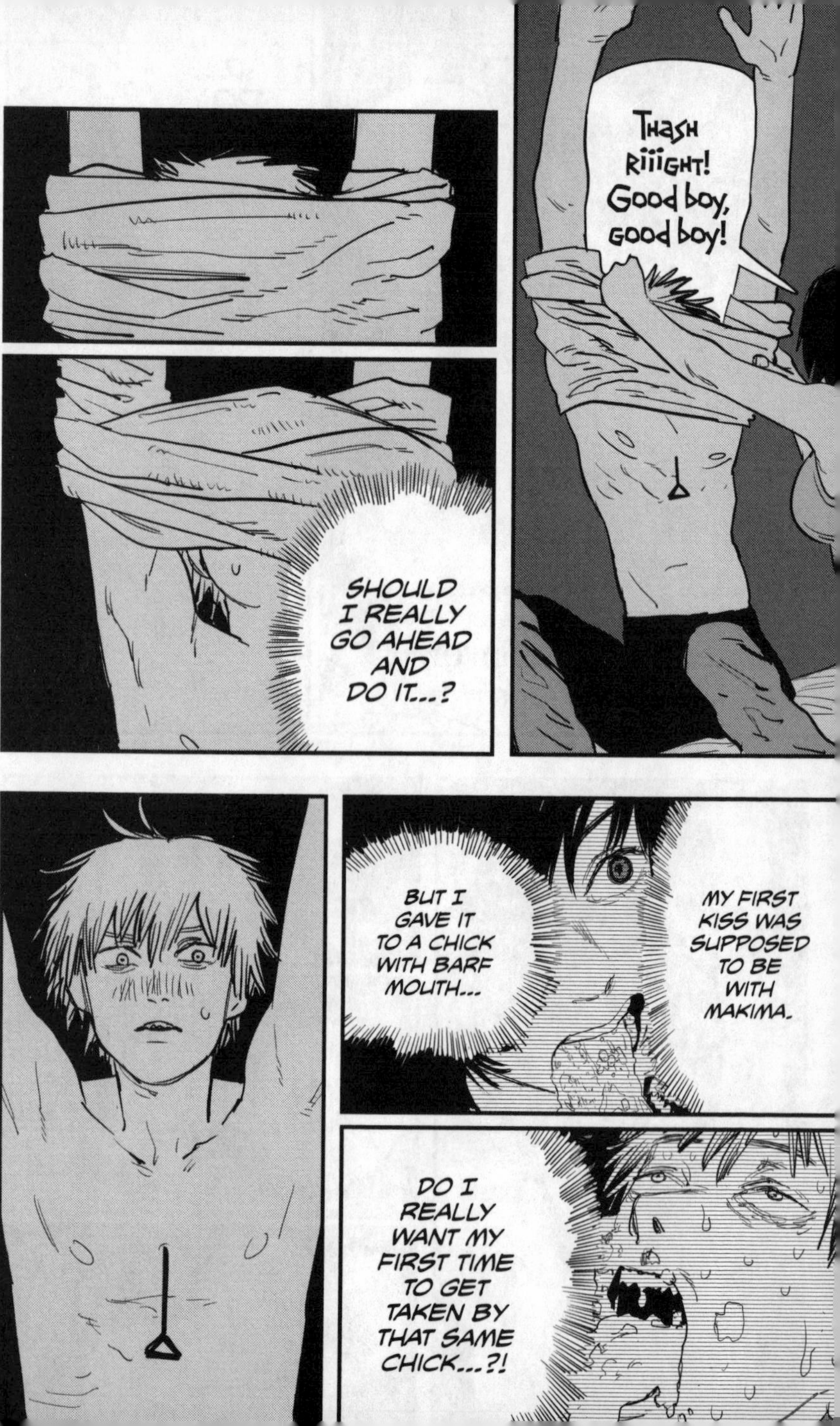
Thash riiight! Good boy, good boy!
SHOULD I REALLY GO AHEAD AND DO IT...?
MY FIRST KISS WAS SUPPOSED TO BE WITH MAKIMA.
BUT I GAVE IT TO A CHICK WITH BARF MOUTH...
DO I REALLY WANT MY FIRST TIME TO GET TAKEN BY THAT SAME CHICK...?!

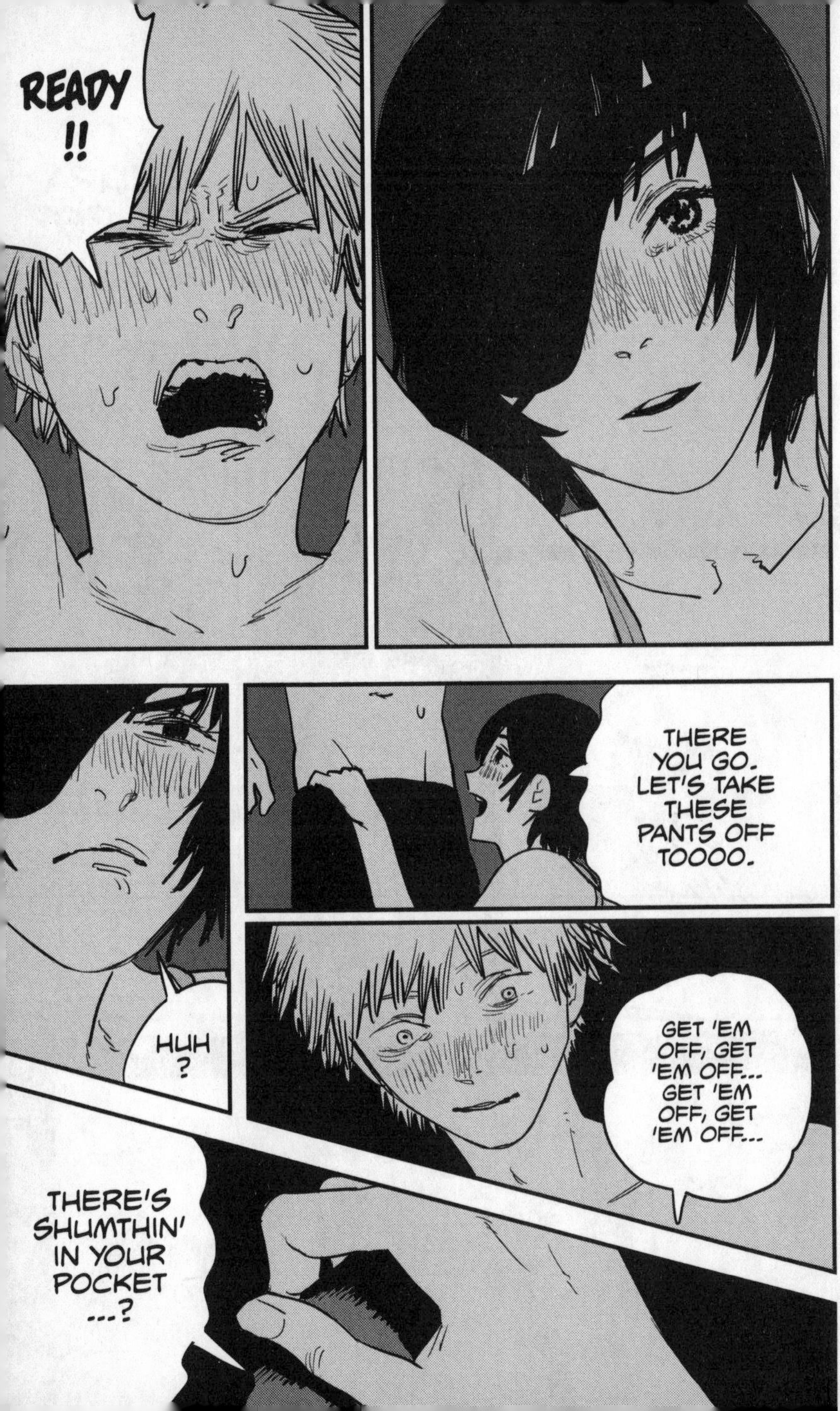
READY !!
THERE YOU GO. LET'S TAKE THESE PANTS OFF TOOOO.
GET 'EM OFF, GET 'EM OFF... GET 'EM OFF, GET 'EM OFF...
HUH ?
THERE'S SHUMTHIN' IN YOUR POCKET ...?

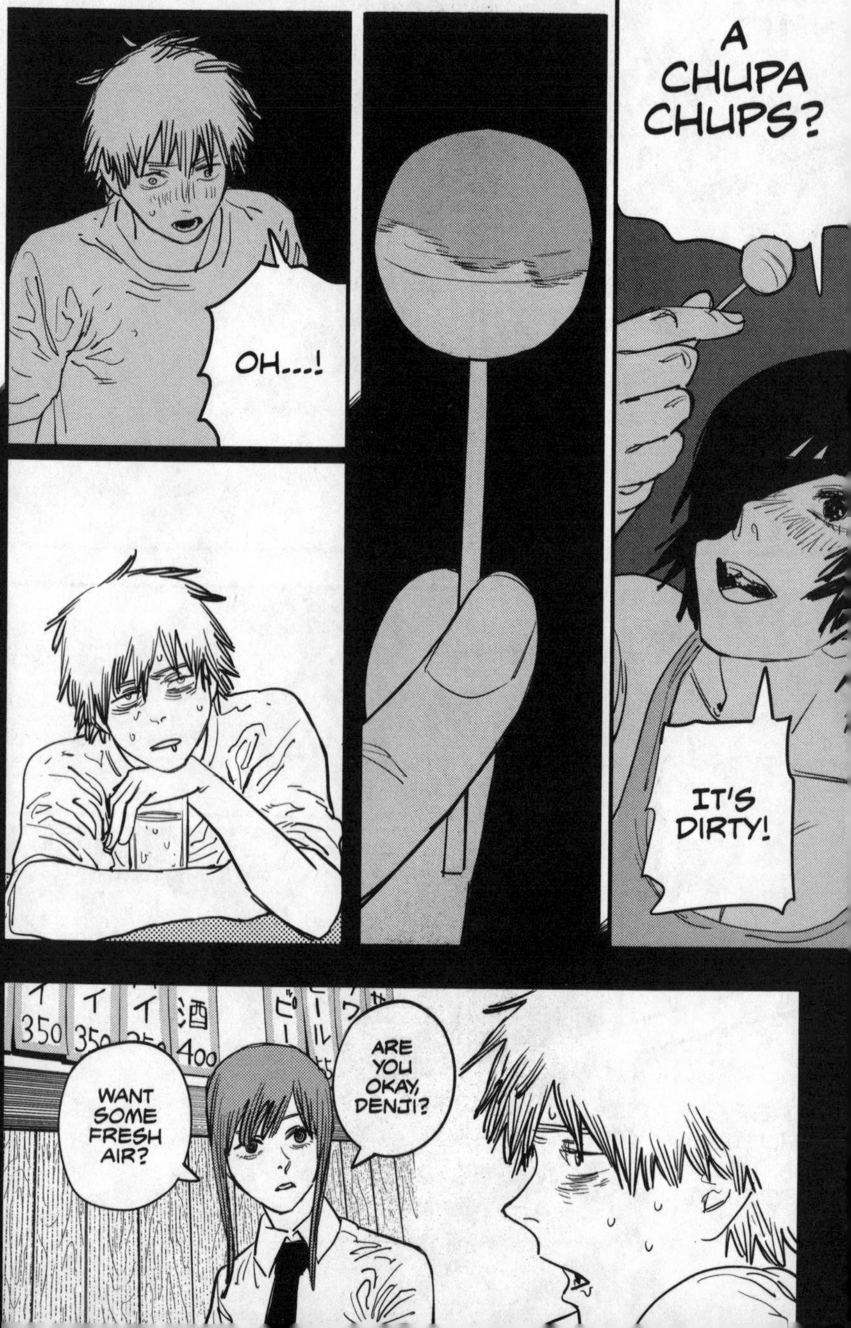
A CHUPA CHUPS?
IT'S DIRTY!
OH...!
ARE YOU OKAY, DENJI?
WANT SOME FRESH AIR?

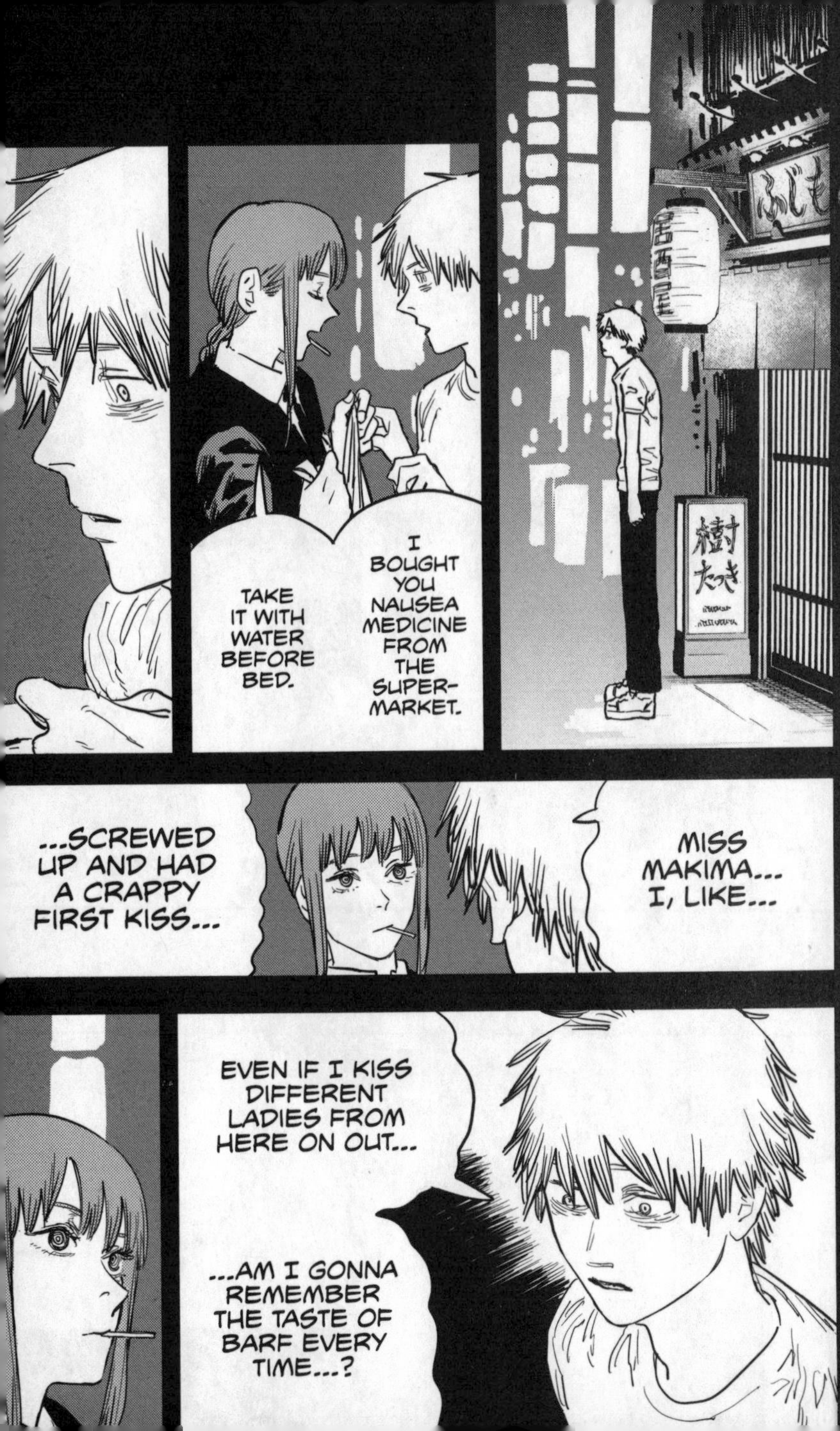
ふじも
I BOUGHT YOU NAUSEA MEDICINE FROM THE SUPER-MARKET.
TAKE IT WITH WATER BEFORE BED.
MISS MAKIMA... I, LIKE...
...SCREWED UP AND HAD A CRAPPY FIRST KISS...
EVEN IF I KISS DIFFERENT LADIES FROM HERE ON OUT...
...AM I GONNA REMEMBER THE TASTE OF BARF EVERY TIME...?

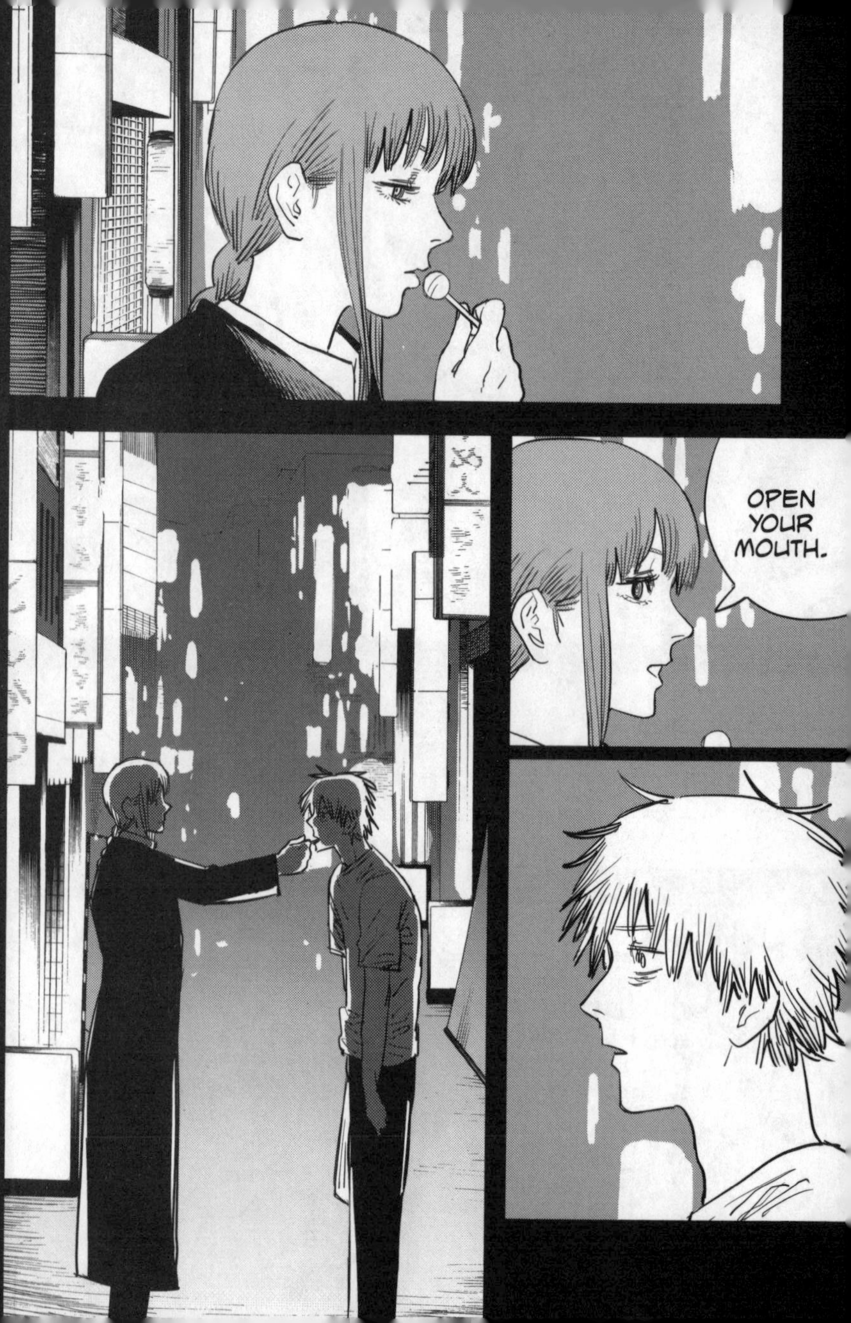
OPEN YOUR MOUTH.

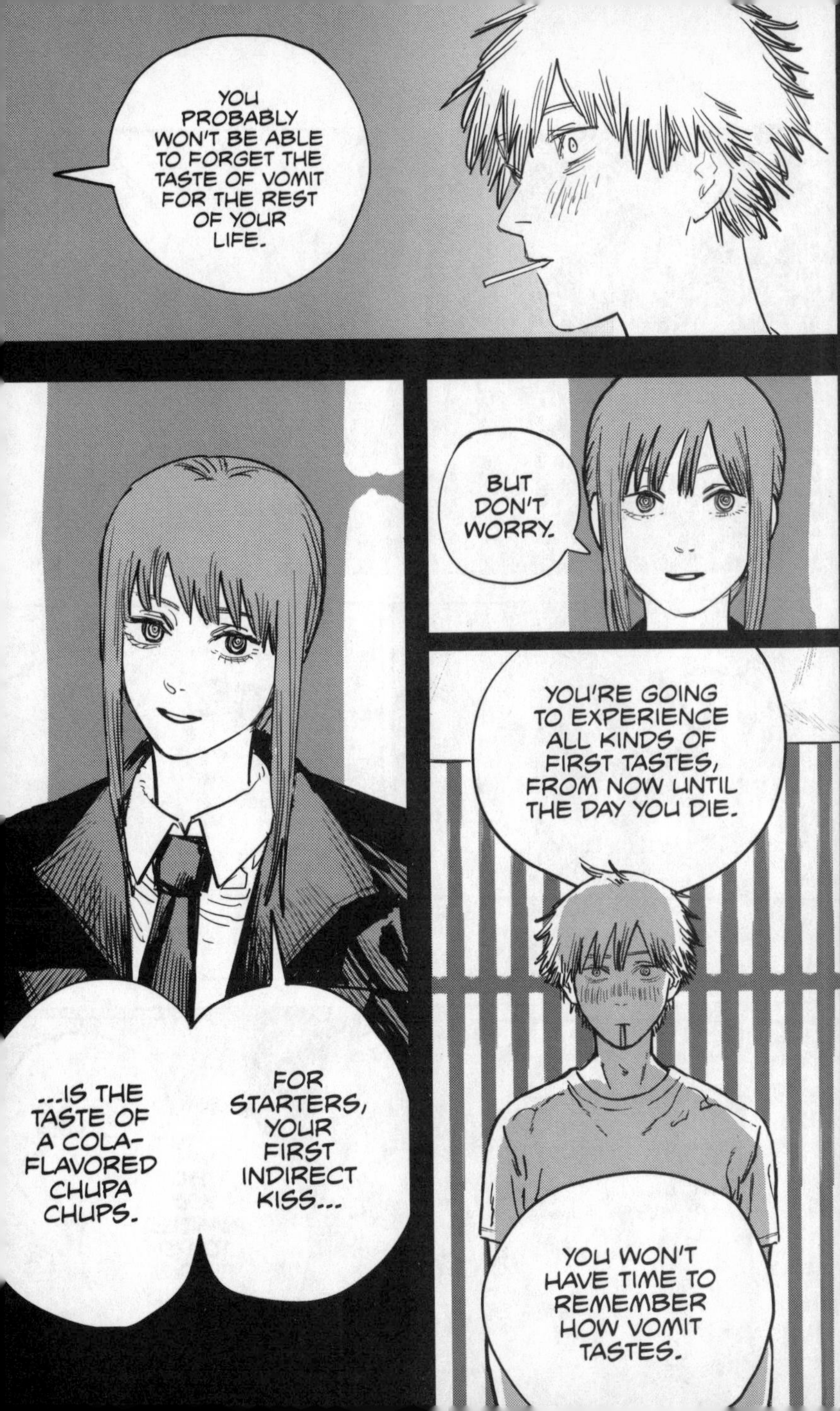
YOU PROBABLY WON'T BE ABLE TO FORGET THE TASTE OF VOMIT FOR THE REST OF YOUR LIFE.
BUT DON'T WORRY.
YOU'RE GOING TO EXPERIENCE ALL KINDS OF FIRST TASTES, FROM NOW UNTIL THE DAY YOU DIE.
YOU WON'T HAVE TIME TO REMEMBER HOW VOMIT TASTES.
FOR STARTERS, YOUR FIRST INDIRECT KISS...
...IS THE TASTE OF A COLA-FLAVORED CHUPA CHUPS.

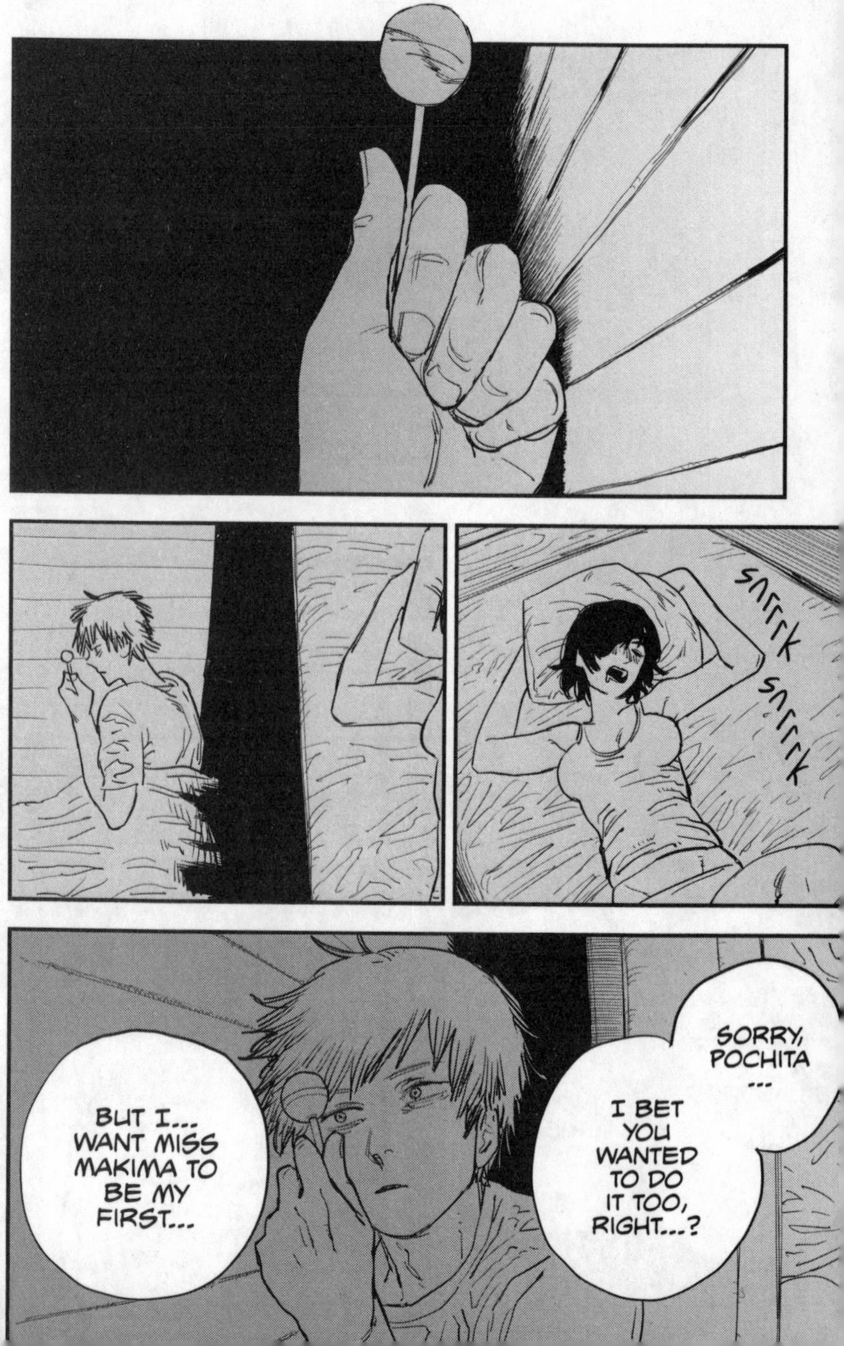
SNRRK SNRRK
SORRY, POCHITA...
I BET YOU WANTED TO DO IT TOO, RIGHT...?
BUT I... WANT MISS MAKIMA TO BE MY FIRST...

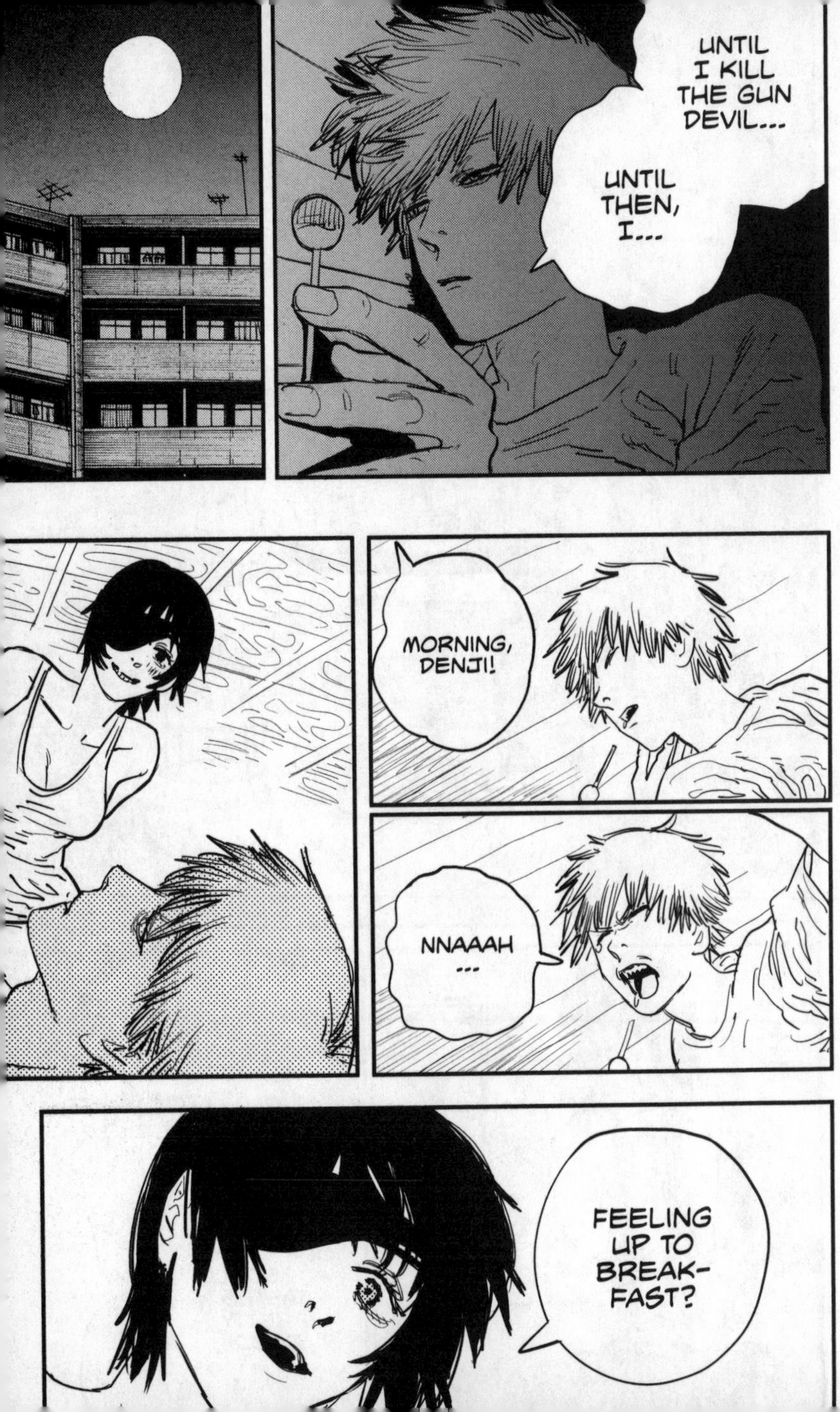
UNTIL I KILL THE GUN DEVIL...
UNTIL THEN, I...
MORNING, DENJI!
NNAAAH ...
FEELING UP TO BREAK-FAST?

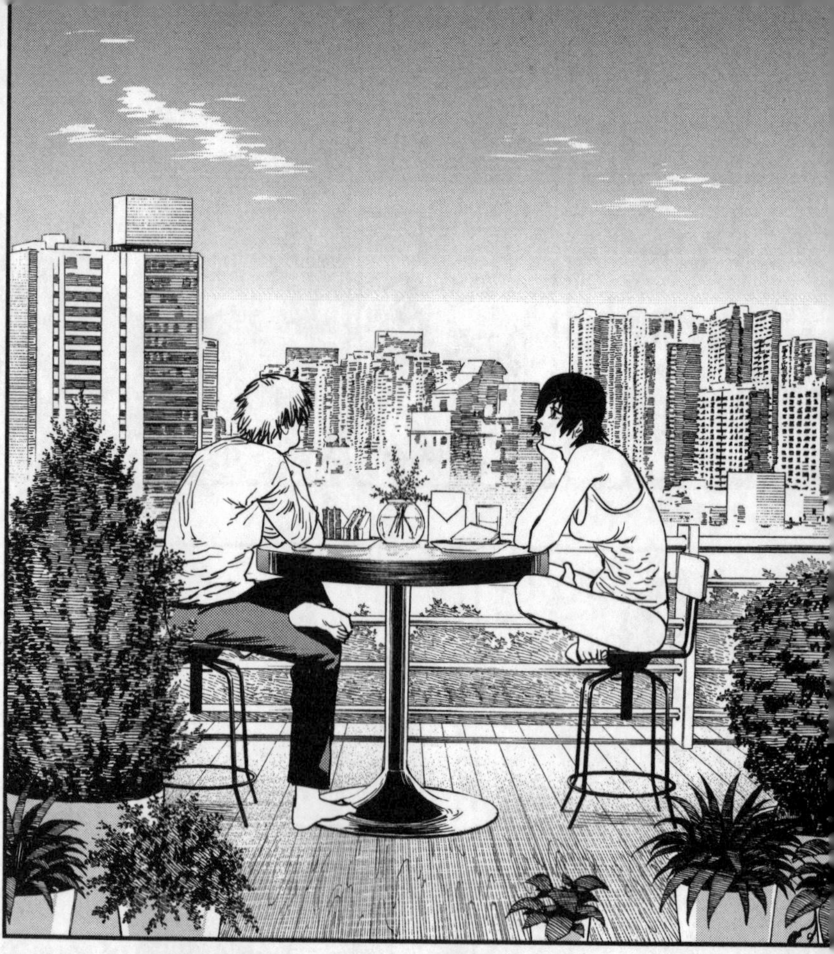
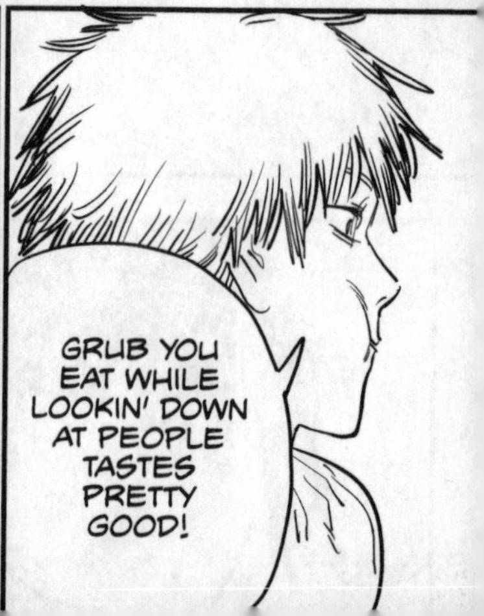
GRUB YOU EAT WHILE LOOKIN' DOWN AT PEOPLE TASTES PRETTY GOOD!
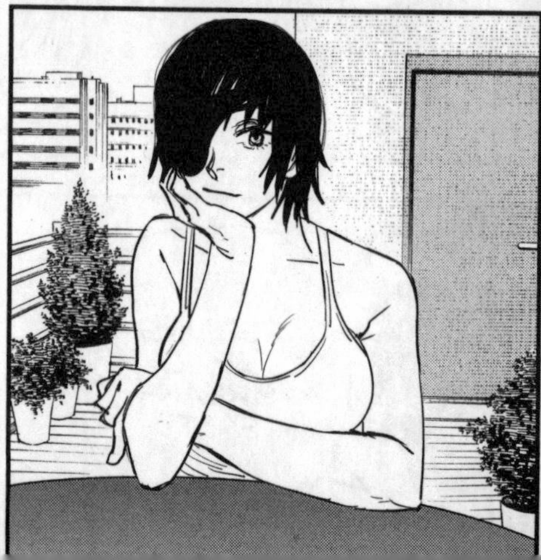

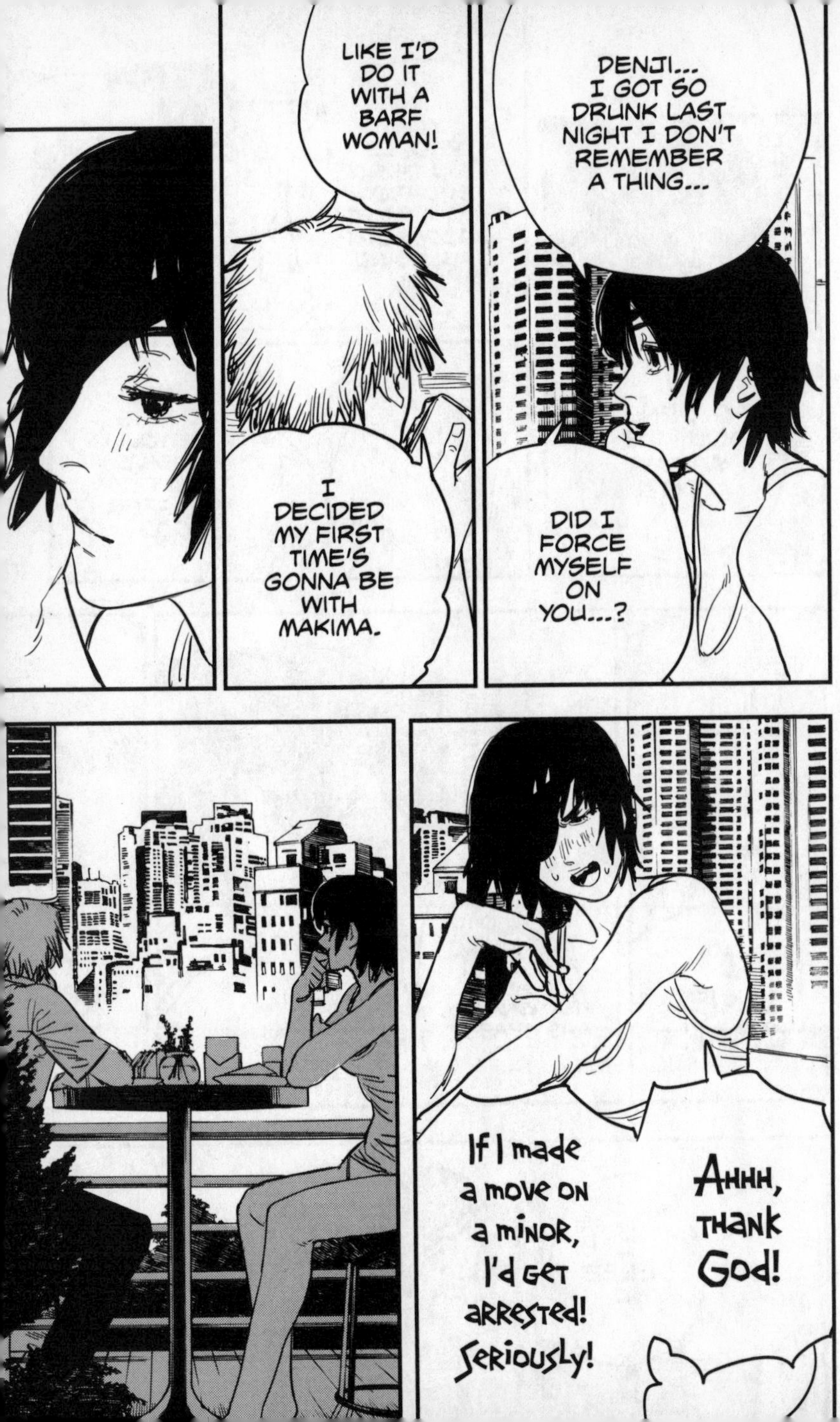
DENJI... I GOT SO DRUNK LAST NIGHT I DON'T REMEMBER A THING...
DID I FORCE MYSELF ON YOU...?
LIKE I'D DO IT WITH A BARF WOMAN!
I DECIDED MY FIRST TIME'S GONNA BE WITH MAKIMA.
AHHH, THANK GOD!
If I made a move on a minor, I'd get arrested! Seriously!

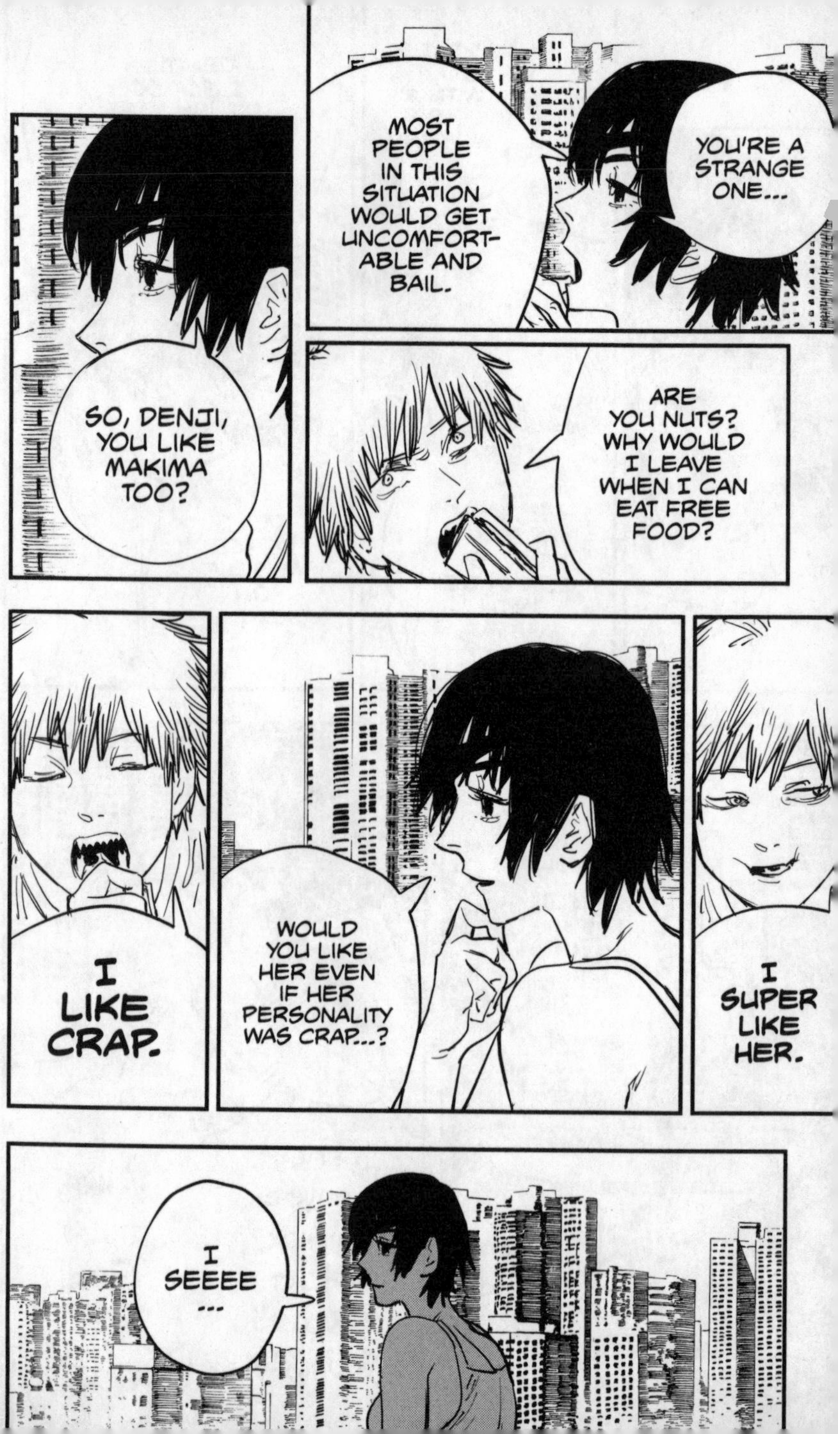
YOU'RE A STRANGE ONE...
MOST PEOPLE IN THIS SITUATION WOULD GET UNCOMFORTABLE AND BAIL.
ARE YOU NUTS? WHY WOULD I LEAVE WHEN I CAN EAT FREE FOOD?
SO, DENJI, YOU LIKE MAKIMA TOO?
I SUPER LIKE HER.
WOULD YOU LIKE HER EVEN IF HER PERSONALITY WAS CRAP...?
I LIKE CRAP.
I SEEEE ...

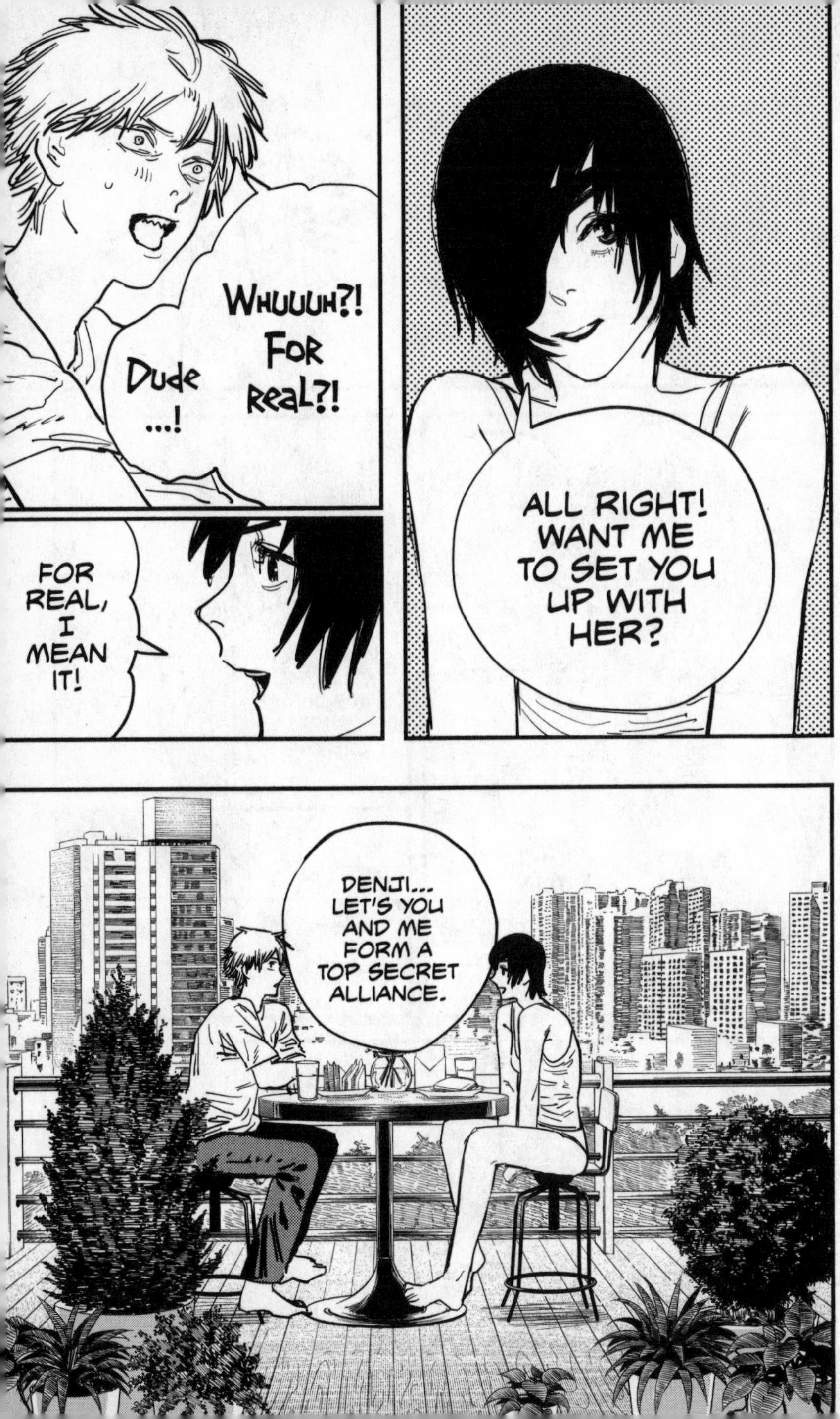
ALL RIGHT! WANT ME TO SET YOU UP WITH HER?
WHUUUH?! FOR REAL?!
Dude ...!
FOR REAL, I MEAN IT!
DENJI... LET'S YOU AND ME FORM A TOP SECRET ALLIANCE.

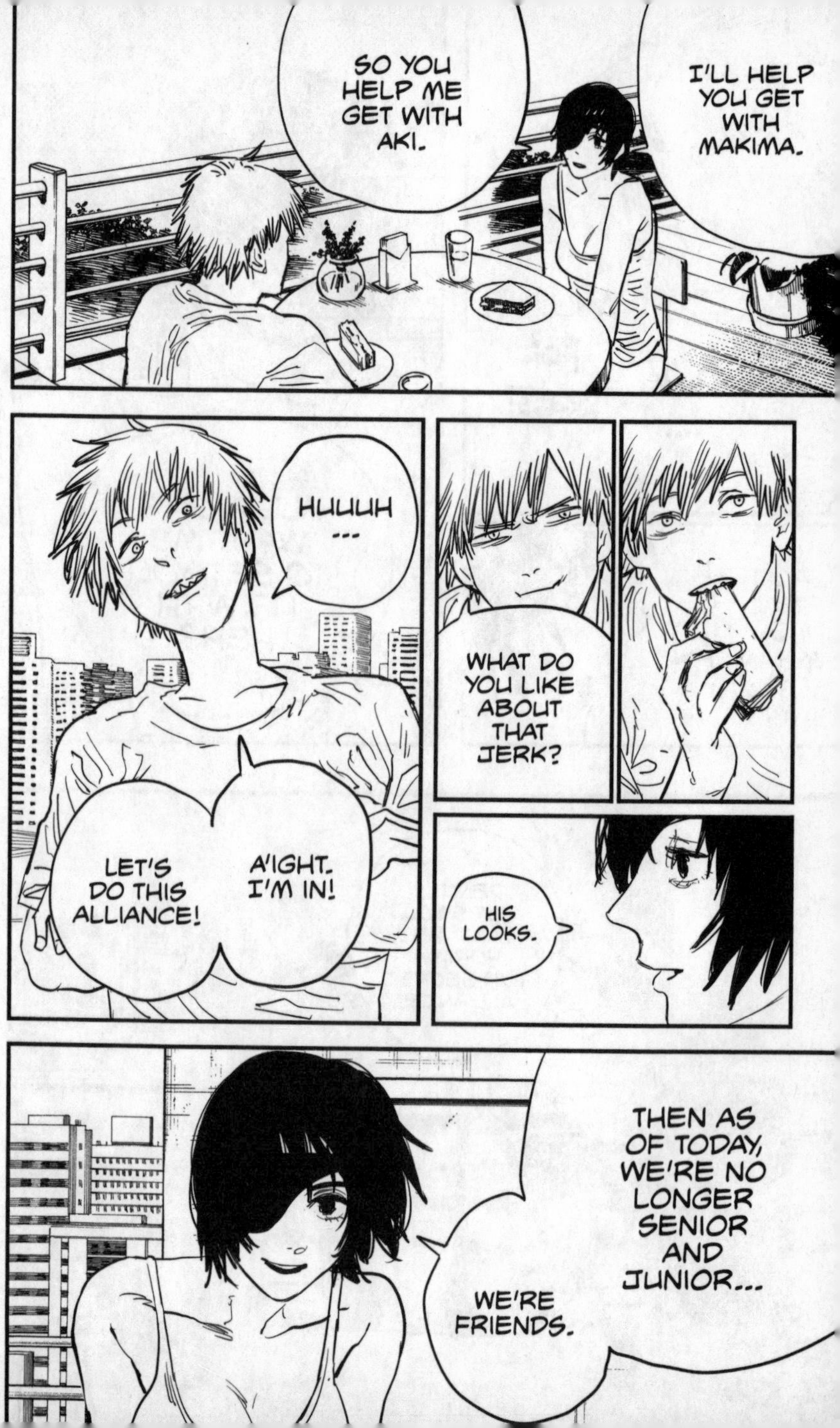
I'LL HELP YOU GET WITH MAKIMA.
SO YOU HELP ME GET WITH AKI.
WHAT DO YOU LIKE ABOUT THAT JERK?
HIS LOOKS.
HUUUH ...
A'IGHT. I'M IN!
LET'S DO THIS ALLIANCE!
THEN AS OF TODAY, WE'RE NO LONGER SENIOR AND JUNIOR...
WE'RE FRIENDS.

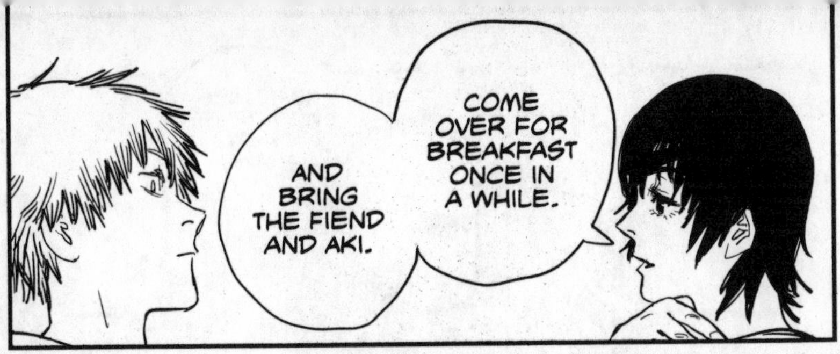
COME OVER FOR BREAKFAST ONCE IN A WHILE.
AND BRING THE FIEND AND AKI.

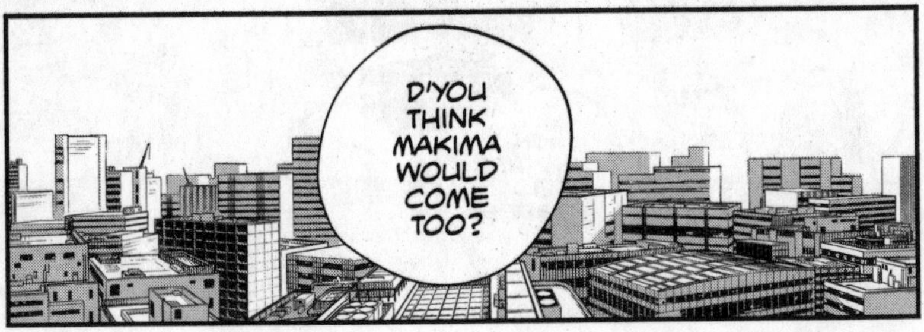
D'YOU THINK MAKIMA WOULD COME TOO?

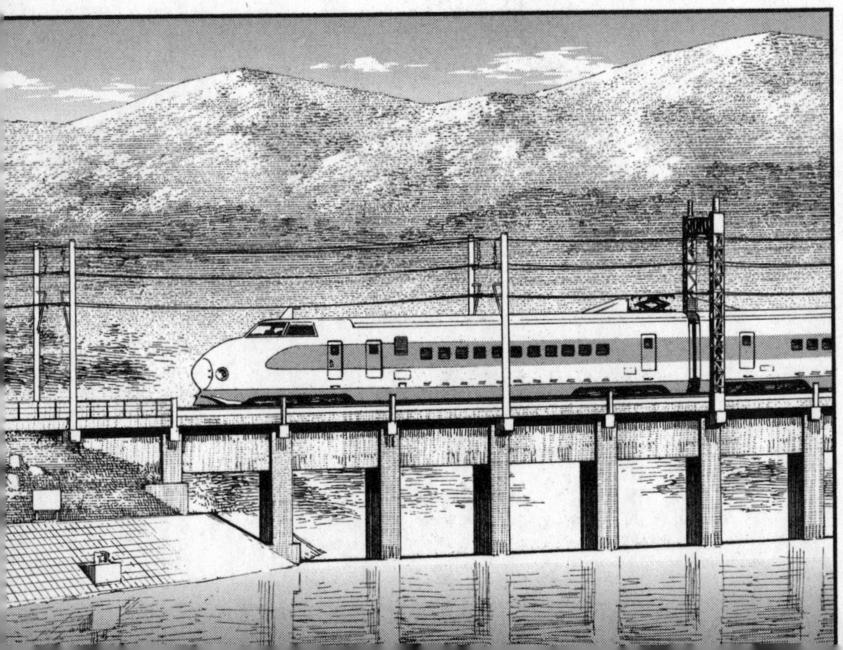

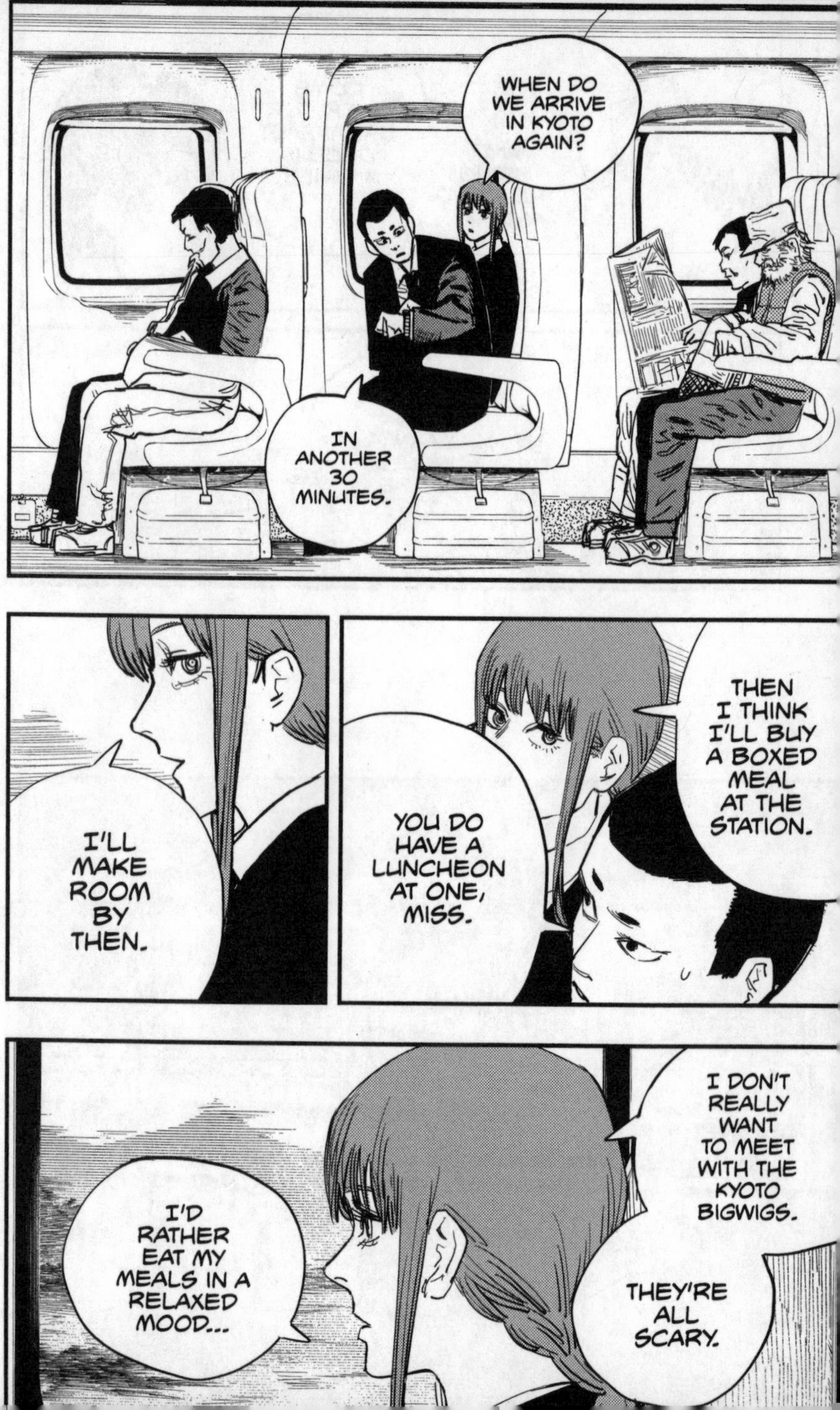
WHEN DO WE ARRIVE IN KYOTO AGAIN?
IN ANOTHER 30 MINUTES.
THEN I THINK I'LL BUY A BOXED MEAL AT THE STATION.
YOU DO HAVE A LUNCHEON AT ONE, MISS.
I'LL MAKE ROOM BY THEN.
I DON'T REALLY WANT TO MEET WITH THE KYOTO BIGWIGS.
THEY'RE ALL SCARY.
I'D RATHER EAT MY MEALS IN A RELAXED MOOD...

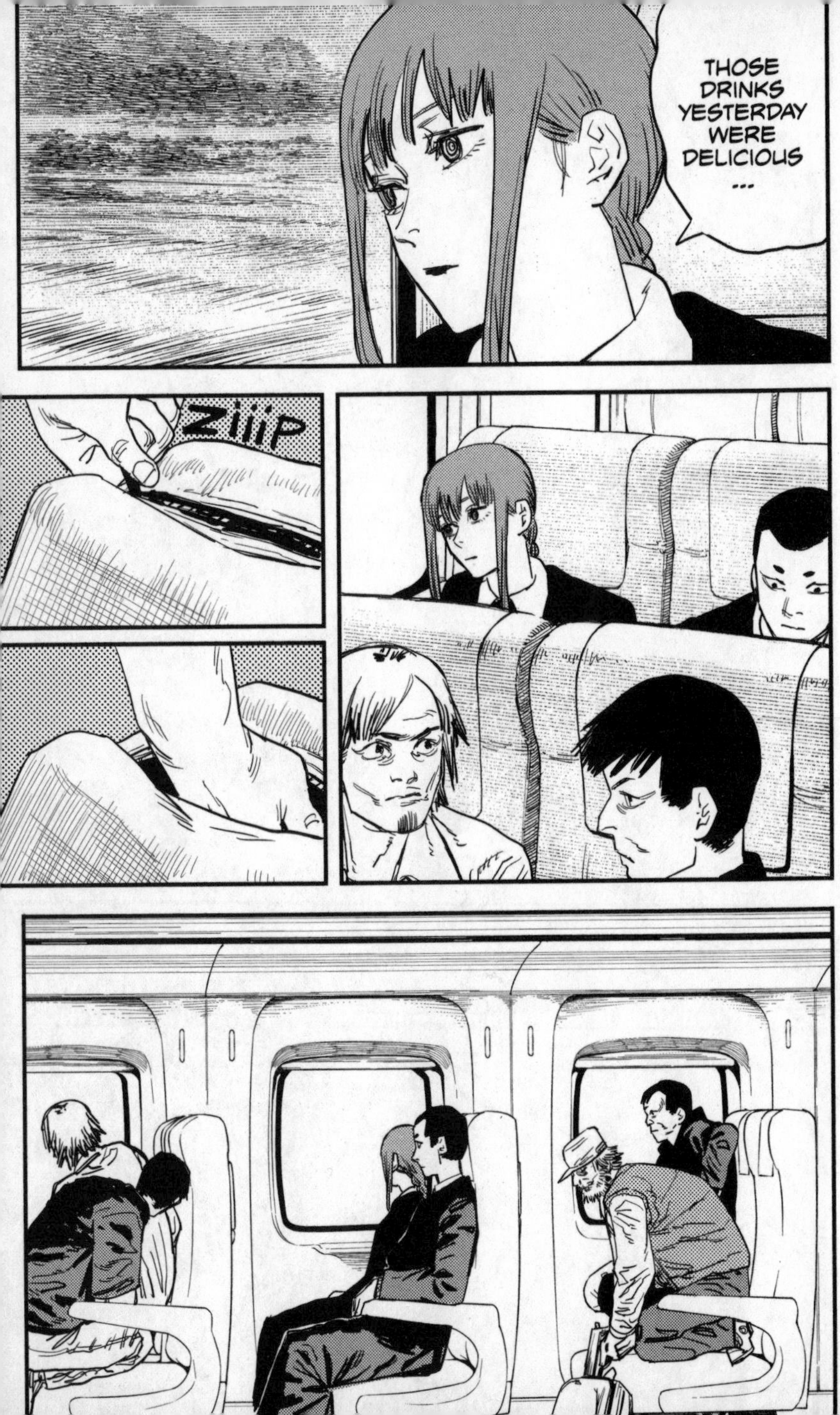
THOSE DRINKS YESTERDAY WERE DELICIOUS ...
ZIIIP

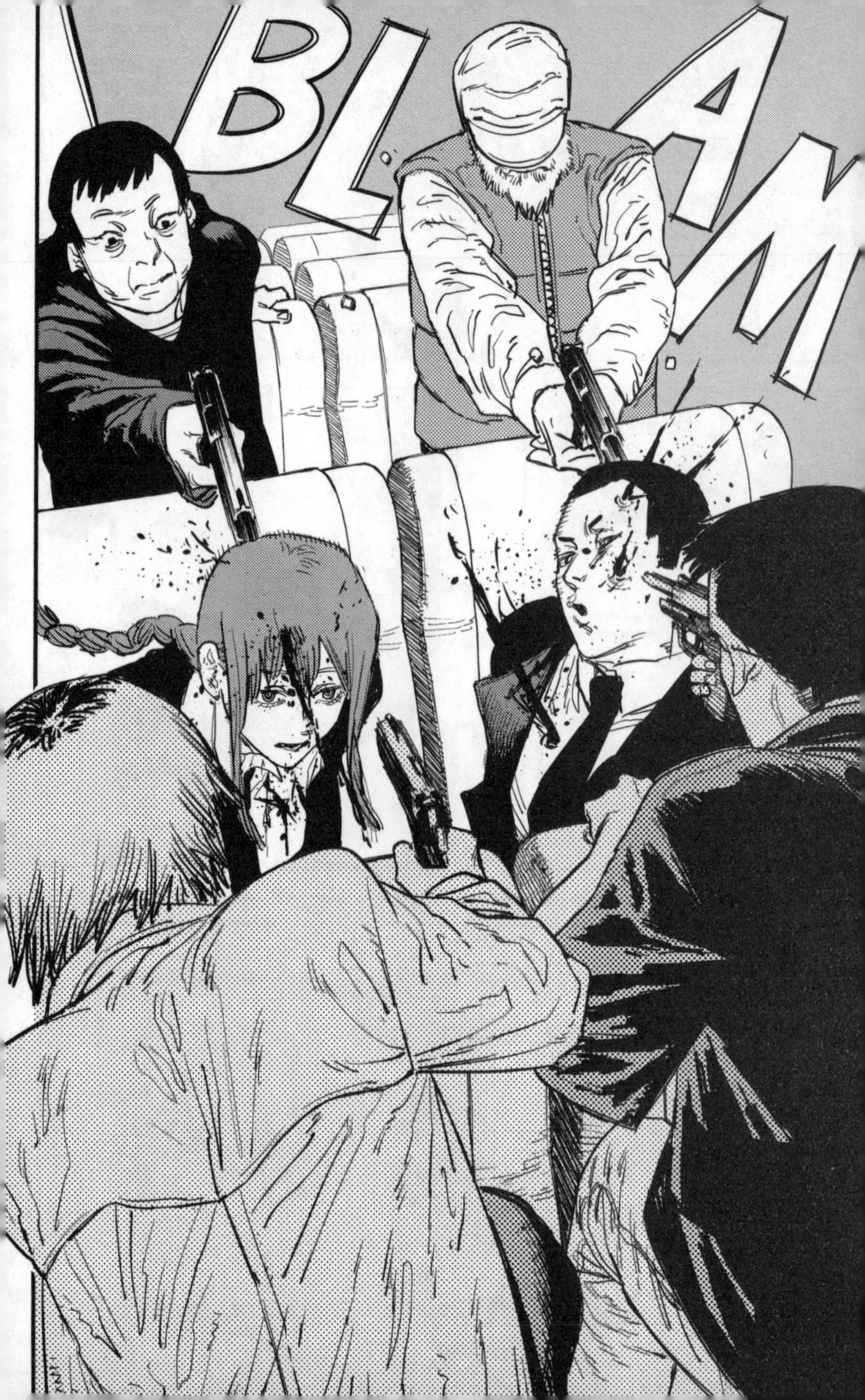
BLAM

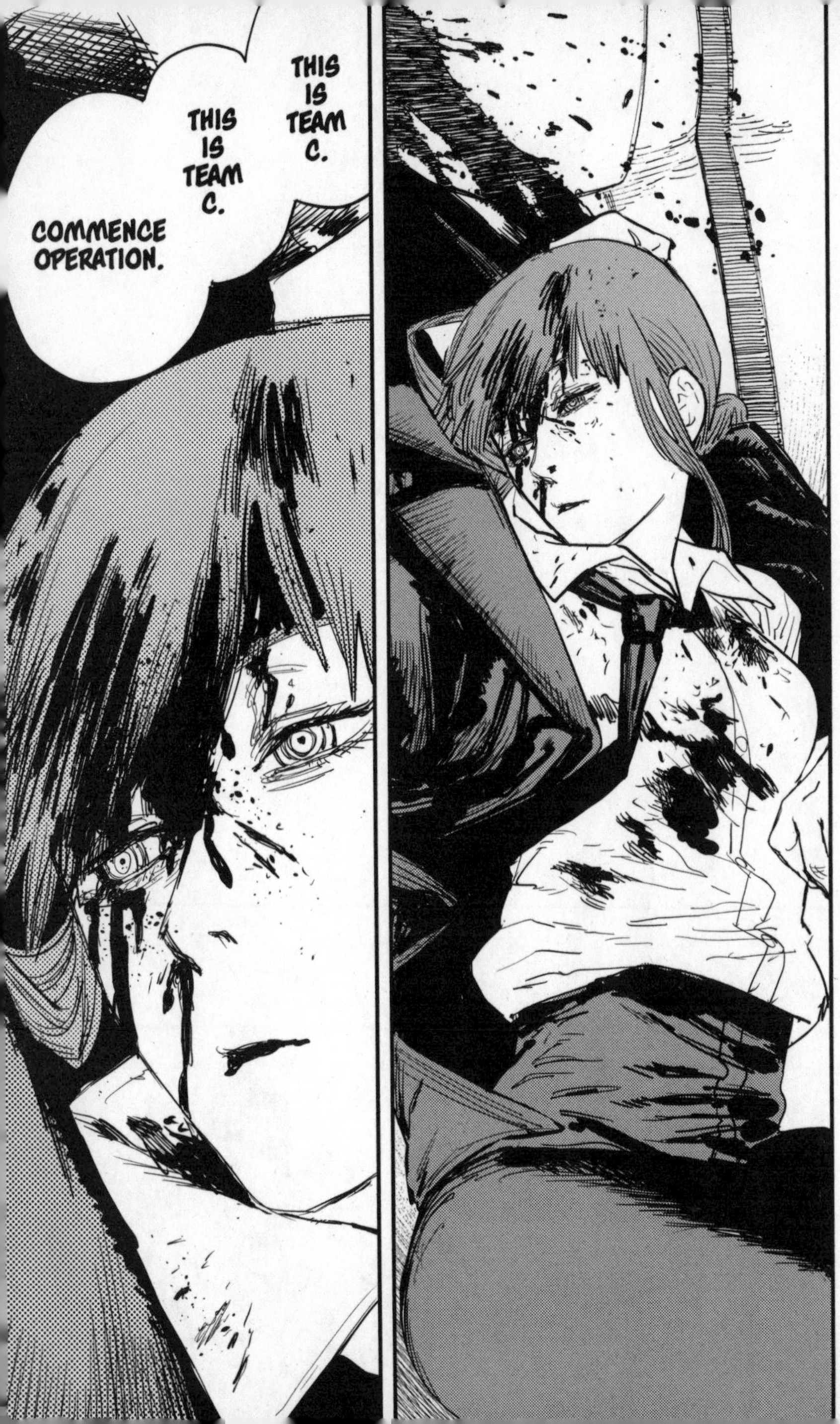
THIS IS TEAM C.
THIS IS TEAM C.
COMMENCE OPERATION.

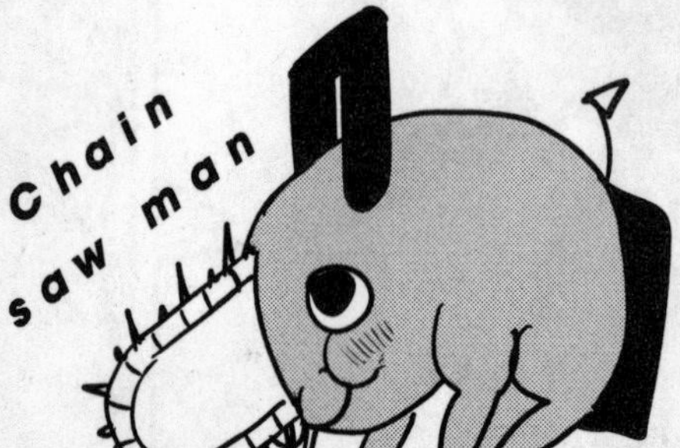
Chain
saw man

Chapter 23: Gunfire

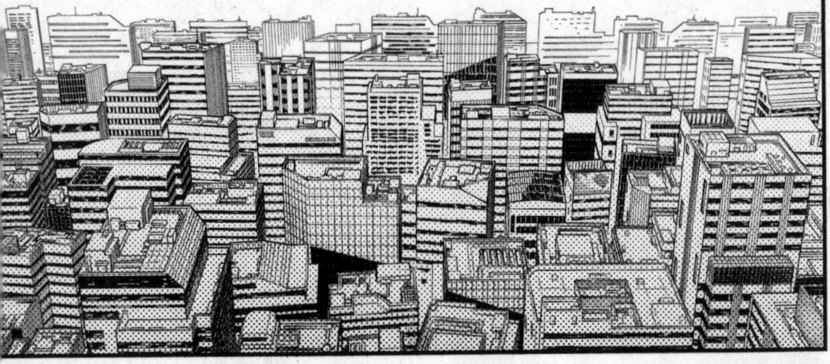

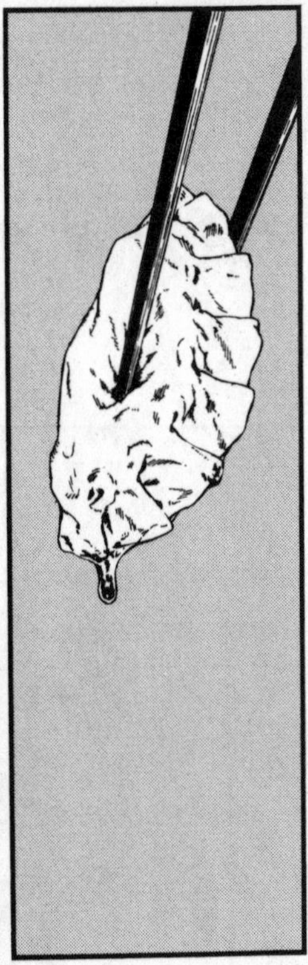

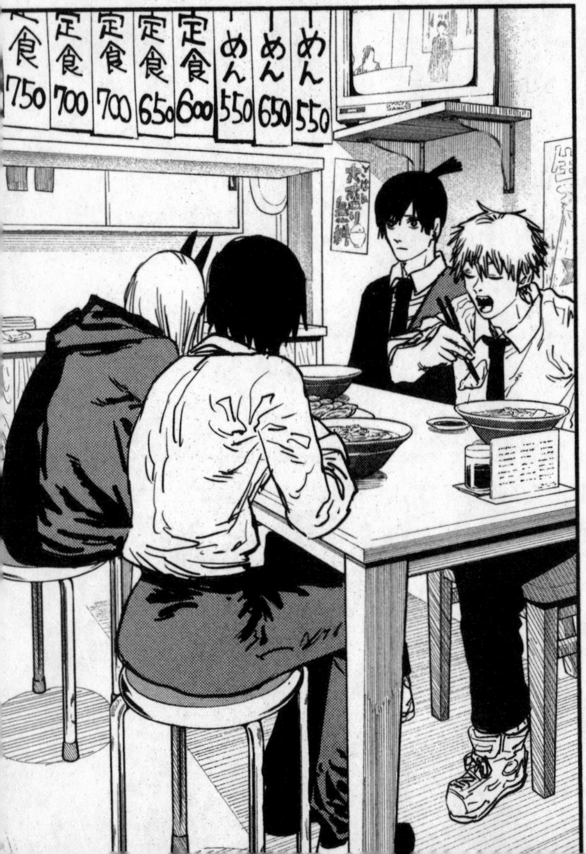
食 750
定食 700
定食 700
定食 650
定食 600
めん 550
めん 650
めん 550

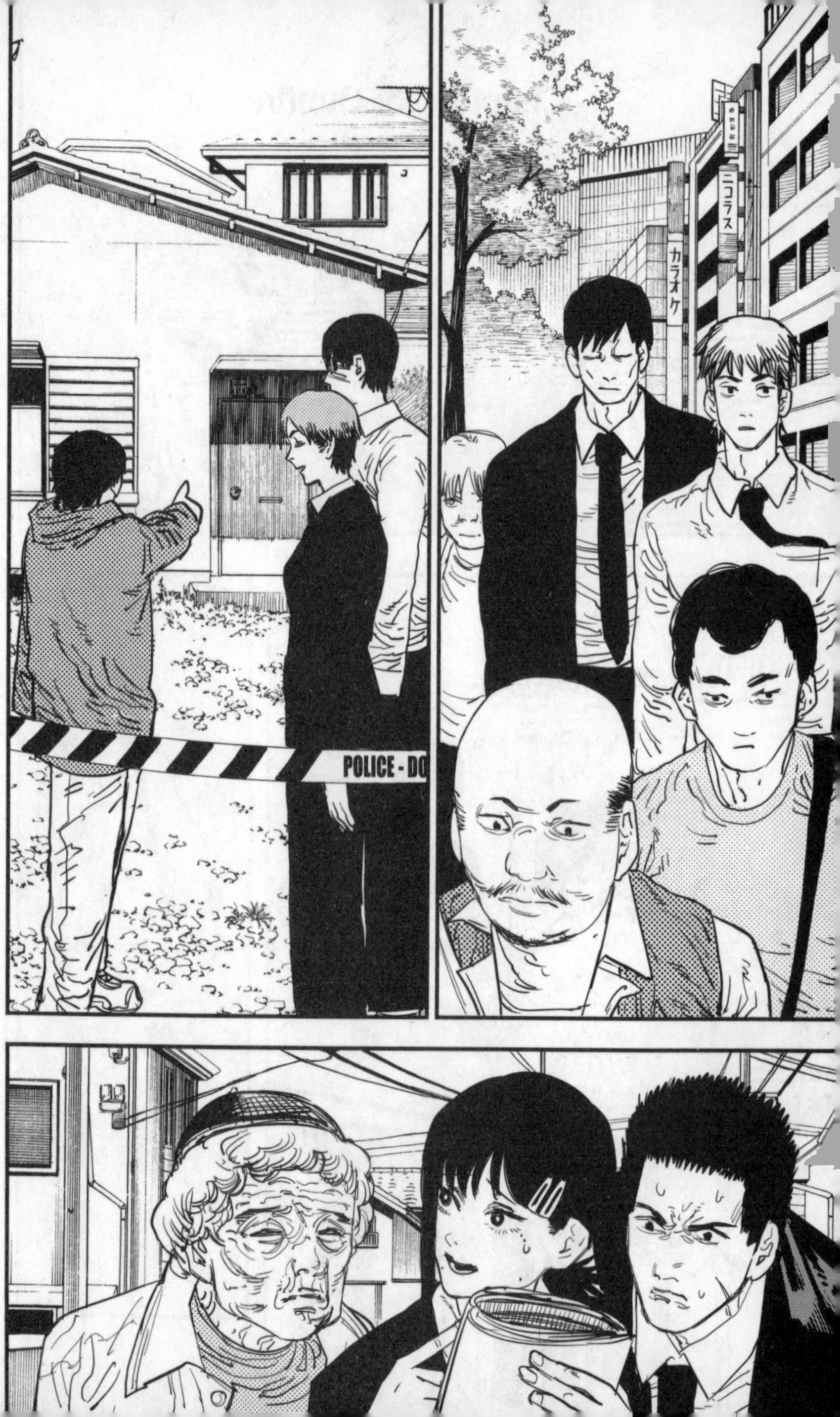
ニコラス
カラオケ
POLICE - DO

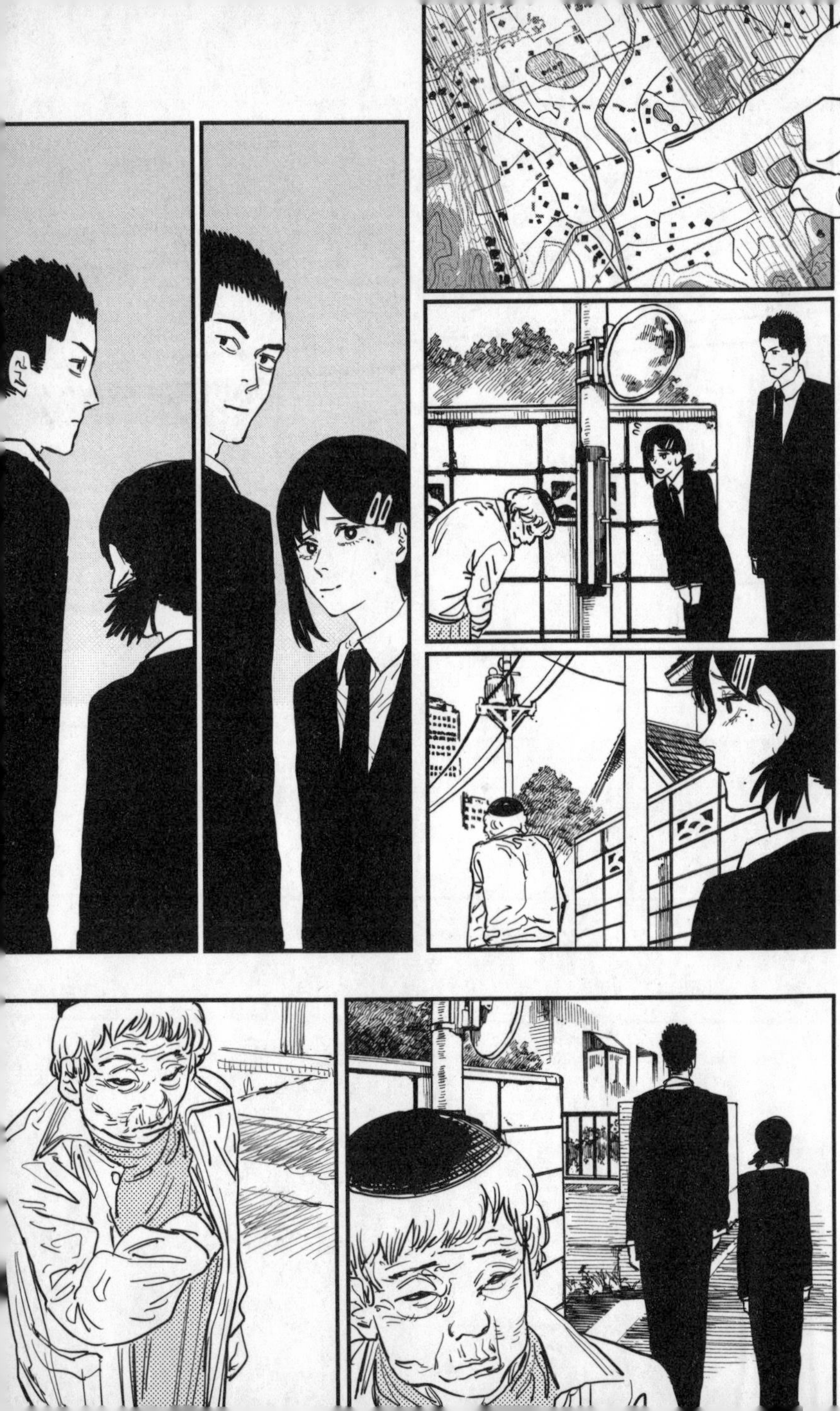

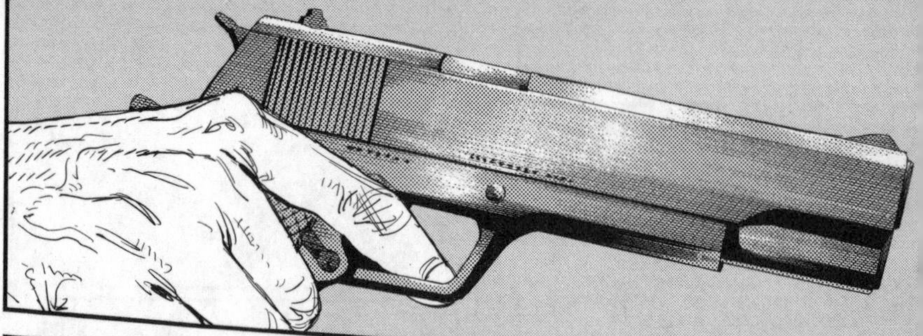
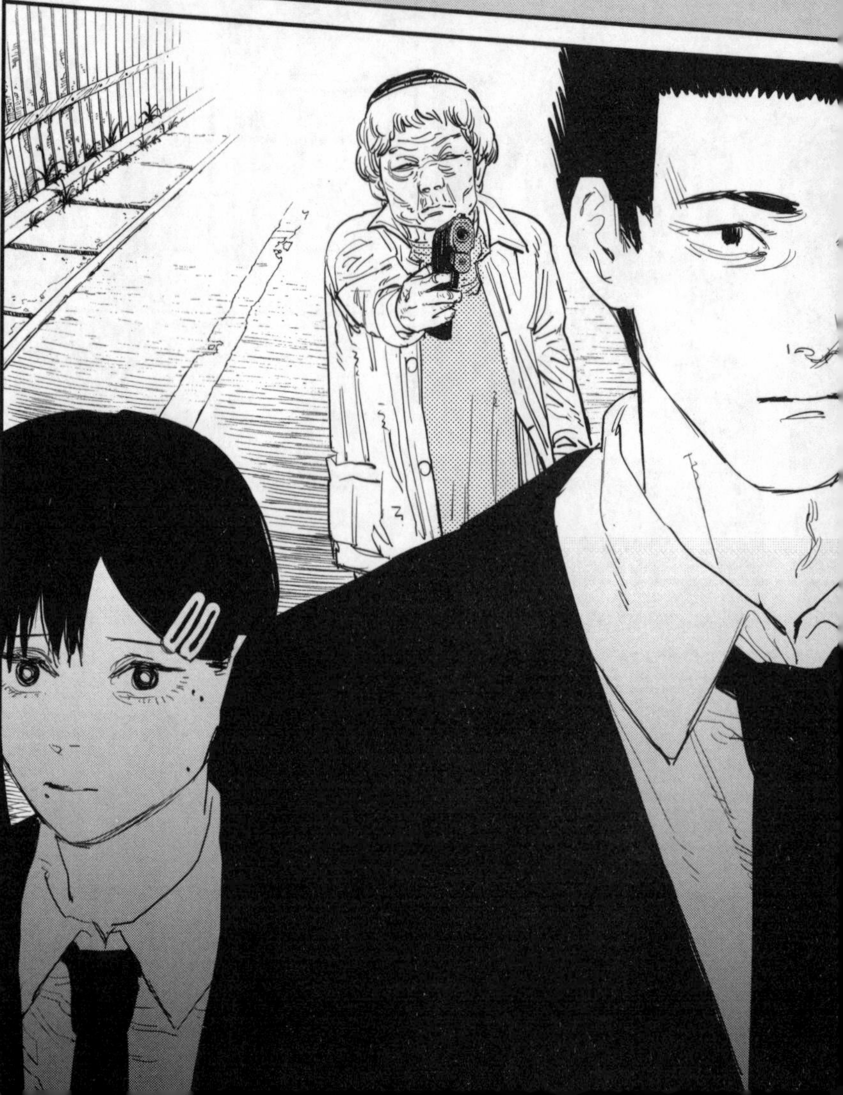

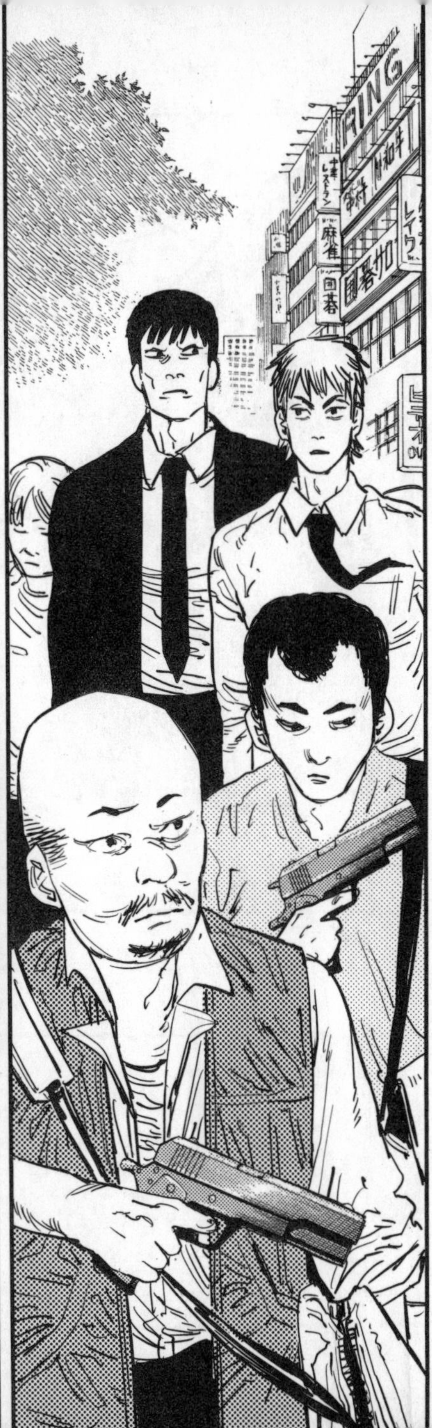
麻雀
囲碁
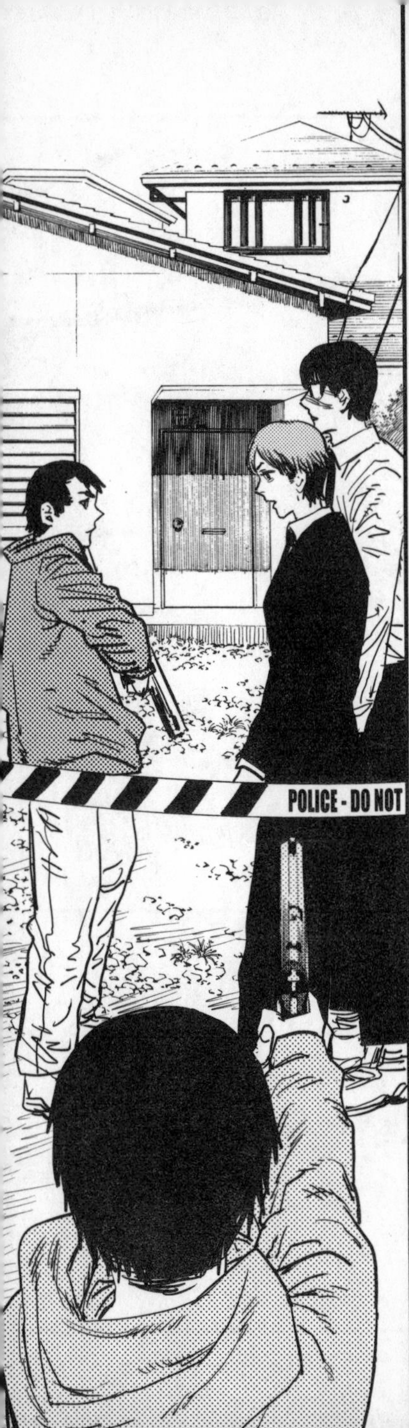
POLICE - DO NOT

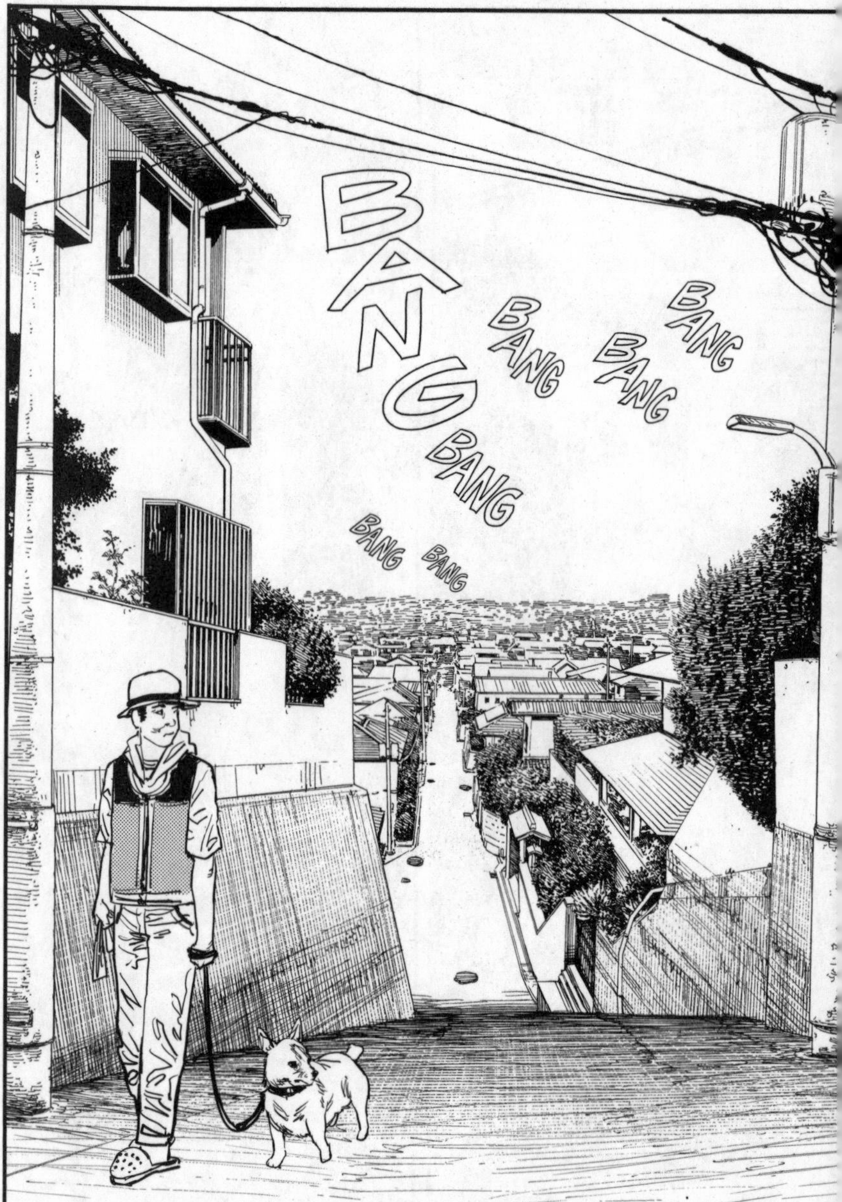
BANG
BANG
BANG
BANG
BANG
BANG
BANG

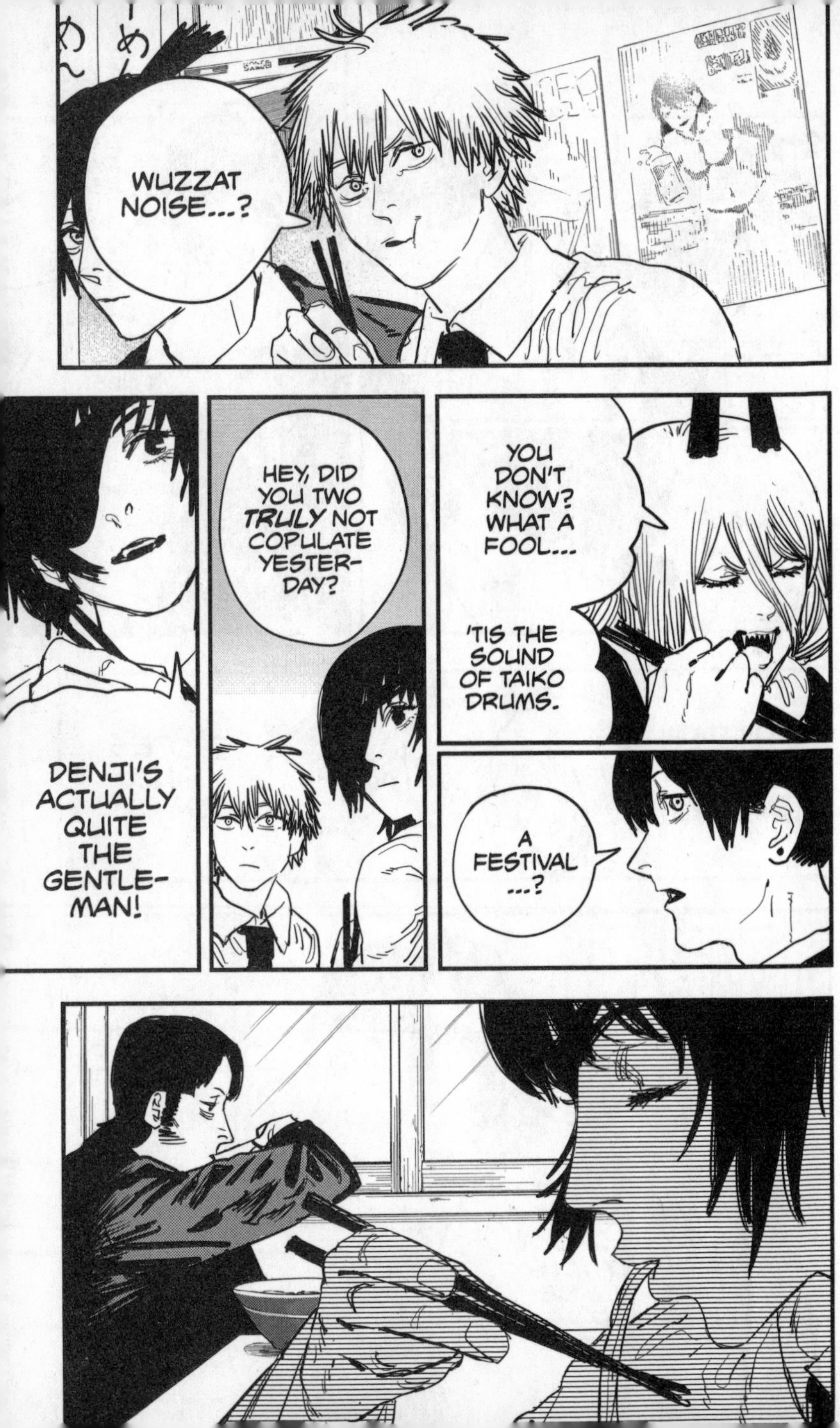
WUZZAT NOISE...?
YOU DON'T KNOW? WHAT A FOOL...
'TIS THE SOUND OF TAIKO DRUMS.
A FESTIVAL ...?
HEY, DID YOU TWO *TRULY* NOT COPULATE YESTERDAY?
DENJI'S ACTUALLY QUITE THE GENTLEMAN!

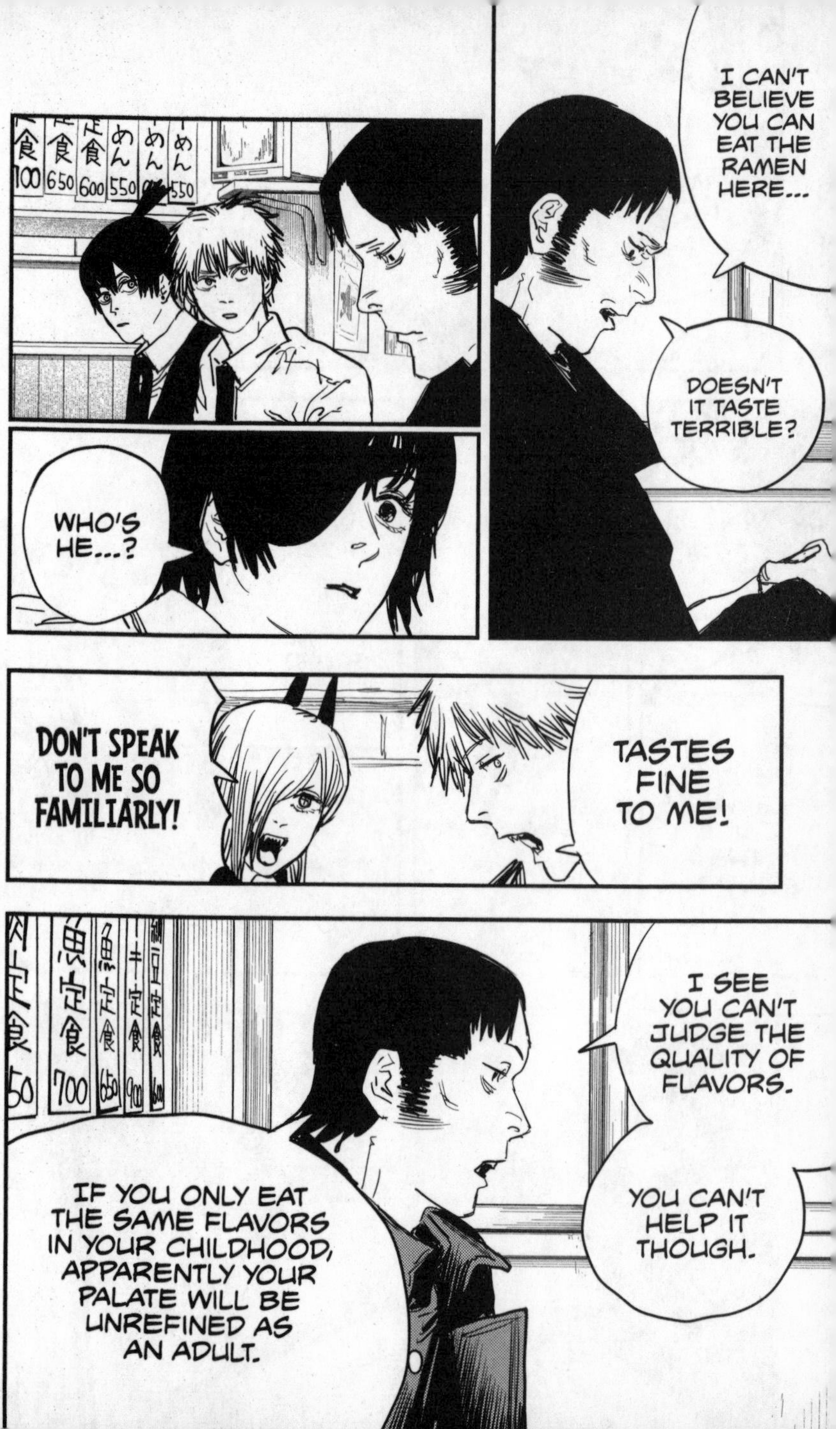
I CAN'T BELIEVE YOU CAN EAT THE RAMEN HERE...
DOESN'T IT TASTE TERRIBLE?
WHO'S HE...?
TASTES FINE TO ME!
DON'T SPEAK TO ME SO FAMILIARLY!
I SEE YOU CAN'T JUDGE THE QUALITY OF FLAVORS.
YOU CAN'T HELP IT THOUGH.
IF YOU ONLY EAT THE SAME FLAVORS IN YOUR CHILDHOOD, APPARENTLY YOUR PALATE WILL BE UNREFINED AS AN ADULT.

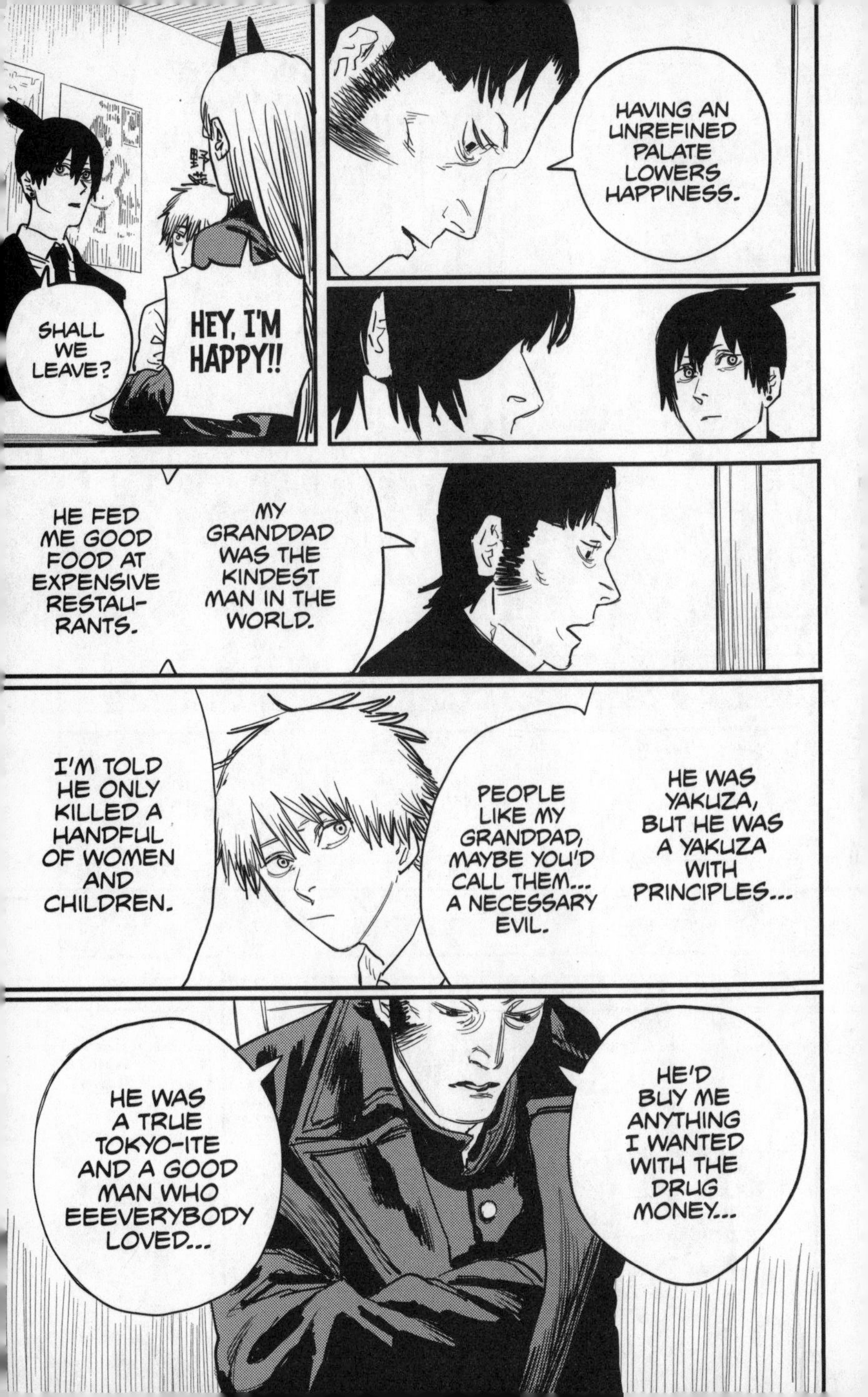
HAVING AN UNREFINED PALATE LOWERS HAPPINESS.
HEY, I'M HAPPY!!
SHALL WE LEAVE?
MY GRANDDAD WAS THE KINDEST MAN IN THE WORLD.
HE FED ME GOOD FOOD AT EXPENSIVE RESTAU-RANTS.
HE WAS YAKUZA, BUT HE WAS A YAKUZA WITH PRINCIPLES...
PEOPLE LIKE MY GRANDDAD, MAYBE YOU'D CALL THEM... A NECESSARY EVIL.
I'M TOLD HE ONLY KILLED A HANDFUL OF WOMEN AND CHILDREN.
HE'D BUY ME ANYTHING I WANTED WITH THE DRUG MONEY...
HE WAS A TRUE TOKYO-ITE AND A GOOD MAN WHO EEEVERYBODY LOVED...

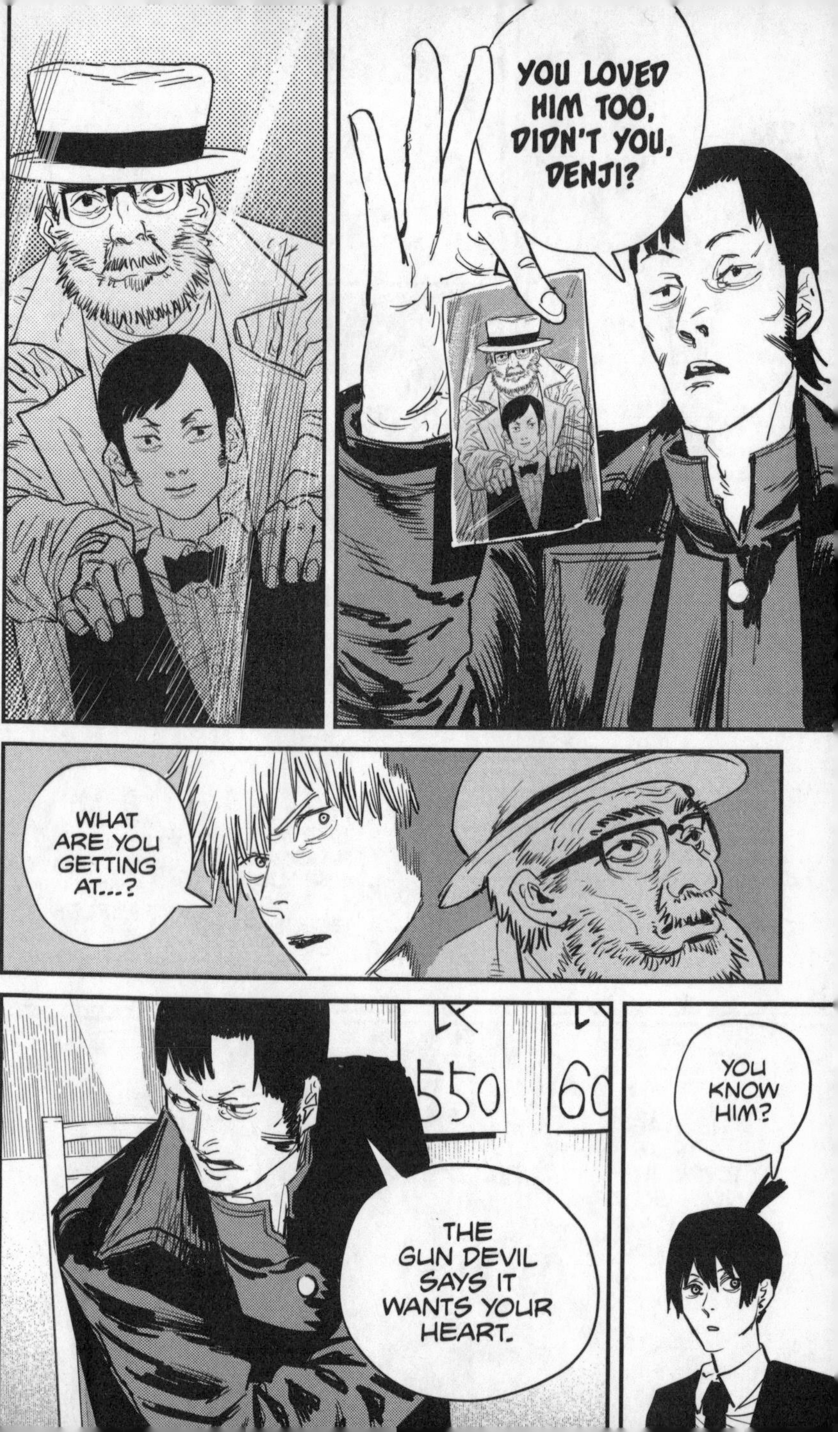
YOU LOVED HIM TOO, DIDN'T YOU, DENJI?
WHAT ARE YOU GETTING AT...?
YOU KNOW HIM?
550
THE GUN DEVIL SAYS IT WANTS YOUR HEART.

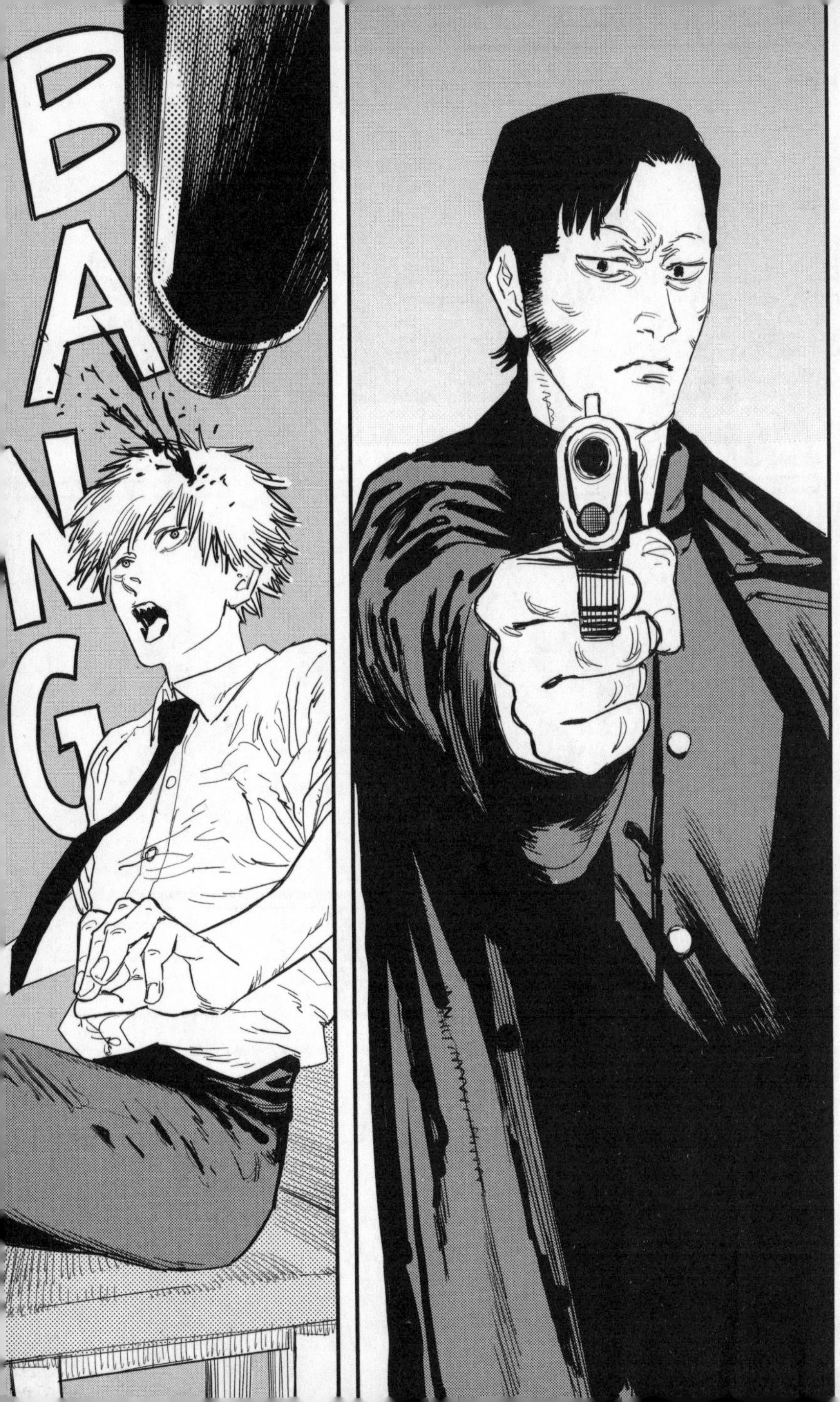
BANG

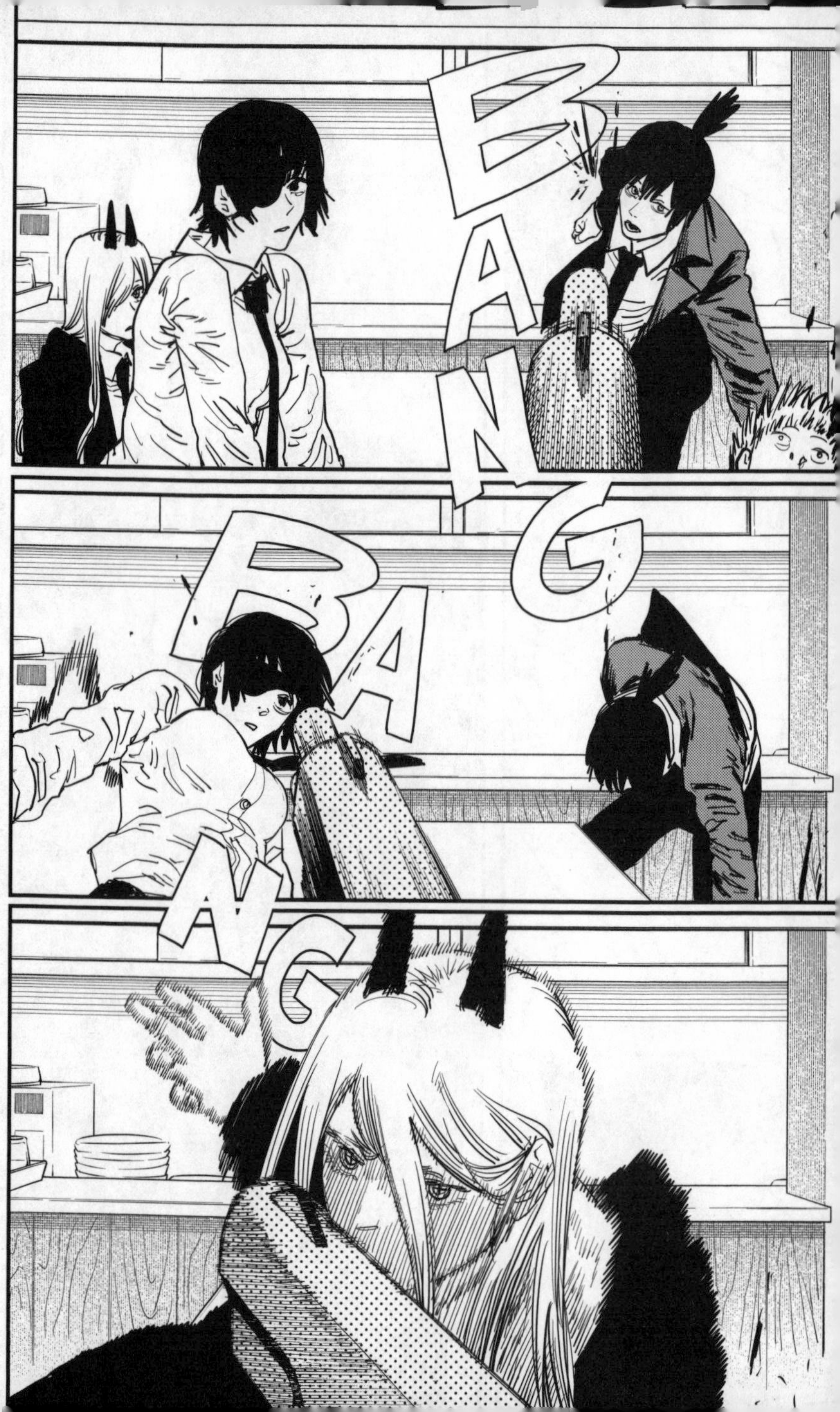
BANG
BANG

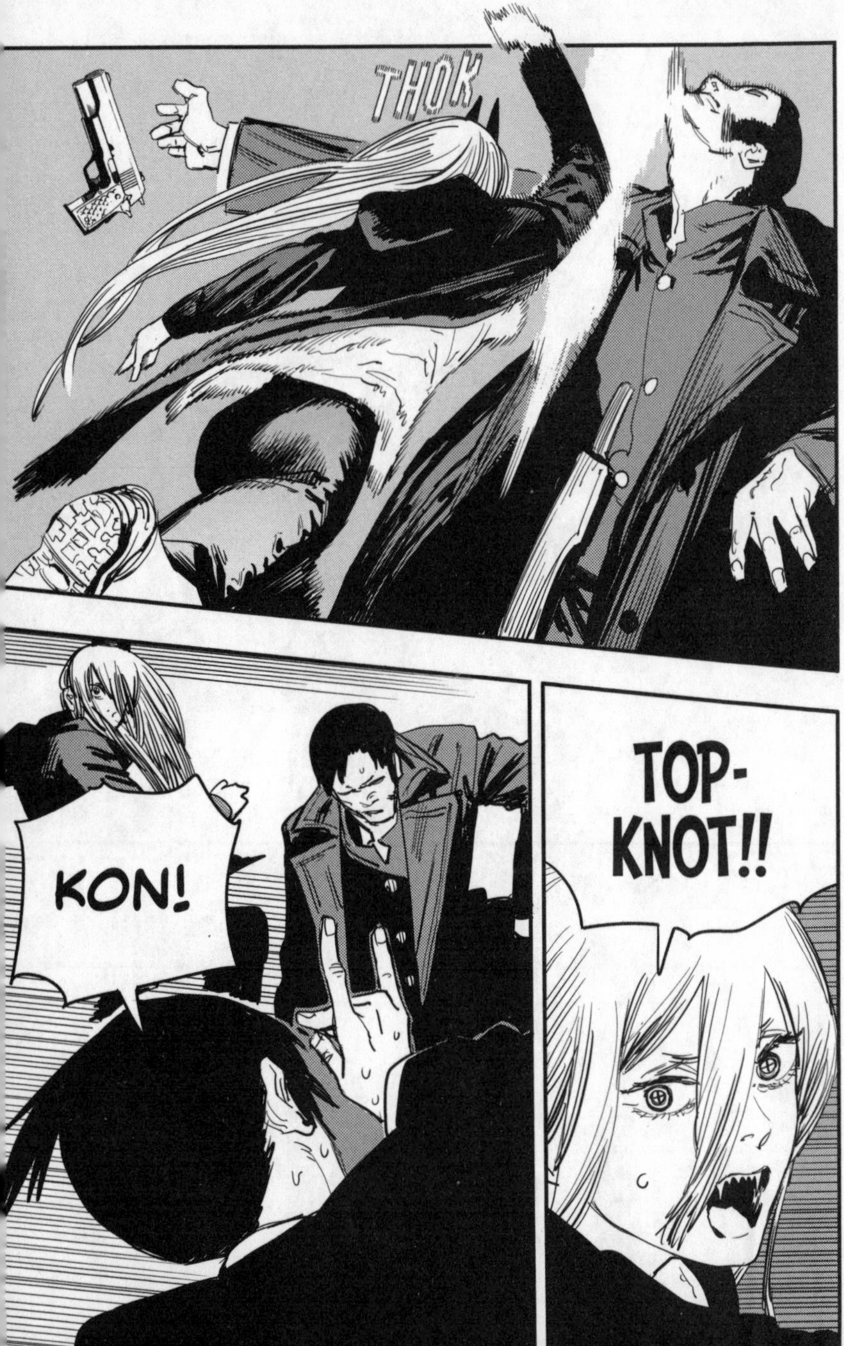
THOK
TOP-KNOT!!
KON!

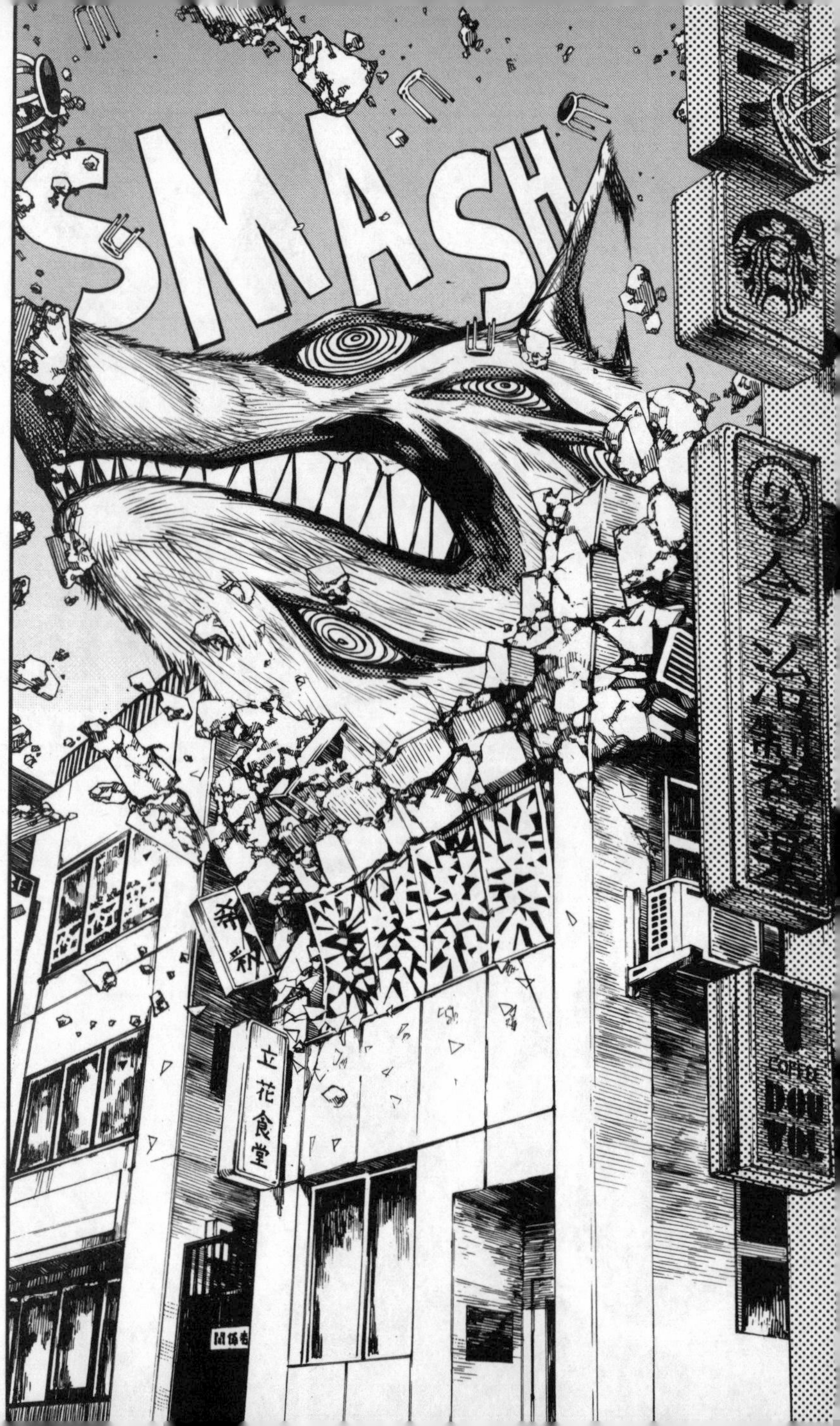
SMASH
立花食堂
COFFEE

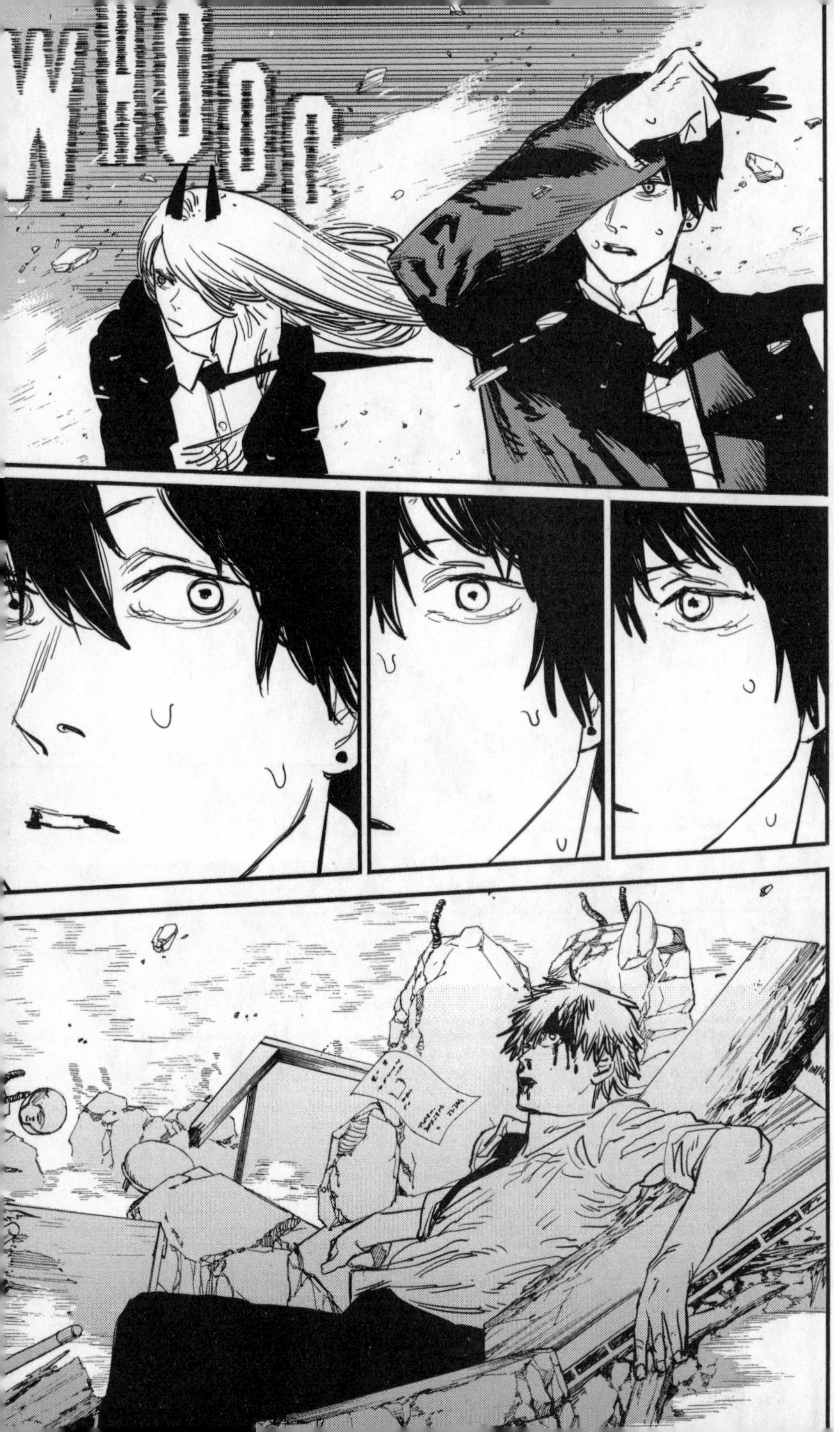
WHOOO

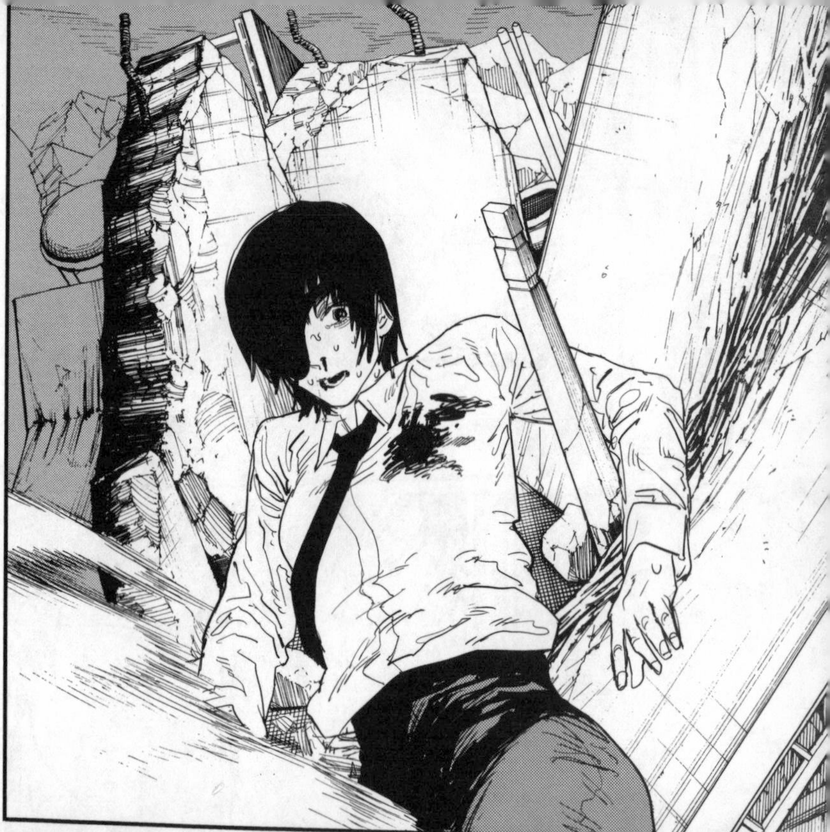
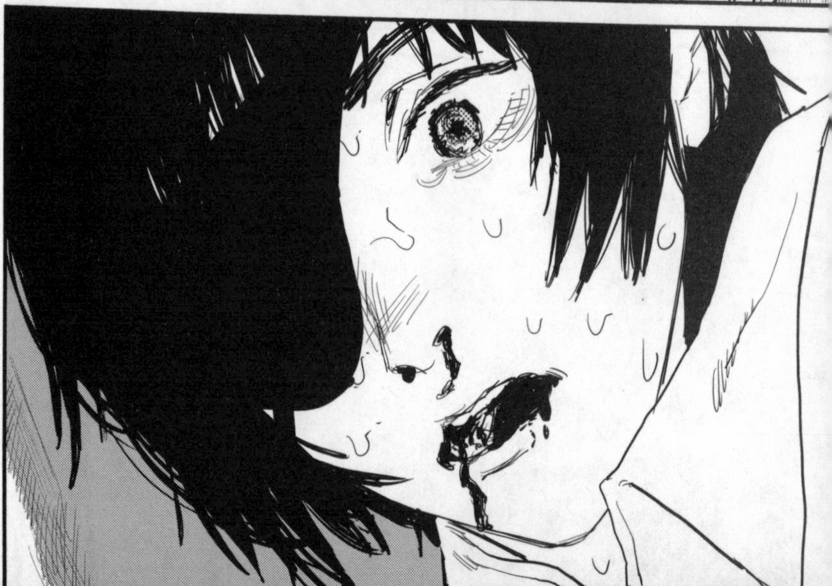

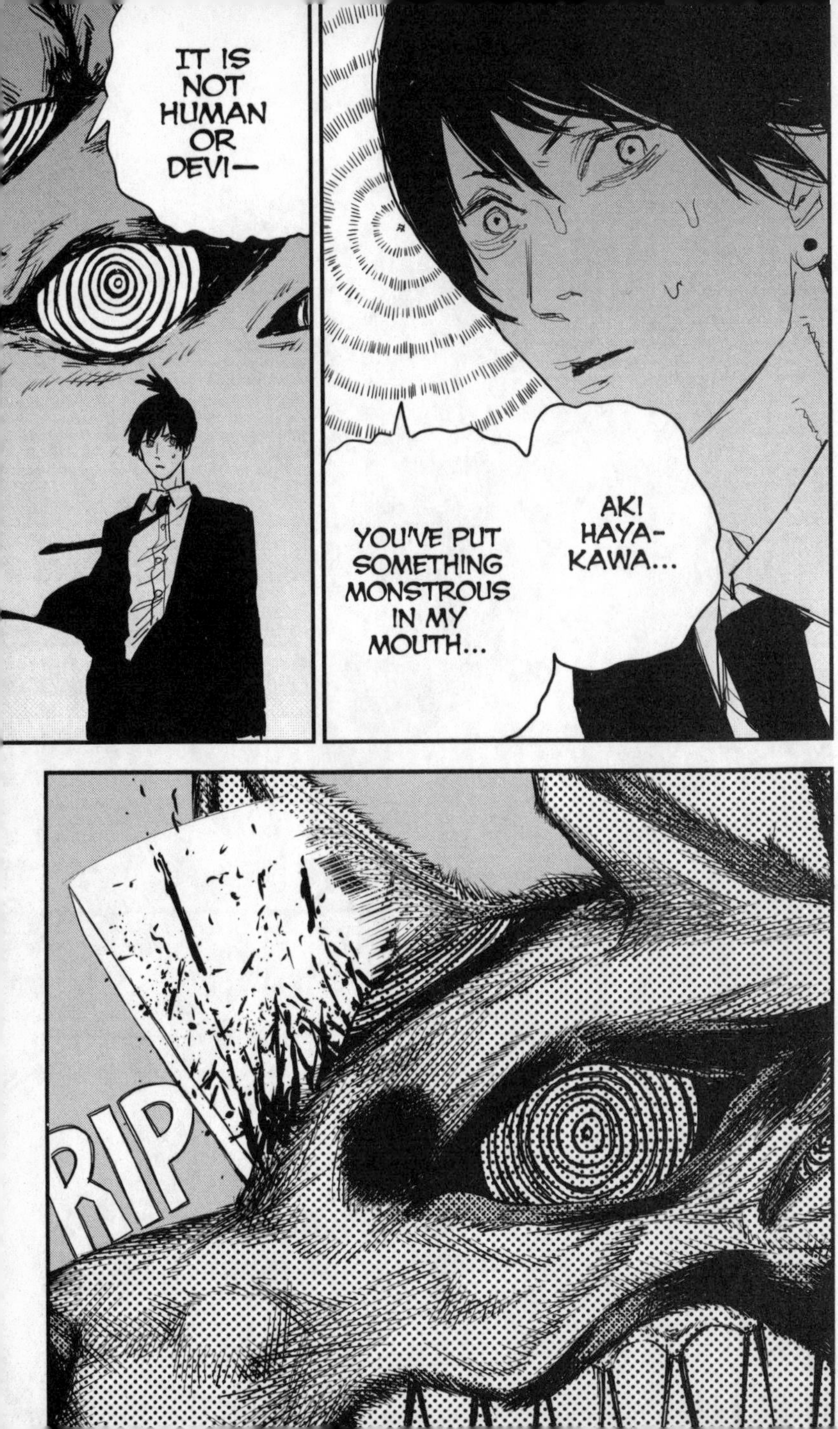
AKI HAYA-KAWA...
YOU'VE PUT SOMETHING MONSTROUS IN MY MOUTH...
IT IS NOT HUMAN OR DEVI—
RIP

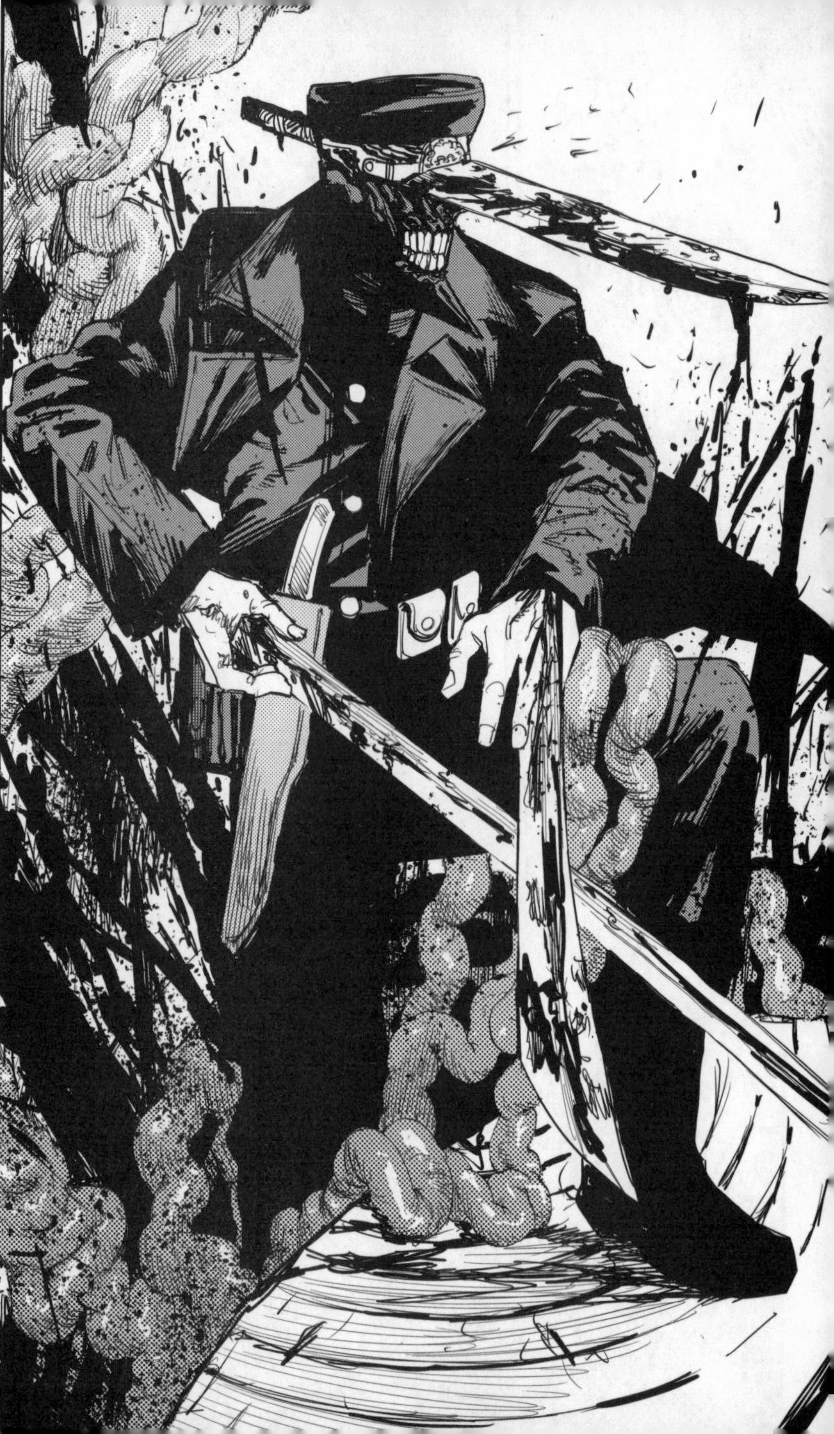

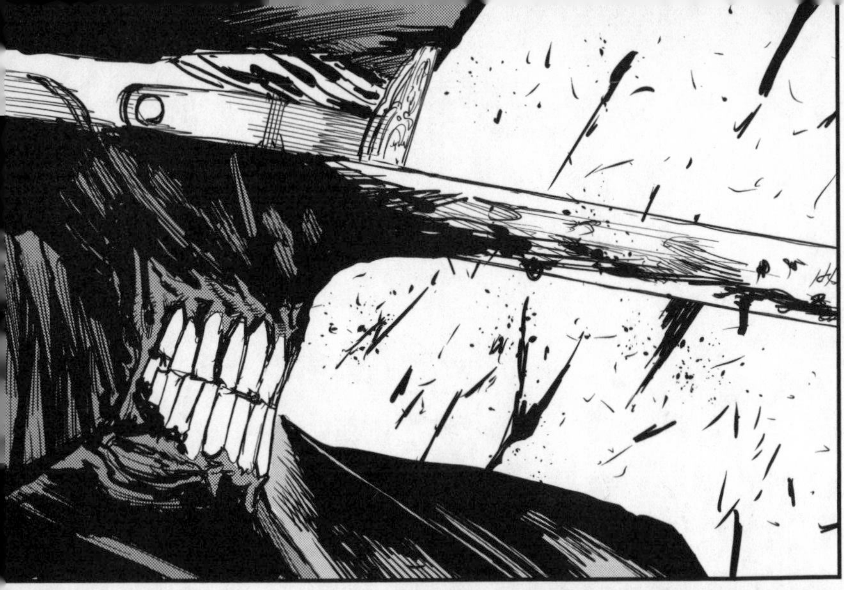

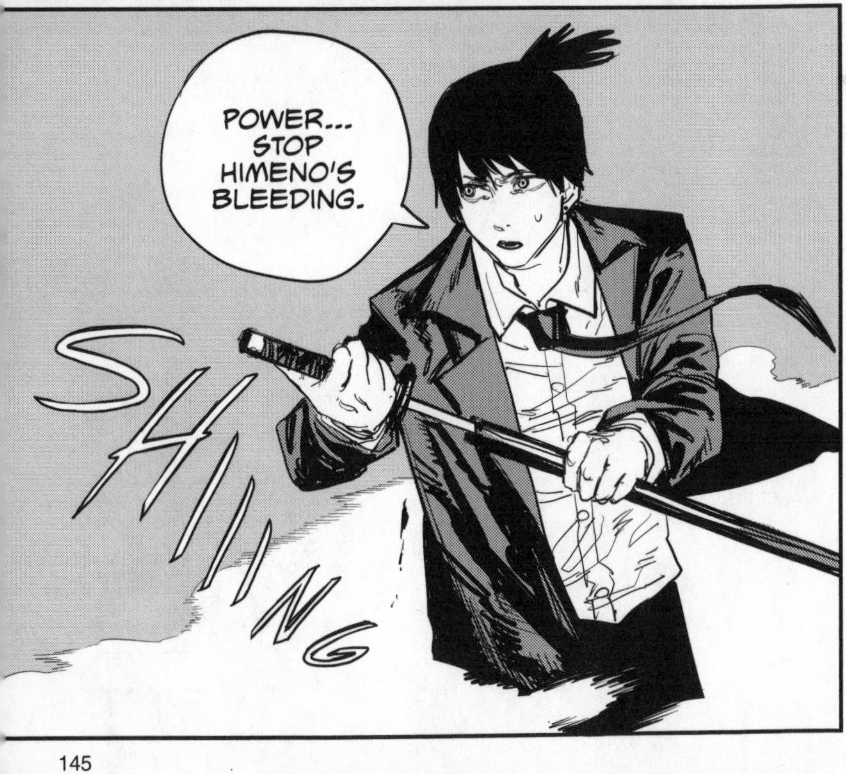
POWER... STOP HIMENO'S BLEEDING.
SHIING

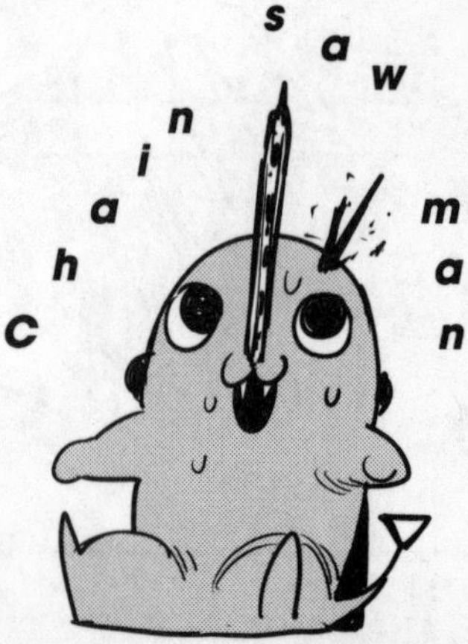
Chainsaw man

Chapter 24: Curse

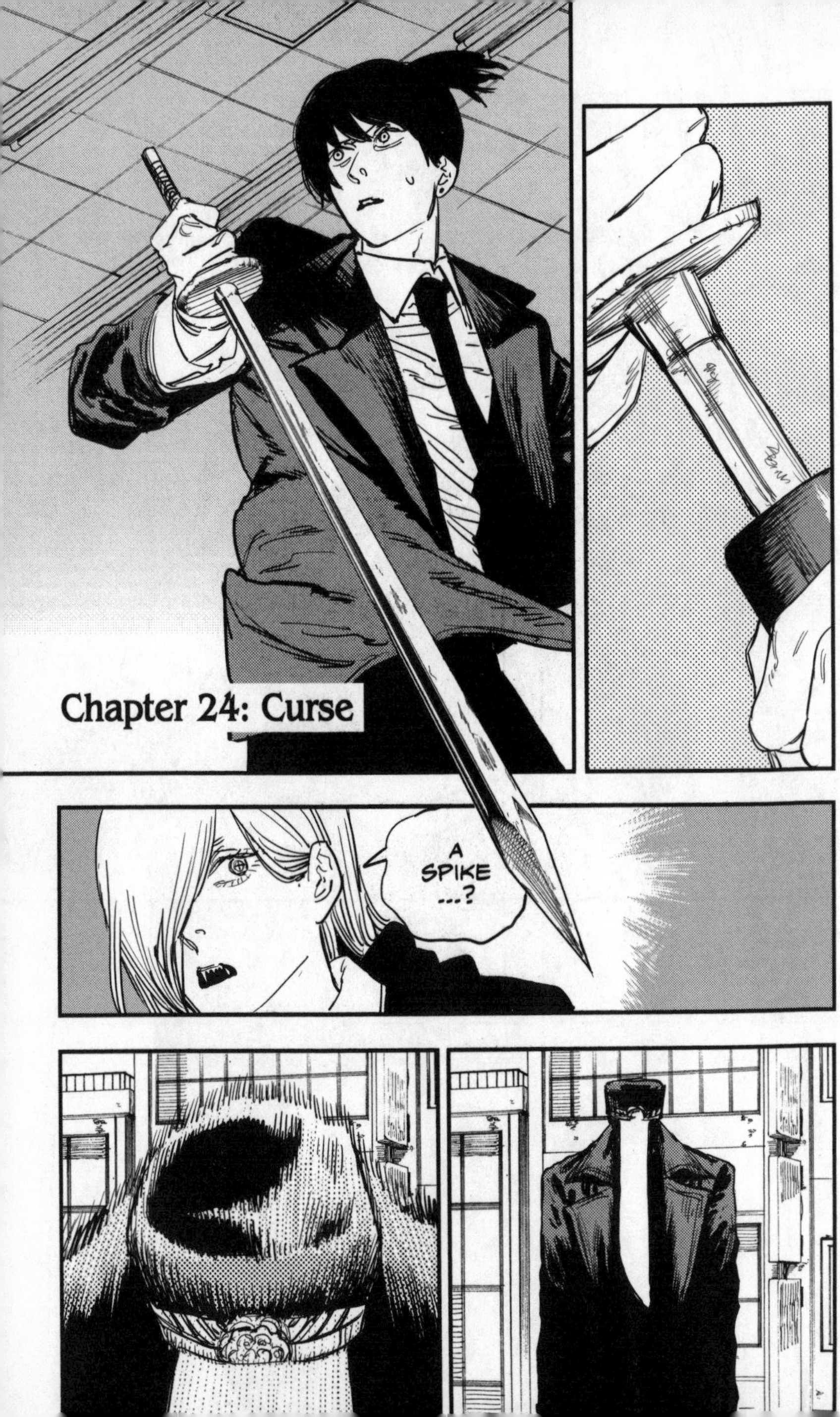
A SPIKE ...?

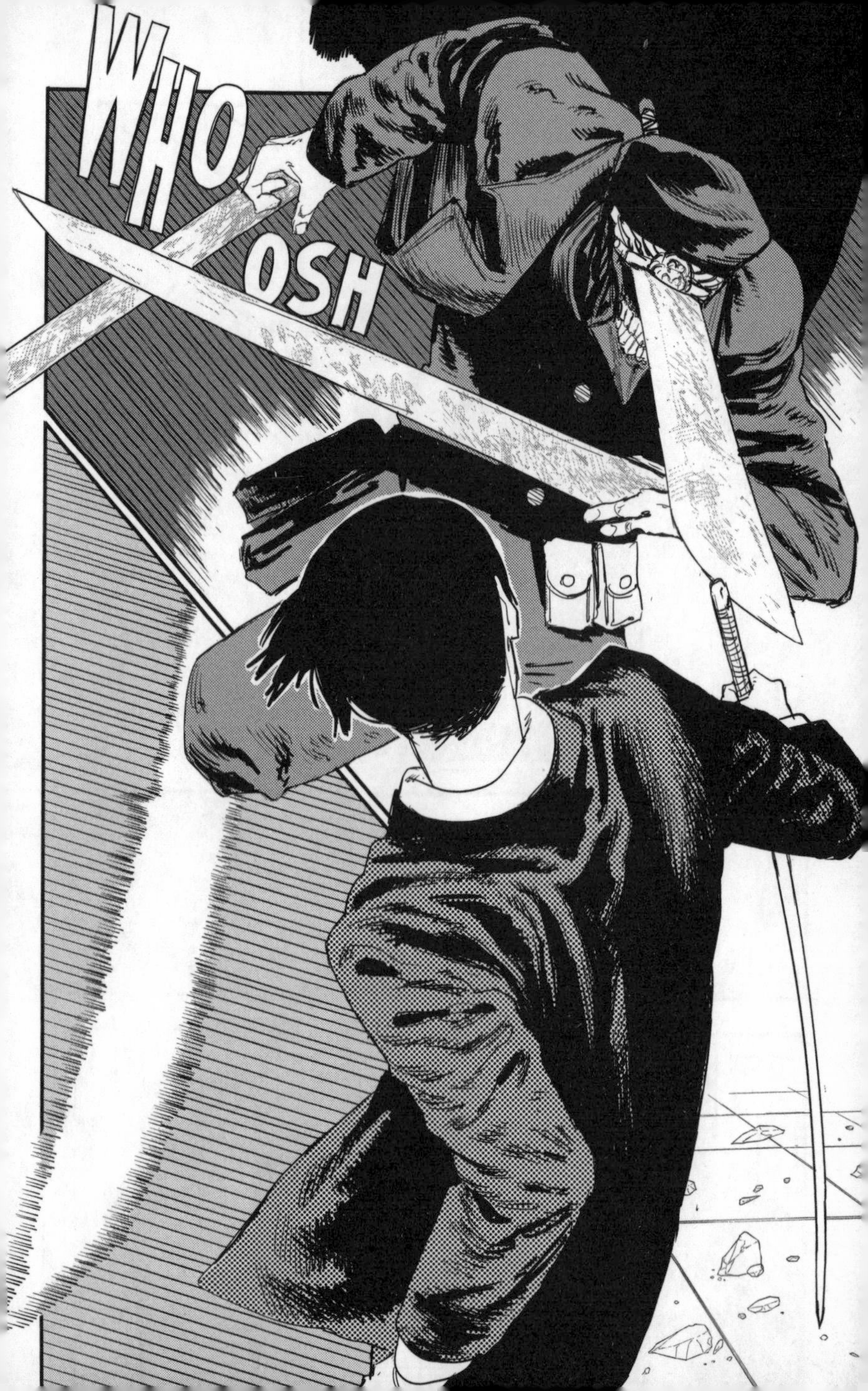
WHOOSH

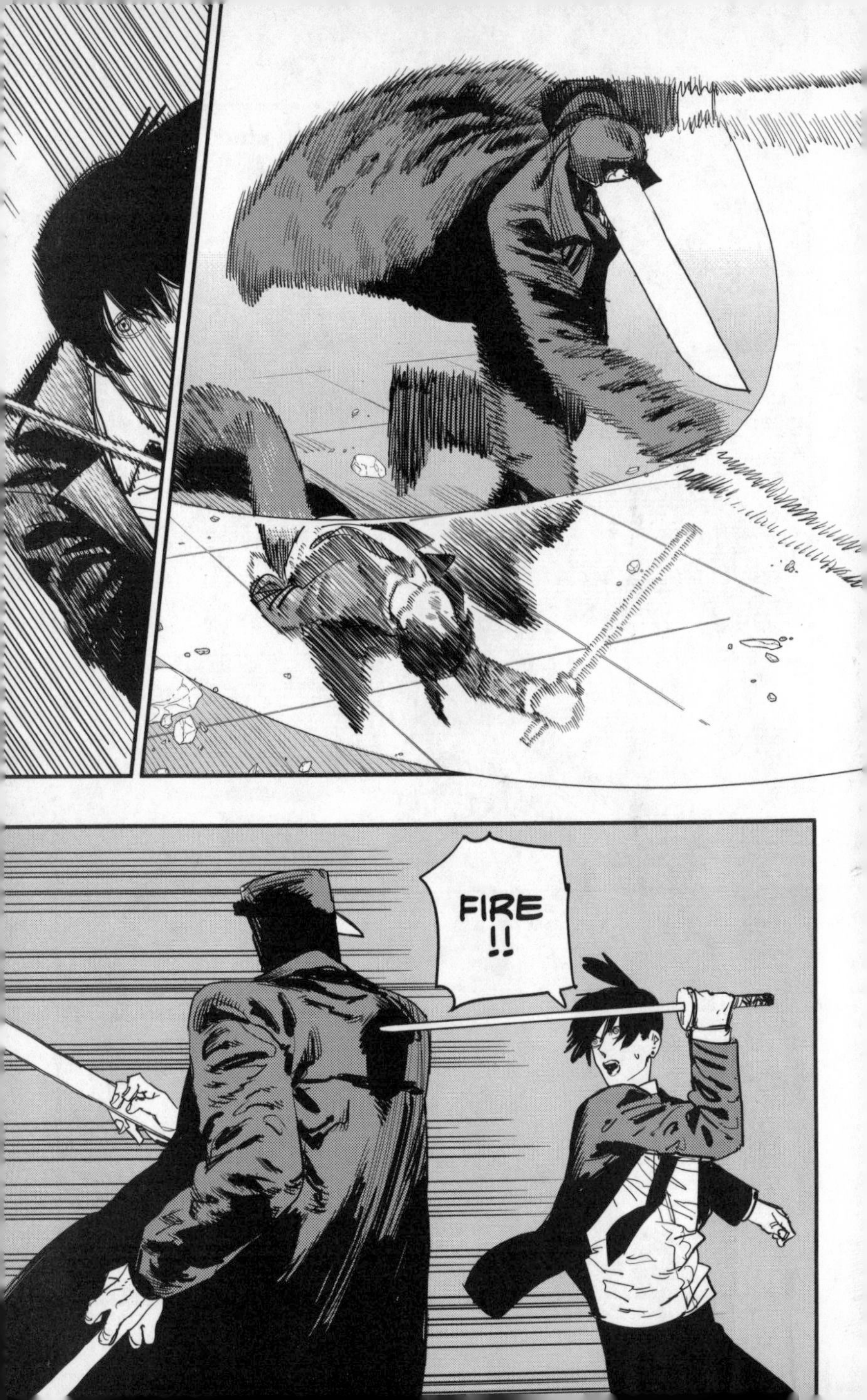
FIRE !!

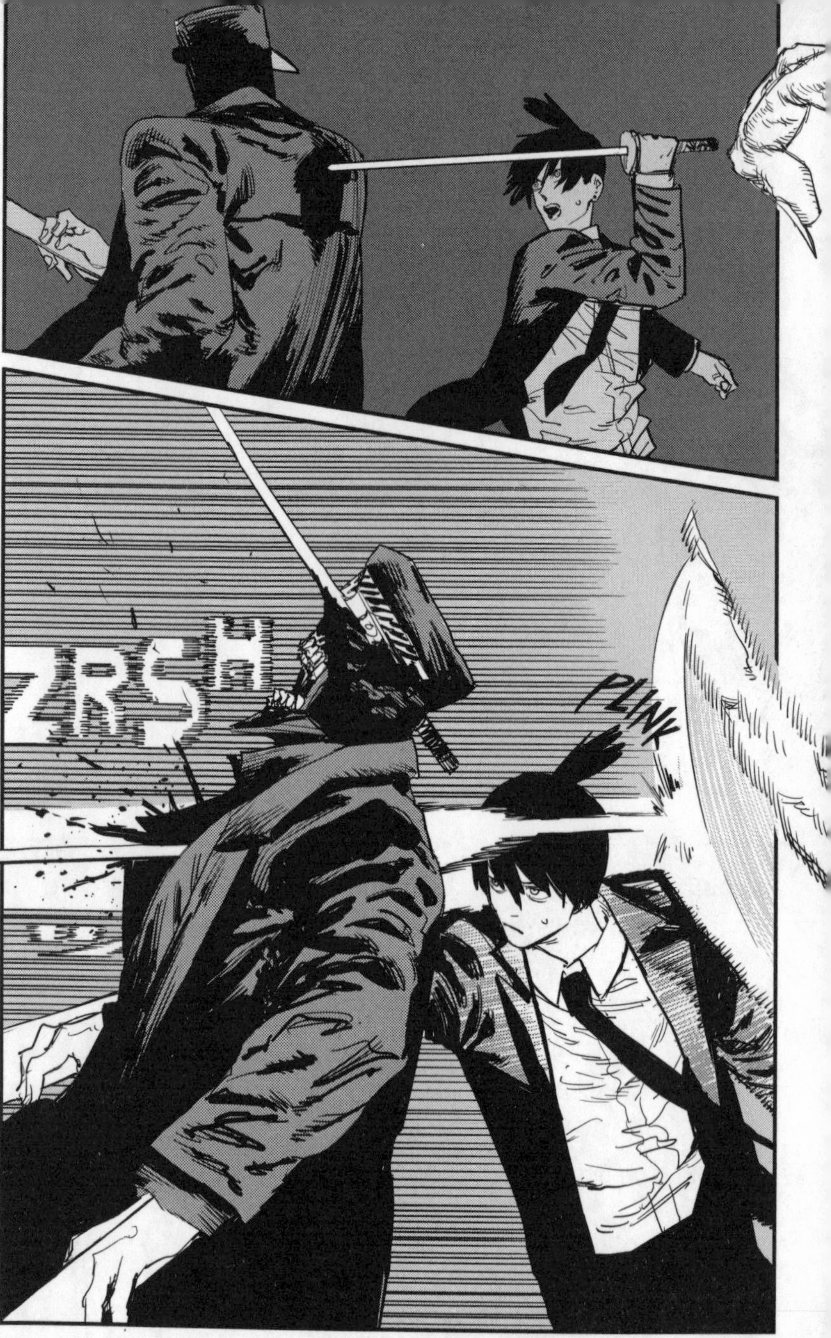

ZRSH
PLINK

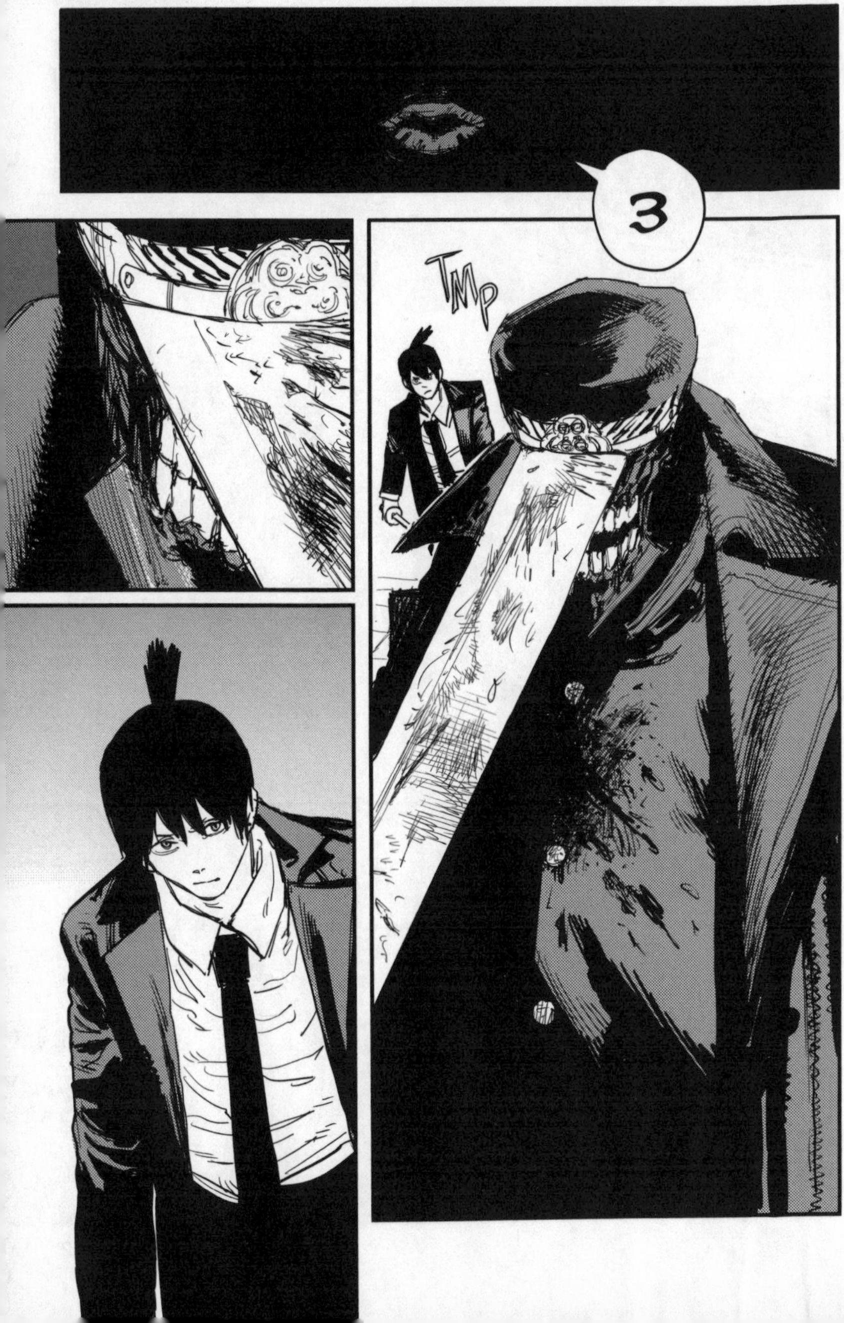
3
TMP

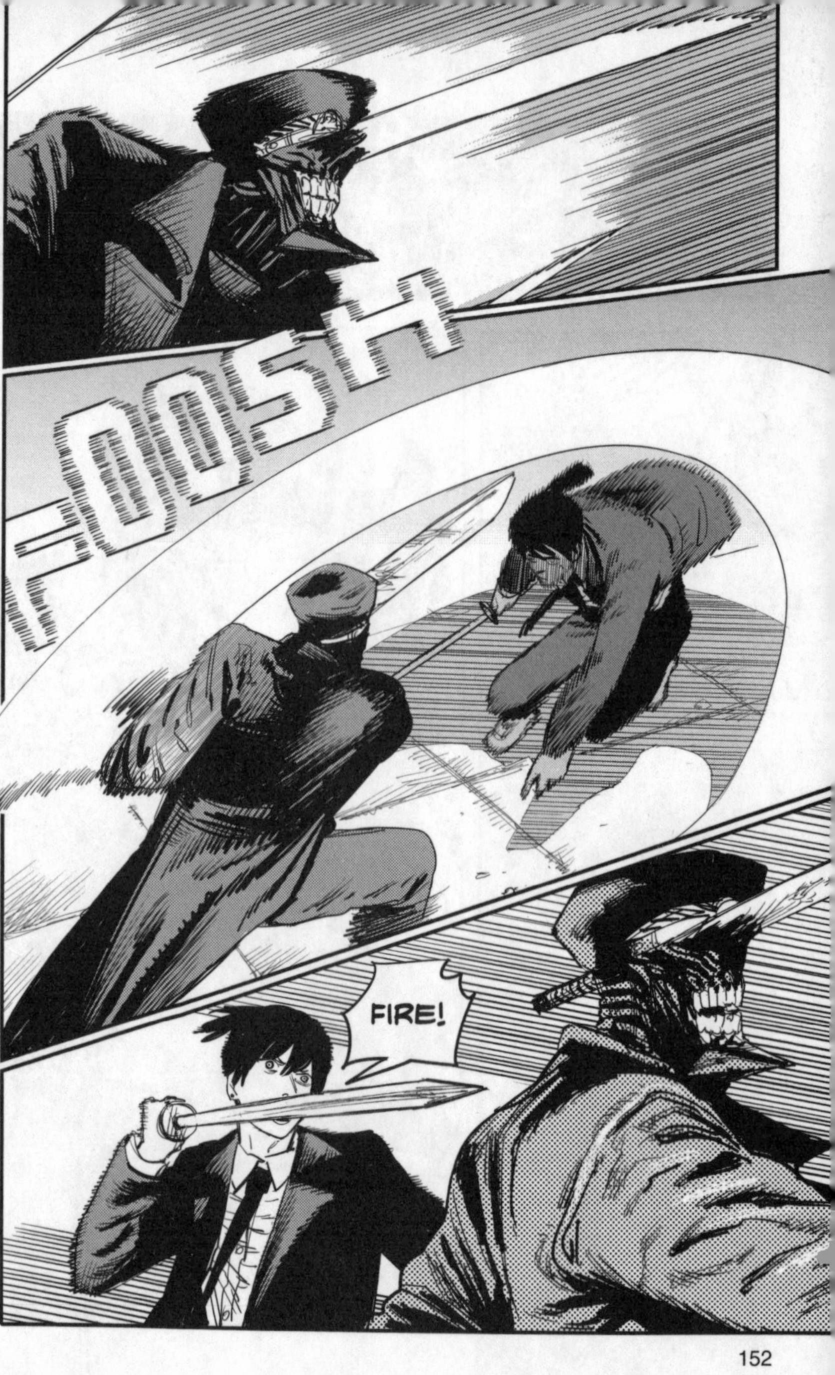
FOOSH
FIRE!

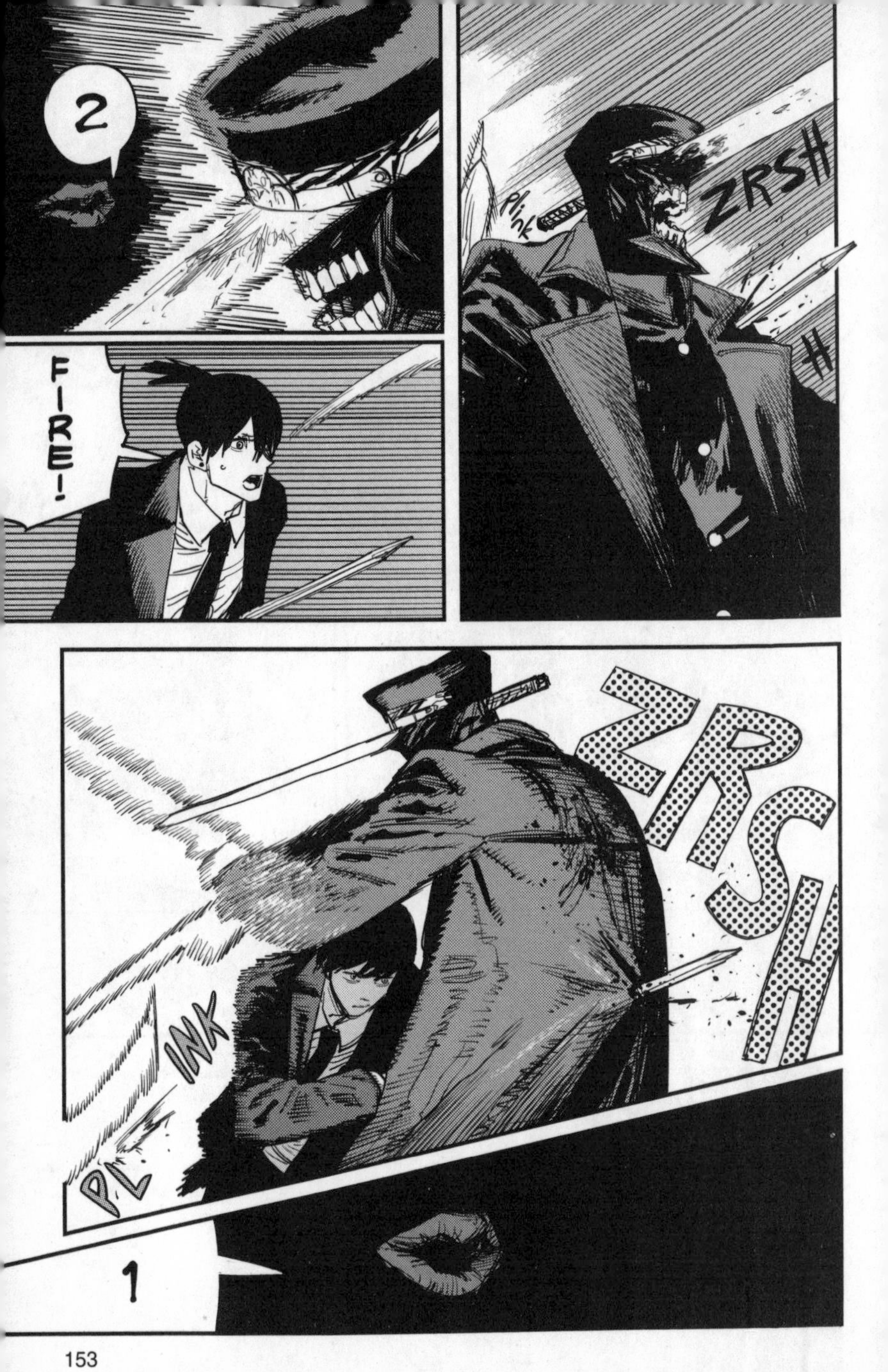
ZRSH
PLINK
2
FIRE!
ZRSH
PLINK
1

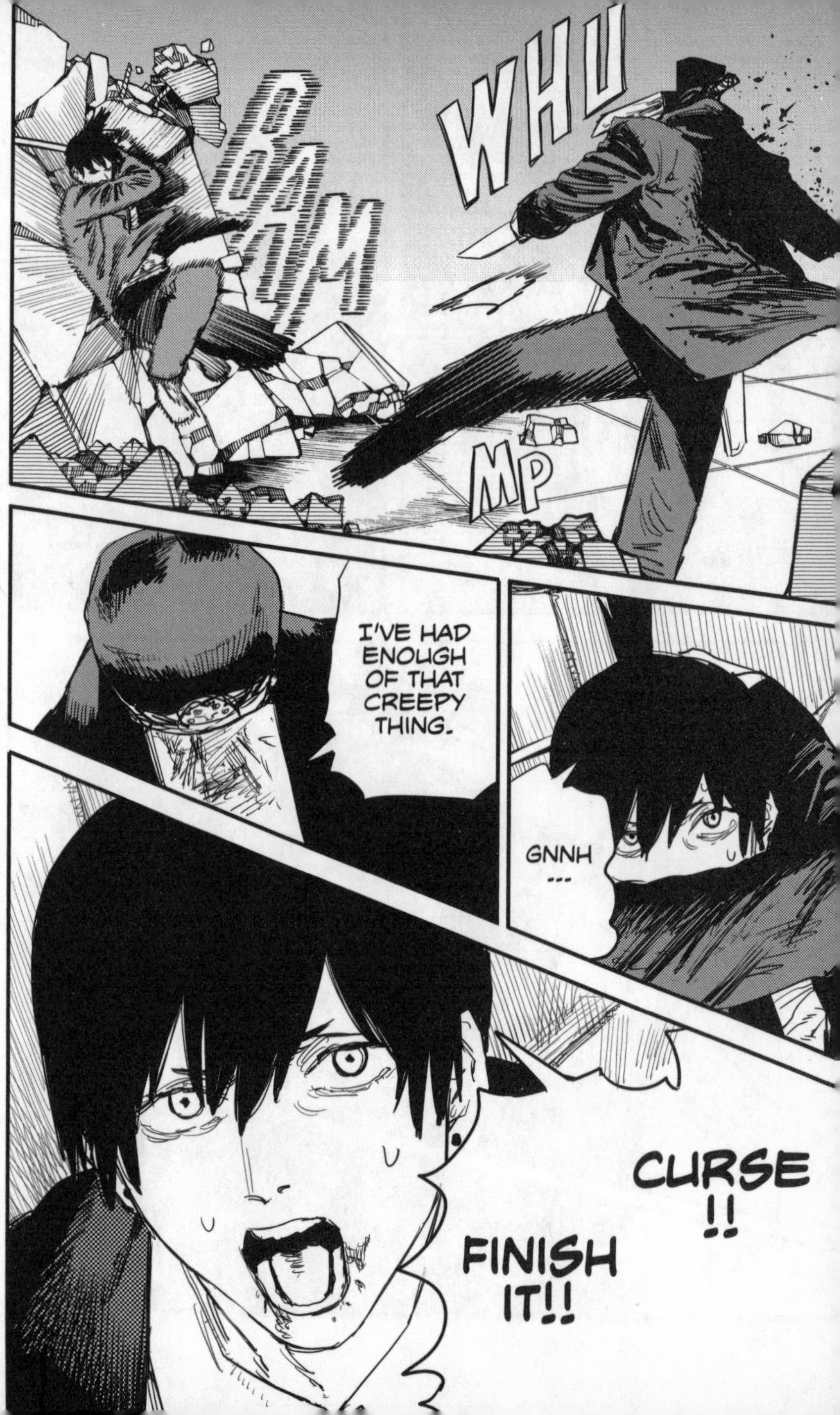
WHU
MP
BOOM
I'VE HAD ENOUGH OF THAT CREEPY THING.
GNNH ...
CURSE !!
FINISH IT!!

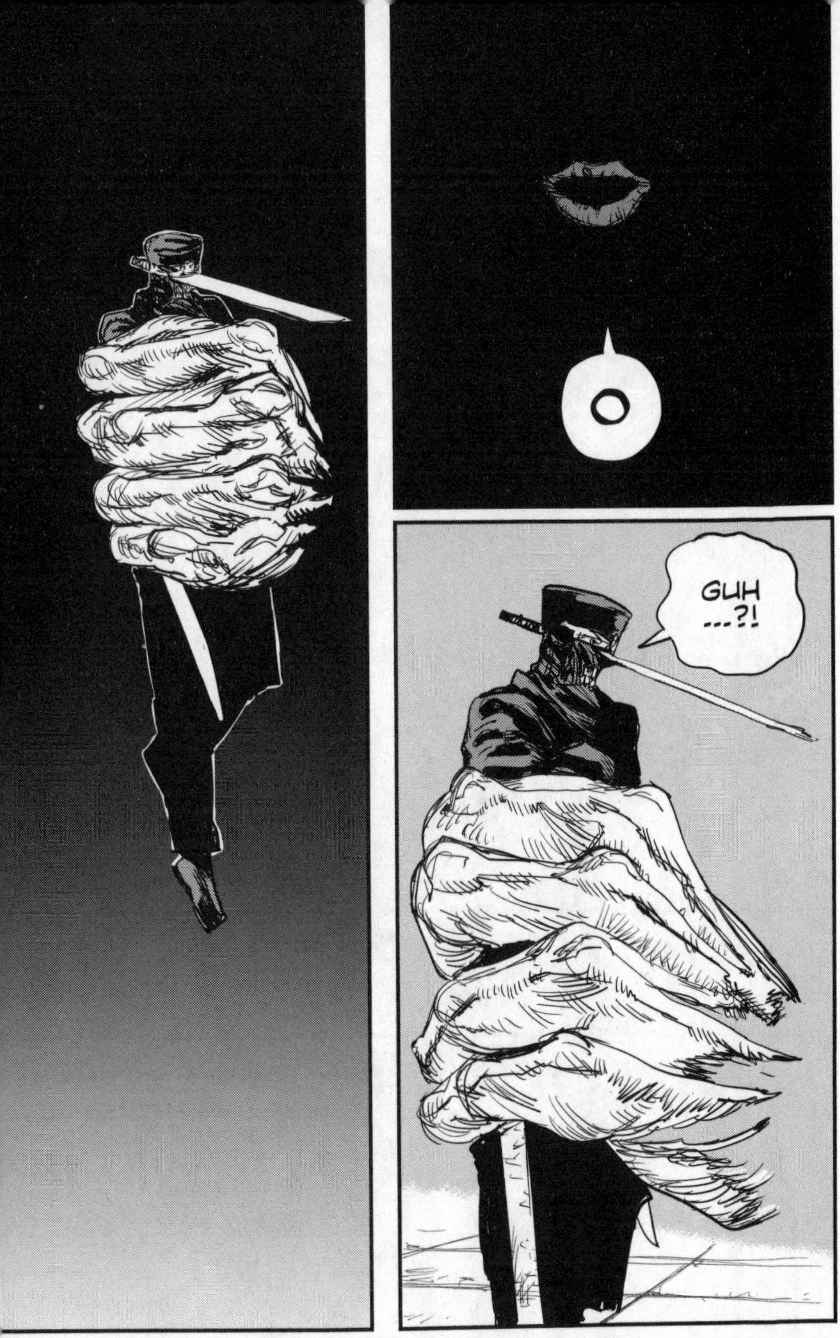
GUH
---?!

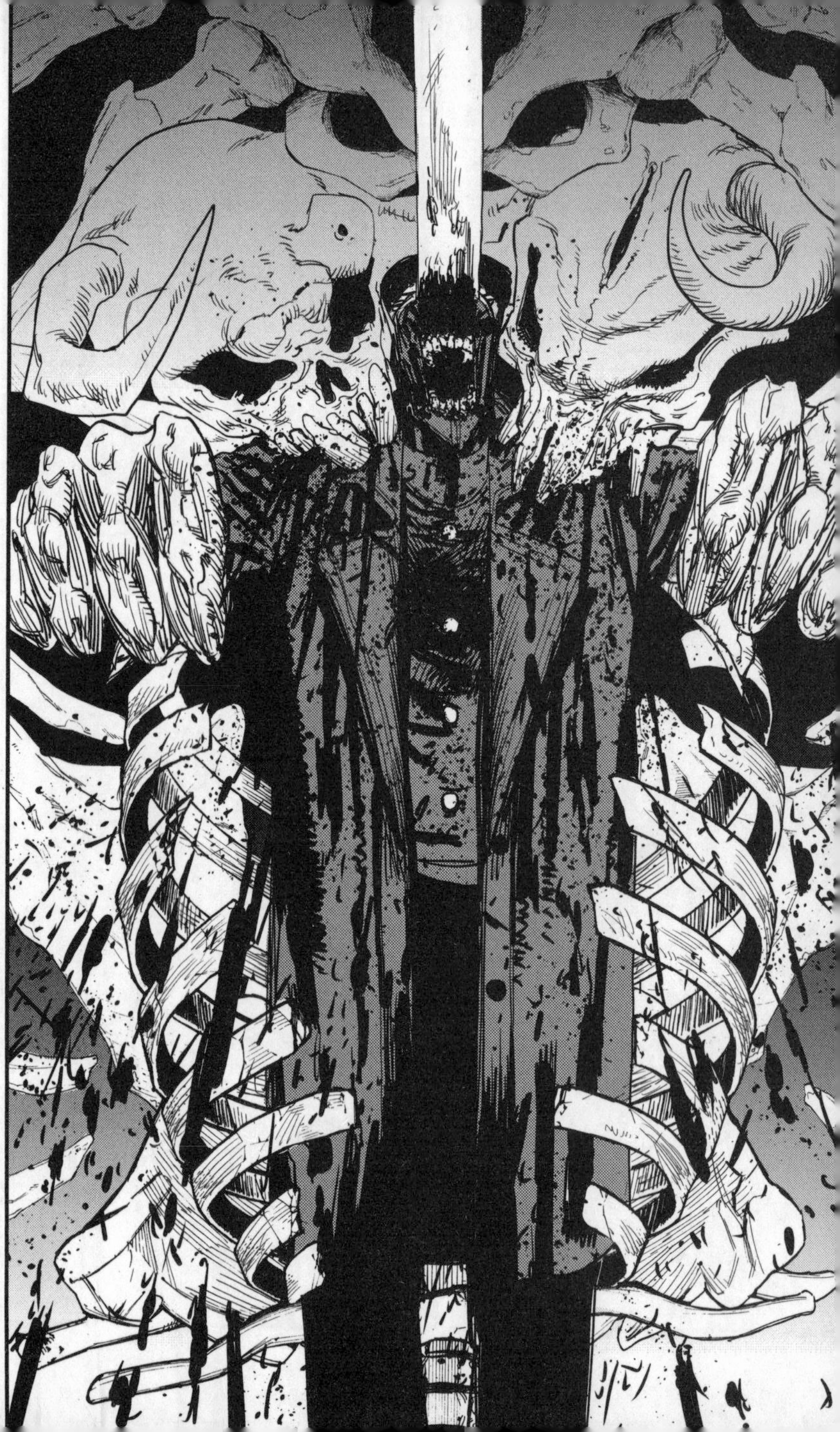

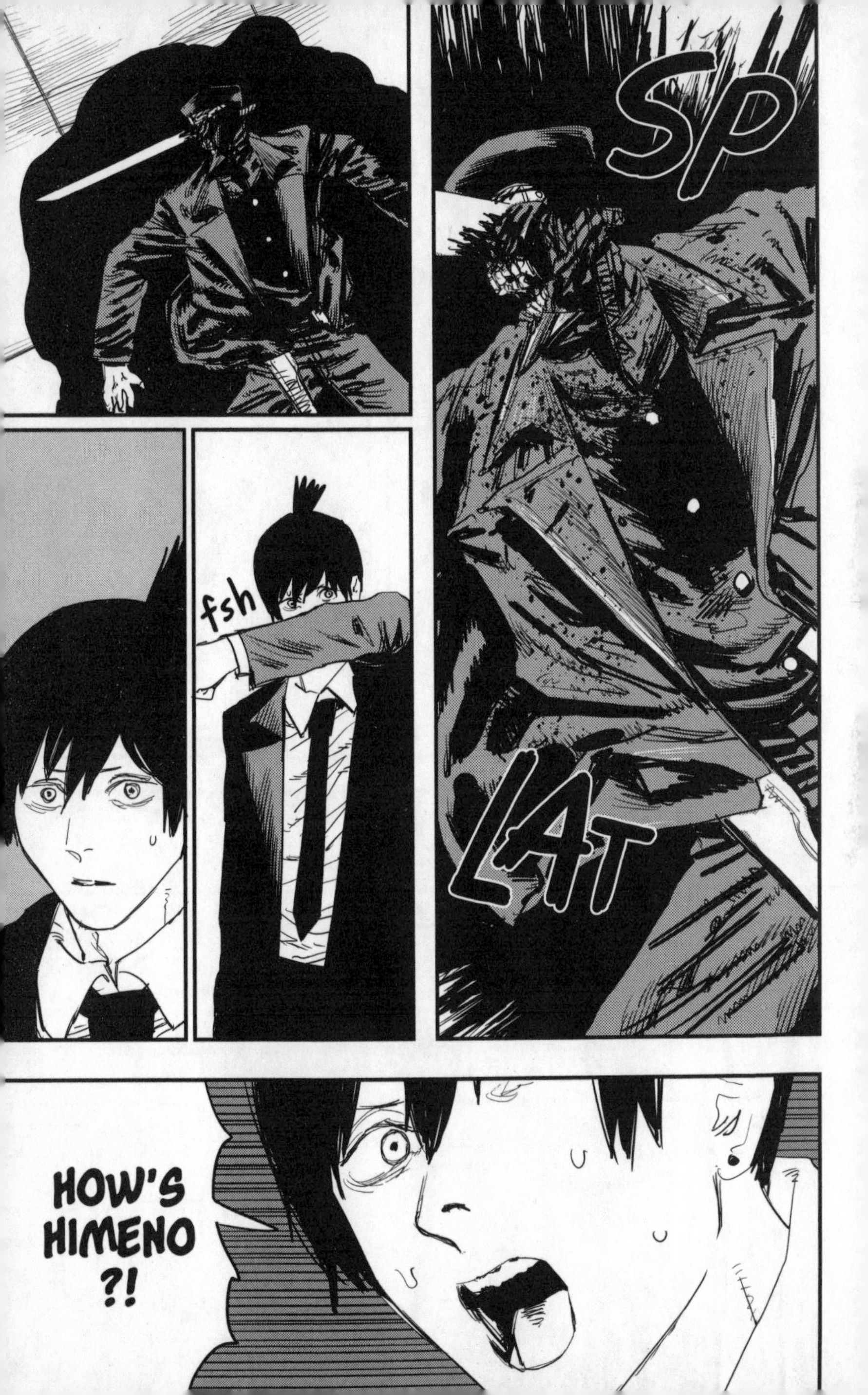
SP
LAT
fsh
HOW'S HIMENO ?!

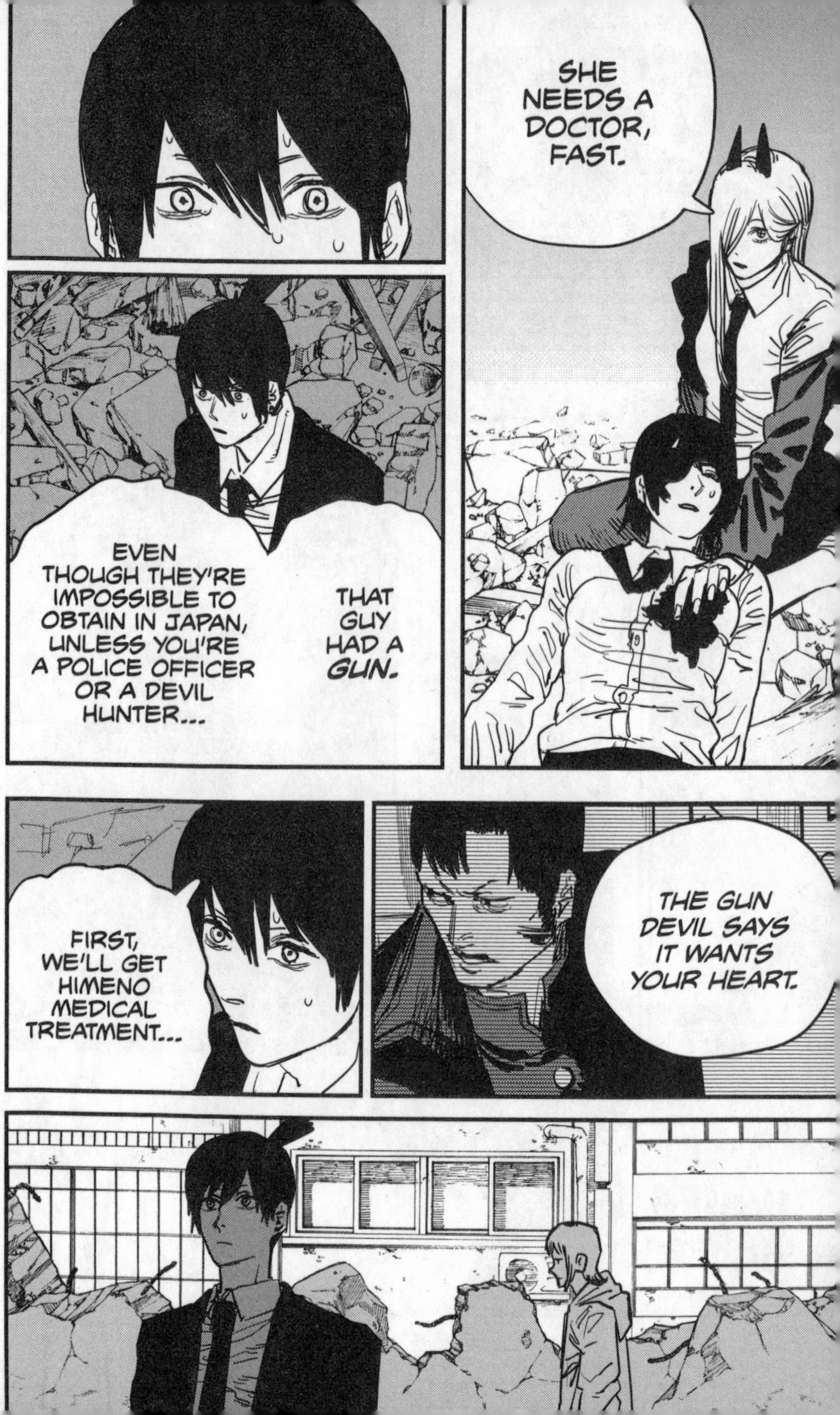
SHE NEEDS A DOCTOR, FAST.
THAT GUY HAD A GUN.
EVEN THOUGH THEY'RE IMPOSSIBLE TO OBTAIN IN JAPAN, UNLESS YOU'RE A POLICE OFFICER OR A DEVIL HUNTER...
THE GUN DEVIL SAYS IT WANTS YOUR HEART.
FIRST, WE'LL GET HIMENO MEDICAL TREATMENT...

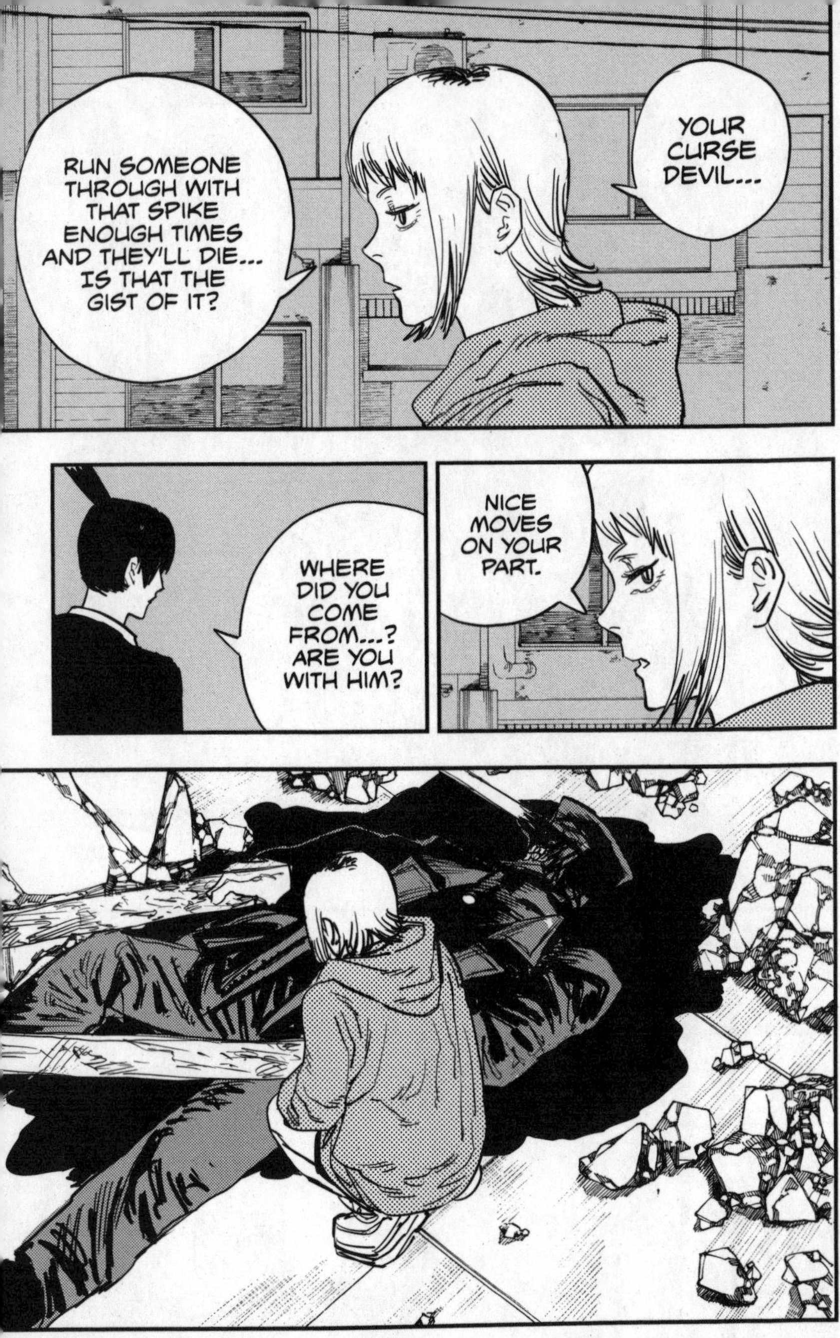
YOUR CURSE DEVIL...
RUN SOMEONE THROUGH WITH THAT SPIKE ENOUGH TIMES AND THEY'LL DIE... IS THAT THE GIST OF IT?
NICE MOVES ON YOUR PART.
WHERE DID YOU COME FROM...? ARE YOU WITH HIM?

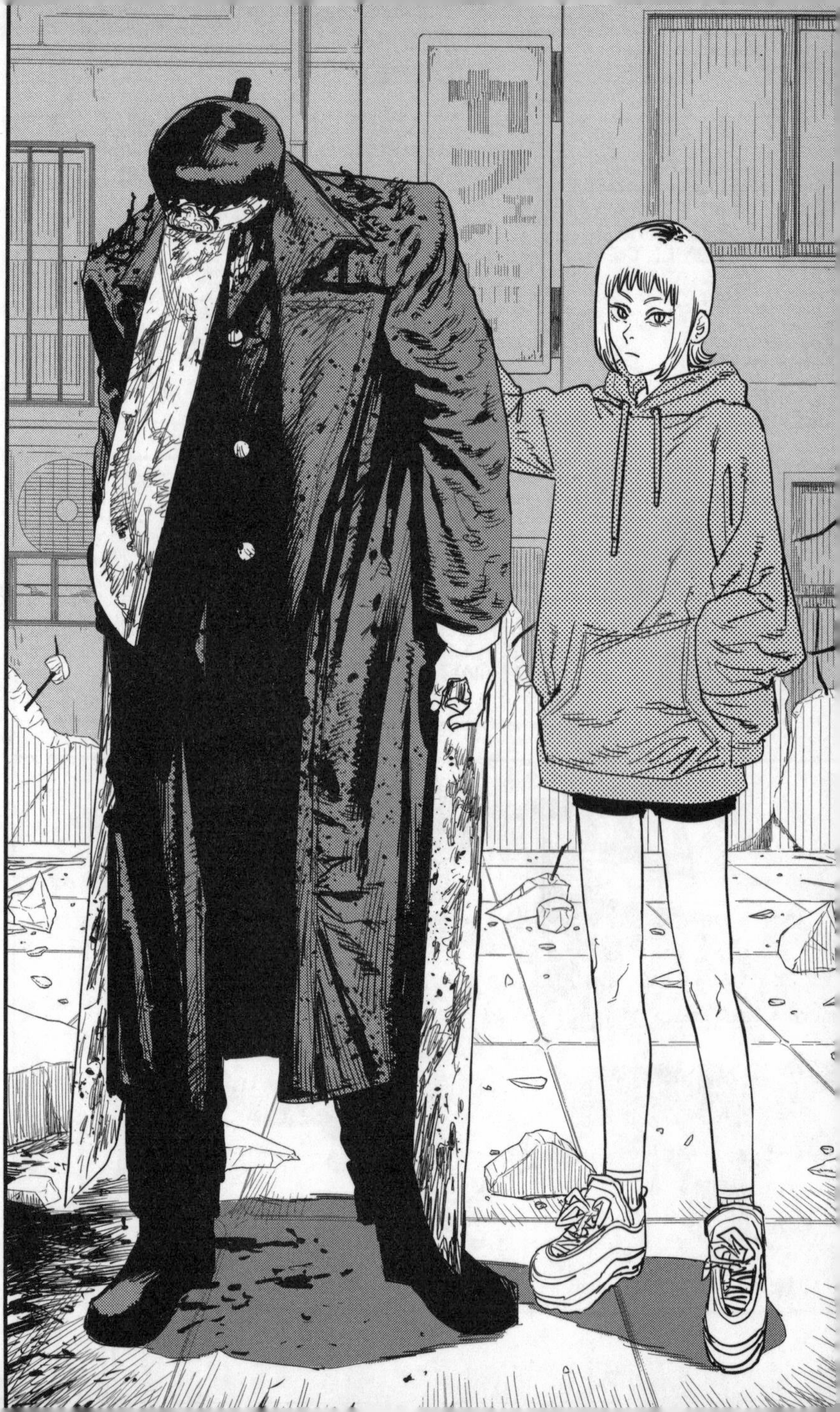

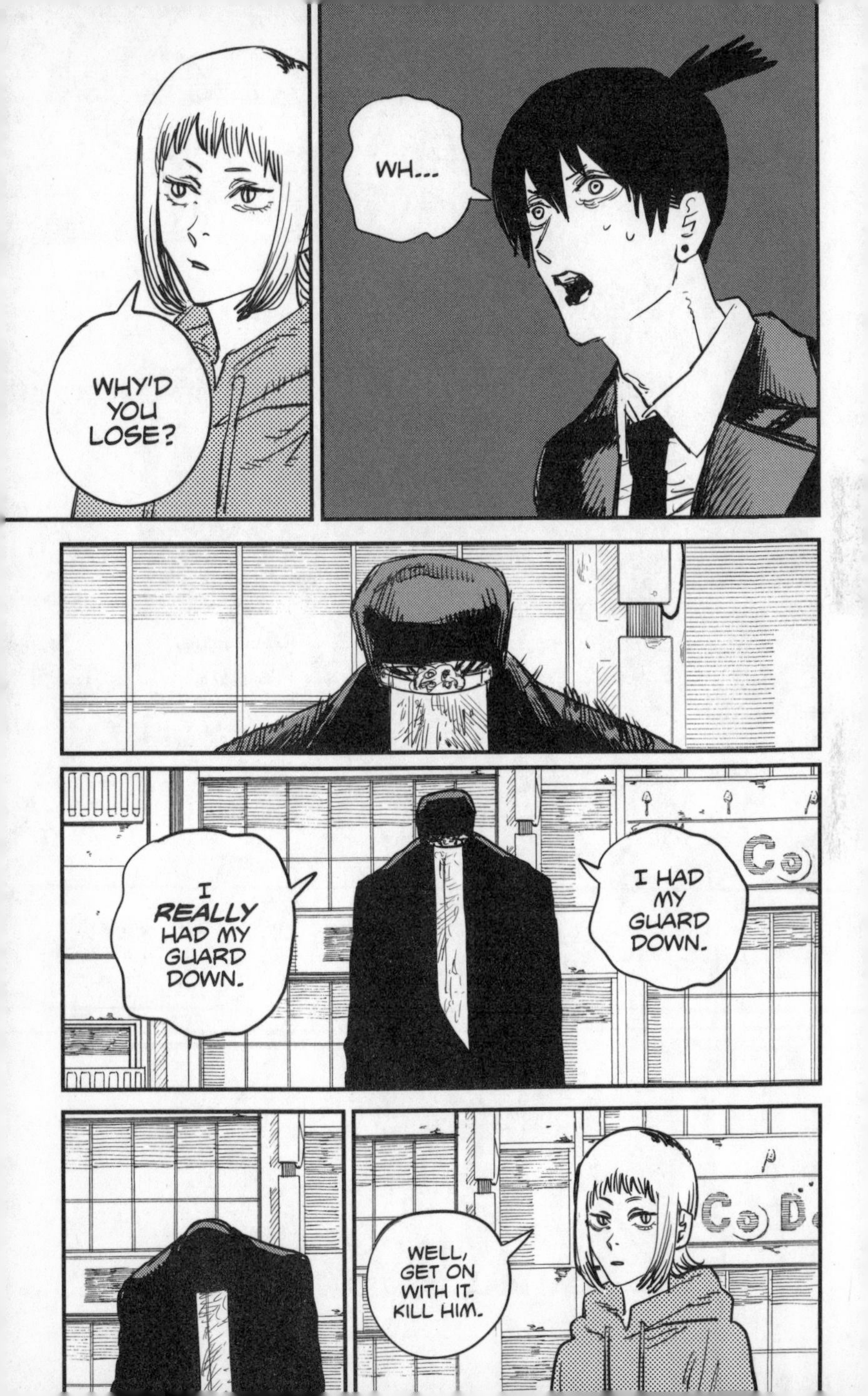
WH...
WHY'D YOU LOSE?
I HAD MY GUARD DOWN.
I REALLY HAD MY GUARD DOWN.
WELL, GET ON WITH IT. KILL HIM.

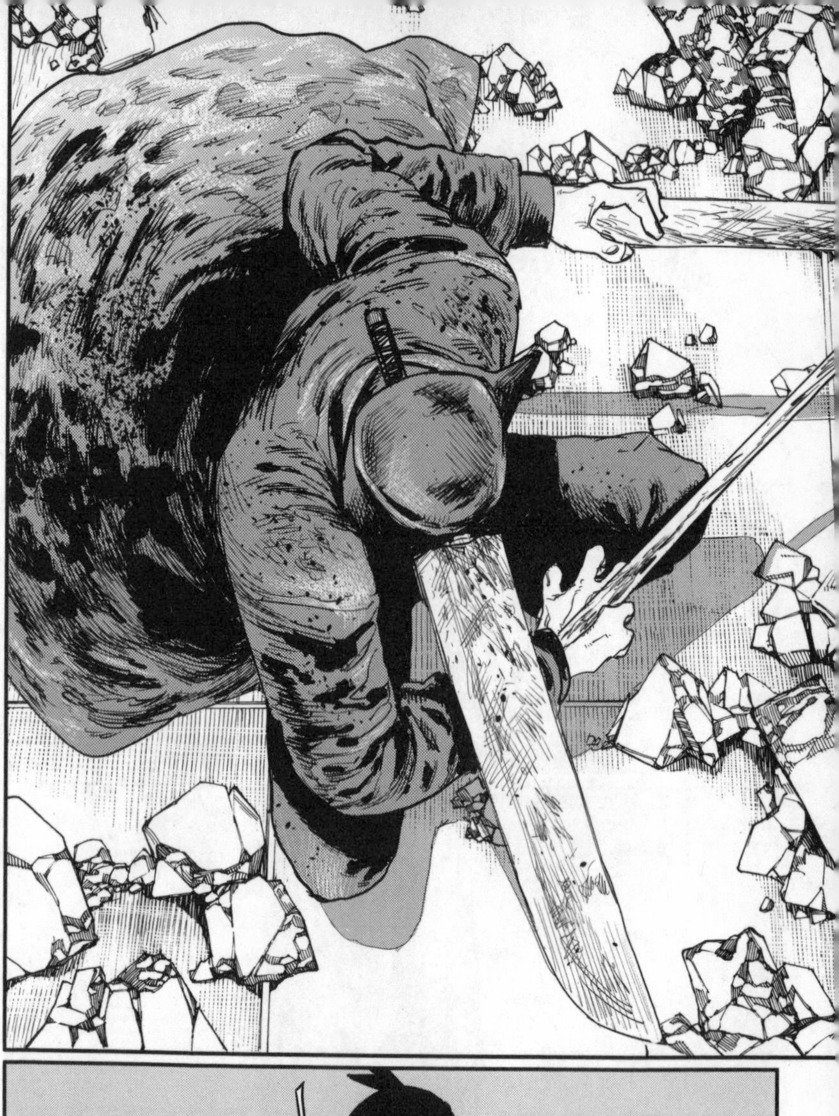
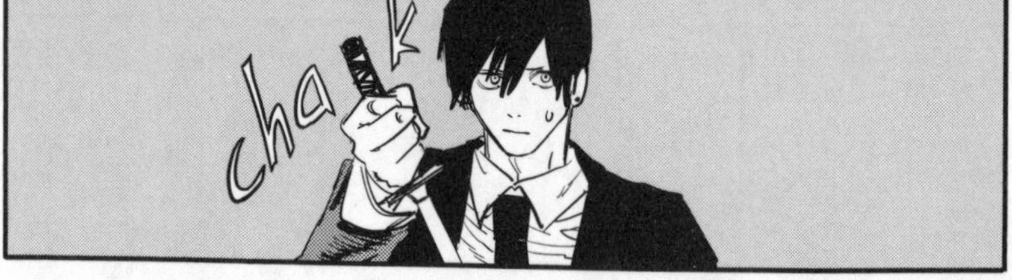
chak

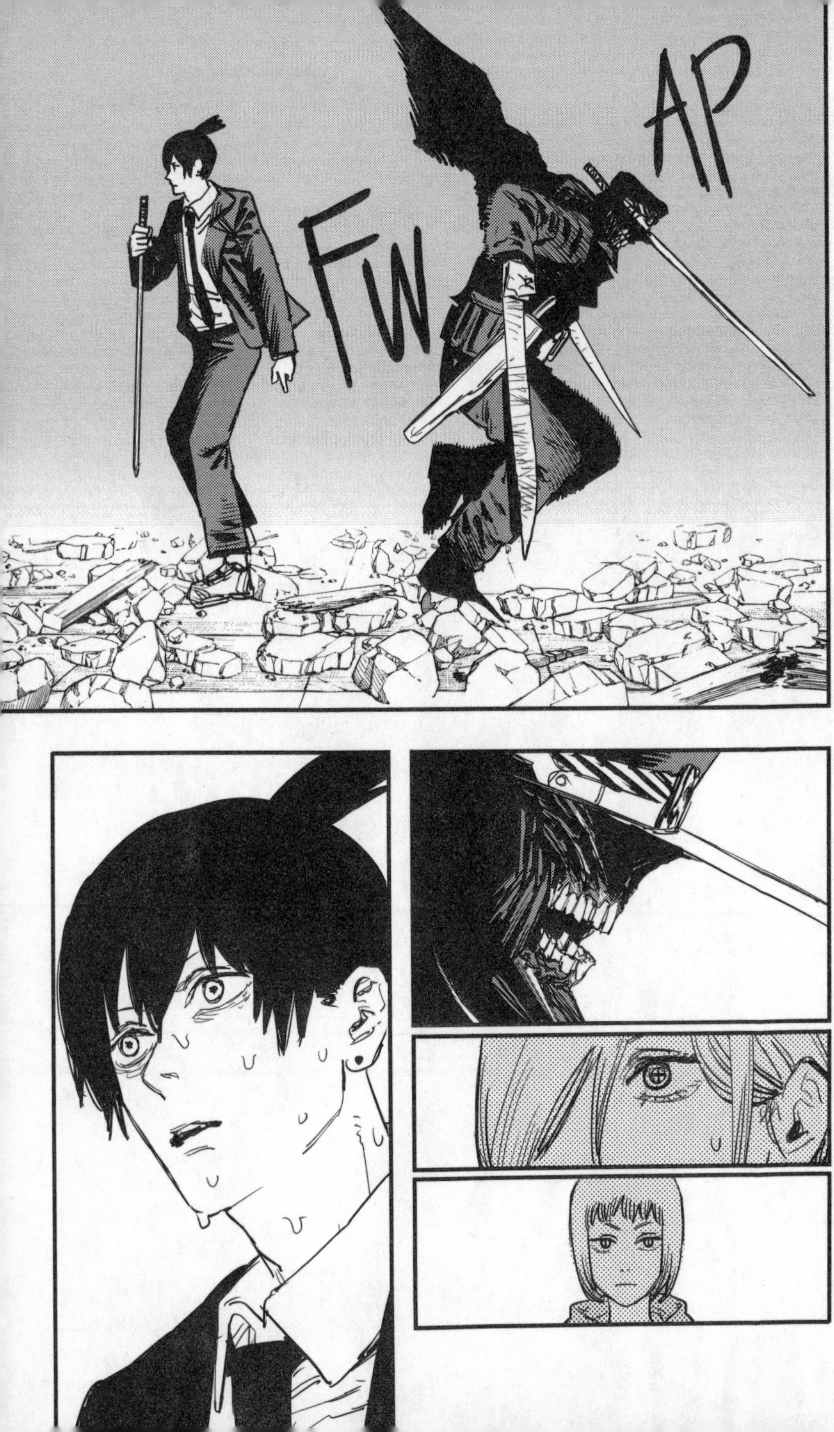
FWAP

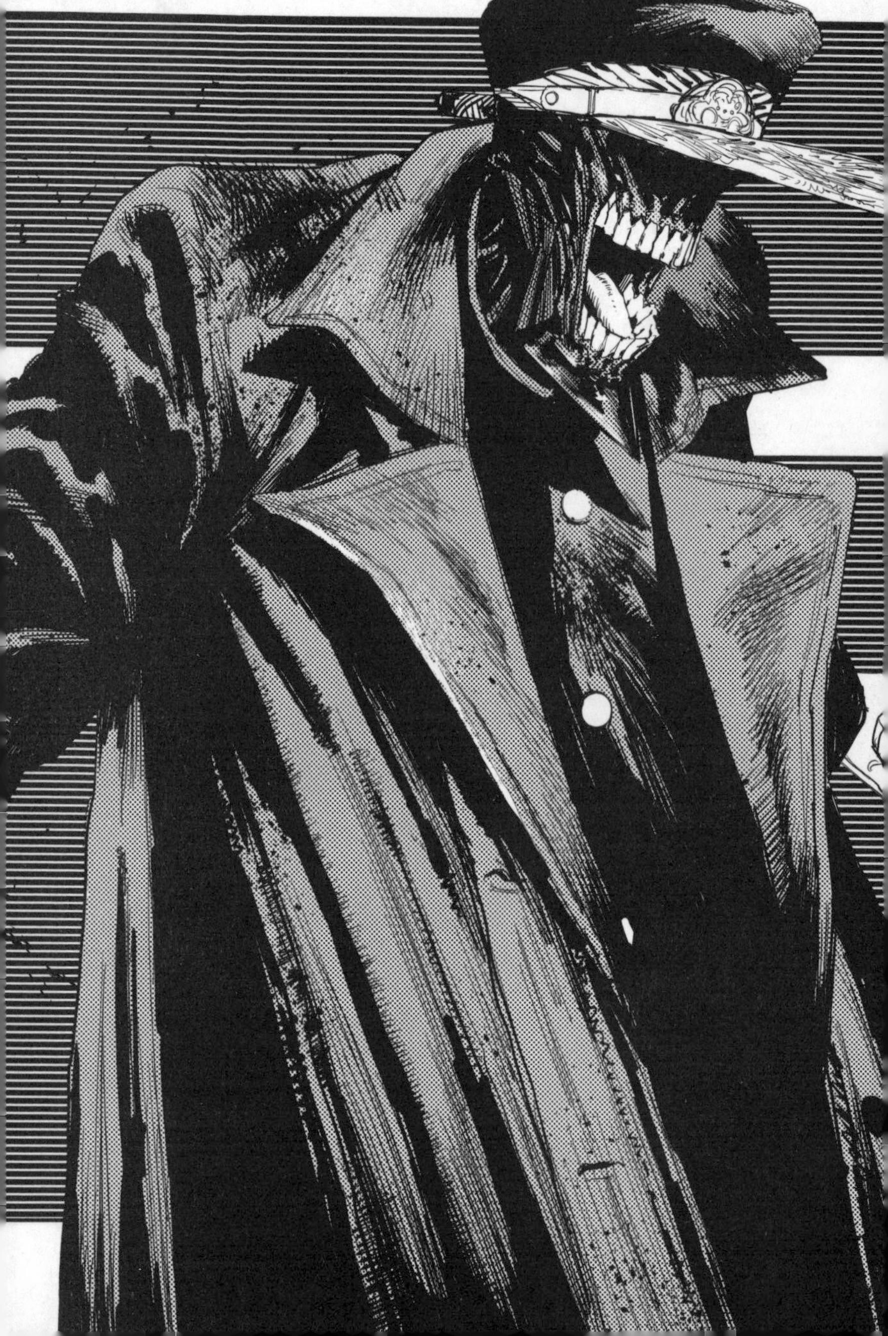

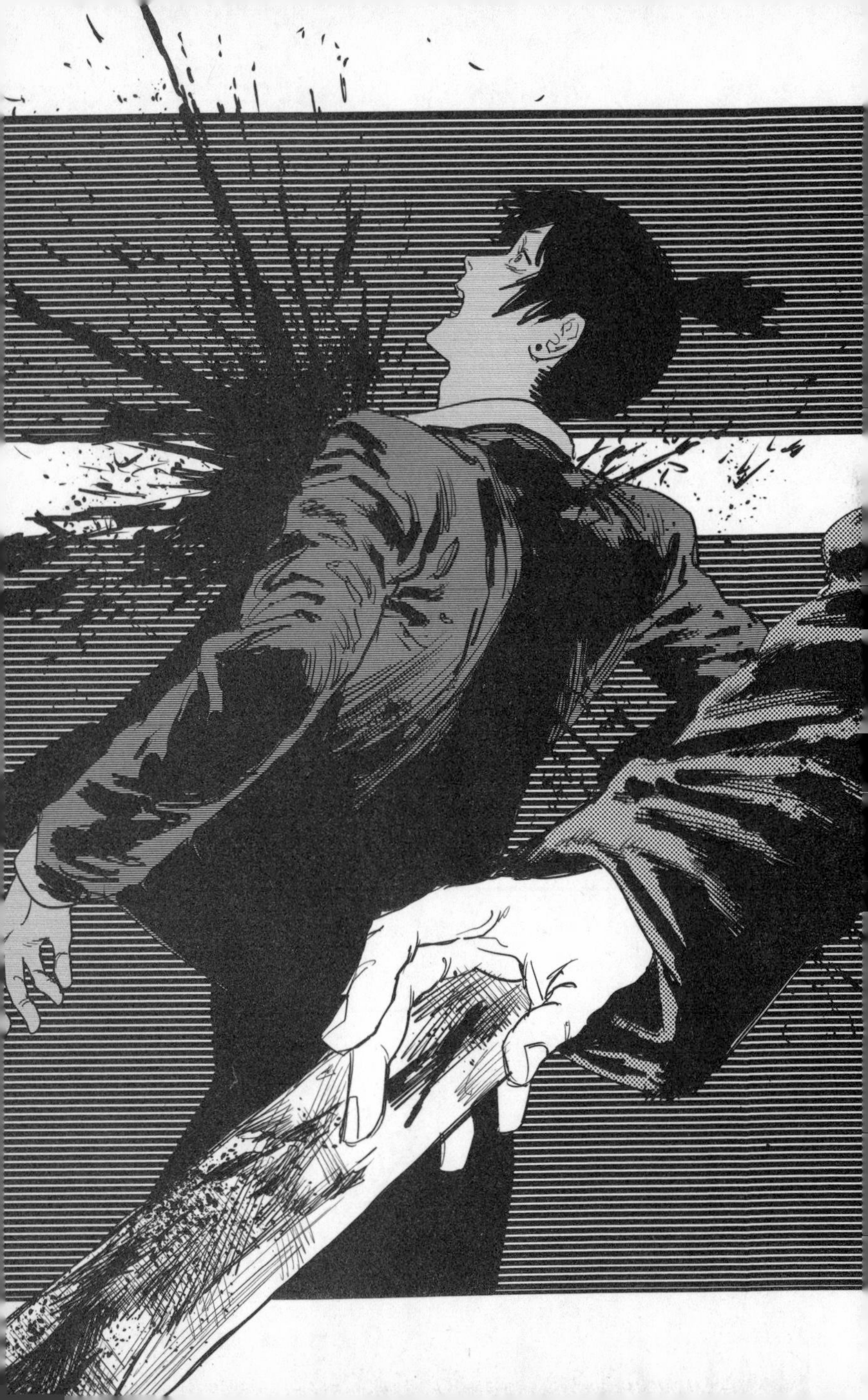

Chain saw man

Chapter 25: Ghost, Snake, Chainsaw

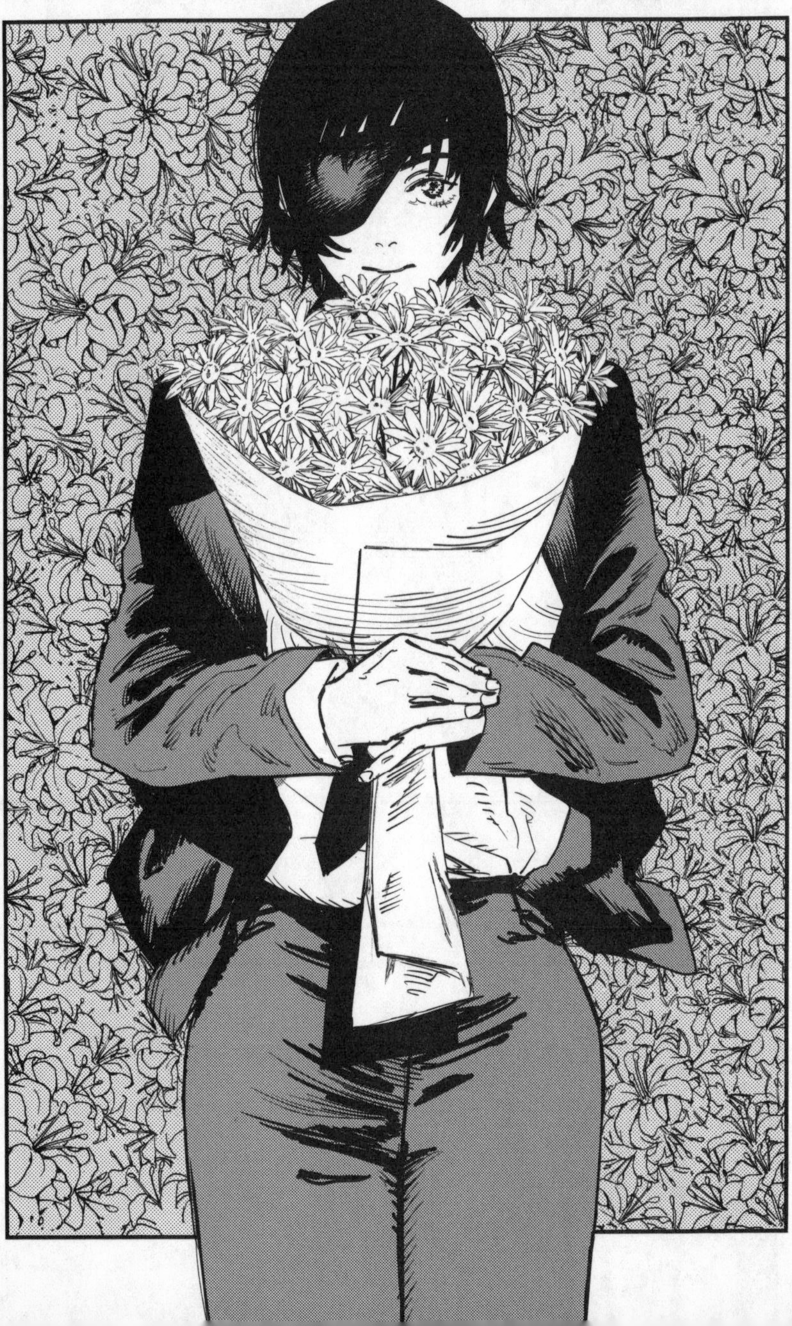

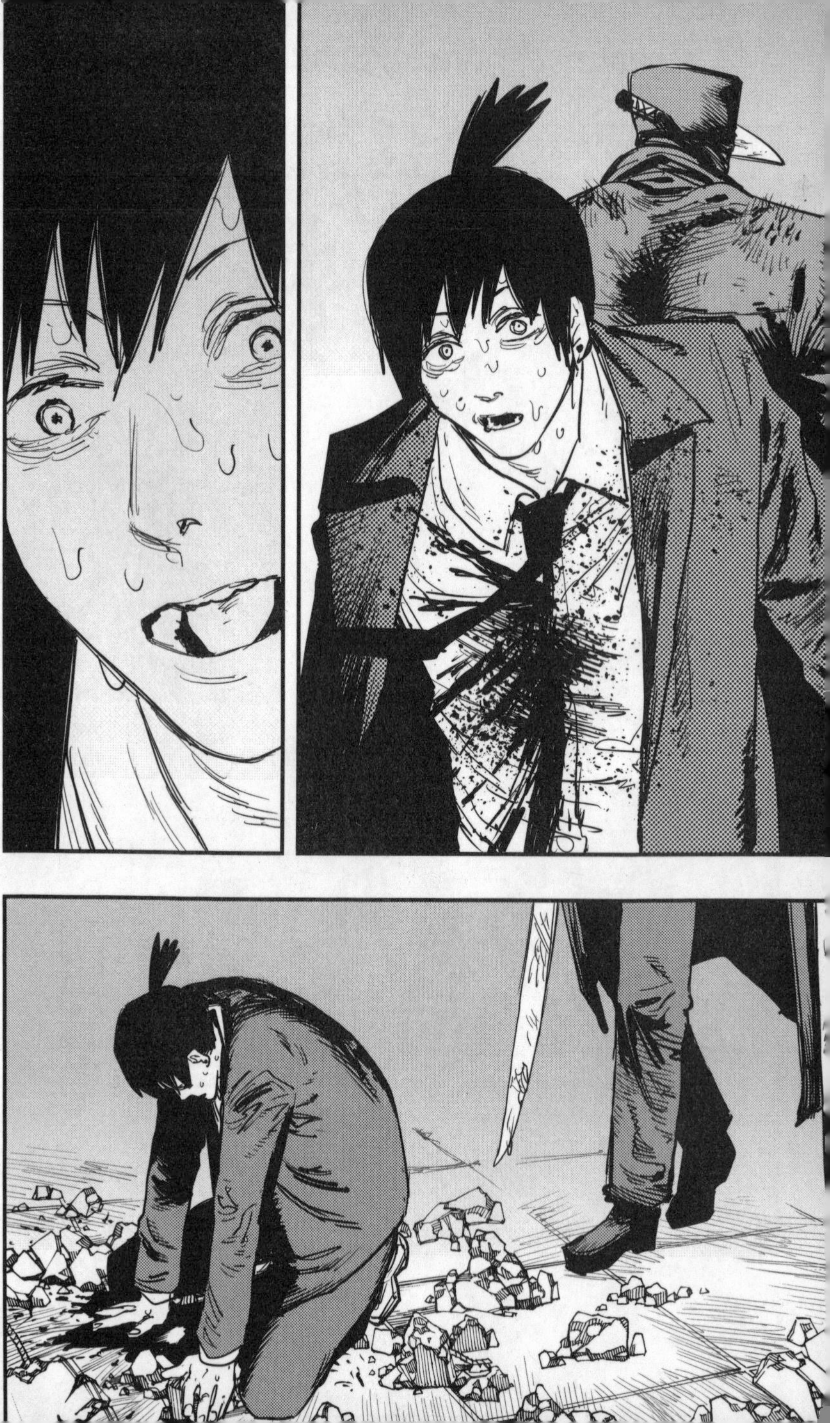

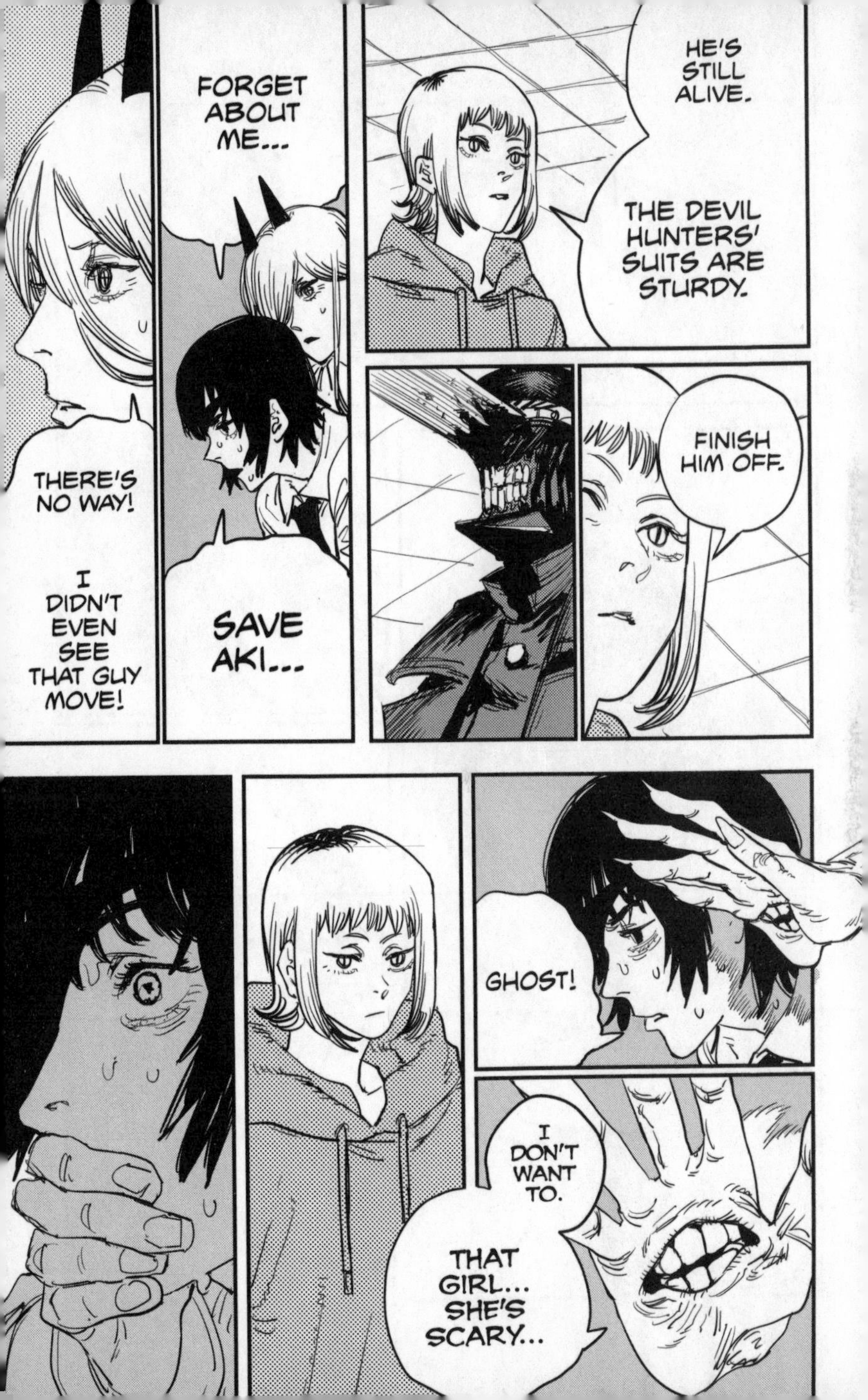
HE'S STILL ALIVE.
THE DEVIL HUNTERS' SUITS ARE STURDY.
FINISH HIM OFF.
FORGET ABOUT ME...
SAVE AKI...
THERE'S NO WAY!
I DIDN'T EVEN SEE THAT GUY MOVE!
GHOST!
I DON'T WANT TO.
THAT GIRL... SHE'S SCARY...

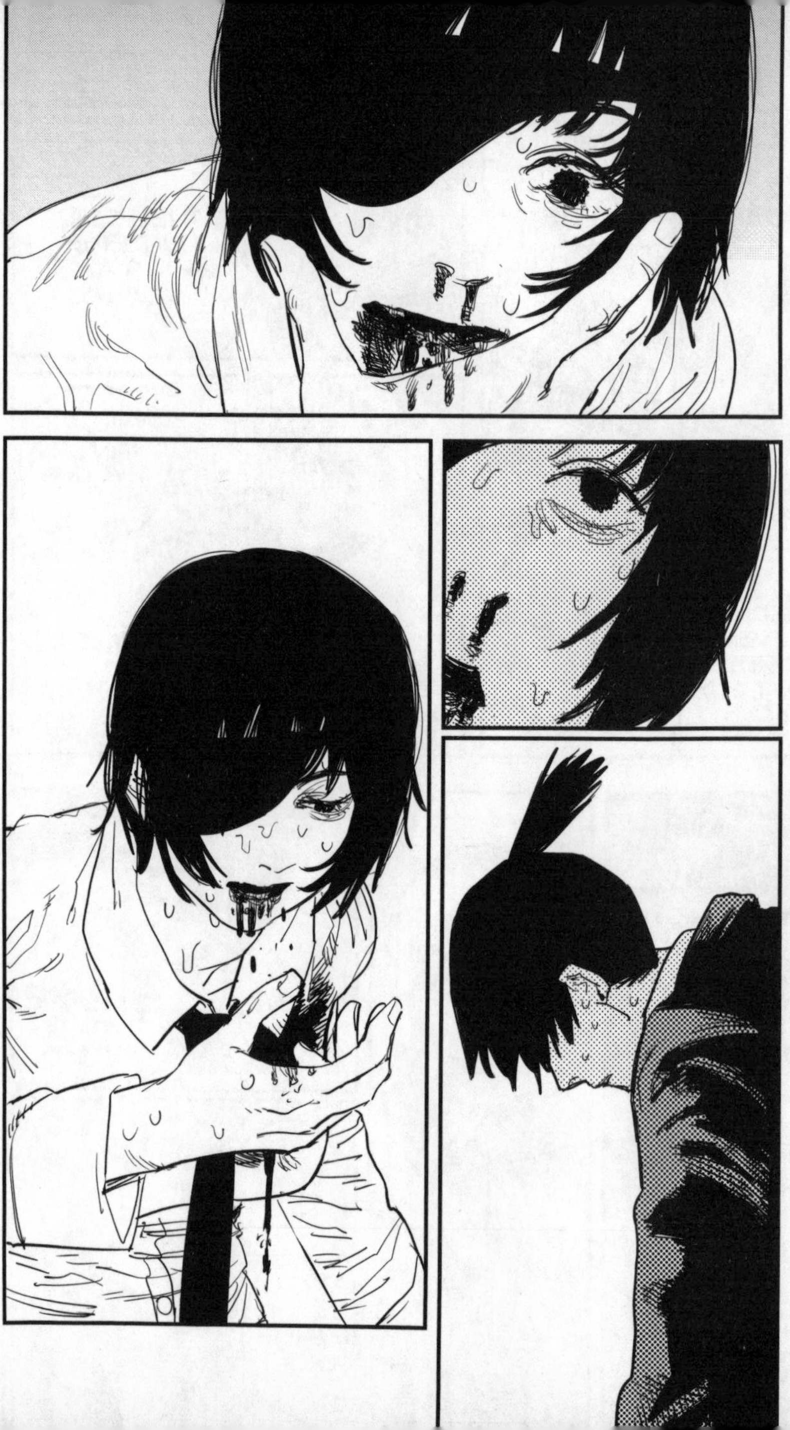

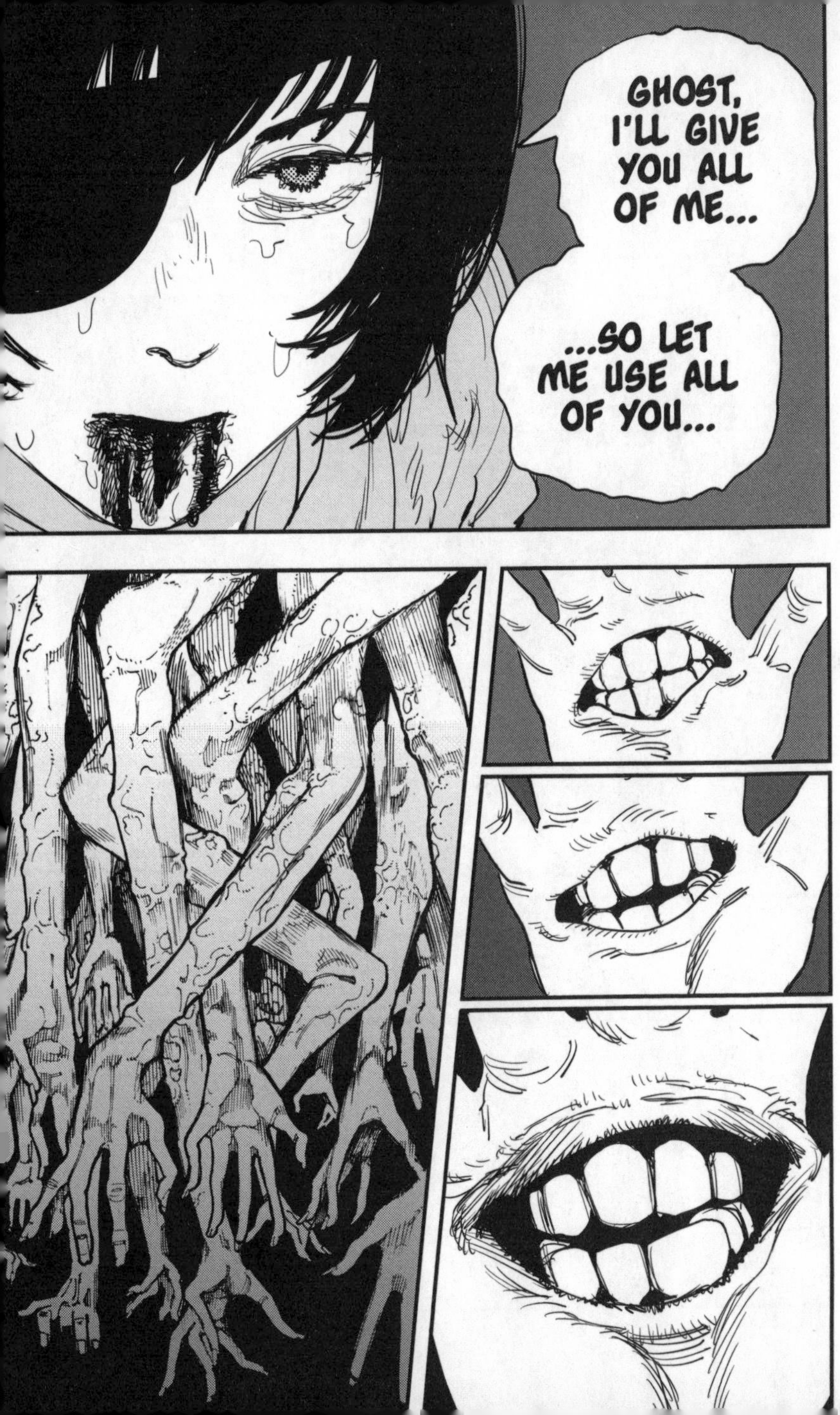
GHOST, I'LL GIVE YOU ALL OF ME...
...SO LET ME USE ALL OF YOU...

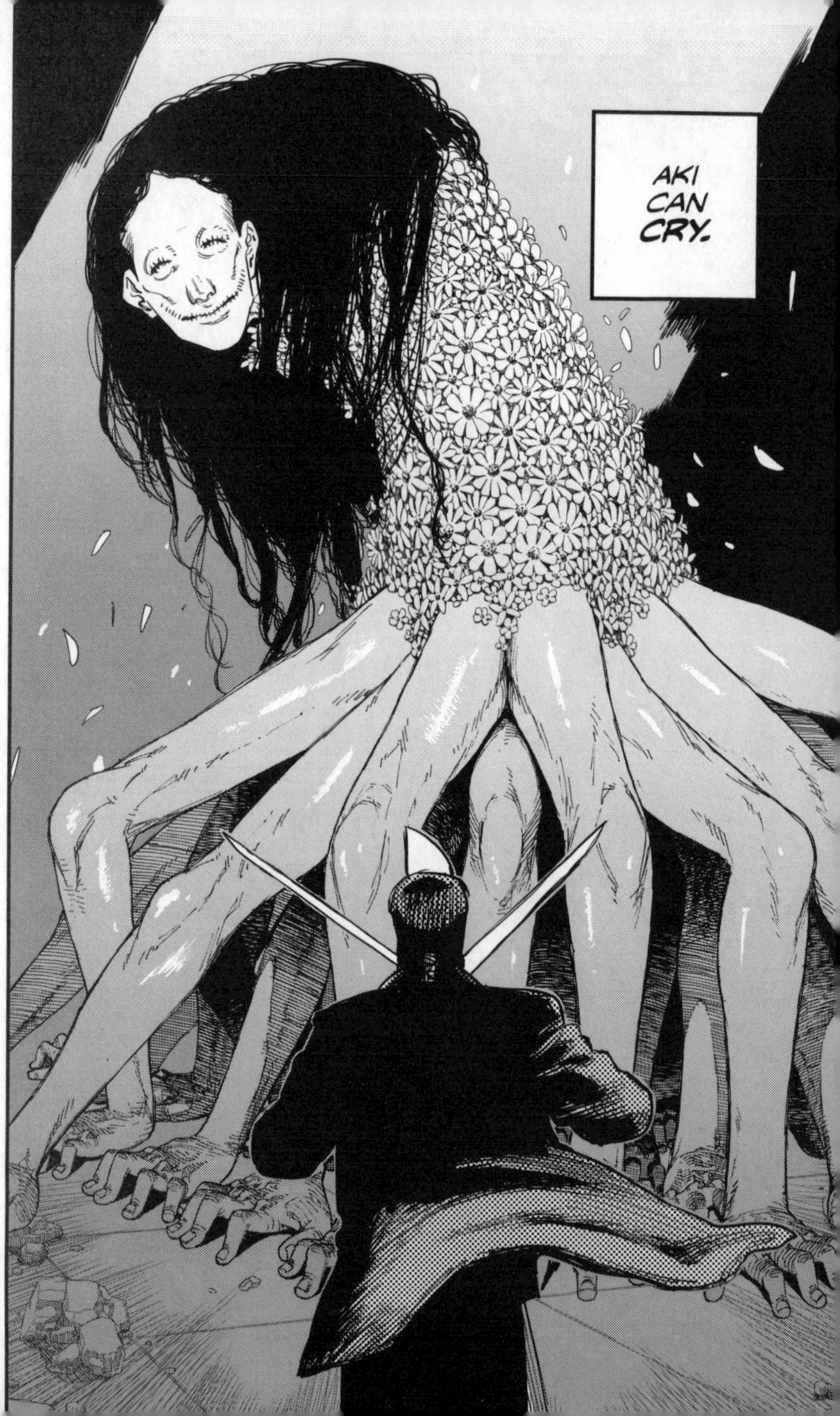
AKI CAN CRY.

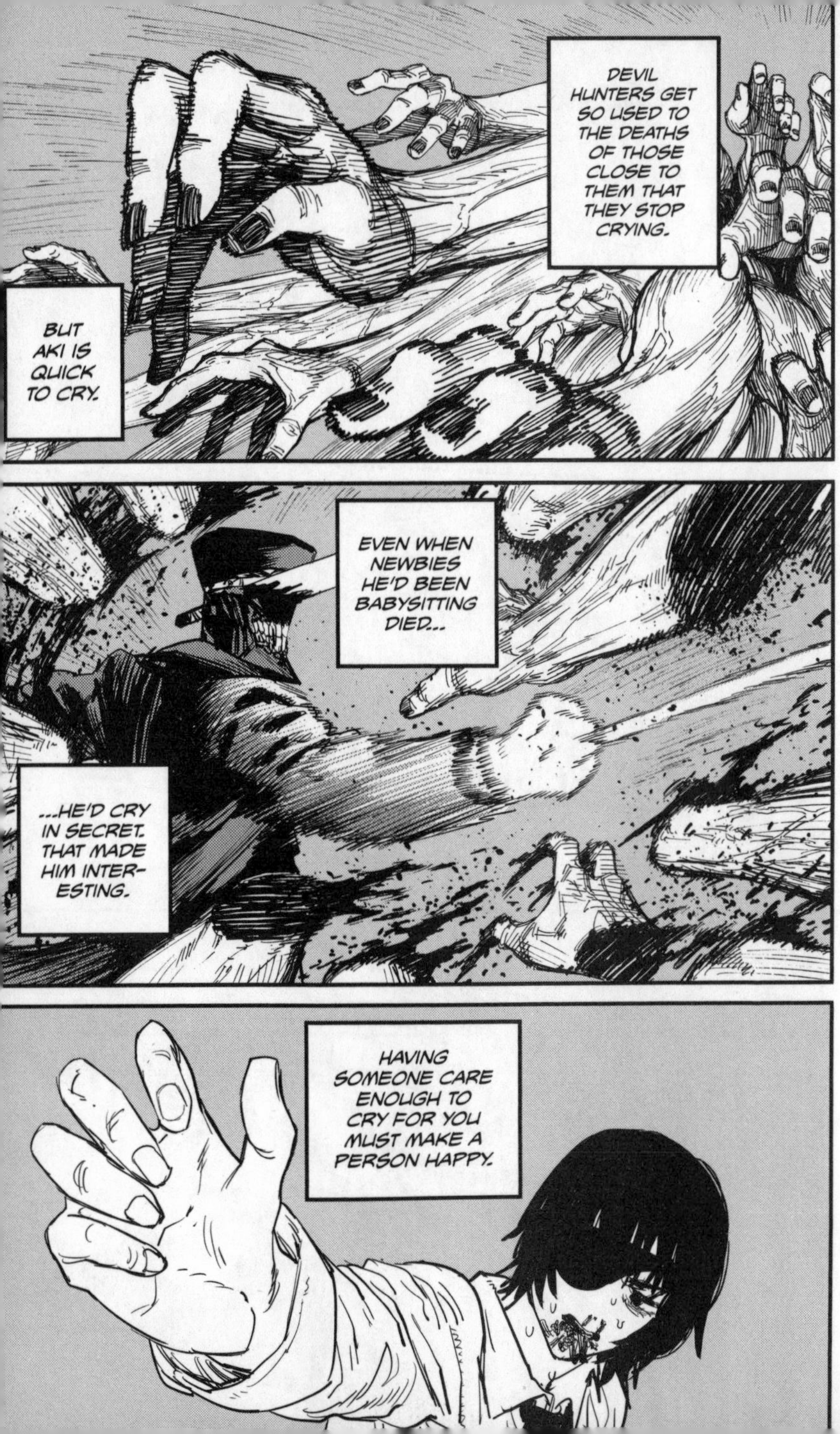
DEVIL HUNTERS GET SO USED TO THE DEATHS OF THOSE CLOSE TO THEM THAT THEY STOP CRYING.
BUT AKI IS QUICK TO CRY.
EVEN WHEN NEWBIES HE'D BEEN BABYSITTING DIED...
...HE'D CRY IN SECRET. THAT MADE HIM INTER-ESTING.
HAVING SOMEONE CARE ENOUGH TO CRY FOR YOU MUST MAKE A PERSON HAPPY.

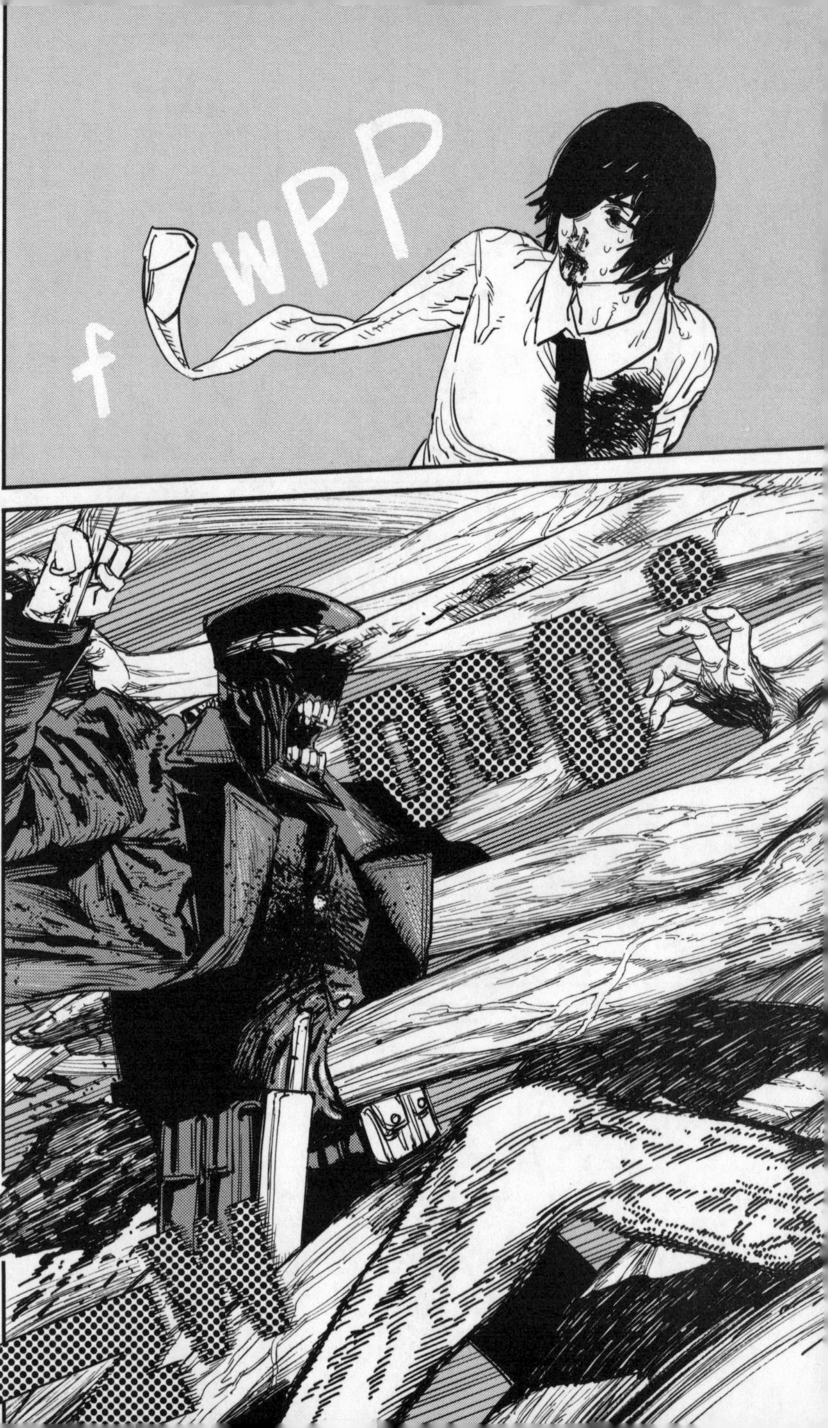
fwPP

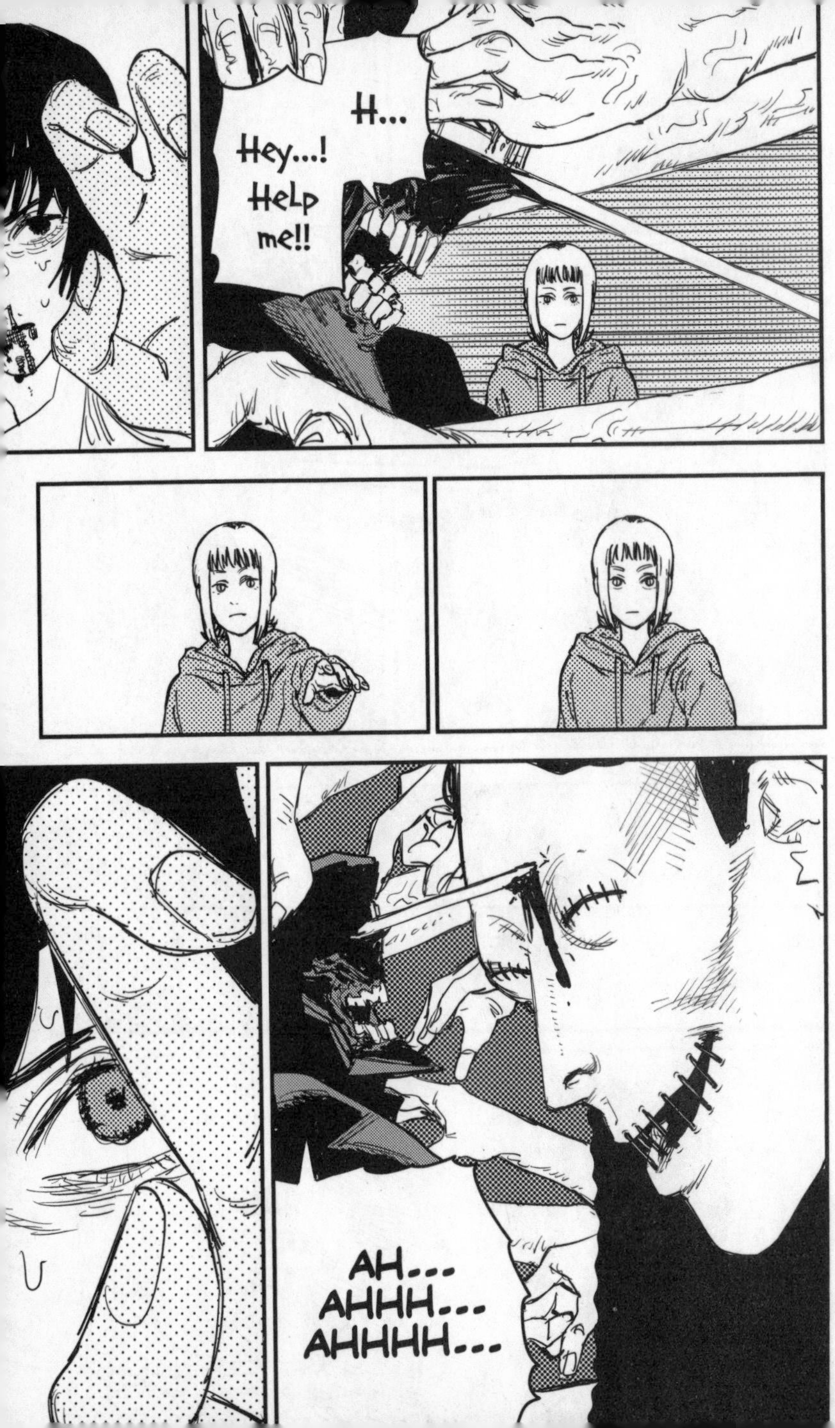
H...
Hey...! Help me!!
AH... AHHH... AHHHH...

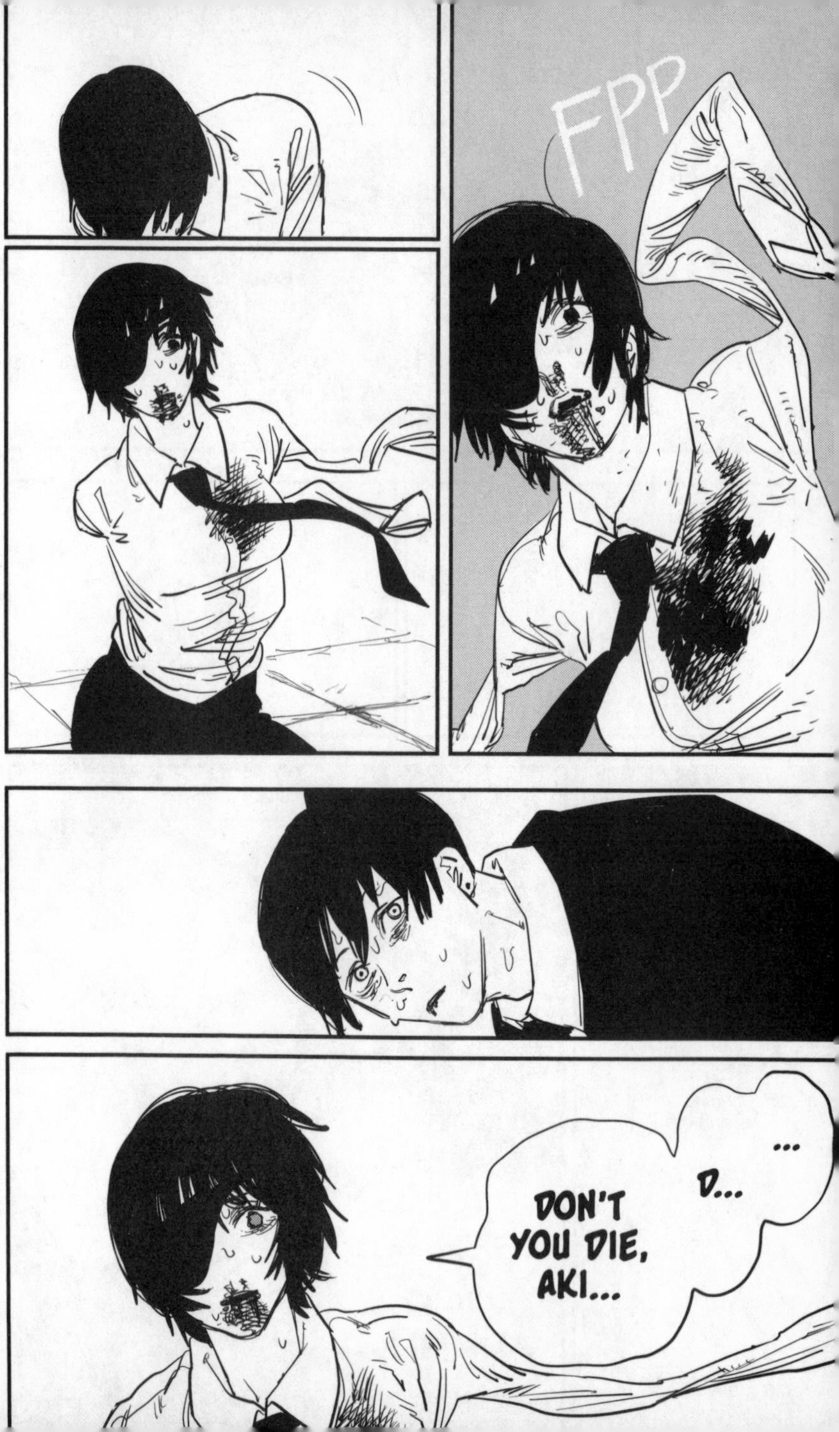
FPP
...
D...
DON'T YOU DIE, AKI...

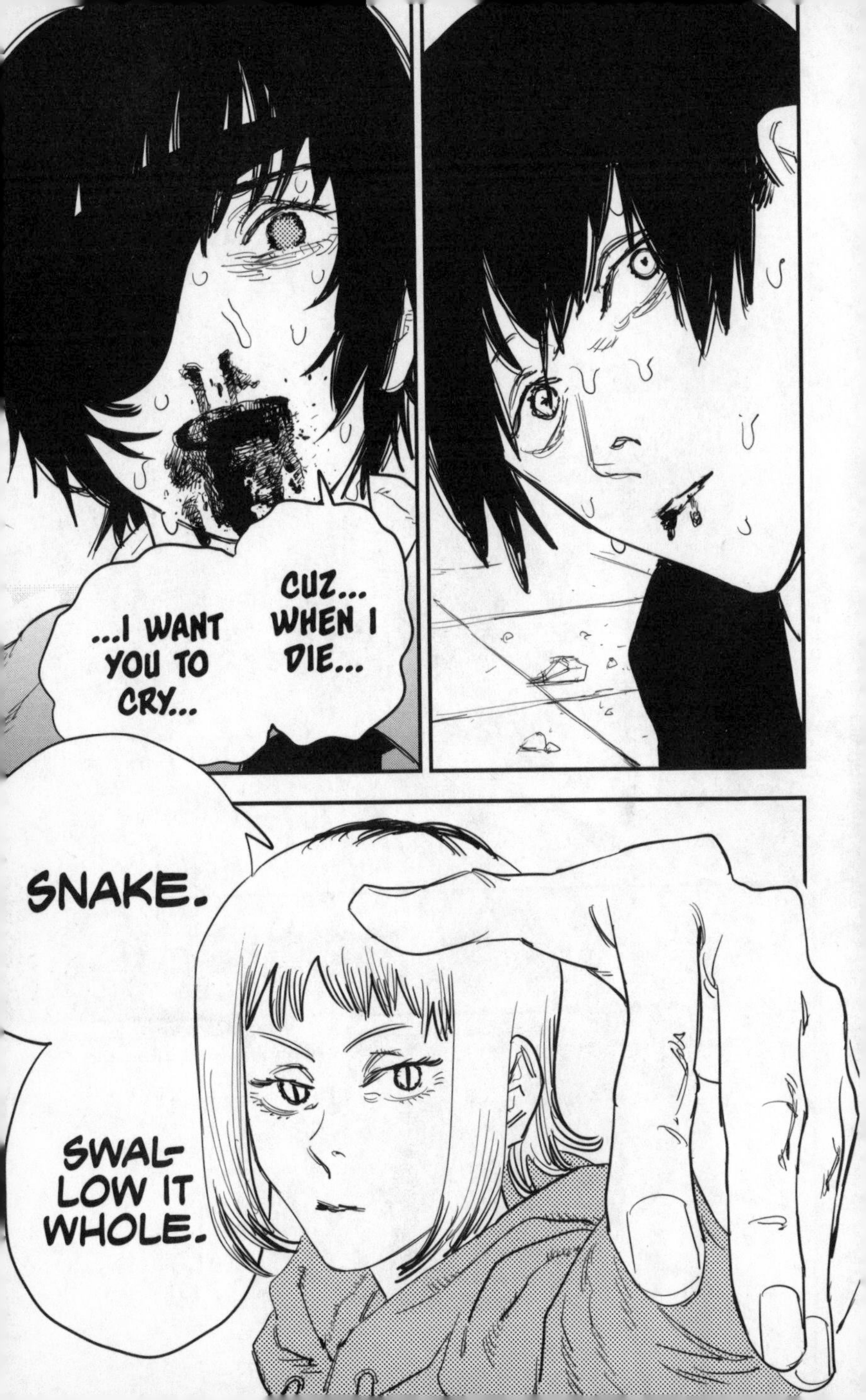
CUZ... WHEN I DIE...
...I WANT YOU TO CRY...
SNAKE.
SWAL-LOW IT WHOLE.

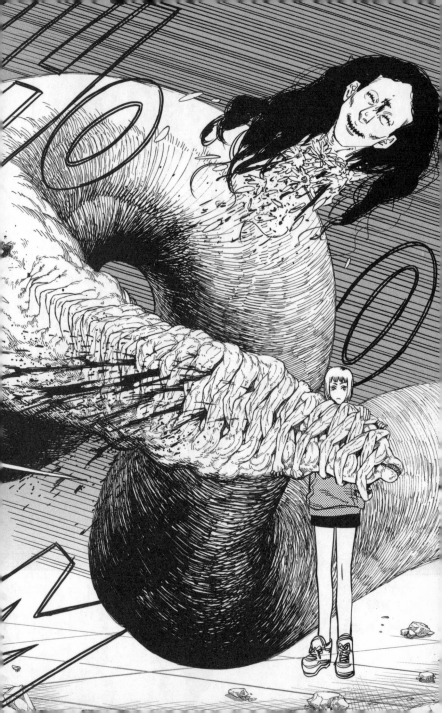

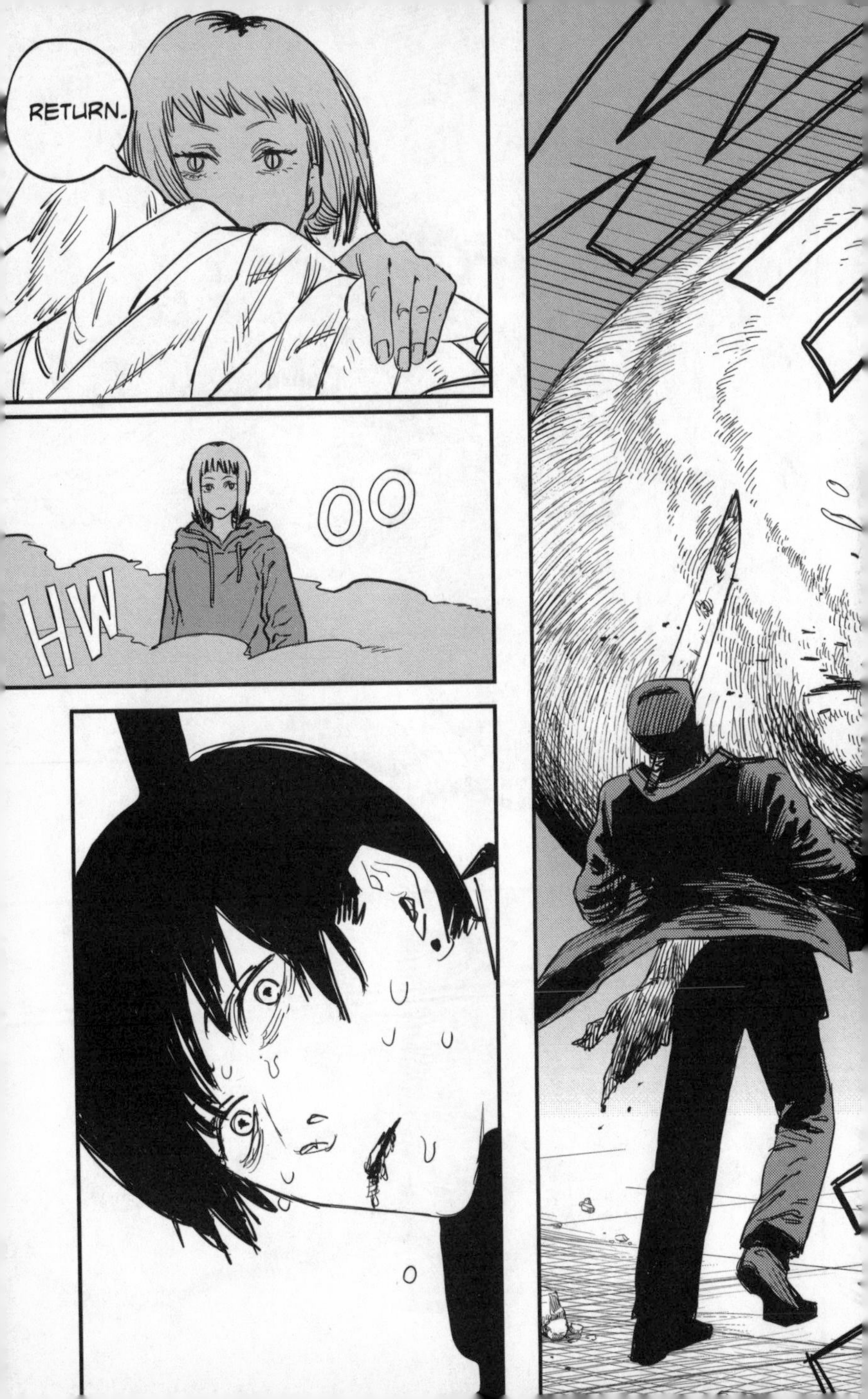
RETURN.
HWOO

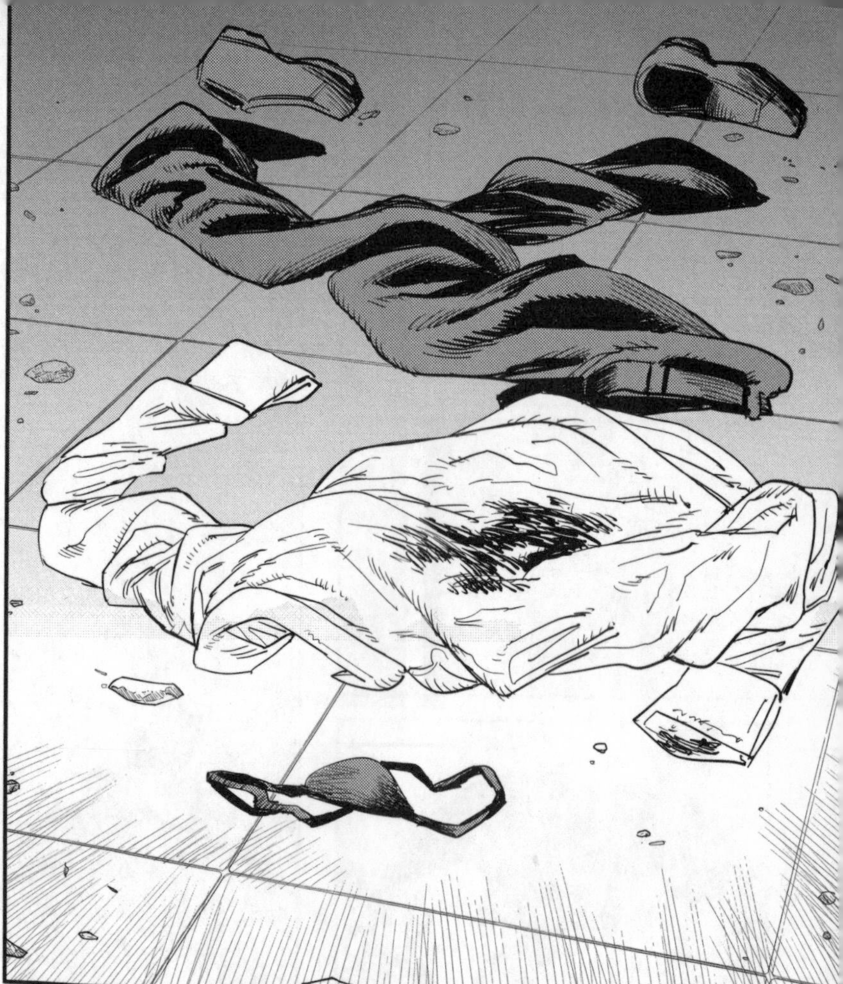
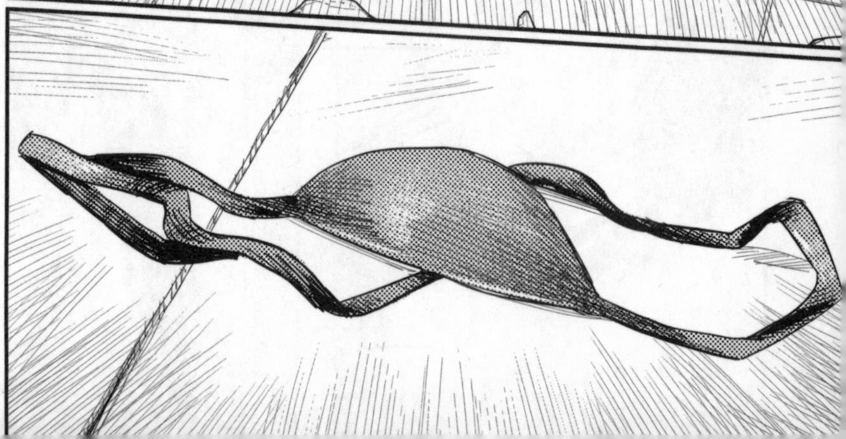

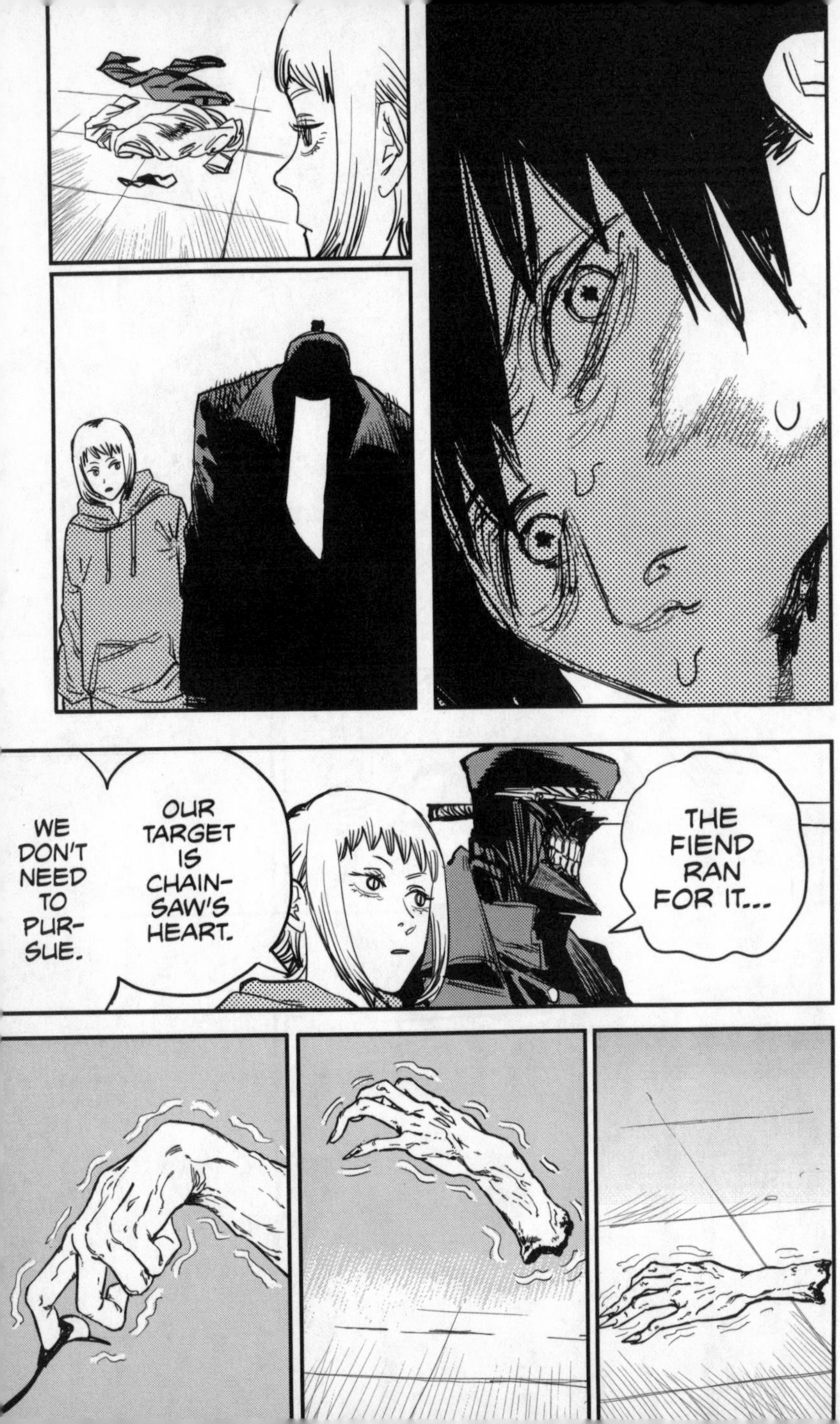
THE FIEND RAN FOR IT...
OUR TARGET IS CHAIN-SAW'S HEART.
WE DON'T NEED TO PUR-SUE.

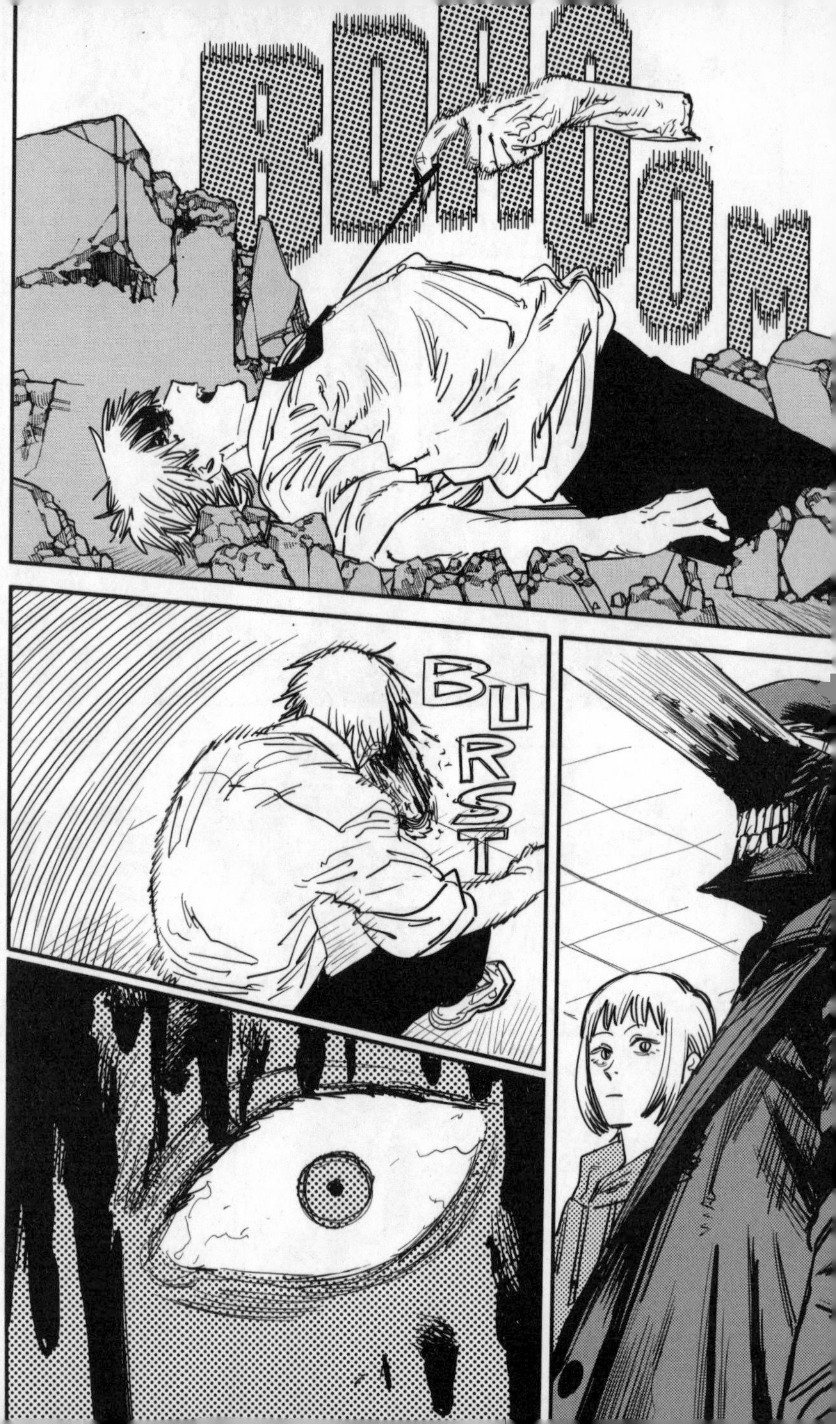
BOOOM
BURST

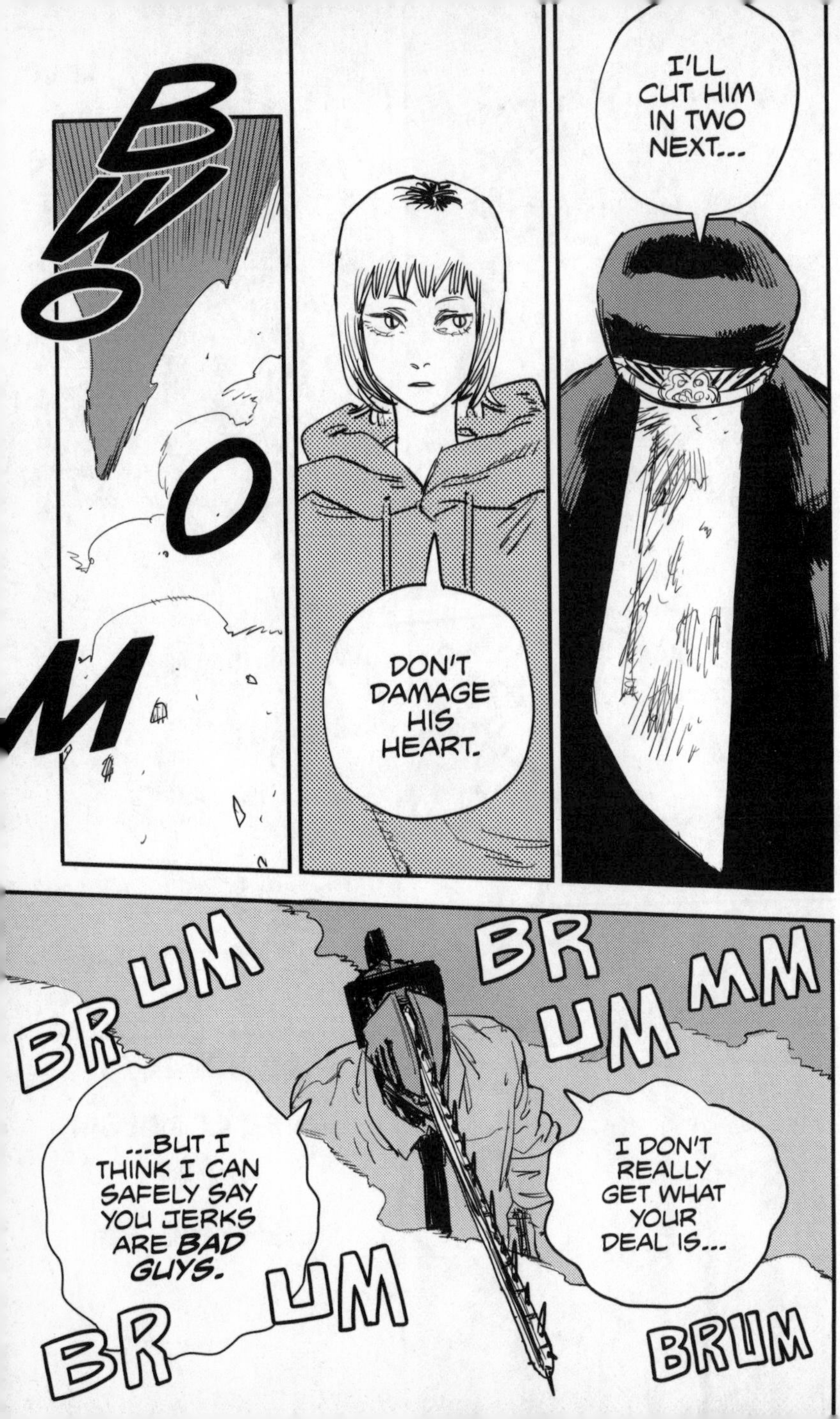
I'LL CUT HIM IN TWO NEXT...
DON'T DAMAGE HIS HEART.
BWOOM
BRUMMM
BRUM
I DON'T REALLY GET WHAT YOUR DEAL IS...
...BUT I THINK I CAN SAFELY SAY YOU JERKS ARE *BAD GUYS*.
BRUM
BRUM

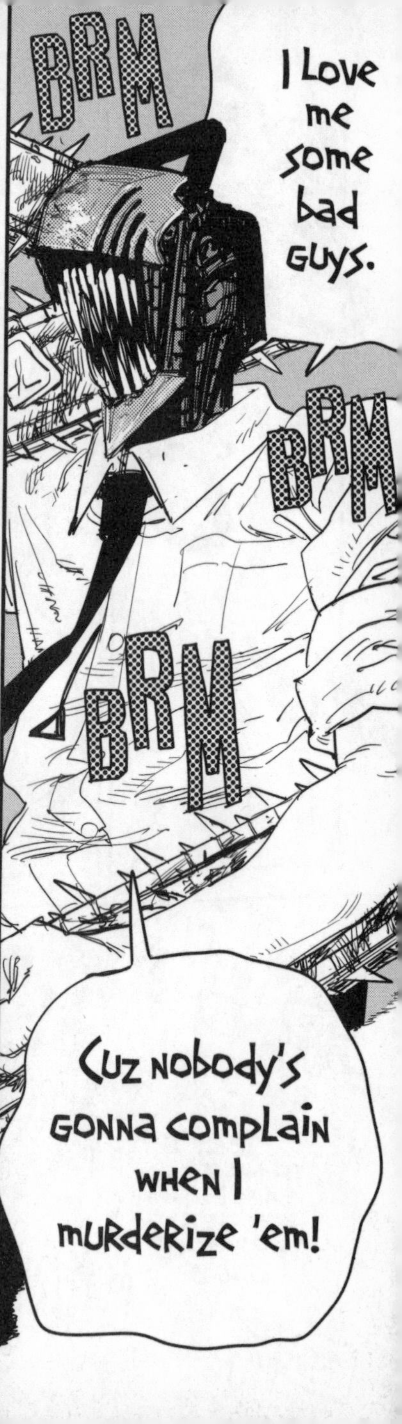
BRM
I Love me some bad guys.
BRM
BRM
Cuz nobody's gonna complain when I murderize 'em!

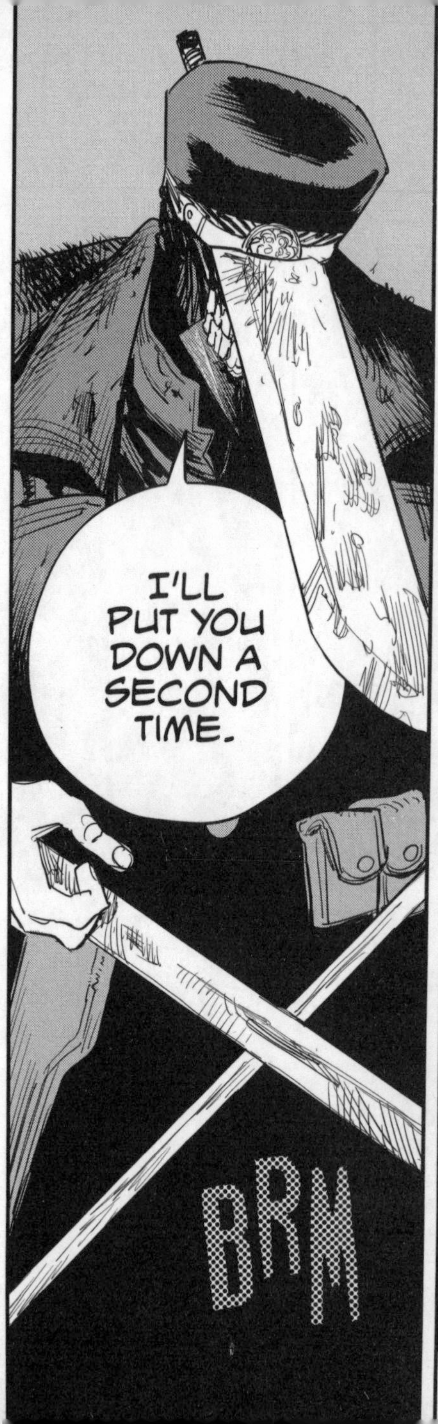
I'LL PUT YOU DOWN A SECOND TIME.
BRM

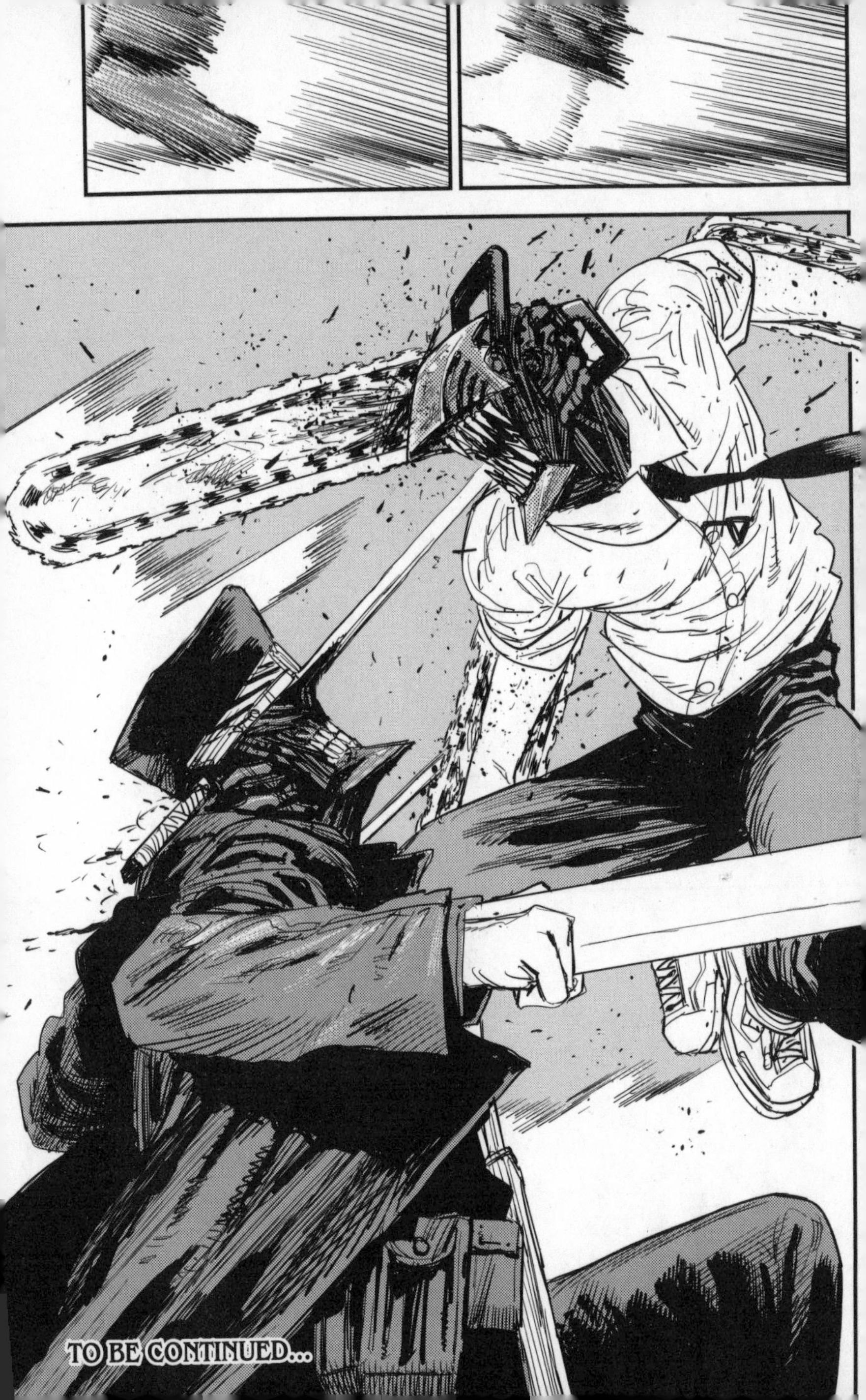
TO BE CONTINUED...

Chainsaw man

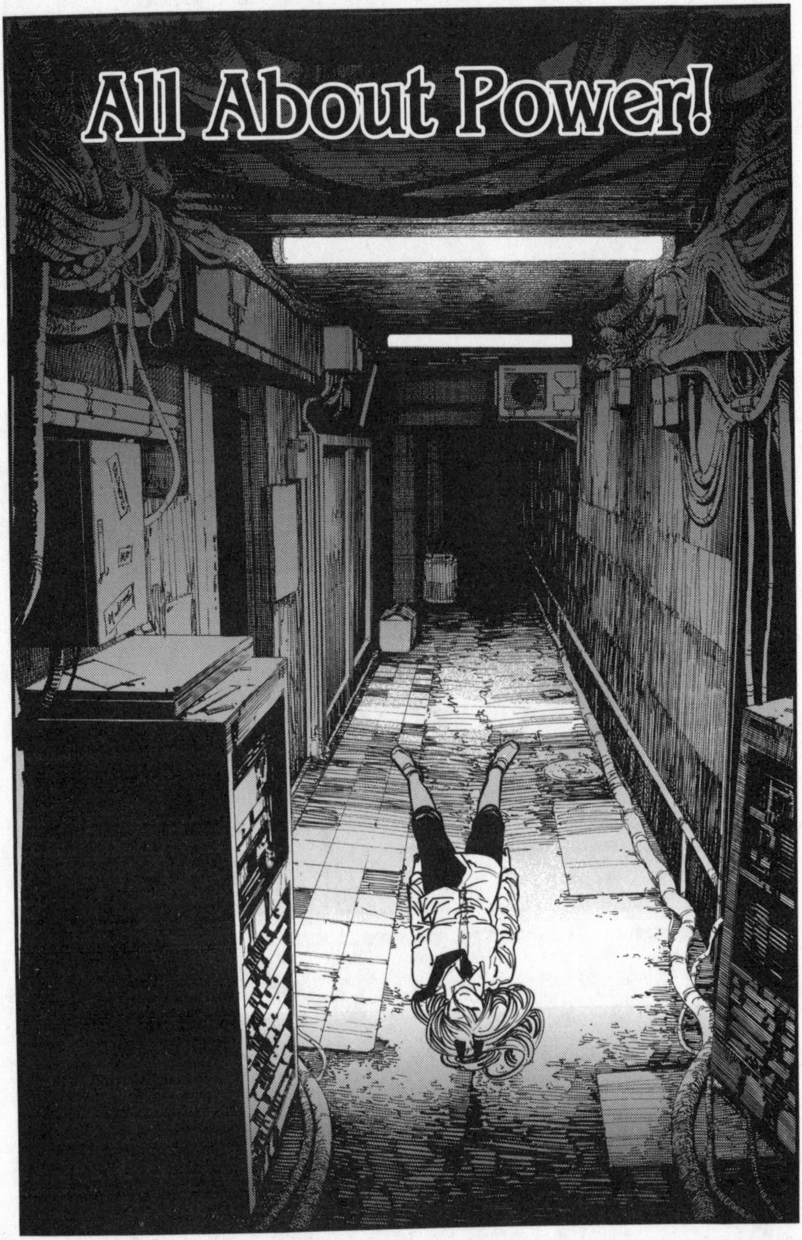
All About Power!

① She's a Pathological Liar!

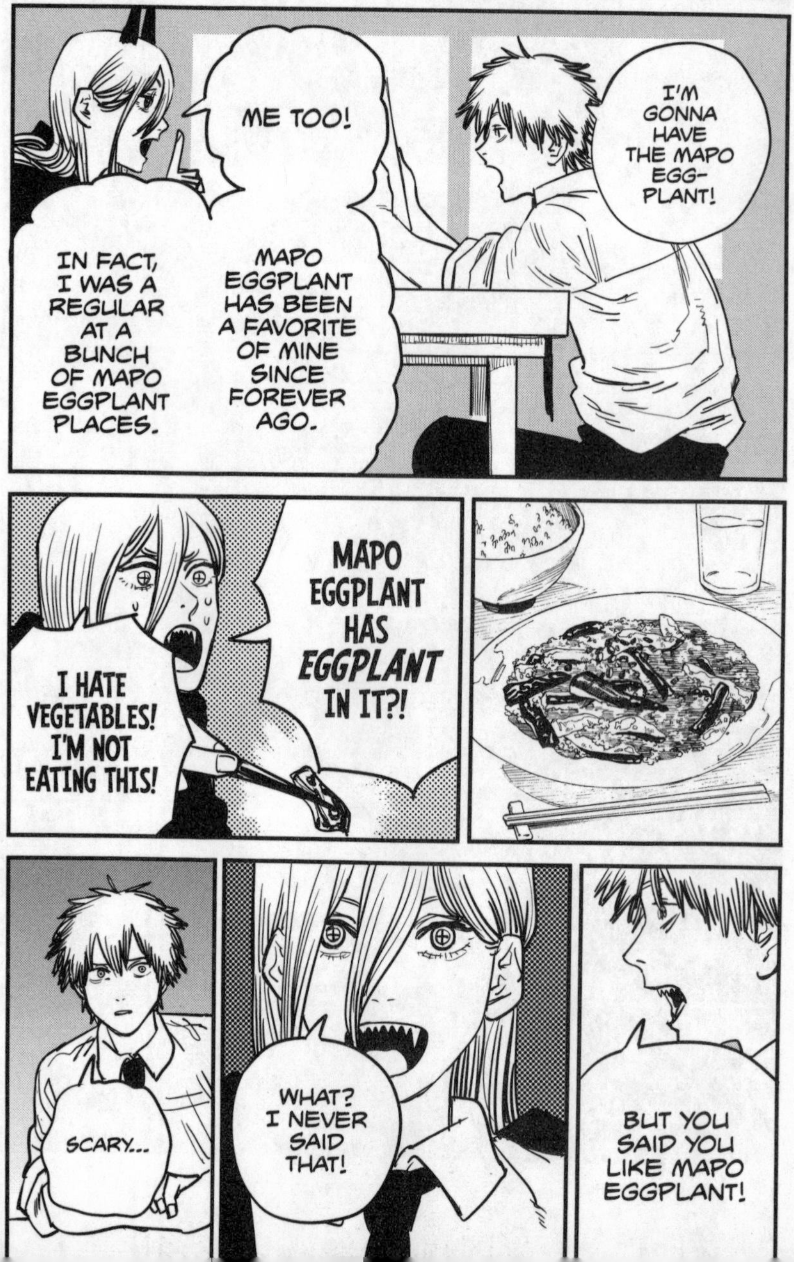
I'M GONNA HAVE THE MAPO EGG-PLANT!
ME TOO!
MAPO EGGPLANT HAS BEEN A FAVORITE OF MINE SINCE FOREVER AGO.
IN FACT, I WAS A REGULAR AT A BUNCH OF MAPO EGGPLANT PLACES.
MAPO EGGPLANT HAS *EGGPLANT* IN IT?!
I HATE VEGETABLES! I'M NOT EATING THIS!
BUT YOU SAID YOU LIKE MAPO EGGPLANT!
WHAT? I NEVER SAID THAT!
SCARY...

② She's a Show-Off!

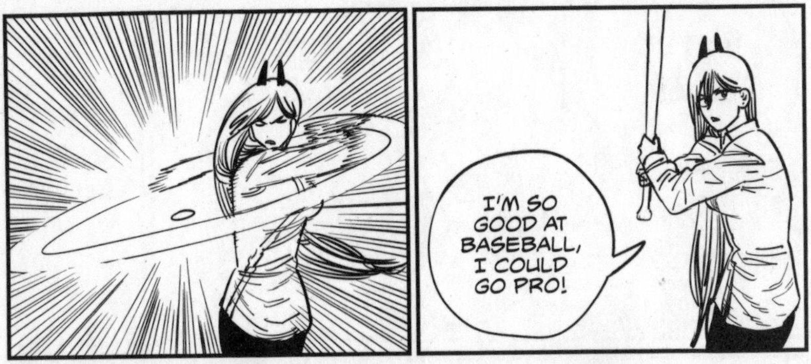
I'M SO GOOD AT BASEBALL, I COULD GO PRO!

③ But She's Actually a Scaredy-Cat!

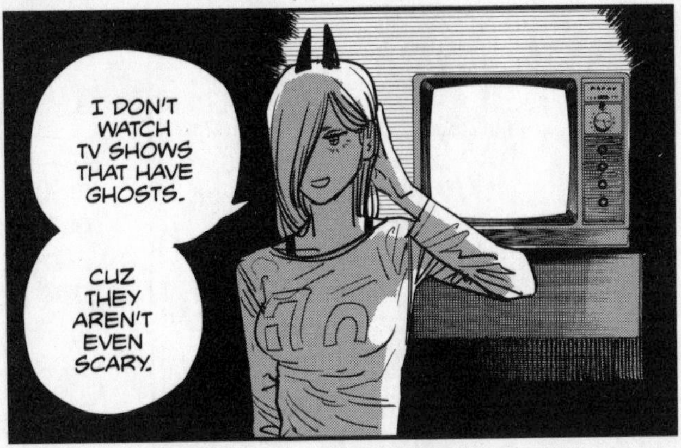
I DON'T WATCH TV SHOWS THAT HAVE GHOSTS.
CUZ THEY AREN'T EVEN SCARY.

④ She'll Use Your Loyalty Cards Without Asking!

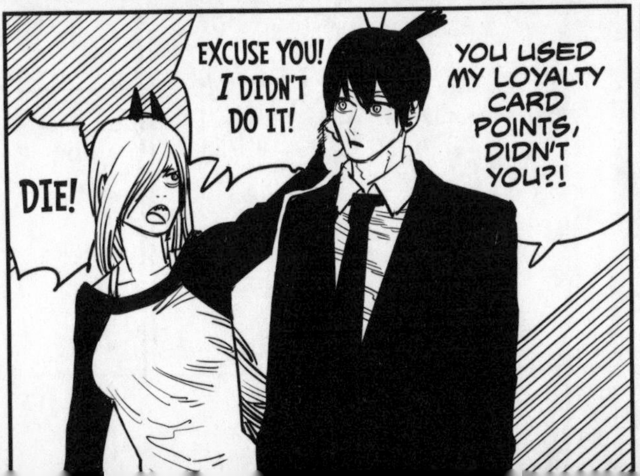
YOU USED MY LOYALTY CARD POINTS, DIDN'T YOU?!
EXCUSE YOU! I DIDN'T DO IT!
DIE!

⑤
She's a Racist!

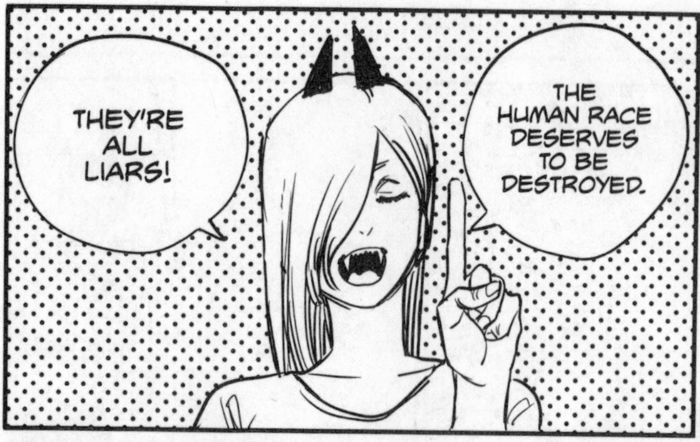
THE HUMAN RACE DESERVES TO BE DESTROYED.
THEY'RE ALL LIARS!

⑥
She'll Drink Your Blood on the Sly!

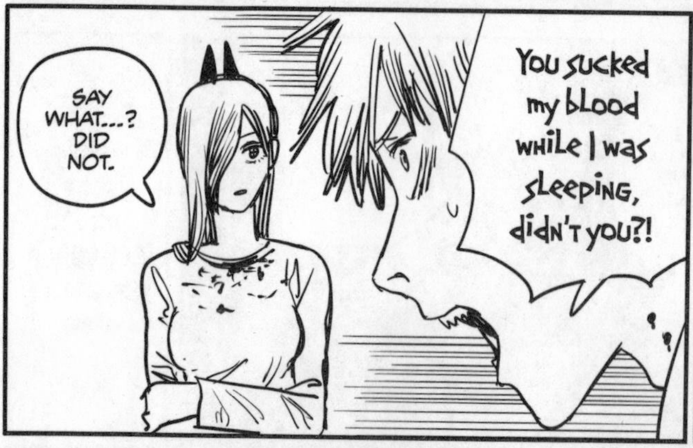
You sucked my blood while I was sleeping, didn't you?!
SAY WHAT...? DID NOT.

⑦
She Loves to Kill Bugs!

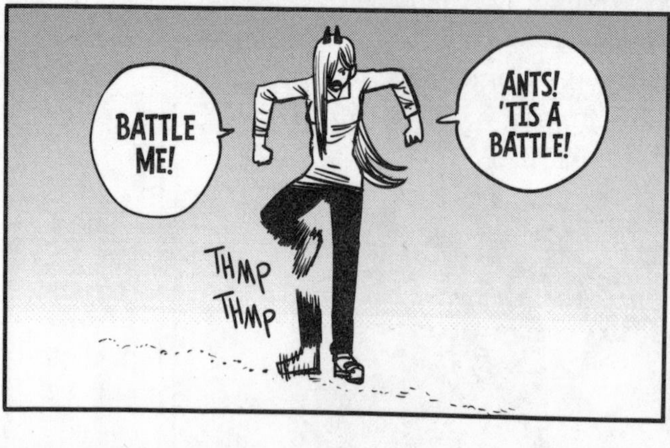
ANTS! 'TIS A BATTLE!
BATTLE ME!
THMP THMP

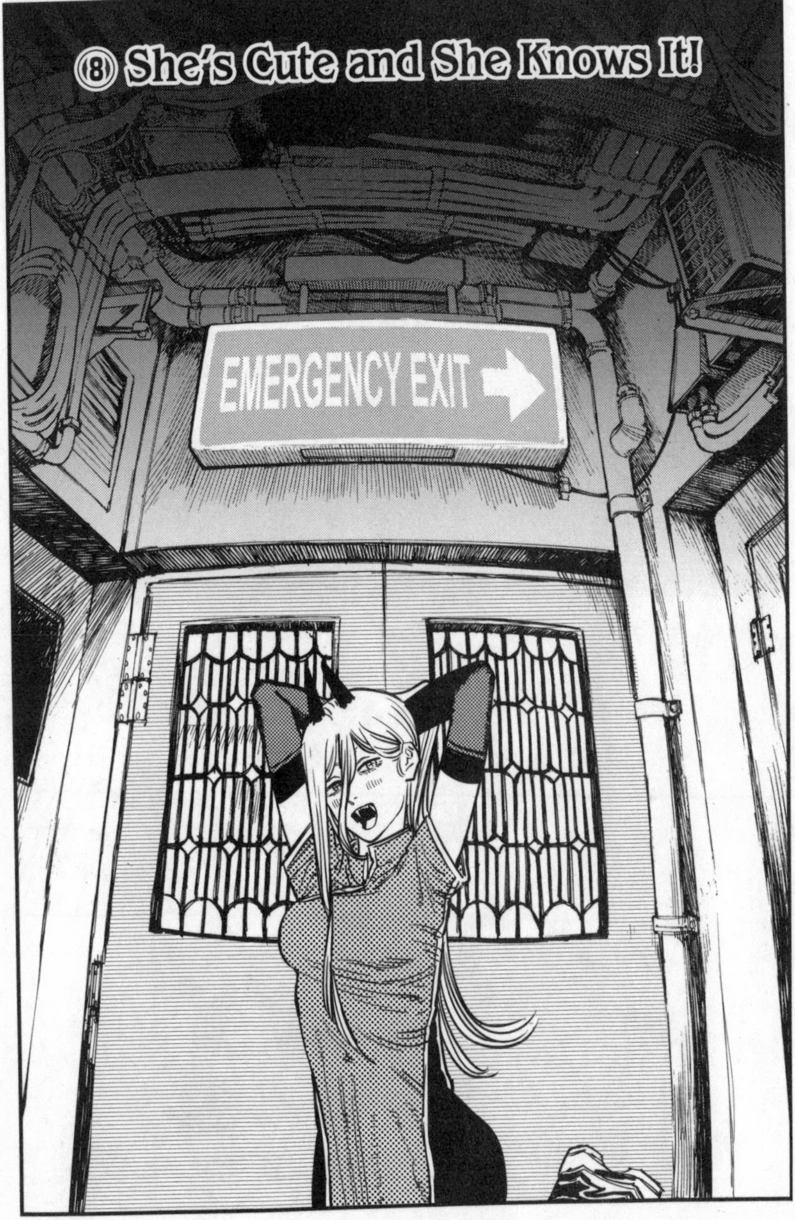

⑱ She's Cute and She Knows It!
EMERGENCY EXIT

YOU'RE READING THE WRONG WAY!

CHAINSAW MAN

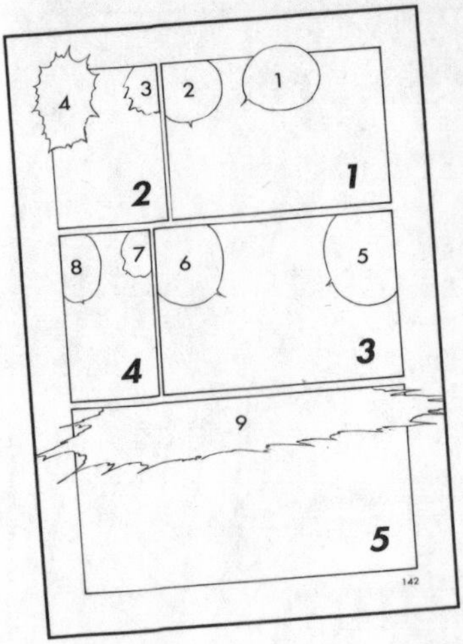

1
1
2
3
4
2
5
6
7
8
3
4
9
5
142

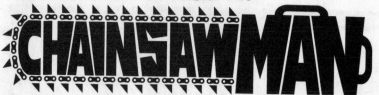

Chainsaw Man reads from right to left, starting in the upper-right corner. Japanese is read from right to left, meaning that action, sound effects and word-balloon order are completely reversed from English order.

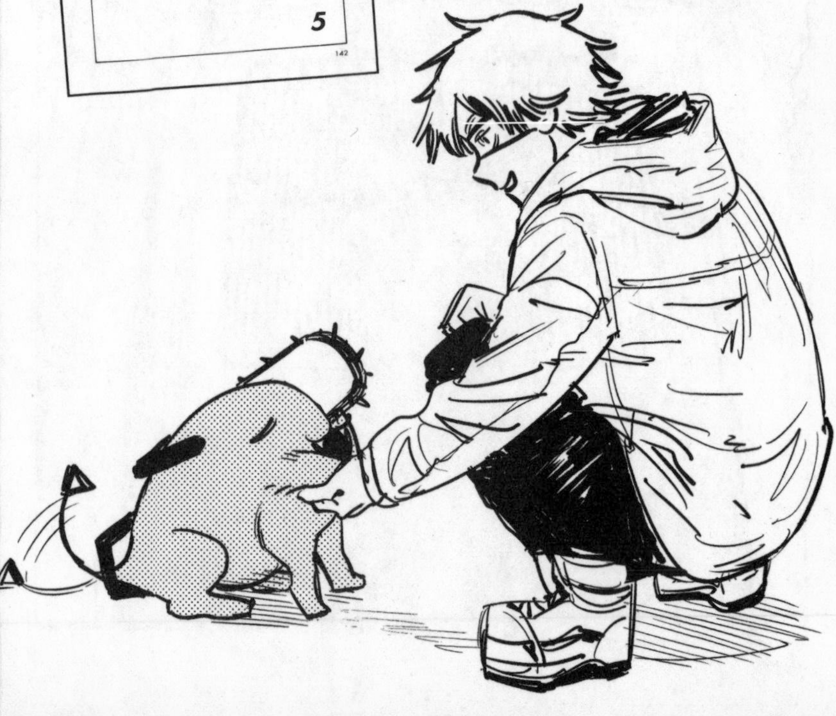